Puritans
and
Libertines

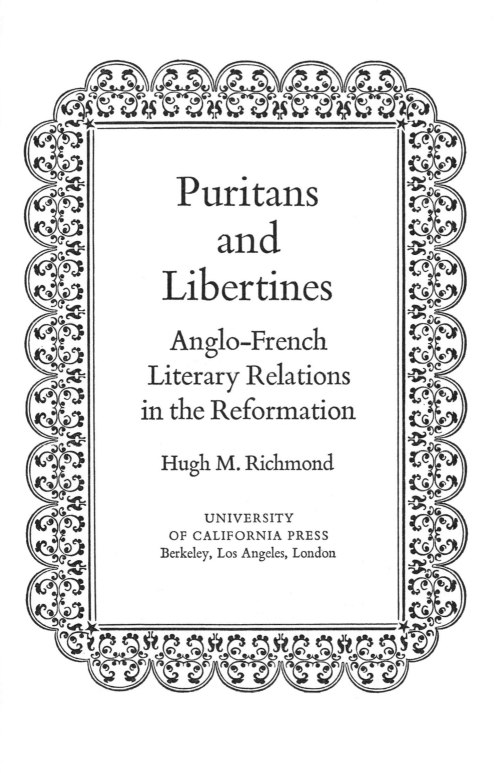

Puritans
and
Libertines

Anglo-French
Literary Relations
in the Reformation

Hugh M. Richmond

UNIVERSITY
OF CALIFORNIA PRESS
Berkeley, Los Angeles, London

University of California Press
Berkeley and Los Angeles, California

University of California Press, Ltd.
London, England

© 1981 by
The Regents of
the University of California

Printed in the United States of America
1 2 3 4 5 6 7 8 9

Library of Congress Cataloging in Publication Data

Richmond, Hugh M
   Puritans and libertines.

   Bibliography: p.
   Includes index.
   1. English literature—Early modern, 1500–1700—French
influences. 2. French literature—16th century—History
and criticism. 3. Great Britain—Civilization—16th
century—French influences. 4. France—Civilization—
1328–1600. 5. Reformation in literature. I. Title.
PR129.F8R5   820'.9'003   80–28864
ISBN 0–520–04179–8

à la famille Baïssas,
en amitié éternelle

Si vous lisez ceste oeuvre toute entière,
Arrestez-vous, sans plus, à la matière.
MARGUERITE D'ANGOULÊME

Contents

Acknowledgments

SINCE THIS MATERIAL HAS INTERESTED ME FROM 1946, IT IS IMPOSSIBLE TO trace all my indebtedness, but certainly the Baïssas family has done most to familiarize me with the nuances of French culture over the last thirty years. I owe them a personal debt which can never be repaid, unless by the tribute to French innovativeness reflected in the thesis of this book. More recently I have been greatly helped by the subtle insights and great kindness of Professor Ian McFarlane of Oxford and of Professor C. A. Mayer of Liverpool, whose own publications have made monumental contributions to our understanding of the civilization of Renaissance France. I have also profited from discussions with Terence Cave, Natalie Davis, Pauline Smith, and Clifford Davies, whose various publications are recognized at appropriate points in the text. Less explicitly, but more generally, those who share my enthusiasm for the scholarship of J. B. Leishman may detect the cosmopolitan spirit of my late mentor as inspiring the book's concerns and methods, if not all the interpretations offered.

Several institutions permitted decisive use (and reproduction) of historical materials: above all the Bibliothèque Nationale (Plates 2, 8, 9, 11, 16), and the library of the Société de l'Histoire du Protestantisme, the Musée de Condé at Chantilly (Plates 1, 3, by Giraudon), the Bodleian Library, the Public Record Office, the British Library (Plates 7, 10), the Newberry Library, the National Portrait Gallery in London (Plate 4), the Victoria and Albert Museum (dust cover), the Musée publique de Genève (Plate 15, by F. Martin), and the Huntington Library. Their staffs often drew my attention to invaluable references. Repeated grants by the University of California have made systematic use of these resources possible, through Humanities Institute fellowships, travel costs, and regular aid with research expenses. Several presentations to the MLA, the Renaissance Society, at London University and the University of Aix-en-Provence, and elsewhere have allowed me to refine my material with the aid of sympathetic and informed discussions.

My selective bibliography may give some sense of my indebtedness within the vast dimensions of the documentation available in this field. If somewhat neglected by English specialists, the resources far exceed possibility of exhaustive survey in French studies, both literary and historical. Incapable of fully recognizing all that is relevant, I must be content to offer simply a few of my more significant starting points in entering a field whose fascinating richness and potentialities invite a lifetime's devotion.

Of course, over many years the goodwill and support of my wife and family have been crucial to the completion of an enterprise on so demanding a scale as this. At least we have shared the pleasures of provincial France together on many occasions, worthy of the authors who inspired them.

France and the Tudors

"WE ARE OBLIGED TO THINK THAT PERHAPS BETWEEN THE SIXTEENTH AND the twentieth century the psychological resources of the West have not stayed the same, but have transformed themselves, evolved, become enriched; that perhaps the men of 1520, of 1530, of 1540 did not perceive exactly like ourselves, did not grasp as firmly as we do the living integration of their personalities. . . . The abrupt reversals in sixteenth-century men, the almost insane speed with which we see them shift, by their own admission and testimony, from wisdom to folly, from restrained moderation to the worst excesses, from what we would consider the humanity of civilized man to the bestiality of an unchained beast—all this cannot be explained by what I would call the cheap psychology of a gossip columnist."[1] Thus speaks Lucien Febvre, confronted by the fact that "the *Heptameron* is the fully authentic record of the ideas, sentiments, and acts of the men and women of the time of Marguerite d'Angoulême, Queen of Navarre." Such an evaluation explains why her impressive collection of *novelle*, in the more or less documentary style of that convention, may serve so well as a starting point from which to measure this progression in human psychologies even by 1650, insofar as they are illustrated in the literary models of the time. It is the contention of this study that while much remained

1. Lucien Febvre, *Amour sacré, amour profane, autour de l'Heptameron* (Paris: Gallimard, 1944), pp. 280–81. The issue is also addressed in Zevedi Barbu, *Problems of Historical Psychology* (New York: Grove, 1960).

I

to develop of our modern literary attitudes after this period, decisive steps were taken in providing psychological models for a more self-aware, integrated, and socially consistent type of personality. Marguerite's own dialogue-commentaries on each tale started this progression, and these reflect some of the intellectual and social forces released by the Reformation, which were expressed even more forcefully in the works of other intellectuals also affected by them like Marot, Ronsard, Montaigne, du Bartas, d'Aubigné, and Théophile de Viau. I have selected five representative French authors (Marguerite herself, Marot, Ronsard, d'Aubigné, and Théophile) to illustrate this progression and its relevance to England, partly on the basis of the shift, indicated by Febvre's comments, in scholarly awareness of and attitudes toward sixteenth-century French literature. These five authors have all re-emerged as more important than was believed in the centuries following their own.

Such positive reevaluations of sixteenth-century French literature have greatly intensified in recent decades, though they started in the nineteenth century. While the status and influence of more familiar major figures like Rabelais and Montaigne may have remained relatively unchanged since the Renaissance and need little further clarification, the contemptuous reaction against their poetic contemporaries such as Marot, Ronsard, and d'Aubigné (led initially by Malherbe and his sympathizers) has increasingly been neutralized. This reappraisal has been aided substantially by the lucid and thorough reediting of the relevant major texts, which has given us easy access and fresh understanding through the scholarship of such works as C. A. Mayer's monumental and invaluable edition of Marot (1958–70); the accessible Pléiade editions of Ronsard (1958) and d'Aubigné (1969), as well as that series' anthologies of sixteenth-century verse (1969) and fiction (1956); the handy new *Heptameron* of Marguerite de Navarre edited by M. François (1967); J. Streicher's scrupulous edition of Théophile de Viau (1951); and also the expository work of scholars like Ian McFarlane, Isidore Silver, Terence Cave, and other French specialists.[2] Such substantial resources have led to significant revisions in our ap-

2. See the relevant sections of the Bibliography for further details.

preciation of the writers involved. If many of their less significant contemporaries (like du Bellay, Desportes, and du Bartas) appear substantially to preserve the character and status traditionally ascribed to
them, scholars' familiar concerns with the neoclassical elements in a
complex author like Ronsard have been refocused on his political and
expository verse, with some lessening of interest in the traditional
Petrarchan aspects of his sonnet cycles. The full range and energy of
Marot's genius have similarly become recognizable now that we have
a clear sense of his work as a whole.

As such French scholarship has evolved, the implications for related
disciplines have also deepened, and a recent review of studies in the
English Renaissance has properly deplored the lack of adequate response in the study of Anglo-French relations in this period.[3] A first
step in remedying this deficiency has been taken in one area by Anne
Lake Prescott in her *French Poets and the English Renaissance*,[4] which
summarizes much of the relevant research undertaken since Sidney
Lee's now dated study, *The French Renaissance in England* (1910).
Prescott has confined herself to overt allusions to the five poets whom
she has selected (Marot, du Bellay, Ronsard, Desportes, and du Bartas),
and she has excluded most broader interpretations of the bearing of
French sensibility on the achievements of the English Renaissance.[5]
Among her French authors two prove marginal in influence: du Bellay's *Regrets*, for example, "had little success in England" (p. 39), perhaps because "he did not often strike such impressive or dramatic
postures" as Ronsard (p. 74); and similarly "English readers may have
sensed in Desportes (all the more because his conceits were so export-
able) a lack of personality or character, a self-effacement in the verse"
(p. 164). As a result there was "near indifference to him as a literary
figure worth a comment" (p. 161). Paradoxically, the figure of du
Bartas presents the opposite problem of an excessively fashionable figure now considered to be aesthetically insignificant. Though numerous

3. See William M. Jones, ed., *The Present State of Scholarship in Sixteenth-
Century Literature* (Columbia: University of Missouri Press, 1978).
4. Anne Lake Prescott, *French Poets and the English Renaissance: Studies in
Fame and Transformation* (New Haven: Yale University Press, 1978).
5. See Prescott, pp. xi, xiii.

scholarly studies have shown that he was immensely popular and widely imitated in England, the exhaustive documentation may lead us to overvalue his interest.[6] He demonstrates the unique importance of the French Huguenot tradition for England, but his works have largely escaped the modern critical reevaluation of his contemporaries' verse: "He cannot come to us across the years" (p. 274), and he now tends to be rated as "an eyesore . . . an inescapable monstrosity" (p. 167). Even in his own time his work dismayed French authors like Ronsard, and it was ridiculed by his own friend d'Aubigné. For all his prominence, du Bartas provides only an archaic and unsatisfactory precedent for the excellencies we now recognize in Elizabethan literature, even while he validates the impression that such French models were at least as crucial as Italian ones in the flowering of Elizabethan sensibility.

The importance of Italy in fostering the evolution of Renaissance English literature has been universally recognized and thoroughly explored,[7] though sometimes with disapproval, as in Ascham's censure in *The Schoolmaster*. Yet while all literary historians must accept the initiatory role of a Petrarch, a Ficino, a Machiavelli, or a Castiglione, not to name the great Italian masters of the fine arts, nevertheless the literary achievements of Renaissance Italy do not fully predetermine the literary character of sixteenth-century Europe, and England in particular. Shakespearean comedies and tragedies consistently transcend their *novelle* sources. Spenser, Donne, Milton, and Marvell only partly resemble such prototypes as Ariosto, Aretino, Tasso, Marino, and others. Literary critics and scholars have often hopefully ascribed these discrepancies to the extraordinary originality of the English authors;[8] but

6. See the footnotes to Prescott's fifth chapter and her article "The Reception of du Bartas in England," *Studies in the Renaissance* 15 (1968): 144–73.

7. See, for example, Donald L. Guss, *John Donne, Petrarchist: Italianate Conceits and Love Theory in the "Songs and Sonets"* (Detroit: Wayne State University Press, 1966).

8. "Shakespeare needed no specific source for his happiest creations." Geoffrey Bullough, ed., *Narrative and Dramatic Sources of Shakespeare*, vol. 2 (London: Routledge and Kegan Paul, 1968), p. 78.

there are some grounds for thinking that T. S. Eliot's sense of the in-escapable importance of tradition is relevant here and that some of the major components of European tradition have not been adequately related to the English Renaissance, and are not registered by Prescott's study either. For literary creativity in the Renaissance laid less stress on the need for originality, personal expression, and imaginativeness than the Romantic period has encouraged us to expect of authors. To the Renaissance writer literary creation certainly involved "invention," but this often came closer to the etymological sense of *invenio*—a find-ing of existing materials for use: "While the original meaning of 'in-vention' involved primarily the idea of 'finding' subject matter (even by imitating or borrowing from other writers) the term later came to suggest, through association with the concept of imagination not so much finding as 'creating'. . . . that poetic substance is generated in the poet's soul."[9] The Renaissance tendency to the former view ap-pears in Thomas Wilson's *The Arte of Rhetorique*: "The finding out of apt matter, called otherwise Invention, is a searching out of things true, or things likely, the which may reasonablie set forth a matter, and make it appear probable."[10] This is why the term *syncretism* is so relevant to the resulting mosaic, even in the case of so powerful an author as Shakespeare.

If the Italians provided rather less of this matter for the English Renaissance than we might expect, it is only natural; to get to Italy (or most other countries) in the first place, most Englishmen had to make a long journey across France, an area which had therefore been the closest European source of cultural interaction with Britain since before the Roman occupation. Moreover, French has characteristically mediated European literary tradition for the English, whatever the original language of a text. In 1598 Robert Dallington censures the current tendency for sophisticates to be satisfied with French versions of any foreign text, since "yee have now almost all Histories, Greek

9. Alex Preminger, ed., *Princeton Encyclopedia of Poetry and Poetics* (Prince-ton: Princeton University Press, 1965), p. 402.

10. Thomas Wilson, *The Arte of Rhetorique* (Oxford: Clarendon Press, 1909), p. 6.

and Latine, translated into French, yea, and the Artes also."[11] Yet the English were no less impressed with France as a self-sufficient source of sophistication in Shakespeare's time. In his copy of *An Excellent Discourse upon the now present estate of France* (1592), Gabriel Harvey lists the current major French writers, such as Montaigne, and concludes that "varieties of accidents, and many pregnant practiques have refined divers French wittes even above the sharpest Italians, or Spaniards at this instant."[12]

Harvey's appraisal seems unexpected since France at that very moment was being torn apart by the Catholic League's desperate attempt to deny the succession to the Protestant Henri IV, which perpetuated the disastrous civil wars described by Montaigne:

> I thinke there is more barbarisme in eating men alive, than to feed upon them being dead, to mangle by tortures and torments a body full of lively sense, to roast him in peeces, to make dogges and swine to gnaw and tear him in mammockes (as we have not only read, but seen very lately, yea and in our owne memorie, not only amongst ancient enemies, but our neighbours and fellow-citizens, and which is worse, under pretence of pietie and religion) than to roast and eat him after he is dead.[13]

Montaigne's unfavorable comparison of his bigoted contemporaries with the cannibals must seem amply justified by events in the French civil wars: the St. Bartholomew's Day Massacre in 1572 was only the most visible of the horrors committed by both sides throughout the century. Yet Montaigne played a prominent (though honorable) part in the administrative and political life of this turbulent period as mayor of

---

11. Robert Dallington, *The View of France* (London: Oxford University Press, 1936), sig. V3r. The point is confirmed by the large number of French books in William Drummond's library: Alfred H. Upham, *The French Influence on English Literature from the Accession of Elizabeth to the Restoration* (New York: Octagon, 1965), p. 7.

12. *An Excellent Discourse upon the now present estate of France*, "faithfully translated out of French, by E. A." (London: John Wolfe, 1592), in MS on the title page of the Huntington Library copy.

13. Michel de Montaigne, *Essays*, trans. John Florio, vol. 1 (London: J. M. Dent, 1942), p. 223-24.

Bordeaux and as an informal ambassador between the warring factions: he was intimately acquainted with both the Protestant leader Henri de Navarre and his Catholic wife Marguerite, flamboyant daughter of the notorious Queen Mother, Catherine de' Medici. Montaigne's own distinctive genius and quietism were distilled from an increasingly intense repugnance to the tumults and tensions through which he lived, and this example may suggest why even T. S. Eliot's gloomy conviction of the ensuing "dissociation of sensibility" in the seventeenth century still permitted him to recognize in the Renaissance the evolution of "a kind of self-consciousness that is new" and which might mark a kind of "progress."[14] This modern interpretation is justified by the contemporary verdict, for "during the formative period in the lives of Sidney and Spenser, France was a battleground of Protestantism, and England grew accustomed to watch every development of the struggle and look to the great Protestant leaders there for inspiration," for reasons their contemporary, Dallington, makes clear: "It is a thing ever observed in great states and kingdoms that they never rise to any greatness, except in their rising they meet with many lets, and are sometimes even brought to such low tearmes, as they are thought past all hope."[15] Dallington continues to anticipate Toynbee in saying that a similar triumph over odds is the prerequisite of greatness in princes like Henri IV. The correctness of Dallington's analysis appears in Henri's founding of the Bourbon dynasty, which reached its climax in his grandson, Louis XIV, but which largely evolved through the efforts of yet another offspring of the civil wars: Cardinal Richelieu.

Indeed, by Dallington's criterion of the need for a challenge to develop a distinctive identity, it seems plausible to assert that what generated much of the achievement of French culture in the sixteenth century was not simply any sustained commitment to the Reformation or to the forces opposing it, but the challenge of a society disrupted by the Reformation. We must beware of forcing on elusive figures like Marguerite de Navarre, Elizabeth I, or Maximilian II the theology of a Luther, or a Zwingli, or a Calvin, for the most potent personalities

14. T. S. Eliot, *Selected Essays* (New York: Harcourt Brace, 1950), pp. 119, 247.

15. Upham, p. 73, and Dallington, sig. G3v.

of the period, like Shakespeare, usually eluded the doctrinaire or partisan commitment of these prophets' supporters or their opponents. But such controversies opened up opportunities for idiosyncratic personal developments which were often intensified by the physical disorders of Reformation politics. Marguerite herself as well as her protégés (such as Marot, Rabelais, perhaps even Calvin) were continually forced to scrutinize their ideas and conduct in the face of psychological, social, and physical pressures and thus seem to have acquired almost involuntarily a deeper sensibility from the adversities and confrontations of the time. Yet many authors who share the Reformation's concern with the Bible (and its doubt of the efficacy of reason and human capacities by comparison with a Pauline sense of redemptive grace) nevertheless elude religious categories, united only in hostility to bigotry, ignorance, and ecclesiastical corruption. Such spirits as Marguerite's "were ultimately of no particular sect"[16] unless coerced by expediency, as were Marot and Théophile. Inevitably, many of the greatest French poets of the Age of Reform were entangled in its religious bitterness on one side or the other formally: du Bartas and d'Aubigné, or Ronsard and Saint-Amant; but any attempt to force them into a narrow and consistent religious category negates the individuality which the era's confusions evoke. To cover the doctrinal roots of the French Reformation and the whole range of interaction between England and France is impossible here, and I shall concentrate not on retracing known relationships, or recapitulating the well-documented scholarly study of the diffusion of Lutheran and Calvinist ideas through France to England,[17] but on the social, psychological, and literary results precipitated by these doctrines' secular effects.

16. Marguerite de Navarre, *Les Marguerites de la Marguerite des Princesses*, ed. Félix Franc (Geneva: Slatkine, 1970), p. 20. The avoidance of religious categories receives more general justification in Ian McFarlane, *A Literary History of France: Renaissance France, 1470–1589* (London: Benn, 1974), pp. 336–37.

17. Extensive bibliographies on the theology and ecclesiastical history of the Reformation can be found in V. H. H. Green, *Luther and the Reformation* (London: Methuen, 1969); T. H. L. Parker, *John Calvin* (London: Dent, 1975); Arthur G. Dickens, *Reformation and Society* (New York: Harcourt Brace, 1966); Richard S. Dunn, *The Age of Religious Wars, 1559–1689* (New York: Norton, 1970).

Any substantial study of French literary sensibilities in the early sixteenth century may start advantageously with the role of Marguerite d'Angoulême, "reine de Navarre." Her influence and that of her mother, Louise de Savoie, became great after the accession of her brother as François I, who was dependent on both women after the early death of his father. As a result of François' devotion to these values, his court made a major contribution to the new sensibility by boldly advancing the status of women. Marguerite was extremely intelligent and receptive to new ideas, whether derived from the Platonism of Italy or the Reformation in Germany, and thus she became the protector of both the new Humanists and the new Reformers in France, whom she also encouraged her brother to favor and protect, with uneven success and some personal risk. In the lively but civilized ambience she sought to create, women became intellectual, autonomous, and morally complex, as the *Heptameron* illustrates in its often historical tales and in the brisk discussions they provoke among their hearers at the end of each episode. We find daughters and sisters asserting their right to free choice, wives rejecting domestic constraints, and a rigorous scrutiny of customary views of marriage. If Marguerite is scarcely a radical feminist, she certainly raises consciousness about women's social roles. We shall see that she thereby fosters a type of intellectual, autonomous woman who alters the history of France and England as well as their literary characterizations, for among Marguerite's protégées were both Catherine de' Medici (whose *escadron volant* provided the model for Shakespeare's aggressive young women in *Love's Labour's Lost*),[18] and Anne Boleyn, who not only dominated the affections and policies of Henry VIII, swaying him toward Reform, but also shattered the facile Petrarchan stereotypes of femininity and courtship in a conservative poet like Wyatt. In this new kind of aggressive, autonomous, self-consciously sexual woman we can also

---

More specifically focused on my concerns are Ralph Roeder, *Catherine de' Medici and the Lost Revolution* (London: Harrap, 1937), and Edith Sichel, *Catherine de' Medici and the French Reformation* (London: Constable, 1905).

18. See Hugh M. Richmond, "Shakespeare's Navarre," *Huntington Library Quarterly* 42 (1979): 193–216.

9

see the prototype for many of Shakespeare's heroines, the Dark Lady, and even ultimately his characterization of Anne Boleyn herself in *Henry VIII*.[19] The *Heptameron* is not a feminist tract, but it invites review of traditional sexual norms, and Marguerite's fame and influence in England ensured that the work and its concerns were well known there.

Henry VIII was fascinated by such dynamic Frenchwomen, and he seriously considered marriage with Marguerite herself on several occasions: in 1505, 1508, and around 1530.[20] In the event, after seducing the French-trained Mary Boleyn, Henry was himself finally vanquished by the acquired Gallic sophistication of her sister, Anne Boleyn. Both women were raised at the Valois court dominated by Marguerite, of whom we know that Anne conserved the fondest memories.[21] Sidney Lee is correct in saying that Marguerite was "adored by Tudor ladies,"[22] for on her death three of them (Anne, Margaret, and Jane Seymour) wrote an elegy to her memory in one hundred Latin quatrains, which achieved such fashionable repute that a French version was published in Paris in 1551, with additions by other admirers, under the title of *Le Tombeau de Marguerite de Valois royne de Navarre faict premierement en distiques Latins par les trois soeurs Anne, Marguerite, et Jeanne de Seymour, princesses en Angleterre*.[23] So famous was the original effusion that this collection included a salutation to the English devotees of Marguerite by Ronsard himself, praising the excellence of such appreciative Englishwomen.[24] This devotion to Marguerite's excellence in fact followed a far more significant precedent provided by the publication, in London in 1548, of a translation of Marguerite's *Miroir de l'âme pécheresse* by another English princess, later to become

19. See Hugh M. Richmond, "The Feminism of Shakespeare's *Henry VIII*," *Essays in Literature* 6 (1979): 11–20.

20. J. D. Mackie, *The Earlier Tudors 1485–1558* (Oxford: Clarendon Press, 1972), pp. 177, 187, 322.

21. See the start of Chapter 3 below.

22. Sidney Lee, *The French Renaissance in England* (Oxford: Clarendon Press, 1910), p. 129.

23. Lee, p. 45.

24. *Odes* V.iii. See Pierre de Ronsard, *Oeuvres complètes*, ed. Gustave Cohen, vol. 1 (Paris: Gallimard, Pléiade, 1950), pp. 589, 1101.

Queen Elizabeth I, who clearly inherited her mother's reverence for Marguerite.[25]

Not only were some of the most influential ladies of the English court thus conditioned by their superiors throughout the century to admire Marguerite, but also this enthusiasm evidently was widely shared elsewhere in England. Among intellectuals like George Puttenham her learning was proverbial, as he shows in his widely read *The Arte of English Poesie*: "Queens also have been knowen studious, and to write large volumes, as Lady Margaret of Fraunce, Queene of Navarre in our time."[26] There is ample proof also that the *Heptameron* provided tales that formed "the favorite reading of English ladies in the first decades of Elizabeth's reign."[27] Among the translations violently attacked by Ascham was William Painter's anthology of stories, *The Palace of Pleasure*. The first volume of this work sold so well in 1566 that the second volume was published in 1567: "Of its immediate and striking success there can be no doubt. A second edition of the first Tome appeared in 1569, . . . a second edition of the whole work in 1575."[28] What is significant here is that "the first Tome might be called the *Heptameron* volume," because the ten stories from the *Heptameron* provided the most substantial and climactic part of the book. Their crucial role in the popularity of the series is proved by the fact that the principal selling point of the second edition of this first volume was the addition of a further five stories from the *Heptameron* to the original ten: the readers clearly wanted more of Marguerite.[29] George Whetstone recognized Marguerite's value in adding a similar tale to his own *Heptameron* collection of 1582, which was twice reprinted, and a further anthology of Marguerite's stories appeared in 1597.[30] Thus Marguerite figured massively in a whole series of popular pub-

---

25. See the start of Chapter 4 below and the bibliography for Marguerite d'Angoulême and the court of François I.

26. George Puttenham, *The Arte of English Poesie*, ed. Gladys D. Willcock and Alice Walker (Cambridge University Press, 1936), p. 22.

27. Lee, p. 129.

28. William Painter, *The Palace of Pleasure*, ed. Joseph Jacobs, vol. 1 (New York: Dover, 1966), p. xxiv.

29. Painter, p. xxviii. 30. Painter, p. lxxiv.

lications throughout Elizabeth's reign, and it is certain that her contribution to Painter helped ensure that his collection's "success was the cause of the whole movement" to publish anthologies of *novelle*, of which his was the major example.[31] The exploitation of the popularity of Marguerite's tales in Painter is apparent also in James Shirley's use of one of them in his *Love's Cruelty*[32] and even more strikingly in the recent discovery of a probable source another provides for the Beatrice and Benedick scenes added (without a previously known original) to the Bandello material of Shakespeare's *Much Ado About Nothing*. This tale may even be based on an episode in Marguerite's own private life, so that it is plausible to see her spirit permanently reincarnated in performances of that play.[33]

To these important signs of recognition must be added the international appreciation directed toward Marguerite's own court of Navarre from 1527 to 1549 at Nérac, where all that was most admired in Renaissance culture was cherished. Figures like Marot, Rabelais, and even Calvin found solace there when pursued for heresy. Marguerite became famous as "la mère poule de la Renaissance," and this fame lasted well into the seventeenth century.[34] Throughout the sixteenth century, ambassadors' reports in the English *Calendar of State Papers, Foreign* show that intellectual and aristocratic young Englishmen flocked to Nérac because of the reputation conferred on it by Marguerite and sustained by the reign of her daughter, Jeanne, and her grandson, later Henri IV.[35] The psychological impact of Marguerite can thus hardly be exaggerated in France and thereby on England, via the emulation initiated by Henry VIII's competition with François on such occasions as the Field of the Cloth of Gold. The dynamic, idiosyncratic personality Marguerite displayed is not only reflected in the women of the *Heptameron* but in the verse of Marot and Ronsard and in the self-

---

31. Painter, p. xxiv.   32. Painter, p. lxxix.

33. See Hugh M. Richmond, "Much Ado About Notables," *Shakespeare Studies* 12 (1979), pp. 49–63.

34. For example see Pierre Olhagaray's comments on her in 1609, at the start of Chapter 3 below.

35. See Chapter 9 below.

assertive behavior of young women trained in the Valois court. Women like Mary and Anne Boleyn were followed by Mary Stuart, who shared this influence with the later Marguerite de Navarre—both raised to self-assertion by the conditioning of Catherine de' Medici. The appearance of a new, assertive, brunette ideal of womanhood in the literature of the century is the result of such models both in life and art, for the Valois princesses were all deep brunettes.[36] As Marot and Wyatt discovered to their pain, and such writers as Shakespeare also, these Dark Ladies were no blonde and bland Petrarchan impassives, but tough, egocentric women, as much a part of the Fallen World as the males of the Reformation era. The archaic, Italianate courtliness of Petrarch or Scève or Spenser[37] is somewhat out of place in such relationships, and a new sexual parity appears in the most advanced and sophisticated works of the late sixteenth century. Ronsard himself increasingly abandons the sentimental Petrarchan mode, for his last mistress, Hélène de Surgères, was also one of the hardened beauties of the *escadron*. It is hardly surprising that Donne's love poetry, often derived from Shakespeare's comedies, shows a strong dash of cynical wit in dealing with such women, for "the mocking tongues of wenches are / As keen as is the razor's edge" (*LLL* V.ii.257–58).

This sharpness and realism extend from the new sexual behavior to the whole range of social relationships and provoke new self-definitions in other authors of the period also. Sexual, theological, and political controversy force the development of new defensive strategies: personality is redefined as a literary shield to be toughened against slander in the autobiographical and polemic poems of the Reformation; it is not irrelevant that Protestant Navarre's motto was the assertive "Sum id quod sum" (I am what I am).[38] From Ronsard to Milton and Marvell,

36. Brantôme ascribes this new type of woman to the impact of Marguerite on feminine sensibility. See the conclusion of Chapter 9.

37. Spenser's relation to conventional French sources has already been explored in A. W. Sattersthwaite, *Spenser, Ronsard, and du Bellay* (Princeton: Princeton University Press, 1960).

38. Imbert de Saint-Amand, *Women of the Valois Court* (New York: Scribner's, 1895), p. 250.

the literary persona of the poet under assault is polished and tempered to a steely norm, flexible and consciously deployed.[39] We perceive that male personality undergoes changes as radical as the female in its literary expression. The complex authorial personae in *Paradise Lost* and "Upon Appleton House" owe a great deal to the defensive tactics developed by Marot, Ronsard, d'Aubigné, and Théophile in the course of protracted religious, political, and amatory controversies: they are introverted, self-sufficient, and increasingly quietist. It is to the documentation of the origin and development of such new psychologies, and the literary means needed to evoke them and their consequences, that this study is devoted. Without the French prototypes matured in the confrontations of the French Reformation, English authors would have lacked essential models and challenges. Shakespeare understood this when he set one of his early comedies, *Love's Labour's Lost*, in Nérac, and finished his career with a portrait of Anne Boleyn.

39. See Hugh M. Richmond, "Personal Identity and Literary Personae: A Study in Historical Psychology," *PMLA* 110 (1975), pp. 209–21.

2

"The Goggle-Eyed Whore": Anne Boleyn and the French Fashion

On the morning of 19 May 1536 the vivacious and sophisticated woman who had been queen of England for nearly three years dressed herself with her customary care in the Tower room where she had spent her wedding eve, through one of those ironies by which Fate mocks Aristotelian probability. Her husband had been no less attentive to detail, sending for the best professional expert to handle this climactic occasion of her career, an expert who proved to reside in northern France. In executions, as in many other things, Henry VIII regretfully found that contemporary taste rated French performance supreme; and when it came to chopping off the head of an attractive young woman, propriety seemingly required the services of this specialist in elegant executions by sword, whom he promptly brought over from Calais at great expense. Anne Boleyn herself was in complete agreement. A somewhat baffled Kingston, governor of the Tower, reports that: "She said, 'I heard say the executor was very good, and I have a little neck' and she put her hand about it, laughing heartily. I have seen many men and women executed, and all they have been in great sorrow, and to my knowledge this lady has much joy and pleasure in death."[1] Numerous anecdotes confirm this strange mood of the victim. Philip Sergeant notes that after her arrest "in the midst of her sorrow she fell into a great laughing which, Kingston comments, she has done several times since."[2] Sergeant judges this to have been a hysterical reaction to her fall, like her emotional fits of weeping when first sent to the Tower; but this view does not fit her behavior earlier, or thereafter. During her trial "Anne behaved herself with great dignity from all accounts," and a French commentator observes of her self-defense: "Her speech made even her bitterest enemies pity her."[3] The testimony of Eustache Chapuys illustrates this well—for he was the ambassador of the Emperor Charles V, whose sister Anne had supplanted as queen. Chapuys reports how Thomas Cromwell "greatly praised the intelligence, wit and courage of the concubine and her brother."[4] He also records his own macabre anecdote about the affair: "On her last night Anne had said that the jesters would find no difficulty in finding a nickname for her in history—'la Royne Anne sans-tete'—and then she laughed heartily."[5] Even on the scaffold, Sir Thomas Wriothesley saw that Anne delivered her last words "with a goodly smiling countenance."[6] Whatever momentary despair Anne may have felt, her last days fully confirm the earlier verdict of Chapuys: "She is braver than a lion."[7] Perhaps her laughter in her last days was involuntary self-mockery at the grimly paradoxical climax of a meteoric career on which she had lavished so much virtuosity and effort.

The conflicting verdicts passed on her ever since suggest that Anne's tough and agile mind presents a problem in the evaluation of personality which we are scarcely better able now to arbitrate than were her baffled contemporaries. A modern biographer observes that she had "a sharp and sometimes uncannily accurate instinct, a quick but entirely illogical mind. Her judgement on superficial matters of taste, court lyrics, dress, was acute; her assessment of politics haphazard and subjective."[8] Perhaps the sheer unintelligibility of her behavior and not

1. Philip W. Sergeant, *Anne Boleyn: A Study* (London: Hutchinson, 1934), p. 269.

2. Sergeant, p. 252.   3. Sergeant, p. 264.   4. Sergeant, p. 272.

5. Sergeant, p. 269.   6. Sergeant, p. 271.   7. Sergeant, p. 117.

8. Mary Louise Bruce, *Anne Boleyn* (New York: Warner, 1973), p. 26.

just fear of Henry may explain in part the unanimous verdict of "guilty" passed upon the elusive evidence by the jury. As George Wyatt (the poet's grandson) observes, it is "incredible that she, that had it her word as it weare the spirit of her mind, as hathe been said that she was her Caesars all, not to be toucht of others, should be held with the foul desier of her brother."[9] Yet to curious English minds such as Sir Thomas Wyatt's, so alien if hypnotic a personality might indeed seem capable of anything, including incest. Traditional norms of behavior were irrelevant. After all, when Wolsey fell the Boleyns' clique came to include Thomas Cromwell, "perhaps the first English student of Machiavelli, having read the famous 'Prince' in manuscript several years before it was printed."[10] The outmaneuvering of Cardinal Wolsey suggests that Anne Boleyn's talent was above crude lapses into treasonable sensuality, and it proves Chapuy's fear of Anne's "dissimulation or love of intrigue of which she is an accomplished mistress."[11] Not for nothing was her grandfather William Boleyn knighted by Richard III at his coronation, while her father was one of the most coldly cunning and influential politicians in the England of his time. And of course her handling of Henry himself, until the last phase, marks out her own virtuosity. Chapuys gloomily notes that Henry's promiscuousness is no source of hope in frustrating her marriage, "considering the King's changeable character and the craft of the Lady, who knows well how to manage him."[12] Throughout their courtship we must agree with Sergeant that Anne "played a most difficult game with extreme skill. Considering that the other player was an amorous autocrat, who had power of life and death over her whole family, and that she withstood him, without losing him for six years, Anne Boleyn's story is one of the most remarkable instances of a woman's finesse."[13] Whatever our point of view, the genius of so unusual and talented a personality merits our interest and understanding, for it is central to an awareness of the impact of French sensibility on the English Renaissance.

Among fresh influences which might account for the emergence of such novel personalities as Anne's in the early sixteenth century, the

9. George Wyatt, *The Papers* (London: Royal Historical Society, 1968), p. 187.
10. Sergeant, p. 120. 11. Sergeant, p. 109.
12. Sergeant, p. 206. 13. Sergeant, p. 56.

importance of Luther can scarcely be overestimated. Bruce feels Anne's Lutheran interests were "originally awakened in France,"[14] and Sergeant in turn asserts that Anne's "sympathies with the Reformers undoubtedly helped in her ruin."[15] Her sexual and matrimonial difficulties inevitably encouraged her to accept the more dynamic and flexible view of marriage which Luther favored both on personal and institutional levels. Even earlier, when the youthful Anne had become attracted to Lord Henry Percy (himself "suspected of sympathy with the Reformers"),[16] Wolsey's ruthless disruption of the match seems likely to have reinforced Anne's hatred of the cardinal and what he stood for institutionally. Henry's shift from the stiff orthodoxy of Catherine of Aragon to the skeptical flexibility of Anne Boleyn thus epitomizes the shift in religious and social values of his reign, as J. S. Brewer has observed:

> Times were hard at hand when the old Faith was fast losing its influence. A new Faith, apparently less rigid and severe, denouncing the ancient strictness as needless and ungodly, was making rapid advances, especially among the gay and cultivated votaries of the Court. Protestantism found two sets of partisans —those who rejected the formalities of fasts and legal observances of the old Church, as unsatisfactory to their sense of righteousness . . . and those who hated restraints of every kind. . . . So, for opposite reasons, whilst Protestantism had acceptance with the godly, it was equally acceptable to the scoffer and the licentious. The greatest favourers of the Reformation in France, from which Anne Boleyn had just returned, were the King himself and his darling sister, Marguerite.[17]

While urbanity and good nature tempered their sensuality, François and Marguerite were by no means at odds with the tone of the early Reformation. Luther's sanction of a bigamous marriage by the syphilitic and promiscuous Landgrave Philip of Hesse illustrates Protestantism's enforced blend of flexible morality, licentiousness, and political expediency.

14. Bruce, p. 55.   15. Sergeant, p. 54.   16. Sergeant, p. 44.
17. J. S. Brewer, *Letters and Papers Foreign and Domestic of the Reign of Henry VIII*, vol. 4 (London: Longmans, 1867), p. ccxli.

These new attitudes were carried over to England by Anne Boleyn, in whom "French acquired a powerful and enthusiastic patroness. Anne was entirely French by education and tastes. She had been brought up by a French governess."[18] It becomes plausible to assert that Anne's early exposure to French culture at a moment of transition was the decisive element in both her unexpected rise and predictable fall. Until the last decade of the sixteenth century, English popular attitudes to France were largely those of sustained hate, mingled with morbid fascination and reluctant admiration for French virtuosity. Despite an inconclusive episode like the Field of the Cloth of Gold, the French ambassador reported with some justice that "all England" was hostile to the French. J. S. Brewer observes that

> the irrepressible jealousy and excessive dislike with which France, its ambition, its habits, its fashions, its activity under all forms, were then regarded by the mass of the English people, are barely intelligible to us now, to whom conquest of France has ceased to be more than a dim and idle tradition, stirring no blood, awakening no memories and no regrets. But in those days men still talked over by the fireside the deeds of their forefathers in the fields of France.[19]

Yet France was England's most important neighbor and its primary source of cosmopolitan resources: even Italian and classical influences were often mediated through French versions, like Innocent Gentillet's caricature of Machiavelli or Jacques Amyot's translation of Plutarch. It may be more than coincidence that the shift around 1590 from indignant bafflement by French culture to sophisticated understanding of its virtues and defects is matched by the full flowering of English civilization. Surely Brewer is right when he asserts that "no nation has ever become great, which from local position or other causes has kept apart from the general current of human interests."[20] The toughest, most cunning and influential minds in the courts of Henry VIII and Elizabeth realized this, and despite xenophobic popular tastes one is tempted

18. Kathleen Lambley, *The Teaching and Cultivation of the French Language in England During Tudor and Stuart Times* (Manchester: Longmans, 1920), p. 71.
19. Brewer, vol. 3, part 1, p. cx.   20. Brewer, vol. 4, p. clxxxvii.

to assert strong positive correlation between interest in and understanding of France and intellectual or cultural distinction in sixteenth-
century Englishmen. It is probably of no significance that the great-
grandfather of Henry VIII, Owen Tudor, married the widow of Henry
V, Catherine de Valois, about 1429, so that Henry VIII was remotely
related to his rival François I. But Henry's father spent the second fourteen of his first twenty-eight years at the courts of Brittany and France,
and Henry's principal minister Wolsey powerfully reinforced such
Anglo-French interaction. In developing England's international role
and in strengthening her political and cultural ties with France, Wolsey
led the way. And if the Boleyns were Wolsey's opponents in religious
matters, they shared and perpetuated his concern with France and involved themselves intimately in its politics and society.

Both Sir Thomas Boleyn and his son George were ambassadors to
France, and the two daughters, Mary and Anne, completed their education by prolonged stays at the French court, which gave them their
major social attraction on their return to England, for

> the knowledge of the French tongue was at that time by no means
> common. . . . To be able to speak French, [even] if it was no
> better written French than Anne Boleyn's, was a powerful rec-
> ommendation at all courtly festivities, where it was the fashion
> to pair off an English lady with a French or Italian gentleman
> to dance and to mask with. The reputation of her accomplish-
> ments was enhanced by the fact that she was selected by the King's
> sister, Mary, [previously] the French Queen, to take part in a
> small and select circle with whom royalty conversed. . . . In a gay
> and lively court where amusements were so much in vogue, a
> young girl freshly returned from France and its fashions would
> not long for admirers.[21]

George Cavendish describes such an affair: "These lady maskeresses
took each of them a French gentleman to dance and mask with them.
Ye shall understand that those lady maskeresses spake good French,
which delighted much these gentlemen."[22] Before her return to Eng-

21. Brewer, vol. 4, p. ccxxxvi. See a similar account in Bruce, p. 38.
22. George Cavendish, *The Life and Death of Cardinal Wolsey* (New Haven:
Yale University Press, 1962), p. 76.

land, a French admirer had appreciated Anne's demeanor at the Valois court, dominated by "Marguerite, the outrageous, adored, intellectual Duchess of Alençon, author of that classic collection of bawdy tales, the *Heptameron* and of passionate love poems to her own brother," by whom Anne "was encouraged to have confidence in and voice her own judgements on subjects which at the English court were usually reserved for men only."[23] Reviewing Anne's attractions, her French admirers noted her as "pretty and of an elegant figure. But most attractive of her features were her eyes, which she well knew how to use, holding them sometimes still, at others, making them send a message, carrying from her heart the secret witness. And in truth such was their power that many a man paid his allegiance."[24] It is clear that, in the tradition of Marguerite, "love was a game to Anne," albeit a dangerous one, and her "elusiveness suggested she would make an exciting quarry" at the English court.[25]

Her French sophistication, therefore, rather than her physical endowments, gave Anne her fascination, for most accounts minimize her beauty. The hostile Londoners who favored Queen Catherine called Anne a "goggle-eyed whore."[26] An ungallant Venetian who observed her dancing with François at Calais on 26 October 1532 wrote that: "Madame Anna is not the most beautiful woman in the world, of middling height, dark complexion, long neck, big mouth, and flat chest, and in fact she has nothing but the English King's great appetite and her eyes, which are black and beautiful."[27] Like most of the Valois princesses, through whom a new ideal was evoked, Anne failed to conform to the traditional Hellenistic stereotype of blonde beauty, inviting instead allusions to her "Irish descent" as "a little, lively, sparkling brunette, with fascinating eyes and long black hair, which contrary to the sombre fashion of those days, she wore coquettishly floating loosely down her back, interlaced with jewelry."[28] A bitter contempo-

23. Bruce, p. 26.

24. Bruce, p. 25. Sergeant suggests this admirer was "L. D. Carles" (p. 30).

25. Bruce, p. 58.

26. Garrett Mattingly, *Catherine of Aragon* (New York: Vintage, 1941), p. 346. See also Plate 4.

27. Bruce, p. 205.   28. Brewer, vol. 4, p. ccxxxvi; similarly in Bruce, p. 43.

rary critic of her ecclesiastical impact, the Catholic Dr. Nicholas Sanders still concedes that "she was handsome to look at, with a pretty mouth, amusing in her way, playing well on the lute, and was a good dancer. She was the model and mirror for those at Court, for she was always well-dressed and every day made some change in the fashion of her garments."[29] She brought back from France with her the conversational ease and informal candor which made François and Marguerite irresistible, thus provoking prim moralists over the centuries to share her lovers' censure of her because

> after she became Queen she permitted herself to be addressed by her inferiors with a freedom of language repugnant to the dignity of her sex; and she even interchanged jests with them when they ventured to express their regard for her. . . . and her own equivocal position with the King lowered the whole moral tone of the circle in which she moved, and lent encouragement to laxity and licentiousness no English court had witnessed before.[30]

No wonder both Wyatt and Henry VIII turned surly.

Hostile commentators like Sanders do not hesitate to enlarge on this free manner to the extent of asserting "that Anne Boleyn was known in France, for her shameless behaviour as 'the English mare.' "[31] However, the best evidence suggests that it was her elder sister Mary who earned an evil reputation at the French court, where the papal nuncio, Bishop Ridolpho Pio of Faenza, refers to Mary as "una grandissima ribalda et infame sopra tutte."[32] Mary's erratic and ultimately rather pathetic career after her return from France seems to corroborate her probable explusion from its court. James Gairdner dryly comments that

> it is curious, certainly, that if Mary Boleyn was too bad for the French court, there should have been at this very time an outcry against the prevalence of French manners at the English court. Yet so it was; and so strong was the feeling on the subject that

29. Sergeant, p. 40.   30. Brewer, vol. 4, p. ccxliv.

31. James Gairdner, "Mary and Anne Boleyn," *English Historical Review* 8 (1893), pp. 53–60.

32. Gairdner, p. 55.

the lord chamberlain was instructed to call before the Council
Nicholas Carew and some other gentlemen of the privy chamber and banish them from the court. The young gentlemen had
all been in France where one of their amusements had been to
ride through the streets of Paris along with the French king in
disguise, 'throwing eggs, stones, and other foolish trifles at the
people.'[33]

In his *Chronicle*, Edward Hall indignantly describes how they returned
from France "all French in eating, drinking and apparel, yea and in
French vices and brags, so that all the estates of England were by them
laughed at; the ladies and gentlemen were dispraised, so that nothing
by them was praised but if it were after the French turn." Similarly
Polydore Vergil censures the English ladies who participated in the festivities at the Field of the Cloth of Gold. There, as a modern French
historian eagerly notes, "the women of France, the noble ladies of the
estates, shone much brighter than the Englishwomen. Their fashions
were adopted in London: wholly *décolletées*, they showed their fresh
breasts, which excited the envy of the Englishwomen who were but-
toned up to the throat."[34] Vergil more sourly comments that in exposing their busts in this French fashion the English ladies lost more on
the side of modesty than they gained on that of gracefulness.[35] Indeed,
as with Anne Boleyn, the modest elevation of English busts was the
subject of some pity among French connoisseurs.

Such were the facile manners that Mary Boleyn, at least, brought
back after several years in France, in something like disgrace. Not only
was she finally "cast off" by her father for her loose behavior, but, after
a hasty, romantic, and unwise marriage to William Carey in her father's
absence, only the intervention of Henry VIII at her sister's instigation
ensured that her father "must needs take her his natural daughter now
in her extreme necessity."[36] It must be mentioned here that Henry's

33. Gairdner, p. 57.

34. Jean B. H. R. Capafigue, *Francois 1er et la Renaissance, 1515–1547*, vol. 1
(Paris: Amyot, 1845), p. 331.

35. Robert de la Mark, *Mémoires* (Paris: Michaud, 1838), p. 71. See Polydore
Vergil, *Historia Anglica* (Menston: Scolar, 1972), p. 661.

36. Brewer, vol. 4, p. ccxxvii.

concern with Mary was probably less indirect than this occasion suggests. Throughout his career Henry VIII showed a strong sexual predilection for women of French background. Quite early in the discussion of his divorce there was talk of reviving an earlier proposal of his marrying Marguerite d'Angoulême herself.[37] Not only was Anne sufficiently well trained by Queen Claude of France for a contemporary French source to assert that she had "so improved her graces that you would never have judged her English in her fashions but native French,"[38] but it also seems possible that Jane Seymour, her successor as Henry's queen, spent several years at the court of François.[39] Moreover, when Henry later happened to find himself widowed again, "he sent hastily to France for a new bride." Five great French ladies were proposed to him and their portraits submitted, but Henry said, "By God, I trust no one but myself—the thing touches me too near. I wish to see them some time before deciding." The irritated French ambassador then sarcastically "suggested that he sleep with each in turn, keeping the one who performed best, as the Knights of the Round Table treated the ladies of this land in time past." The French court was indignant, and François supposedly commented that "it was not the custom in France for demoiselles from such families to be shown off like hackneys for sale."[40] The image may recall us to the point that Henry's fascination with the French brand of female sexuality seems to have extended to bedding "the English mare," Anne's promiscuous sister, since this is the most plausible explanation for Henry's curiously intense anxiety to secure authorization of changes in the English laws of consanguinity in 1533 before he married Anne—for if he had bedded her sister even illicitly this would have made his marriage to Anne a violation of the existing canon law.[41]

37. J. J. Scarisbrick, *Henry VIII* (Berkeley and Los Angeles: University of California Press, 1968), p. 10; A. Mary F. Robinson, *Margarete of Angoulême, Queen of Navarre* (London: Allen, 1886), p. 81.

38. Sergeant, p. 35.

39. Hester W. Chapman, *The Last Tudor King: a Study of Edward VI* (London: Cape, 1961), p. 18.

40. Desmond Seward, *Prince of the Renaissance: The Life of François I* (London: Cardinal, 1974), p. 199.

41. Scarisbrick, p. 349.

In the context of such passionate concern with French manners, Henry's extravagant preoccupation with Anne Boleyn becomes more intelligible, since she must have epitomized for him all the sophistication and charm which he so envied in the French court. It is certain that Anne spent at least three formative years there (1519–22), first under the supervision of Queen Claude, the wife of François, and later, according to Herbert of Cherbury, with the "Duchess of Alençon," Marguerite d'Angoulême, the king's sister. However, L. D. Carles, bishop of Riez, says that Anne first went to France in the train of Mary Tudor on her way to marry Louis XII in 1514, and later French sources confirm this. She probably traveled with her father and her older sister, for she herself was only seven years old, and seems likely to have lived at first, not at the court, but with the family of Philippe de Moulin, Seigneur de Briis-sous-Forges (near Rambouillet), a friend of Sir Thomas Boleyn.[42] The testimony about her raising in France from the age of seven to fifteen years is substantial enough to explain why she seemed so thoroughly "native French," even to a Frenchman, and why Henry's love letters to her are in French. In any event, the decisive flowering of her personality obviously took place during her adolescence at the French court, and this environment must be explored if we are to understand not only its influence on Anne but on most other significant English personalities until the end of the century; for if Marguerite d'Angoulême risked becoming Henry's wife and trained his mistresses, she also helped to tune the sensibilities of his daughter Elizabeth and to set the tone for her court playwright, William Shakespeare, in whose last play Marguerite's pupil, Anne Boleyn, would achieve a literary apotheosis.[43]

42. Sergeant, pp. 30–33; Bruce, pp. 17–33.
43. See Richmond, "Feminism of *Henry VIII*," pp. 11–20.

"The Monster":
Marguerite d'Angoulême

je suis Serf d'ung Monstre fort estrange,
Monstre je dy, car pour tout vray elle a
Corps femenin, Cueur d'homme et Teste d'Ange.
(Marot)[1]

(I am the slave of a very strange monster,
monster I say because quite truly she has
feminine body, man's heart, and head of angel.)

WITH HER CAREER PAST ITS APOGEE, AND ALREADY SENSING HER IMPENDING ruin, Anne Boleyn inevitably reverted to thoughts of happier times. A French correspondent reported to Marguerite d'Angoulême that "the Queen said that her greatest wish, next to having a son, is to see you again."[2] It is clear that this fascination extended to most of Marguerite's contemporaries, and it has since never faded. In 1609, fifty years after her death, we find Pierre Olhagaray writing that "Marguerite, who had been the precious violet in the garden of this house, and whose scent had drawn to Béarn (as thyme does bees) the best spirits of Europe, with whom insofar as she surpassed the most skillful, she conferred on serious subjects that she handled so much of the philosophy, theology,

1. Clément Marot, *Les Epigrammes,* ed. C. A. Mayer (London: Athlone, 1970), p. 97.
2. Sergeant, p. 229.

as of the history that she loved uniquely."[3] The only possible dissidents to this enthusiasm were her obtuse first and volatile second husbands, her neglected daughter, and the faculty and students of the Sorbonne —who would gladly have burnt not only her books but indeed herself as a notorious heretic, as they actually did or sought to do to many of her sympathizers and protégés: Bonaventure des Périers, Jean Calvin, Étienne Dolet, and Clément Marot. But while the impact of Luther was a crucial factor in the formation of Marguerite's personality and influence, her family antecedents provided no less significant elements in the distinctive ensemble which made her such a seminal figure in English, no less than in French, cultural history. As so often in the extravagant praises of Renaissance courtiers like Brantôme, contemporary flattery may have overestimated Marguerite's physical charms— she is certainly attractive and lively but not uniquely beautiful in many surviving portraits (Plates 1 and 2). Similarly her erudition may well have been overrated by Olhagaray, though perhaps Lucien Febvre now grades her too harshly: "She knew no Greek. She knew a little Latin, so little that it seems she could not read easily in the Roman poets, orators, and historians, and learn from them."[4] Febvre would rate her scarcely better than a Shakespeare or even than her protégé Marot, whose supposedly gross ignorance of Greek and Latin retarded the classical revival in France and England, according to such severe judges.[5] Yet Marguerite's intelligence was compelling to a degree considered unusual even in a woman of her rank by ambassadors and intellectuals, which is why it is often asserted that her model served to enhance and condition the perhaps less gifted mind and personality of her younger brother, the king.

The family ties between her ambitious mother, Louise de Savoie, her brother François, and herself were exceptionally close: "one heart in three bodies."[6] The mother, Louise, "belonged to a classically French

3. Pierre Olhagaray, *Historie de Foix, Béarne, et Navarre* (Paris: Douceur, 1609), p. 505.

4. Febvre, p. 73.

5. See the discussion of "The Complaint of Sigebert" in "The Mirror for Magistrates," Upham, p. 104.

6. See Marguerite de Navarre, *Les Marguerites*, pp. 16–17; and Seward, p. 75.

type, with a slight wiry figure, thick dark hair and metallic black eyes. Highly strung, her strength stemmed from nervous energy and an iron will. She was widely read, with a love of books unusual for a lady of her day."[7] After the early death of a beloved husband, Louise's passionate nature sublimated its drives in the career of her son, later François I, who depended on her energetic loyalty at such moments as his Italian campaigns, during which he left her as regent of France. Unfortunately, Louise's emotions also found other outlets, and her frustrated lust for the aloof constable of France, Charles de Bourbon, turned to a hatred which made him one of her son's greatest enemies. Some see in the "anagram" of Louise's name, Oisille, borne by the oldest lady of the *Heptameron*'s narrators, a suggestion that her personality is portrayed there.[8] If so it is less frantic, egotistic, and exploitative than its original. Fortunately, Marguerite's personality was richer and more flexible than her mother's: "Her humour was an odd mixture of earthiness and courtliness, of obscenity and piety, half Gallic, half Italian—a peculiarly Valois mixture," and "her court contained the whole world of letters, as complex and strange as her own temperament. Indeed, many of the contradictions in her own self-expression reflected the contradictions of French artistic and intellectual society as it struggled to assimilate the achievement of Italy."[9] Such complexity has often caused Marguerite to be seen as "the genius of the future, the modern woman."[10] Perhaps this unconventional personality derived in part from a family background initially more provincial than most royal families because of its indirect line of succession to the throne, caused by the failure of Louis XII to leave an heir. Lucien Febvre claims, "There is in her at bottom something of the parvenue, of the outsider, of the accidental, and to some extent of the unranked."[11] This appears in her writings and in her beliefs: "Marguerite lived her religion, a religion she made up for herself, little by little, with adjust-

7. Seward, p. 15.

8. Marguerite de Navarre, *L'Heptameron*, ed. Michel François (Paris: Garnier, 1967), pp. xii, 447.

9. Seward, p. 75; J. M. Plumb, *The Renaissance* (Harmondsworth: Penguin, 1964), p. 306.

10. Saint-Amand, p. 7.   11. Febvre, p. 20.

ments, reversals, corrections, continual adaptations which modified the form of her ideas."[12] Pierre Bayle agrees: "I would not know by what ways this queen of Navarre raised herself to so high a level of judgment and reason. . . . It must therefore be that the beauty of her mind and the greatness of her soul revealed to her a road that no one knows."[13] This unique synthesis resulting from her eclecticism makes her a valuable and distinctive illustration of the effects of the new ideas of her time, in a way superior to the personalities and compositions resulting from narrower minds and loyalties.

The lack of conditioned orthodoxy left her particularly open to the emotional influences of Lutheranism: "The direct, real, warm and human style of the great German populariser had a immediate appeal of which traces reappear in the style of such French works as the *Miroir de l'âme pécheresse* of Marguerite de Navarre."[14] Yet her characteristic lack of narrow commitments not only kept her free of the shackles of religious orthodoxy which so clearly limit Oisille's role in the *Heptameron*, it also left her sufficiently free of formal Lutheranism to avoid entrapment by its French persecutors from the Sorbonne. Her art, like her religion, is also too rich to fit classic categories and formulae: her "fervent syncretism . . . presupposes a free will that dominates choices and actions, strongly buttressed by an empirical view of life; on a literary level, it inevitably produces composite, amorphous works that on the surface defy the Aristotelian concept of order."[15]

She recognizes but never surrenders to classic attitudes and sources of any kind. Just as she fostered and protected the new ideas of the Reformers in France without binding herself to their cause, "it was in large part the queen [of Navarre] who was responsible for the diffusion and the vogue of Platonism around 1520." Yet again Marguerite stopped short of full commitment: "It is not possible to say that the

12. Febvre, p. 194.

13. Marguerite de Navarre, *Les Marguerites*, p. 21.

14. F. C. Spooner, "The Reformation in Difficulties," in *The New Cambridge Modern History*, vol. 3, *The Reformation*, ed. G. Elton (Cambridge: Cambridge University Press, 1958), p. 212.

15. Marcel Tetel, *Marguerite de Navarre's "Heptameron": Themes, Language, and Structure* (Durham: Duke University Press, 1973), p. 3.

queen fully accepted the theories of Platonic love," for she perceived that "Neoplatonism was too alien to the French temperament."[16] Still, Italian Neoplatonism formed one part of that system for the refinement of manners and true spiritual nobility which was to make the court not merely elegant and polite, but "a school of true virtue and knowledge, an example for all France."[17] A new code of manners crystallized out of this synthesis: "At the court, and even in the city, everyone became fascinated by questions of sexual psychology inspired by the new theories imported from Italy."[18] In consequence, "as it became in good taste to maintain platonic friendships to the knowledge of all the world, the courtiers flaunted these extra-marital liaisons in the style of the English Milord who bore his lady's glove on his breast" (in the fifty-seventh story of the *Heptameron*).[19] François followed his sister's lead in encouraging this mode of service, according to Brantôme: "I have heard some say that he wished strongly that the worthy gentlemen of his court should never be without a mistress."[20] This high value set on women's roles in the court of François was "a great novelty"[21] and began that shift to the highest authority and sophistication which makes the aristocratic ladies of later sixteenth-century France the best precedents for modern autonomous women and provides in them models for Shakespeare's witty and dynamic heroines, who are their best literary correlatives.

With this higher status of women in the Valois courts there were drastic shifts in manners and ethics from those of the sober, unimaginative society of Louis XII. A new flamboyance and emotional indulgence became common, which baffled or scandalized more conservative observers, as we saw in some English reactions to such manners when they were carried across the Channel by the Boleyn sisters. Indeed the Valois courts are not exempt from the censure of modern prudishness:

16. Émile V. Telle, *L'Oeuvre de Marguerite d'Angoulême, reine de Navarre, et la querelle des femmes* (Toulouse: Lion, 1937), pp. 253–54, 175.

17. Telle, p. 210. 18. Telle, p. 91.

19. Telle, p. 208. 20. Telle, p. 71.

21. Francis Ambrière, *Le Favori de Francois 1er: Gouffier de Bonnivet, amiral de France* (Paris: Hachette, 1936), p. 97. However, Brantôme's *Life of Anne de Betagne, Wife of Louis XII* credits her with schooling court ladies.

"This age had no more knowledge of modesty than of good taste. There was every freedom in morals. The sexes lived at the court in the strangest intimacy . . . intrigues were in fashion."[22] It is now commonplace to see the relaxed manners of Rabelais' Thélème as modeled on those of the court, evolving into a feminist norm for French aristocratic society. We may judge from the memoirs of Henri de la Tour d'Auvergne, duc de Boüillon (an associate of Marguerite's grandson Henri IV), the rigid authority given the ladies of French society a little later in the century over young men of rank:

> We had at that time a custom that it sat ill in young people of good family if they lacked a mistress, who was not chosen by them, and even less by their affection, but either they were assigned by some relative or superior, or they themselves chose those by whom they wished to be served. A little after I was at the Court, Monsieur le Mareschal d'Anville, who is at present constable of France gave me Mademoiselle de Chasteau-neuf as mistress, whom I served most attentively as much as my freedom and age permitted me. I was careful to please her and to serve her as much as my governor would allow me by pages and servants. She made herself very concerned about me, correcting me in everything which seemed to her I did improperly, indiscreetly, or discourteously, and this with a natural seriousness which she was born to, so that no other person has aided me so much in introducing me to the world, and in acclimatizing me to the court than this lady, I having served her, and in all honor, until Saint Bartholomew's Day. I cannot disapprove of this custom in so far as one sees or hears nothing but worthy things in it.[23]

Throughout the *Heptameron* we find bizarre permutations on this female sovereignty, in which a man may simultaneously serve a wife, a "Platonic" mistress (or socially superior lady), and a bedpartner (for cruder physical sexuality). Interestingly enough, just such a triad threat-

22. Francis Decrue de Stoutz, *La Cour de France et la société au XVIe siècle* (Paris: Firmin Didot, 1888), p. 177.

23. Henri de la Tour d'Auvergne, *Mémoires* (Paris: René Guignard, 1666), pp. 30–31.

ens to form around a talented young man in the *Heptameron*'s sixty-third story, which apparently deals with a planned escapade of King François, who seeks three companions to make love to four dashing Parisiennes. The young man has a well-domesticated wife, and he has served since before his marriage, like the duc de Boüillon, one of the finest ladies of the court. In the story he happens to escape bedding yet another beauty; but the women listening to the tale seem a little edgy about his split allegiances, while the men by contrast find the whole idea of a chaste mistress suggests dubious satisfaction. The moral refinement and intellectual superiority of Marguerite led to social changes permitting such rather strange aberrations. These extended not only to the debauching of chaste wives like Françoise de Foix, whom she had brought to court as a favor, against the husband's wishes, and thus unwittingly exposed to her brother's attentions. They even led to an attempted rape of Marguerite by an oversexed courtier who failed to maintain a dutiful service, as the fourth tale circumstantially recounts, according to Brantôme's sources.[24]

Marguerite's eccentric relationship with her aggressor in this latter case will serve to illustrate the way in which her personality, roles, relationships, and writing set the tone and provide possible sources for the plots, themes, psychology, and societies reflected in the works of such later authors as Shakespeare. Brantôme says that the would-be rapist was Guillaume Gouffier de Bonnivet, amiral de France. After a childhood friendship with François and Marguerite he became the king's official favorite. His "excessive amorousness" was notorious[25] and extraordinarily comprehensive; at one time he was "enslaved by Louise de Savoie," Marguerite's mother, who used him to destroy Charles de Bourbon.[26] Brantôme says he "had a good reputation in arms and wars beyond the mountains [in Italy] where he served his apprenticeship, and for this François had great friendship for him, being very charming and of subtle wit, very skillful, very fluent, very handsome and agree-

24. Marguerite de Navarre, *Heptameron*, pp. 453–54.

25. *Nouvelle Biographie Génèrale*, vol. 6 (Copenhagen: Rosenkilde and Bagges, 1964), pp. 645–46.

26. *Biographie Universelle*, vol. 5 (Paris: Desplaces, 1843), p. 43.

able."[27] Bonnivet powerfully reinforced the king's interest in Italy, and the reconquest of Milan was Bonnivet's favorite project, for his social and sexual successes there were enormous: "Brilliant at table, in games, at the ball, as at war, he was the darling of all the great Milanese ladies. He shared himself among them equitably. He promised, embraced, betrayed, begged forgiveness, pleaded, drove all hearts to despair, and passed through every bed. As soon as he encountered a hostile woman, it was naturally she who was the object of all his cares."[28] His sexual ambition was boundless, and he even succeeded in bedding François' own mistress, the comtesse de Chateaubriand, while the king still favored her, leading to the famous episode in which François interrupted Bonnivet's lovemaking, forcing him to hide behind the greenery ornamenting the bedroom's spacious fireplace while the king replaced him in his lady's arms—and afterwards (accidentally?) urinated all over his concealed rival before leaving. Bonnivet was a past master at sexual exploits and once disguised himself as the would-be lover of a Milanese *grande dame*, thus historically achieving the supposedly improbable bed-switch often exploited in Shakespeare. This escapade is ascribed explicitly to Bonnivet in the account of it which appears as the fourteenth tale of the *Heptameron*.

Bonnivet also aspired to "the vainglory of seducing the first princess of France," and initially "Marguerite let herself be deceived the more willingly because she had a repressed attraction to the favorite."[29] Failing to consummate the relationship, Bonnivet supposedly contrived the secret trapdoor to her bedroom by means of which he unsuccessfully sought to rape Marguerite when she was his guest at his new chateau with her brother. Inevitably there was a great cooling in Marguerite's attitude to Bonnivet thereafter, even though she wisely rejected the idea of public punishment of her assailant. However, Le Roux de Lincy, among others, has conjectured that another tale in the *Heptameron*, the fifty-eighth, might illustrate her revenge for bad treatment[30]—and this has the more interest since we find some amusing

27. *Biographie Universelle*, p. 42. See Plate 3.
28. Ambrière, p. 32.   29. Ambrière, p. 132.
30. Marguerite de Navarre, *Heptameron*, p. 491.

analogues and precedents in the tale for Shakespeare's Beatrice and Benedick, with Bonnivet anticipating Benedick's role. We know Shakespeare read this tale in Painter's anthology, from which he took details of stories printed on either side of Marguerite's story. The setting evokes a lady as elusive and talented as Marguerite, for historians have conjectured that "though Marguerite had no lovers, she had more brothers by alliance, sons by alliance, platonic enthusiasts, and adoring protégés than any other queen in Europe:

> Par alliance ay acquis une soeur
> Qui en beauté, en grace et en doulceur
> Entre ung millier ne trouve sa pareille;
> Aussi mon coeur à l'aymer s'apparreille
> Mais d'estre aymé ne se tient pas bien seur.[31]

(By a marriage, I have acquired a sister who is without peer in beauty, in grace, and in sweetness, among a thousand; also my heart prepares to love her, but it is not really sure of being loved back.)

Such indeed is the heroine of the fifty-eighth tale:[32]

> In the court of King François I, there was a lady of very lively wit who, by her good nature, worthiness and pleasing conversation had gained the heart of many suitors without dishonor, entertaining them so agreeably that they did not know what to make of her, for the most confident were in despair, and the most despairing were encouraged by her. All the same, in mocking most of them, she could not avoid loving one of them a great deal, whom she called her "cousin," so that this name would justify a deeper understanding. And as nothing is fixed, often their love turned to anger, and then returned more strongly than ever, so that the court could not ignore it.

Brantôme specifically mentions Marguerite's tendency to confer the

---

31. Robinson, p. 89.

32. Marguerite de Navarre, *Heptameron*, pp. 357–59. For a fuller discussion of this material, see Hugh M. Richmond, "Much Ado About Notables," pp. 49–63.

title of "cousin" on attractive young men, with whom she flirted as coolly as Beatrice does in the play.[33]

The lady in this fifty-eighth tale is provoked once too often by being jilted, just as Beatrice is affronted by Benedick for winning her heart "with false dice" (*Much Ado About Nothing* II.i.251) and then throwing her over: "You always end with a jade's trick. I know you of old" (I.i.129).[34] Marguerite's heroine explains to her friends, "You know how many wicked tricks he has played on me, and that when I loved him most he made love to others, from which I had more pain than I let appear. Well, now God hath given me the means to revenge it." The other court ladies are attracted to the idea of humiliating the lover because, like Benedick in his "merry war" with Beatrice, "there was no gentleman more committed to war against the ladies than he, and he was so loved and admired by everyone that no one dared risk becoming the victim of his mockery." The plotters agree that the witty gallant shall be convinced that his alienated mistress has once again fallen victim to an ungovernable passion for him. He is to be entrapped into preparing to make love to her and then, at the last moment, ridiculed before the whole court for believing himself so irresistible. The plot is successfully carried out, to general amusement, "but he had his responses and ripostes so neatly that he made them all think that he was not keen on the enterprise and that he had agreed to visit the lady just to give them amusement. . . . But the ladies would not accept this truth, of which there are still grounds for disbelief."

One sees how the lively court of François and Marguerite prefigures the witty domination of Shakespeare's comedies by their heroines. Even the famous church scene in *Much Ado* seems to parallel some unnerving consequences of such self-assured women's roles. Beatrice seeks to revenge her friend Hero's honor by inviting Benedick to "kill Claudio," Hero's accuser, and follows this invitation up with her aggressive reproaches: "O that I were a man! . . . O God that I were a man! I would

33. Pierre de Bourdeille de Brantôme, *The Lives of Gallant Ladies* (London: Elek, 1961), p. 358.

34. All Shakespeare references are cued to William Shakespeare, *Complete Works*, ed. Alfred Harbage (Baltimore: Penguin, 1969).

eat his heart in the market-place. . . . O that I were a man for his sake! Or that I had a friend would be a man for my sake. . . . I cannot be a man with wishing, therefore I will die a woman with grieving" (IV.i.285ff.). The words are almost identical to those with which two notorious ladies of the Catholic League spur on an admirer to revenge their faith: "If they were men or if they could be transformed into men that they might have accesse to the tirant, they would find it in their hearts to stabbe him: that is a special point of honor which they do proffer him to doo such a famous deed . . . hee is a man endowed with strength, they have been his good Ladies, they have favoured him greatly and pleasured him in anything that ever he requested. What, will he not do so much at their request: they must die . . . what a good deede it is to save the lives of Princesses, Ladies."[35] One can see how drastic an evolution was provoked by the religious strife, from Marguerite's playful revenge to this murder, of which Shakespeare read in Antony Colynet's *The True History of the Civill Warres of France*. Yet both the playfulness of Beatrice and her militant savagery are part of that shift in women's roles and initiatives set in motion by Marguerite and documented in her *Heptameron*. It is piquant to consider that some of Marguerite's personal traits can be seen on the modern stage in the liveliness which they have contributed to the role of Beatrice, whatever its harsher notes.

François himself also illustrates the mixed potentialities of such a cult of the sophisticated woman. The awkwardness of his first sexual adventure with a very steely bourgeoise is detailed in the forty-second tale of the *Heptameron*, and this affair was not successfully consummated. However, "further adventures were not so platonic. By 1512 his mother was writing of a disease in her son's secret parts—fortunately soon cured. His heart was seldom engaged. He enjoyed a woman in two ways. First with a simple, uncomplicated sensuality. Second, on an aesthetic level. Quite apart from his sexual appetites, Francis regarded pretty women as works of art, like some modern master of *haute couture*—he loved to see them beautifully dressed against beautiful back-

35. Antony Colynet, *The True History of the Civill Warres of France* (London: Woodcock, 1591), p. 403. See the start of Chapter 9 below.

grounds."[36] And if he thought women fickle and changeable, nevertheless he "insisted on their being accorded great honor and respect," according to Brantôme.[37] For François, "till the day he died, his sister was his ideal of what a woman should be.... He may well have learned his own charm and grace from her."[38] For if he was "ugly by most standards ... he made up for his strange face not only by a magnificent physique and presence, and the gorgeous clothes of the Renaissance, but by high spirits, superb manners, and unusual gifts as a conversationalist; the latter, enhanced by a pleasing voice, charmed everyone who met him." Castiglione saw in him "a certain lovely courtesy"[39] which François did not hesitate to exploit in seducing any woman who caught his eye. However, the dependence of François on women was not just condescendingly aesthetic or sensual. His mother regularly served with ruthless efficiency as regent during his absences from France; and when François languished in a Spanish jail after his defeat at Pavia, he depended on his mother and sister to restore his nerve and fortunes: Brantôme tells us that he "often said that without Marguerite he would have died."[40] Despite intermittent persecutions, his relative benevolence to Protestantism during much of his reign reflects her moderating influence and subtle conditioning. The ladies of his court sang the translations of the psalms of her poet, Clément Marot, "so enthusiastically that it has been said that the court of François I became Lutheran without knowing it."[41]

The court's ambivalence on the matter of religion matched its aesthetic discontinuities. Just as Marot's art balances precariously between such late medieval models as his father, Jean Marot, or Villon and the new fashion flowing through Lyons from Italy, so in magnificent artifacts like the palace of Chambord, "though the detail is Italian, the overall effect is that of some fantastic production of the late Gothic ... like some enchanted castle."[42] At this period in France, "French and

---

36. Seward, p. 33.   37. Brantôme, p. 386.
38. Seward, p. 33.   39. Seward, p. 32.
40. *Nouvelle Biographie Génèrale*, vol. 32 (Paris: Fermin Didot, 1967), p. 567. See also Saint-Amand, pp. 35–43.
41. Seward, p. 169.   42. Seward, p. 97.

Italian ideas remained distinct while existing side by side—they had yet to coalesce."[43] Indeed this rich ambivalence made the court an accurate microcosm of the syncretism of the whole country: "In the absence of an organic, authoritarian system both general and effective, everything or nearly everything in sixteenth-century France expressed its social disparity."[44] The lack of enforced consistency, such as each of the Tudors characteristically sought, explains the wild and veering qualities of both official and private attitudes in France, "the abrupt tacks of sixteenth-century men . . . from wisdom to folly, from disciplined moderation to the worst excess."[45]

This erratic and unpredictable world was that of Marguerite and, as we have seen, it is accurately reflected in the *Heptameron*. King François often appears under his own name in a surprisingly dubious light, above all when his sexual escapades are the subject of such tales as the twenty-fifth, or the forty-second, or the sixty-third. He emerges with more dignity and self-sufficiency in those with a political slant, as in the outmaneuvering of a traitor in the seventeenth tale. In addition to conscious and accidental corroborations by authors like Brantôme, scholarship has unearthed plausible historical antecedents for many of the other stories in actual events associated with the court, and Marguerite has usually sought to give plausibility to her tales by contemporary allusions to appropriate historical personalities, even when archetypal plots are involved, like the frequent fabliau treatments of the sexual misadventures of clergy, as in the thirty-first tale. While often ornamenting truth by fiction, and vice versa, the *Heptameron* still vividly evokes the texture of Marguerite's own environment, based as the stories are largely on "the tragedies of her life and her observation of the life about her, notably at court."[46]

It is by no means a cheerful picture of human nature that she presents: "A frank depiction of the world of sham she saw about her leads to a fatalistic viewpoint. In fact a study of the language of the *Heptameron* reveals this world of sham, the contradiction between intent and action, between thought and expression, to the extent that

43. Seward, p. 113.
44. Marguerite de Navarre, *Les Marguerites*, p. 18.
45. Febvre, p. 281.   46. Tetel, p. 10.

the words offer their multifaceted, often contrasting meanings in order to unveil the duplicity and multiplicity of thought and action."[47] As a result, while the structure and even the content of the *Heptameron* are clearly derived from the model of Boccaccio's *Decameron*, as Marguerite's prologue openly avows, the subtler potentialities of many originally medieval narrative techniques are developed in the work, even more vividly than in Castiglione's famous dialogue, *The Courtier*. Because many of the events and attitudes conveyed in the stories and in the interplay of comments following them epitomize the intense confusions of life at the dawn of the Reformation in France, the *Heptameron* reveals a calculated complexity and relativism far more unqualified than any medieval analogue, even *The Canturbury Tales*: "The queen's multifarious outlook on life converges into a narrative technique that juggles and purposely confuses the concepts of fiction and reality into a Pirandellian interplay."[48] The seeming anachronism of this parallel merits more sympathy than is often the case in modern criticism, and my argument seeks to suggest that Marguerite's popular work does display a new and influential sensibility from which much that fascinates us in later writers may derive, whether we talk of Shakespeare or Pirandello, not to mention French authors.

Anyone knowing Norman Rabkin's theory of the irresolvable complementarity of values in Shakespeare must be struck by how readily parallel concepts can also be imposed on the *Heptameron* by a critic like Marcel Tetel: "Protagonists who find themselves in a situation where they are forced to make a choice never make the right one; otherwise the tragic sense surrounding man's condition along a Pauline line would cease to exist, as would all irony heightening this basic human incapacity."[49] Each of these two theories overstates the ambivalence of the author by inflexibly imposing a consistent modern agnosticism on sixteenth-century sensibilities, which are incapable of such unqualified skepticism. Just as many Shakespearean figures do *learn* to make valid choices—like Malcolm, Edgar, and Cassio to mention the major tragedies alone—so in many of Marguerite's stories virtue triumphs

47. Tetel, p. 14.   48. Tetel, p. 15.

49. Tetel, p. 121. Compare Norman Rabkin, *Shakespeare and the Common Understanding* (New York: Free Press, 1967), p. 7.

without a doubt, as when the young woman rejects François' suit in the forty-second story or when François himself puts a traitor to flight in the seventeenth. In such contexts hostile comments about the stories by any of the listeners tend merely to rebound against themselves, as with Hircan's contemptuous comments on female virtue after the Platonic sentiments of the twenty-sixth tale. There, Nomerfide reacts sardonically: "What a pity you have an honest wife, since you not only despise virtue in anything, but try to prove it vicious."[50] Moreover the text, through various persons, consistently resolves the paradox that virtuous acts exist even in a world true to the Lutheran dogma that all humanity is victim to Original Sin. Parlamente agrees that Hircan may be right when he says of his spouse: "I believe she and I are children of Adam and Eve, whence, in perceiving ourselves well, we will not have need to cover our nudity with leaves, but rather to confess our frailty."[51] Parlamente accepts that "we all have need of the grace of God for we are all sealed in Sin," and asserts that "it is impossible that the victory over ourselves be made by ourselves, without a marvelous pride which is the vice that each must most fear, for it engenders the death and ruin of all the other virtues." Hircan himself describes in the thirtieth tale the complex double incest achieved by a woman whose trust in her own strength to reform her son achieves effects excelling even those of Oedipus. Geburon comments, "That man is wise who knows no enemy but himself and who holds his own will and his own counsel suspect."[52]

However, whenever this idea is wholeheartedly accepted by a character, virtue becomes possible even to those swept toward adultery by overpowering passions, such as the heroine of the twenty-sixth story who rejects both her lover's flattery of her virtues and his kisses. Similarly the virtuous wife marooned in the sixty-seventh novella, "who depended on God alone," is rescued by seeming chance because God "did not permit the virtue which he had set in this woman to be unknown to men."[53] In introducing the twenty-second story Geburon ex-

50. Marguerite de Navarre, *Heptameron*, p. 220.
51. Marguerite de Navarre, *Heptameron*, p. 221.
52. Marguerite de Navarre, *Heptameron*, pp. 233–34.
53. Marguerite de Navarre, *Heptameron*, p. 393.

plains that "if there is good, one should attribute it to him who is the source of it and not to his creatures, an error by which, through granting too much glory and praise, one esteems oneself something virtuous, most people mistakenly."[54] He tells the story of Marie Heroet, a nun whom a clerical reformer tried unsuccessfully to debauch. Against all the odds his campaign to blacken her reputation fails, and his own seeming virtue is discredited, leading Geburon to conclude "that God confounds the strong by the feeble" and that "without God's grace there is no man of whom one can believe anything good."[55] Oisille sets this fideistic frame for the whole cycle as early as the second story, about the virtuous wife of a muleteer. Oisille admonishes her hearers that such lowly virtue shows the hand of God: "For his graces are not given to men for their nobility and wealth, but as it pleases his goodness: which is no respecter of persons, who chooses whom he wishes; for whom he has elected honours him with his virtues. And often he elects the low to confound those whom the world esteems high and honorable."[56] Though the sentiments are quite orthodox and date back as far as Paul and Augustine, there is a certain irony in the attribution of so Lutheran an emphasis to the aging traditionalist Oisille. Indeed there is a strong emphasis throughout the book on the subversive social impact of Pauline sentiment that "he who thinks himself wise is a fool before God" and that "no one is wiser than he who knows his nothingness."[57]

Such recurring emphases indicate that Marguerite was sympathetic to the balance against good works in favor of grace which Lutheranism stressed, but they scarcely explain the psychological interest and excitement generated by many of the tales in which these principles are applied to the full gamut of sexual relations, from the most idyllic and ideal to the most macabre and bathetic. The moral intensity with which

54. Marguerite de Navarre, *Heptameron*, p. 175.
55. Marguerite de Navarre, *Heptameron*, p. 185.
56. Marguerite de Navarre, *Heptameron*, p. 21.
57. Marguerite de Navarre, *Heptameron*, pp. 272, 226. Compare St. Paul, I Corinthians 1.19–28. Stress on these aspects of Paul's thought was characteristic of St. Augustine's influence on the Reformation; see Henri Marrou, *Saint Augustine and His Influence* (London: Longmans, 1957), p. 165.

these frequently historical circumstances are scrutinized shows the desire to map out systematically a fresh pattern of ethical psychology, often by studying tests of humanity taken to its breaking point. After the fifth story, of a virtuous ferrywoman who fights off two lecherous clerics in midstream, Geburon contrasts her authentic but uninstructed virtue, which met the true test, with the untried worth of carefully nurtured ladies, "which should rather be called habit than virtue."[58] The sentiment is one which anticipates Milton in *Areopagitica*, a hundred years later, where he criticizes those who sink into a "pool of conformity and tradition. A man may be a heretic in the truth; and if he believes things only because his pastor says so . . . without knowing other reasons, though his belief be true, yet the very truth he holds becomes his heresy."[59] Marguerite anticipates Milton's sentiments when he asserts in the same work that "the knowledge of good is so involved and interwoven with the knowledge of evil." Therefore, he asks, "As therefore the state of man now is, what wisdom can there be to choose, what continence to forbear without the knowledge of evil?"[60] Longarine avoids a quarrel with Saffredent, to whom she has ascribed knowledge of evil, by saying, "You know the ugliness of vice so well that you know better than any how to avoid it."[61] Similarly Parlamente diplomatically interprets Hircan's affected approval of promiscuity by saying, "Hircan, it is quite sufficient that you should know how to commit evil."[62] Such issues reach a climax in the twenty-sixth tale, in which the virtuous wife resists a terrible temptation to commit adultery after being unwittingly ordered by her husband to receive her suitor in her bedchamber. The young man is at first shocked by her dexterous avoidance of his embrace and is then contemptuously admonished by his mistress: "Sir, did you dare to think that opportunities could move a chaste heart? Believe that just as gold purifies

58. Marguerite de Navarre, *Heptameron*, p. 37.
59. John Milton, *Complete Poems and Major Prose*, ed. Merrit Y. Hughes (New York: Odyssey, 1957), p. 739. All later Milton references are based on this edition.
60. Milton, p. 728.
61. Marguerite de Navarre, *Heptameron*, p. 331.
62. Marguerite de Navarre, *Heptameron*, p. 364.

itself in the furnace, so a chaste heart in the midst of temptations finds itself there more strong and virtuous, and becomes more severe the more it is attacked by its contrary."[63] The Lady in *Comus* could speak no more toughly, and *Areopagitica* exploits the same imagery: "Assuredly we bring not innocence into the world, we bring impurity much rather; that which purifies us is trial, and trial is by what is contrary."[64]

Part of my argument depends on the suggestion that Marguerite's self-awareness in such controversial matters results from her own similar experiences, for "always Marguerite was suspected of heresy."[65] Not only was her *Miroir de l'âme pécheresse* condemned by the Sorbonne in 1531 and temporarily placed on the list of forbidden works (until François forced this to be rescinded), but the university's "young members performed a farce which mocked Marguerite de Navarre and her sympathizers. Montmorency, always a champion of orthodoxy, rebuked her to her face."[66] Her capacity to protect sympathetic figures like Calvin and Marot depended largely on her brother's personal affection for her, and it was very uncertain, even when she withdrew to her own estates at Nérac. She earned the title of "mother-hen of the Reformation" by such associations as her early friendship with Bishop Guillaume Briçonnet, who fostered a Humanist center vaguely sympathetic to Reform at Meaux.[67] This group also suffered from the excessive negative reaction of the Sorbonne and Parlement, which extinguished the moderate, humanist Reform movement within the Catholic Church of France by resorting readily to imprisonment, torture, and execution at the least sign of reforming spirit, such as the breaking of Lenten fast regulations, a favorite trip-wire for Protestant inclinations, as Marot learned (it is interesting that this sixteenth-century preoccupation is used by Shakespeare to emphasize the Lollard views of his Oldcastle-Falstaff figure in *Henry IV, Part 1* I.ii.104ff.). While anticlericalism was almost a reflex in medieval writers like Chaucer and Boccaccio, not to mention Dante and Petrarch, Marguerite's use of the convention of the wicked Franciscan approached extravagance, as she

63. Marguerite de Navarre, *Heptameron*, p. 216.
64. Milton, p. 728.   65. Seward, p. 233.
66. Seward, p. 183.   67. Seward, p. 115.

herself realized: "My God, will we never run out of accounts of these damned Franciscans," groans one of the listeners to the forty-eighth story.[68]

Her first editor finds himself constrained to tone down the "Protestant" nature of many of the text's comments on the clergy and theology to avoid offense to Catholic readers, but there is no doubt that the *Heptameron* achieved great popularity as soon as it was published in 1558. Yet its writer's views have continued to offend the devoutly orthodox ever since: Génin considers Briçonnet's correspondence with the Queen as resembling "the work of a maniac," and, while he concedes Marguerite talent in profane literature, "she always preferred theology, a singular predilection in a woman whose name evokes only ideas of spiritual frivolity and anti-Christian abandon."[69] Of course, at first sight many of the stories seem flippant, or just perverse, as in the eleventh, in which the court lady, feeling an urgent call of nature, gets stuck in a convent privy and is rescued in some disorder, requiring her to strip naked; or in the thirty-second, about the adultress whose husband punishes her by confining her to the bedchamber with the skeleton of her murdered lover—his skull afforded as her sole drinking cup; or in the thirtieth, of the mother who bears her son's daughter, whom he later marries himself. In fact these tales are properly included in a work which approaches in scale and purpose the accumulation of case histories of modern psychologists like Freud, Jung, Laing, or Fromm, not to mention the even closer parallels of Berne and Goffman. It is accurate to say that Marguerite's stress on the authenticity, currency, and nonliterary nature of her raw material is part of a conscious and systematic attempt to evoke the new pattern of social relationships precipitated in the sixteenth century by the collision of the Renaissance and the Reformation with medieval survivals: "In spite of inevitable failure, attempts at synthesis must be made to seek knowledge about oneself and the world about us. The symposia at the end of

68. Marguerite de Navarre, *Heptameron*, p. 317.
69. Marguerite de Navarre, *Lettres*, ed. F. Génin (Paris: Renouard, 1841), pp. 3, 6.

the novellas provide a means to arrive at a composite and ever-changing synthesis."[70]

In the case of the flippant or perverse stories mentioned earlier one should see that our modern sensibility can accept possible serious aesthetic and ethical intentions for their inclusion. After all, a recent distinguished expositor has reemphasized the familiar cloacal aspect of Luther's discovery "of the meaning of the phrase from Romans when he was sitting on the stool. . . . It is fair to stress that Luther's personal experience was a strong blend of mind, body and soul. Throughout life too he suffered much from constipation as from anxiety; in such circumstances a successful evacuation could be a physical and almost a spiritual liberation."[71] The court lady who gets stuck to the lavatory seat is thus not just a quaint antecedent of the modern jingle about the three similar victims. Like Rabelais' prude on whom all the dogs of Paris urinate, she epitomizes that humiliating encounter with gross reality which Luther stressed and which Milton sees in a relevant turn of phrase as a salutary shock to untouched innocence. This he calls, paradoxically to our ears, "an excremental whiteness" of the kind which lends no dignity to the worth of those untouched by the "dust and heat" of life.[72] Similarly the incestuous mother of the *Heptameron*'s thirteenth story achieves disaster, like the characters in *Oedipus*, from too strenuous an attempt to avert evil, "instead of humbling herself and recognizing the inadequacy of our flesh, which without the aid of God can only do sin, wishing by herself and her tears to correct the past and by her prudence avoid the evil of the future."[73] The overstrenuous concern to protect her son's innocence leads to the worst conceivable results: "There, my ladies, is what happens to those who rely on their own powers and virtue to conquer love and nature . . . by thinking to do well all this evil has resulted."[74]

It says much for the range and subtlety of Marguerite's own sensibility that her stories are so compatible with the fashionable modern cult of

---

70. Tetel, p. 131.   71. Green, p. 60.   72. Milton, p. 729.
73. Marguerite de Navarre, *Heptameron*, p. 231.
74. Marguerite de Navarre, *Heptameron*, p. 233.

irony and skepticism: her "search for a constant produces ambiguity because it creates an acute realization of the inadequacy of human judgment."[75] This recognition is one she shares with Rabelais and above all with Montaigne: "The one dominant is absolute suspension of judgment: 'for this reason one must only judge oneself,' "[76] as she writes in the sixty-fifth tale. Inevitably, objective values tend to be replaced by subjective ones as Simontault decides after a debate about sexual decorum: "The best that I can see in this is that everyone should follow his own feelings."[77] Yet this sentiment, equally worthy of Montaigne, certainly does not emerge unscathed in the *Heptameron* either. Ennasuitte is warned by Nomerfide, "Beware of loving your husband too much: too much love will betray him and you, for everywhere there is a mean; and by lack of full understanding one often engenders hate by love."[78] The moral of the fiftieth story is "that extreme love brings another misfortune."[79] Such psychological views may explain the recurring pattern of ruined love: "As the most beautiful couple in Christendom and the greatest and most perfect love, Fortune, envious of two people so much at ease, would not suffer them to enjoy it but raised up an enemy for them."[80] On the whole romantic love is not fortunate or sustained in the *Heptameron*: "Ultimately love is equated with a malady, a spiritual disorder, causing a depressed state completely beyond human cure or reason"[81]—and characteristically this disease is fatal to one or both lovers in the stories. Negative imagery is often associated with love in them. As often in Shakespearean plays like *Antony and Cleopatra*, in the *Heptameron* "food . . . lends itself naturally to serve as an emblem of the sexual needs of the body; moreover it evidences a wilful ambivalence by suggesting the opposite spiritual needs."[82] Again, as in *The Merchant of Venice* or *Cymbeline*, classic images of love are pessimistically reversed: "The ring can mean perfection and eternity,

---

75. Tetel, pp. 108–9.   76. Tetel, p. 109.

77. Marguerite de Navarre, *Heptameron*, p. 115.

78. Marguerite de Navarre, *Heptameron*, p. 395.

79. Marguerite de Navarre, *Heptameron*, p. 325.

80. Marguerite de Navarre, *Heptameron*, p. 275; see also pp. 266, 312 for parallels.

81. Tetel, p. 188.   82. Tetel, p. 43.

or in the context of love, fidelity after marriage. However, from Marguerite's point of view it has the opposite significance: it is the object of deception and disappointment that does not fulfill its stated purpose,"[83] as in the eighth or twenty-fifth stories (or in Marguerite's own misuse of the stolen ring of the husband of Françoise de Foix to bring her to court and thus into her brother's adulterous embraces).

In such a pattern of sexual uncertainty, simple sincerity is rarely sufficient or even possible; Marguerite frequently talks specifically of role playing in our current sense: in the fifteenth tale an aging husband "begins to change his role, taking that which for a long time he had forced his wife to play,"[84] that of pursuer. Many of the women in the stories resemble the one in the fifty-ninth "who knew her role by heart."[85] Not for nothing was Marguerite herself a playwright. Feigning and disguise, both physical and psychological, are often the marks of wise, civilized, or at least sophisticated personalities throughout the *Heptameron*:

> Perfect or ideal love can go on only when two individuals involved are discreet about their relationship. This prerequisite condition she calls a good dissimulation. Given the nature of man, though, he leans more often toward a bad dissimulation, one that screens unvirtuous intention. The tragedy lies in the fact that the difference between the two is frequently indiscernible.[86]

This is a world anticipating that of Shakespeare's lovers, full of confused identities and appearances; personalities are either masked or are masks. For Marguerite:

> As a rule the mask conceals the lasciviousness or hedonism of an individual: Marguerite has in mind here the carnival tradition. . . . Bonnivet wears a mask as he pursues his female prey. . . . Concealing one's face, then, with a mask or any other object means to be devoured with carnal appetites; these protagonists

83. Tetel, p. 70.
84. Marguerite de Navarre, *Heptameron*, p. 119.
85. Marguerite de Navarre, *Heptameron*, p. 361.
86. Tetel, p. 84.

do not want to expose their loss of reason and measure. The naked face would become a metaphor of honesty.[87]

In observing these patterns the English literary critic finds the precedents they provide for Shakespeare unavoidable. This last theme of masked faces is one of his most intense preoccupations, as in the *Sonnets*:

> For since each hand hath put on Nature's power,
> Fairing the foul with art's false borrowed face,
> Sweet beauty hath no name, no holy bower.
>
> (127)

Marguerite's consistent suspicion of masks and makeup is a plausible source for Shakespeare's own frequent association of them with viciousness, sensuality, or at least ominous passion. It is an authentic bit of local color that the Frenchwomen in *Love's Labour's Lost* treat their suitors with (to us) unjustified hostility for dressing up as Russians:

> And will they so? The gallants shall be tasked:
> For, ladies, we will every one be masked,
> And not a man of them shall have the grace,
> Despite of suit, to see a lady's face.
>
> (v.ii.126–29)

After his humiliation, Berowne professes a new frankness and honesty: that he will "never come in vizard to my friend" (V.ii.405). The same negative effects of masking appear in the humiliation of Benedick by Beatrice during the masked ball in *Much Ado* (II.i). Psychological disguises can also be extremely dangerous in the later author, whether we talk of Richard III, Angelo, Iago, or Iachimo. In Marguerite no less terrifying disguised personalities appear, like the cuckolded husband of the thirty-sixth tale, who affects to ignore all the evidence only to achieve his wife's murder without appearing to have sought vengeance. The previous story is about another husband, potentially a cuckold, "but he, who was wise, disguised his anger,"[88] and assuming the clerical garb and role of the lover taught his wife an acutely painful lesson which

87. Tetel, p. 89.
88. Marguerite de Navarre, *Heptameron*, p. 256.

48

successfully reformed her. This deception, like the young men's lies to avoid accompanying François in debauch in the sixty-third story, is contrastingly classed in the *Heptameron* as "a good and holy hypocrisy," a "disimulation" which averts evil.[89] Parlamente even defends the discretion of women who are attacked by Simontault for putting on masks so that they can laugh at improper conversations which they affect to abhor when without these concealments, thus exposing herself to the charge of "praising women's hypocrisy as much as their virtue."[90]

Inevitably then, no simple solutions to the problem of integrating sexuality and moral standards are proposed by Marguerite; indeed, "the *Heptameron* stresses the relativism of truth and the difficulty people have in communicating with one another because of the impossibility of discerning the real facts or motivations behind human behaviour."[91] The only sexual relationship which does have some objective, permanent attributes in the *Heptameron* is an explicit, legal contract: "Only marriage offers an immutable synthesis of the multifarious and evanescent nature of love."[92] Marguerite's expositors approach this relationship with a blunt emphasis on its superiority to mere whim or sensuality; it must be sanctioned by the objective approval of family, friends, and other suitable judges, as with the young man in the sixty-fourth story whose intent "was to accept marriage with the approval of his friends, who, being assembled to this purpose found the marriage very reasonable."[93] Misfortune is precipitated in this case because the girl, for some elusive whim, refuses to accept the objective verdict. The pathetic story of Rolandine in the fortieth story seems to imply that she is the victim of a sadistic brother, who kills the young man she has secretly married; but Parlamente assigns a very different moral: "I pray God, my ladies, that this example may be so profitable to you that none of you may wish to marry for your pleasure without the consent of those to whom one owes duty; for marriage is so longlasting a condition that it should not be begun lightly or without the verdict of our best friends and relatives. Even then it cannot be done so well that there may not

89. Marguerite de Navarre, *Heptameron*, p. 381.
90. Marguerite de Navarre, *Heptameron*, p. 335.
91. Tetel, pp. 12–13.   92. Tetel, p. 9.
93. Marguerite de Navarre, *Heptameron*, p. 383.

be at least as much pain as pleasure."[94] Oisille coldly adds that the story should teach girls "not to marry by their own choice." In another commentary, Oisille savagely attacks the idea that it should be "permitted to everyone to marry whom they please," asking "whether it is to be supposed that a young man and a girl of twelve or fifteen should know what is best for them?"[95] In this passage she ridicules the idea of premarital intercourse and trial marriages which the relevant love story (excised by the first edition) has carefully raised, asserting that sentimental affairs only slowly give recognition to mistakes, while those obliged to marry at the discretion of the more experienced tend to make unexpectedly pleasant discoveries in their spouses.

Marguerite herself, with her inadequate marriages, is no good argument for Oisille, but nevertheless she aligns herself with most Protestants, including English authors such as Spenser, Shakespeare, and Milton, in believing that the marriage contract is central not only to all ethical systems, but to the very survival of the social structure itself, as modern sociology is only now reluctantly beginning to realize. Again Marguerite offers us a norm against which to measure Shakespearean archetypes. The volatile lovers of *A Midsummer Night's Dream* bitterly repudiate any marriage which "stood upon the choice of friends —Oh Hell! To choose love by another's eyes" (I.i.139-40). Yet they scarcely do much better on their own unstable initiatives, which are far less rational and objective than they assert. Similarly, the affair of Romeo and Juliet conforms to the ominous pattern of liaisons which are not public and socially sanctioned. In fact some of the details of their affair resemble closely a disastrous secret marriage in the fifty-sixth tale. The friar who arranges this concealed match admits, "It is true there is an inconvenience that only I know of the fiancé, which is that in wishing to save one of his friends whom another sought to kill, he drew his sword, thinking to separate them, but by misfortune his friend killed the other, so that he though he did not strike once is a fugitive from his city because he participated at a murder with his

94. Marguerite de Navarre, *Heptameron*, p. 277.
95. Marguerite de Navarre, *Heptameron*, pp. 437-38.

sword drawn. . . . And for this reason the marriage should be kept secret."[96] In fact the lack of any public celebration which he pretends to justify here ultimately proves almost as agonizing in its results as the concealed marriage of another Juliet of Shakespeare, who becomes pregnant by Claudio in *Measure for Measure*. The managed courtship of Ferdinand and Miranda seems more hopeful in this context, which also serves to suggest grounds for optimism in the author when he describes the manipulated affair of Beatrice and Benedick. Marguerite's views would encourage us to think so, for in the *Heptameron* "some couples, a few, succeed in marriage if they are able to close their eyes to each other's faults and make the best of the ups and downs of life; these individuals find a measure of happiness."[97] Marguerite is careful to stress this view in several tales which end hopefully; but more immediately, at the end of the fourth day there is a long discussion of marriage, which she concludes with a paean in the praise of virtuous marriages by Parlamente, who is applauded by all (if perhaps a shade sardonically by some of the male listeners), after which all retire to bed: "And I believe those who were married did not sleep as long as the others—recalling their previous loves and reenacting them in the present."[98]

Such moments of satisfaction do not imply that marriage is an easy solution to all the sexual problems of society, for the tensions and disasters of marriage figure as prominently in the *Heptameron* as those of courtship. To succeed in one requires almost as much dexterity as in the other, for Simontault grimly asserts: "Who has well thought out the nature of marriage will not esteem it less oppressive than an austere religion."[99] The exact balance of marital responsibility requires more concessions to sexual parity than most men and some wives are capable of; in the *Heptameron* it would seem that every man married to an

96. Marguerite de Navarre, *Heptameron*, p. 349. Shakespeare's source, Brooke's *Romeus and Julet*, does not include this accidental killing, perhaps suggested by Marguerite.

97. Tetel, p. 130.

98. Marguerite de Navarre, *Heptameron*, p. 281.

99. Marguerite de Navarre, *Heptameron*, p. 387.

honest wife should emulate the husband in the thirty-seventh tale where, "as he should, he trusted her in all matters."[100] Even this long-fortunate marriage is finally tainted with adultery, until the husband is shamed out of it by a trick of his wife, "and from that time they lived together in such great friendship that even the past faults, as a result of their happy outcome, increased their contentment."[101] Still, in the course of a fairly tortuous intrigue in the fifteenth tale, the double standard receives severe handling (in somewhat analogous terms to those used in equally confusing circumstances by Adriana when she is addressing her supposedly adulterous husband in *The Comedy of Errors* II.ii.132ff.): "And you sir, who are the sole cause of my misfortune, would you take vengeance for an act for which you have so long set me the example?"[102] It is true that by an act of sexual virtuosity the husband in the forty-fifth tale saves his marriage by recreating with his wife the distinctive sexual orgy which he discovers he had just perpetrated with a chambermaid before witnesses; but the comments by the listeners reject such superhuman talents, agreeing that the true sexual satisfaction of one's wife should suffice for normal desires, agreeing with Parlamente that if "reciprocal love does not satisfy a heart nothing else can."[103]

Nevertheless, many tales confirm that both husbands and wives are bound to tolerate sexual adventures in the hope of transcending them sooner or later; forgiveness is a recurring creative resolution for tales like the thirty-eighth and, more strikingly, the thirty-second, in which the sadistic husband who forces his wife to cohabit with her lover's skeleton finally restores her to her dignities, allowing Ennasuitte to point out a Christian, indeed a rather Protestant, precedent: "Tell me if the Magdalen has not more honor among men now than her sister who remained a virgin?"[104] Indeed, Marguerite does not hesitate to include a tale, the fifty-ninth, in which a court lady proves that a husband should happily accept the fact that a virtuous wife may have ad-

100. Marguerite de Navarre, *Heptameron*, p. 266.
101. Marguerite de Navarre, *Heptameron*, p. 268.
102. Marguerite de Navarre, *Heptameron*, p. 123.
103. Marguerite de Navarre, *Heptameron*, p. 308.
104. Marguerite de Navarre, *Heptameron*, p. 246.

mirers without his acquiring the right to revenge himself in any way:
"A beautiful and honorable woman is no less virtuous for being loved.
. . . Therefore her husband would never prevent her from going to court
nor object if she has suitors."[105] The beginnings of female emancipa-
tion can surely be detected here, and only a woman exposed to the
fresh currents of belief and ideology of the Reformation and the Renaissance could have explored the options open to women as effectively as
Marguerite did in the *Heptameron*. It is the foundation on which many
literary treatments of sexual roles depended during the rest of the century. And behind these tales lie as often as not the historical experiences
of Marguerite's contemporaries, not just literary precedents. The *Heptameron* is a self-conscious encyclopedia of the new sexuality, accurately
reflecting the fresh experiences and perspectives of its author: "She had
the presentiments, the intuitions of the future . . . she was a woman
essentially modern in her aspirations, ideas, morals."[106]

Without her, much of Renaissance literature would not have taken
the exact form it did, not least because, through her example, the role
of women begins to shift decisively; she was the intellectual and artistic
peer of the male Humanists and Reformers of her time, and she was
also their social and political superior and, as such, one major "origin of
feminism."[107] Her witty poise and good nature are important, perhaps
even specific, models for the self-confident heroines of Shakespeare's
comedies, as we shall see repeatedly. The praises which are devoted to
her are full of important anticipations of his virtues—not only in a
concern with "the analysis of feelings" based on "acute powers of observation," but in the skeptical shrewdness which anticipates Montaigne
in its suspicion of high sentiment:

> Many of the tales describe the break-up of an imperfect person-
> ality in the grip of human love which acts as a corrosive. . . .
> may well undermine reason and will power. . . . The characters
> are well motivated, and better still, are seen to act from multiple
> pressures and indeed inconsistent urges: the human condition is
> contemplated with neither cynicism nor morbid fascination, but

105. Marguerite de Navarre, *Heptameron*, p. 363.
106. Saint-Amand, p. 10.
107. Telle, p. 41.

with level-headed insight, sympathy often, and a desire to limit the damage.[108]

In such a fortunate temperament, resulting from the tensions of her lifetime, Marguerite affords both a major precedent and a standard by which to evaluate the kindred spirits who shared her outlook and experience during the Reformation.

108. McFarlane, pp. 243–48.

4

The *Heptameron* and the New Sensibility

Marguerite's eminent social position, progressive religious views, and political influence inevitably ensured that her tastes and values received broad recognition and close imitation, as when her *Miroir de l'âme pécheresse* was devotedly translated by the youthful Princess Elizabeth of England (and ceremoniously published in London in 1548). We have also seen that the *Heptameron* was excerpted in William Painter's *The Palace of Pleasure* (1566–67) and again partly translated in 1597. The *Heptameron* became part of "the favorite reading of English ladies in the first decades of Elizabeth's reign."[1] Marguerite's narratives were also widely noted by professional writers, even though they were not necessarily divergent from other French fiction of the time written by authors associated with (and even perhaps helping) Marguerite's work. In such a man as Bonaventure des Périers "the spirit of the French Renaissance, in its more cultivated and refined representatives, comes out very strongly . . . as a kind of cultivated sensuality, ardently enamoured of the beautiful in the world of sense, while fully devoted to intellectual truth, and at the same time always conscious of the nothingness of things, the instant pressure of death, the treacherousness of mortal delights."[2] While des Périers was one of

1. Lee, *French Renaissance in England*, p. 129. See Chapter 1 above.
2. George Saintsbury, *A Short History of French Literature* (Oxford: Clarendon Press, 1901), p. 163.

Marguerite's protégés, she could not shield him from orthodoxy's persecution of intellectuals sympathetic to Reform, and his suicide is usually attributed to the fears thus aroused in him. However, his work does indicate that Marguerite's writing is an authentic expression of the literary sensibility of the period, and it has even been suggested that the anecdotal form of the *Heptameron* permits it to assimilate the writings submitted by other members of her court, like des Périers, without strain or falsification. Such a sustained corporate effort might help to explain the range and virtuosity of the *Heptameron*, even though it is still ultimately the expression of Marguerite's own choices and tastes.

The general enthusiasm which greeted the *Heptameron* in France and England after its first publication in 1558 indicates how truly it reflected and reinforced the literary ideals of European sensibility around the time of the accession of Elizabeth. The nominal recognition by English literary historians of an Italian tradition called "Petrarchism" and of an associated set of ideas called "Neoplatonism" has gradually been replaced by a more exact sense of the most evolved writing of sixteenth-century Italy;[3] but the literary effect in England of the still closer civilization of Renaissance France tends to be identified with the most obviously "classic" authors like the Pléiade, Rabelais, and Montaigne, even though scholars of Shakespeare are aware of his dependence on sources in French popular fiction. Marguerite's work affords a much more comprehensive illustration than Belleforest and his fellows, or most of the Pléiade, of the moral and cultural resources which French society could offer to the succeeding generation of English authors in Elizabeth's reign. Shakespeare was born six years after the *Heptameron*'s first publication, and many of the complexities of situation, personality, and value usually considered to be distinctively his are prominently prefigured in the *Heptameron*. This collection of tales serves much better than Petrarch, Boccaccio, and the other Italian models as a measure both of Shakespeare's direct dependence on and his advances beyond such literary resources of his time.

3. See for example Guss, *John Donne, Petrarchist*; Hugh M. Richmond, *The School of Love* (Princeton: Princeton University Press, 1964); Rosalie Colie, *The Resources of Kind* (Berkeley and Los Angeles: University of California Press, 1973), etc.

The seminal pattern of Marguerite's own witty, skeptical, yet well-meaning personality has affinities with Shakespeare's comic heroines, for example Beatrice; likewise, her brother's distinctive character offers precise sources for Shakespeare's sonnet cycle. The high emotional intensity of the relationship to the young man in the *Sonnets* resembles sexual passion yet avoids sensuality and possessiveness to a paradoxical degree. The tolerance of failures, betrayals, and deficiencies depends on a relativism of values irreconcilable with conventional ethics, which has led scholars like Stephen Booth to deny that the sonnets can be definitively explicated.[4] However, their elusive qualities can be better categorized and understood in light of the precise model provided by Marguerite's relationship to her brother, for she was no less intense, tolerant, skeptical, and self-sacrificing to him than was the writer of the sonnets to his younger friend. (See Plate 5.)

Most historians find Marguerite's attitude to François disturbingly self-abusing. She has left abundant testimony of its extravagance:

> Et toy, François, de mon coeur la moitié,
> Amy entier, vray Polion d'aimitié,
> Mon Jonathas, mon fidèle Achates
> Mon vray Pollux, mon syncère Orestes,
> En me voyant, de malheur abbatu
> Ainsi traité, mon frère, qu'en dis-tu?
> Làs, sans t'ouyr, bien présumer je peux
> Que toy et moy n'ayans qu'un coeur tous deux
> Si dans mon corps l'une moitié labeure,
> L'autre moitié dedens le tien en pleur.[5]

(And you, François, the half of my heart, complete friend, true Pollio in amity, my Jonathan, my faithful Achates, my true Pollux, my sincere Orestes, in seeing me crushed with misfortune, treated thus, my brother what do you say? Alas, without hearing you, I can well presume that you and I, having both only a single heart, if one half of it struggles in my body, the other half of it weeps in yours.)

4. See his Yale edition of the *Sonnets* (1978), *passim*.
5. Henri A. Blind, *Marguerite de Navarre dans ses rapports avec la Réforme* (Strasbourg: Heitz, 1868), p. 12.

The intensity of Marguerite's devotion has led to perverse misinterpretations of it as incestuous, a view comparably questionable as the homosexual approach to the sonnets. There is adequate, objective evidence for neither view. Each author's self-abnegation transcends even emotional recompense, let alone sensual satisfaction, and involves the sacrifice of all other relationships: Marguerite's "excessive love for her brother explains well the evasions and the weaknesses which she showed more than once in abandoning her friends and protégés to persecution." [6] Worst of all she repudiated all maternal instincts in surrendering her daughter entirely to the political manipulations of her brother, a submission which modern scholars describe in terms that diminish her humane pretensions drastically. [7] With similar provocativeness Shakespeare matches his creation, Valentine, in *Two Gentlemen of Verona*, when he himself surrenders his mistress to his friend with as good a grace as sophistry can muster (Sonnet 42).

As for the recipient of his sister's uncritical devotion, "François well knew his sister was a slave to his will," and when Anne de Montmorency, constable of France, suggested "exterminating" such "heretics" in the king's own family, François complacently responded: "Don't talk of her any more, she loves me too much, she will never accept any religion dangerous to my state." [8] Indeed no service or acceptance was too humiliating for Marguerite, and this produces a curious portrait of François to emerge in her stories of him—showing him to be equivocal, exploitative, even dishonest—exactly the characteristics which have caused critics [9] to think Shakespeare really is censuring his friend when he writes disturbing sonnets like the ninety-fourth:

> They that have power to hurt and will do none,
> That do not do the thing they most do show,
> Who, moving others, are themselves as stone,
> Unmovéd, cold and to temptation slow;

6. Blind, p. 3.

7. Bernard Nabonne, *Jeanne d'Albret, reine des Huguenots* (Paris: Hachette, 1945), pp. 26–33.

8. Blind, p. 27; Seward, p. 183.

9. Anne Ferry, *All in War with Time* (Cambridge: Harvard University Press, 1975), p. 35.

They rightly do inherit Heaven's graces
And husband nature's riches from expense.
They are the lords and owners of their faces,
Others but stewards of their excellence.
The summer's flower is to the summer sweet,
Though to itself it only live and die;
But if that flower with base infection meet,
The basest weed outbraves his dignity:
>For sweetest things turn sourest by their deeds;
>Lillies that fester smell far worse than weeds.

It is a striking proof of Shakespeare's indebtedness that Marguerite twice expresses the identical sentiment of Sonnet 94's first line for which no source has been noted hitherto. In the twenty-fifth tale of the *Heptameron* it is addressed to Marguerite herself by the prior of a monastery visited as a cover for an adulterous love affair by her brother, the king. The deceived prior has been impressed by the apparent devotion of François, with all his opportunities for worse conduct: "Bien heureux est qui peut mal faire et ne le faict pas"[10] (He is most fortunate who can do evil and does not do it). Marguerite is puzzled by the discrepancy between what she knows of her brother's moderate religious commitment and these nocturnal rituals, "so she went to him and told him the good opinion that the clergy had of him, at which he could not prevent himself from laughing with an expression by which she, who knew him like her own heart, perceived that there was something hidden beneath his devotion, and did not give up until he told her the truth," which is that he was debauching a nearby lawyer's wife. The auditors' reactions to this tale are not those of our modern puritanism; Oisille even says (perhaps reflecting the doting mother, Louise): "Truly, I would that all young aristocrats would follow his example, for scandal is often worse than sin"[11]—a cynical sentiment which Shakespeare echoes in Sonnet 121: " 'Tis better to be vile than vile esteemed." It is worth noting that this authentic tale also fascinated Montaigne, who talks about its historicity in the sixty-sixth essay of

10. Marguerite de Navarre, *Heptameron*, p. 206.
11. Marguerite de Navarre, *Heptameron*, p. 207.

his first book and exclaims against Marguerite's indulgent attitude[12]—
for Parlamente (who often approximates the author's views) notes how
convenient may be the king's return through a monastery after com-
mitting carnal sin: "You should not at all make a judgment about it,
for perhaps in returning, repentance was such that the sin was forgiven
him."[13] The tale epitomizes the *Heptameron*'s blend of sensuality,
irony, wit, and moral sophistication—a blend also prefiguring the bizarre tonalities of *Measure for Measure*.

The sonnet's opening phrase is also used a second time in praise of
François in the forty-second tale, describing his failure to take revenge
on the tough young woman who frustrates his first sexual advances.
She is the sister-in-law of "ung sommelier d'eschansonnerye"[14] (a butler or wine-steward) assigned to François, who finds this sixteen-year-
old brunette has the demeanor of a princess. Despite every kind of
subterfuge François fails to seduce her, even though she admires him
greatly, and when he finally decides to rape her in the forest at the
instigation of the servant and one of his gentlemen, "God willed it"
that his mother Louise keeps him busy elsewhere.[15] The girl detects
the failed plot and turns on her brother, saying, "in extreme fury, that
he was the devil's lackey and that he did more than he was ordered,
for she was sure it was the plot of himself and the gentleman and not
the young prince."[16] When François tries to reconcile her with her
brother-in-law, reproaching her for her severity, she responds "that
he was well indebted to his butler, since he served him not only with
his body and goods but also put his soul and conscience at the prince's
disposition."[17] François then gives up his suit but respects the woman
ever after. The listeners' reactions to the tale are again unexpected.
The narrator, Parlamente, still resembles Marguerite herself in affecting
to be surprised by the girl's toughness: "Have we such low spirits that
we make our servants our masters, since this girl could not be won by

12. Marguerite de Navarre, *Heptameron*, p. 473.
13. Marguerite de Navarre, *Heptameron*, p. 207.
14. Marguerite de Navarre, *Heptameron*, p. 287.
15. Marguerite de Navarre, *Heptameron*, p. 292.
16. Marguerite de Navarre, *Heptameron*, p. 293.
17. Marguerite de Navarre, *Heptameron*, p. 293.

love or persecution? I pray you that, by her example, we should remain victorious over ourselves, for it is the most praiseworthy victory that we could have."[18] Oisille compares the girl to Lucretia, but the cynical Hircan suggests she was probably just satiated by some other lover, and Saffredent claims that her virtue was sheer affectation, a kind of "hypocrisy" masquerading as "honor," for in a corrupt society like theirs honest frankness in love has been lost "so that even those who love perfectly dissimulate, thinking virtue a vice."[19] However, Dagoucin defends the girl's refusal to surrender to her instincts, adding surprisingly that the prince's final moderation reflected even greater credit on him, and Longarine agrees, saying: "He is the more to be esteemed in that he has overcome man's customary viciousness, for he who can do harm and does not do it at all, that man is very fortunate" (Qui peut faire mal et ne le faict poinct, cestuy-là est bien heureux).[20]

These two authentic accounts of François not only provide specific sources for Sonnet 94, they share one of Shakespeare's most profound preoccupations: the erratic behavior of the gifted aristocrat who blends charms and virtues with egotistical sensuality and callousness, concealing beneath a mask of hypocritical honor many antisocial acts which may even invite the charge of criminality. It is not only the young man of the sonnets who matches this pattern, for Prince Hal fully illustrates this disconcerting blend of attributes. And like the brother-infatuated Marguerite, Shakespeare finds himself trapped in Sonnet 94 into admiring the tremendous potentialities of such agile personalities, if they escape deep corruption. The parallelism with François is self-evident: when he seeks to rape the girl he not only risks demeaning himself in comparison to her innocent integrity but also subordinates his actions to the will of his two servants, who seek to exploit his egotism to their own advantage. On the other hand, there is a clear sense in which his use of the monastery as a cover gains him paradoxical advantages and even might literally win "heaven's graces," if we accept Parlamente's hypothesis. If Sonnet 94 seems to us complex, peculiar, and ambivalent, it does so because it closely follows and probably con-

18. Marguerite de Navarre, *Heptameron*, p. 294.
19. Marguerite de Navarre, *Heptameron*, p. 295.
20. Marguerite de Navarre, *Heptameron*, p. 295.

sciously copies such historical precedents embedded in works like the *Heptameron*, which in turn are based on the careers of amgibuous personalities like those of François and his successors on the French throne.

The sonnet cycle's last, sardonic phase, dealing with the Dark Lady, also probably depends directly on the *Heptameron*. Above all the speaker shares many of the paradoxical sentiments of the male narrators in that text, as in the despairing account of his sexuality offered by the misogynist Simontault at the end of the first tale, which deals with the murderous result of a wife's promiscuity:

> I beg you, my ladies, to see what harm comes from a wicked woman and how many evils are made by the sin of such a one. You will find that since Eve made Adam sin all women have undertaken the tormenting, killing, and damnation of men. As for me, I have so much experience of their cruelty that I think I shall only die or be damned by the despair that one of them plunges me. And I am still so mad that I have to confess that such hell is more pleasing to me coming from her hand than paradise given by that of another.

Apparently he loves Parlamente, for the debate goes on thus:

> Parlamente, affecting not to understand at all that it was to her these words were directed, said to him, "Since hell is as pleasant as you say, you should not fear the devil who put you there." But he replied to her angrily, "If my devil became as black as he has always been wicked to me, he would frighten this gathering as much as I take pleasure in seeing it; but the fire of love makes me forget the fire of this hell."[21]

One should carefully distinguish Simontault's deeply ambivalent response from the unqualified misogyny of the medieval moralists which he briefly echoes in his biblical allusion. For while their mistrust of women is doctrinaire and categorical, his is dramatic and psychologically complex, and he is far more cynically angry than any Petrarchan lamenting his beloved's impassivity. He tells of the murders precipitated by a promiscuous wife in order sadistically "to revenge myself on love and on her who is so cruel to me,"[22] presumably one of his

21. Marguerite de Navarre, *Heptameron*, p. 18.
22. Marguerite de Navarre, *Heptameron*, p. 11.

hearers, Parlamente—and by implication Marguerite herself, who often lurks behind this mask and is after all the real narrator of this story. The tale itself bitterly shares the view of lust taken in Sonnet 129 as "perjured, murderous, bloody, full of blame." The young man, who is ultimately murdered because of the adultress, is her preferred alternative to the cleric, who was her first lover and whom she still exploits to employ her conniving husband profitably away from home. When the young man learns of this cynical promiscuity, he is revulsed and sardonically repudiates the doubly corrupt wife, to whom he says wittily "that she was too holy, having touched sacred things, to speak to a sinner like him, whose repentance was so great that he would hope that his sin would soon be forgiven him."[23]

Yet for all his vituperation of women through such an epitome, Simontault admits of his mistress: "I am still so mad that I have to confess that such hell is more pleasing to me coming from her hand than paradise given by that of another"[24]—a dualism which Shakespeare echoes in the face of sexual perversity:

> All this the world well knows; yet none
> knows well
> To shun the heaven that leads men to this hell.
>
> (129)

In another possible debt to the *Heptameron*, the speaker in Sonnet 144 perceives a deplorable sexual tangle very similar to that of the first story of the collection, in which the wife's lover knows he is betraying his own moral obligations, corrupting a marriage, and is probably himself being betrayed for a younger lover. The Dark Lady receives an accusation in Sonnet 152 which could also be accurately leveled at the corrupt wife of the story:

> In loving thee thou know'st I am forsworn,
> But thou art twice forsworn, to me
> love swearing;
> In act thy bed-vow broke, and new faith torn
> In vowing new hate after new love bearing.

23. Marguerite de Navarre, *Heptameron*, p. 12–13.
24. Marguerite de Navarre, *Heptameron*, p. 18.

And while Simontault cannot break with Parlamente because hell with her is more pleasant than others' favors, Sonnet 150 professes "that in my mind, thy worst all best exceeds." Both Marguerite and Shakespeare thus no longer exploit the elegantly formal despair of Petrarchan sexuality, with its clear moral and theological reference points. Each portrays a messy tangle of allegiances and attractions, tightened by the tug of sensuality into a knot beyond rational analysis and disengagement. Nor does Marguerite evoke Simontault's misfortunes and sardonic attitudes only to forget them, for allusions to them recur, as in the prelude to the thirty-third tale for example; and at the end of the twenty-fourth story Saffredent also confesses to a similarly disabused perversity. Rejected by the devil (to whom he had offered himself in despair at the cruelty of his mistress) because his mistress could torment him more skillfully than all the torments of hell, Saffredent admits, "My affection is still such and my error so great . . . that the cruelty of women cannot conquer the love I bear them."[25]

If we cannot certainly detect Marguerite behind the mask of Parlamente, whose moral severity oppresses lovers like Simontault, elsewhere we find Marguerite often appearing overtly in her historical nature and situation, as in the twenty-second story, one of the most circumstantial and historically explicit episodes, in which the participants appear under their own names. This story has a particular interest for Shakespeareans because it offers illuminating models for the technique and content of one of Shakespeare's most eccentric and frequently disliked plays, *Measure for Measure*. Seen in its Reformation context, Shakespeare's play has a very different texture from that suggested by its melodramatic plot—the characters and their language have a cruel realism which has offended many sensibilities but which has rightly won it popular appeal. And even its plot is far less arbitrary if we look at its possible sources in history. The Reformation period was very brutal in regard to the ethics of sex, and the Claudio-Juliet story probably derives from a scandal recorded in Pierre de l'Estoile's journal for 1582[26] concerning just such a Claudio: Claude Touard, who was

25. Marguerite de Navarre, *Heptameron*, p. 201.

26. Pierre de l'Estoile, *Mémoires pour servir a l'histoire de la France*, vol. 45 (Paris: Foucault, 1825), pp. 240–43. Interestingly enough the case is contrasted

sentenced to death for impregnating a government official's daughter. Since the lover was an attractive young man, the girl passionately in love with him, and a marriage possible once financial problems were overcome by his relatives, "all men of spirit" denounced the sentence, and the young man was literally rescued on his way to execution. Those responsible were not discovered, and a notorious crook was seized and executed in the young man's place: "One gave his head for all." The conjunction of the lover's name and the parallels in much of the detail (such as the sexual viciousness of the ruthless official who was the father of the girl, himself guilty of adultery) all suggest that *Measure for Measure* commands attention by its exploitation of the literary capacity which Alessandro Manzoni advocated: "to study the behavior of man in real life . . . in ways contrary to the romantic spirit."[27] L'Estoile's story is exactly the kind of material transcribed by Marguerite into her *Heptameron* a few decades earlier—giving that collection the characteristic vividness and excitement which attracted Shakespeare to its tales and which he recreated by similar realistic allusions.

What George Whetstone lacks in his earlier use of similar material in his *Promos and Cassandra* is this unique Shakespearean talent to clothe the gaunt skeleton of a dramatic (and ultimately historical) story with documentary data, psychological complexities, and juxtapositions which will give it vividness, conviction, and resonance. For instance, the location of Whetstone's melodrama in the Hungarian city of Julio is hardly significant, while the setting of Shakespeare's play in contemporary Vienna is full of historical interest in view of the recent reign of Maximilian II (1527–76) in that city; for the play's new locale marks the first move toward an evocation of specifically Reformation ethical problems which all the sources lack, accepting as they do uniformly traditional standards of morality. Perhaps the "Emperor Maximian" in Giambattista Cinthio's version provides a clue for Shakespeare's detailed references, since the historical Emperor Maximilian II's career, like the skeptical Duke Vincentio's, wavered in its favoring

with a gentler prosecution involving two hypocritical and evil counselors, one called "Malevolus" (pp. 232–33), suggesting a prototype for Malvolio's name, since he is said to have been outsmarted by a "chambermaid."

27. Alessandro Manzoni, letter to Claude Fauriel, 29 May 1822.

of Reformist politics and authorities, and neither figure can be neatly explained, categorized, or fully justified.

It is in stressing such moral uncertainties that the distinctive character of *Measure for Measure* appears, for in comparison with Whetstone's exuberance and the more urbane characters of his source in Cinthio's novella, Shakespeare's "most important innovation"[28] is the introducton of formal religious elements: Isabella's novitiate, the Duke's sacrilegious disguise as a friar, and the intense theological dimension added to many of the debates, which has given them such depth and power. This unique amalgam of current experience and concerns makes the play true to the sixteenth century's sensibility at its most theologically advanced and sophisticated, for much in it which is now put down to authorial eccentricity is actually part of the bizarre Reformation inheritance which it shares with authors like Marguerite d'Angoulême or Rabelais. Measured against the *Heptameron*'s twenty-second story, for example, the Angelo-Isabella plot seems far less willful and contrived, and the tale may well provide a partial source for the provocative characters and sentiments in the play.

The characters in the twenty-second story[29] are recognizable historical identities: Étienne Gentil, prior of St. Martin des Champs from 1508 to 1536; Marie Héroët, who is named, the sister of one of Marguerite's closest associates, the poet (and later bishop) Antoine Héroët; and Marguerite herself, also acting under her own name. The prior's name is not given, but all other details of his career are explicit and verifiable: "His life until the age of fifty was so austere that the fame of his sanctity ran throughout the kingdom, so that every prince and princess paid him great honor when he called on them. And no reform in religion was made except by his hand." As official Visitor and moral censor of the aristocratic convent of Fontevrault, he so terrified the nuns that "they treated him as they would the person of the king, which to begin with he refused; but in the end, approaching fifty-five, he began to find very good the treatment he had despised, and considered himself a public blessing." Despite increasing self-indulgence,

28. J. W. Lever, ed., *Measure for Measure,* by William Shakespeare (New York: Vintage, 1967, p. xliv.
29. Marguerite de Navarre, *Heptameron,* pp. 176–86.

"in all these little things he showed himself so austere that he was feared like a god painted in judgment." The richer diet awakened his sexual appetites, "and with the change of regimen . . . he began to look at faces whose consciences had previously concerned him, and, in seeing those charms which veils make more desirable, he began to desire them." Among the nuns, Marie Héroët's fluent and winning voice by itself attracts his attention and at once traps him in passionate love, confirmed by a glimpse of her face; but love of her is likely "to be difficult because he found her wise with words and of subtle mind." He begins an attempt at physical seduction by calling her attention to her breasts, and when she rejects his caresses he pretends his doctors have prescribed sexual intercourse for him as treatment for a potentially fatal disease: "On my initiative, I would not commit a mortal sin to avoid death, but should someone else get to that point, I know that mere fornication is in no way comparable to the sin of homicide. Therefore if you value my survival, in saving your conscience from that cruelty of homicide, you would save my life." As with Isabella (II.iv.88–110), this variant of the sexual sacrifice proposed to the analogous heroines in Cinthio and Whetstone stresses the theological dimensions of laying down one's body to save another's life. Sister Marie is warned that any refusal is "homicide," just as Angelo observes that her refusal would make Isabella "as cruel as the sentence that you have slandered so" (II.iv.109–10). Marie Héroët is as firm as Isabella in contemptuous rejection of this specious moral obligation, which their more "humane" female analogues in history and literature reluctantly fulfill, to no effect. The prior then tries physical assault and even offers high office to Marie, without success. Next he rigs up false evidence of her sexual relations with another man, accusations which she has to accept in public. In the same way, the innocent Isabella is forced to surrender her reputation for chastity in a public trial (V.i.95–124); thus both obdurately chaste women are made to appear in public as dishonored, and the prior can point out to Sister Marie: "You know the crime of which you are accused and that your affectation of being chaste is useless to you, for everyone knows that you are just the opposite." However, his victim continues to resist his advances, trusting in God's justice. Another attempt at rape by a young cleric having failed, the now nervous prior claims it was simply a test of her chastity. By this time the nun's brother has forced access to her and has learned her wretched story, which he passes on to the horrified sister of the king, Marguerite herself, who feels "such desire to avenge the innocence of this poor girl" that she starts a prosecution of the prior, "who offered no excuse" and says that "if she would stop the case he would confess Sister Marie Héroët a pearl of honor and virginity. The queen of Navarre, hearing that, was so stupefied that she did not know what to say but left the matter there, and the poor man, in great confusion, withdrew to his monastery where he never more wished to be seen by anyone, and only lived one year longer." The king thereupon made Marie abbess "of the convent at Giy near Montargis," which she reformed in harmony with the tough spirit with which she had defended her mind and body from the prior's assaults. The moral drawn by the narrator, Geburon, is "that God by weak things confounds the strong" and "that without the grace of God there is no man of whom one can believe any good, nor so strong in temptation one cannot conquer with his help, as you can see by the confusion of him whom all thought just and by the exaltation of her whom he wished to be found a sinner and wicked."

This theological orientation of the story derives naturally from the emphasis on the victim's vocation as a nun, which she shares with Isabella. Like Angelo, the persecutor is made distinctive as a puritan-ical reformer, and like him the criminal is unexpectedly spared punish-ment after confession, while the victim's professional commitment to virginity survives intact after various kinds of attack which are repulsed with a religious fervor like Isabella's. In his novella, Cinthio softened the original cruel events which were his ultimate sources. Historical accounts of the precedents stress the execution of both the female vic-tim's husband and her successful seducer, but Cinthio spares these men. Shakespeare goes even further in softening the plot and moving the moral pattern toward the fully providential world of the *Heptameron*'s historical story, where even the heroine's chastity is saved and her moral authority vindicated by the king's assignment to replace her would-be seducer as a leader of the Reform movement. Isabella's resilience and self-sufficiency finds its closest precedent not in "Cinthio's humanist heroine, with her trained mind,"[30] but in the intense religious faith of strong-minded women like Marie Héroët, whose superiority to conventional female roles so attracted Marguerite d'Angoulême. They may well be intelligent products of Humanist training, but their moral intensity reflects the Reformation more than the Renaissance.

The violent resentment of enforced sexual intercourse remains characteristic of modern, autonomous women, so that we should be cautious about accepting the tendency of some male scholars to censure Isabella for valuing her chastity higher than a man's life. There is an explicit parallel in Marguerite's own behavior after the attempted rape of her by her host, Bonnivet, which is described in the fourth tale of the *Heptameron*.[31] In her first fury Marguerite exclaims to her lady-in-waiting that "in the morning I shall approach my brother in such a way that the head of this lord shall testify to my chastity." The companion vigorously argues against revealing anything: "If you wish to be revenged on him leave him to love and shame, which will torment him better than you." Public punishment would invite insinuations about her previous familiarity with Bonnivet, who would win sympathy as a victim, and would spread doubt of his failure. As in *Measure for Measure*, expediency and good sense win the argument at the expense of strict justice, as also so often in the *Heptameron*, and Marguerite follows her lady's advice.

Throughout the *Heptameron* there is similar disconcerting alternation and interaction of awkward situations, extravagant personalities, and cynical realism, creating an ensemble which the scholars of later ages have found as consistently unsatisfactory and disturbing as those of Shakespeare's so-called "problem plays," with the result that "Marguerite de Navarre, the writer and storyteller, has received at the hands of her critics for the most part a negative judgment."[32] The same hostility has often been aroused by such sly Machiavellian devices as the switch of bedpartner whereby Angelo's abrupt threat to Isabella is subverted. These are held to be incompatible with the high moral issues

30. Lever, p. xl.
31. Marguerite de Navarre, *Heptameron*, pp. 28–34.
32. Tetel, p. 183.

raised by the play. Yet this blend of sententiousness and expedience is often found in the *Heptameron*, where affronted persons are praised if they avoid forcing the issue, like the husband in the thirty-fifth tale, whose wife is dying to have an affair with a virtuous cleric, but

> who was wise and dissimulated his anger. . . . The gentleman, wishing to test his wife's heart to the full went to the cleric [whom she loved] and asked him for the love of God to lend him his habit. The cleric, who was a worthy man, told him that their order forbade this and that he would not lend it to serve in deception for any price. The gentleman assured him that he did not in the least intend to misuse it and that it was essential for his well-being and salvation. The friar, knowing him to be a good and devout man, gave him the habit.[33]

Dressed in it to resemble her desired lover, the husband courts his own wife but gives her so different a consummation of the affair than any she had expected that she is totally conditioned against further thoughts of adultery with the cleric. Thus for the nominally Catholic Marguerite, as for Duke Vincentio and his accomplice Friar Thomas, the false assumption of a friar's robe can be plausible and proper. Moreover, the lover in the twenty-first tale, who exploits the disguise of a friar, goes further (as does Duke Vincentio in his disguise as a friar during his relations with Mariana [V.i.534]), for he hears his mistress' "confession" as a device to meet her in church against his queen's will: "Honest love, which recognizes no obstacles, was readier to find ways to allow them to speak together than their enemies quick to spy them, and under the disguise of all the cults they could think of continued their honest love."[34]

The same procedure is used, with Marguerite's approval apparently, when her brother exploits the monastery to cover his affair with the lawyer's wife nearby in the twenty-fifth tale. Significantly that episode is preceded by the narrator's careful review of

> the thing which one must use least without extreme necessity, this is lying or dissimulation, which is an ugly and shameful vice

33. Marguerite de Navarre, *Heptameron*, p. 256–57.
34. Marguerite de Navarre, *Heptameron*, p. 163.

particularly in princes and great lords. But there is no prince so great in this world, even if he has all the honors and riches that one might desire, who is not subject to the rule and tyranny of love ... for this glorious god holds no account of ordinary honest things, and his majesty only takes pleasure in doing miracles every day, like weakening the strong, strengthening the weak, giving intelligence to the ignorant, taking sense from the wisest, encouraging passions and destroying reason, and in such mutations the amorous god takes pleasure. And since princes are not exempt from this, so they are not from necessity. Now if they are not free of necessity in which the desire of servitude to love puts them, then by this necessity it is not only permitted but required that they use lies, hypocrisy, and fiction, which are the means to conquer their enemies.[35]

Interestingly this skeptical view of sexuality not only covers François' adultery, it comes close to justifying Duke Vincentio's disguise as friar to defeat the more general siege of his city by the forces of Love (or, at least, of Lust).

Moreover, we find Marguerite's own grandson, Henri de Navarre, echoing her words in Shakespeare's *Love's Labour's Lost* to justify meeting with the beautiful Princess of France: "We must of force dispense with this decree; / She must lie here on mere necessity" (I.i. 144-45). Thereupon Berowne embroiders the concept sardonically to his own advantage in planning further amatory escapades involving dishonesty:

> Necessity will make us all forsworn
> Three thousand times within this three
>   year's space:
> For every man with his affects is born,
> Not by might mast'red, but by special grace.
> If I break faith, this word shall speak for me,
> I am forsworn on "mere necessity."
>   (I.i.146-51)

Ironically this sophistry, like the *Heptameron*'s, almost justifies tricks like the prior's on Marie Héroët, as Saffredent cynically argues ear-

---

35. Marguerite de Navarre, *Heptameron*, p. 202.

lier: "If we show women our real feelings, there are many . . . whom they will hold of no account. But we shall cover our devil with the best angel that we can find. Under this cover before being recognized we shall receive much welcome."[36] It is not surprising that after the prior's story Oisille warns that "often the spirit Satan changes himself into an angel of light so that the exterior eye, blinded by the appearance of sanctity and devotion, remains when it should flee."[37]

Looked at in the light of such analogies, Angelo's macabre soliloquies seem much less peculiar and melodramatic. The prior found that he was attracted to "beauties that the veil made more desirable" and to the nun who was most subtle, fluent, and wise in speech. Angelo exclaims:

> Can it be
> That modesty can more betray our sense
> Than woman's lightness? Having waste
> ground enough,
> Shall we desire to raze the sanctuary
> And pitch our evils there? O fie, fie, fie!
> What dost thou? or what art thou, Angelo?
> Dost thou desire her foully for those things
> That make her good? . . .
> O cunning enemy that, to catch a saint,
> With saints dost bait thy hook: most dangerous
> Is that temptation that doth goad us on
> To sin in loving virtue.
> (ii.ii.168–75, 180–83)

And after the prior's tale Oisille proposes another to reinforce its point: "that the hypocrisy of those who esteem themselves more virtuous than the others, should not enchant your understandings so that your faith, diverted from its right course, should think to find its salvation in some other creature."[38] The indictment might in part cover both Angelo and Isabella, but it is Angelo who most consciously parallels Oisille's

36. Marguerite de Navarre, *Heptameron*, p. 96.
37. Marguerite de Navarre, *Heptameron*, p. 186.
38. Ibid.

awareness of the effect of his "gravity, / Wherein, let no man hear me, I take pride" (II.iv.9–10). Just as ominously he echoes Saffredent's cynical language about the need to "cover our devil with the best angel we can find and under this cover we receive much welcome":[39]

> O place, O form,
> How often dost thou with thy case, thy habit,
> Wrench awe from fools, and tie the wiser souls
> To thy false seeming! Blood, thou art blood.
> Let's write "good Angel" on the devil's horn—
> 'Tis not the devil's crest.
>
> (II.iv.12–27)

This blend of sensuality, moralism, and sardonic observation, which now seems to us so thoroughly Shakespearean, is founded on an awareness like that of Marguerite, stripped of the superfluous prosaicism of her story with no loss of the supple psychology which makes her writing so hypnotic. Marguerite's skepticism was fostered by the threat of persecution by officers of such traditional institutions as the Sorbonne, Parlement, and the Church, by whom intellectuals in Marguerite's court were so often harassed. Marguerite's *Miroir de l'âme pécheresse*, banned by the Sorbonne for its Lutheran emphasis, was chosen by the eleven-year-old Princess Elizabeth of England to translate (perhaps consciously reflecting the love of her mother, Anne Boleyn, for its author), illustrating the relevance of Marguerite's spiritual values to the reign of Shakespeare's queen.

The feminism of the Valois court not only trained the sensibility of Elizabeth's mother and influenced Elizabeth's own mind, it also deeply conditioned the temperament of her arch rival, Mary Stuart (whose expatriate mother, Marie de Guise, had helped to carry French influence to the British Isles). Brantôme says that as an adolescent Mary Stuart gave a Latin speech before the king and queen at the Louvre "proposing, and defending against popular opinion, that it was fitting for women to master literature and the liberal arts."[40] It is fascinating to recognize the tremendous power exercised in Europe by three women

39. Ibid.
40. Tetel, pp. 371–72.

rulers of the generation who matured under Marguerite's influence:
Mary, queen of Scots; Catherine de' Medici, queen regent of France;
and Elizabeth I—who between them provide the modern feminist with
a vivid but by no means coherent vision of what happens when energetic and ingenious women rule a group of European nations. The
intellectuals of the time were extremely conscious of this triad: Ronsard ingratiated himself with all three, and the hypnotic figure of the
powerful woman affects literary characterizations as different as those
of Spenser's *Faerie Queene*, Marlowe's *Massacre at Paris*, and even
Macbeth and *Antony and Cleopatra*. But one of the liveliest literary
illustrations of the impact of the feminism of the French courts of the
sixteenth century probably lies in *Love's Labour's Lost*, where the
Princess of France approximates Marguerite's namesake and successor
as queen of Navarre: the daughter of Catherine de' Medici. The later
Marguerite was herself a magnetic creature, but Shakespeare's heroine
has a serenity and wisdom which makes us remember the figure of her
great aunt, whose Lutheran sentiments Shakespeare makes the later
Marguerite echo sardonically, in view of her historical Catholicism,
when she mocks facile flattery:

> See, see—my beauty will be saved by merit.
> Oh, heresy in fair, fit for these days.
>
> (iv.i.21–22)

This sly and witty princess and the incisive young women of her
court are prefigured in and consciously modeled on the autonomous,
incisive, and skeptical ladies who more than hold their own with the
men with whom they have to deal in the dialogues and narratives of the
Heptameron. In many obvious ways *Love's Labour's Lost* indicates how
thoroughly immersed in French manners the young Shakespeare was,
skillfully exploiting the fashionable enthusiasm for the cause of Henri
IV in his campaign to impose his regal authority on the ultra-Catholic
League.[41] The French wars of religion provide explicit materials for a
score of polemical Elizabethan plays like Marlowe's *Massacre*, but in
a less narrowly partisan comedy like *Love's Labour's Lost* it is natural
to recognize a broader historical horizon. Certainly King "Ferdinand"

41. See Chapter IX for detailed discussion.

of Navarre is the archetypal youthful ruler—as much relevant to Henry V, or François I, as to Henri IV. The campaign against the four French beauties in which Ferdinand leads his friends has an analogue in the *Heptameron*'s sixty-third tale,[42] where François, with two other companions, seeks to involve an unwilling fourth in a campaign to seduce four beautiful Parisiennes at a festival. The seduction fails, but not before the reluctant and wise fourth lover (who already has a loyal wife *and* a mistress) eludes the enterprise because he "decided to dissimulate," affecting a sickness, which his wife naturally enough considers "a good and holy hypocrisy." In the end the mass seduction is abandoned anyway because the king's duties abruptly call him away, and "the deception by this young lord was never perceived by the king."

In many ways this enterprise offers a precedent for the king's campaign against the four beauties of *Love's Labour's Lost*. The comments made by the tale's listeners also anticipate the play's ascetic opening, with the king's call to his court to "war against your own affections" (I.i.9). In the *Heptameron* story Oisille suggests that the young man's chastity (within somewhat liberal conventions) is not improbable in idealistic minds: "When one's heart is in it, nothing is impossible for the body." Hircan sardonically observes that she must be talking about spirits in heaven, but Oisille is emphatic: "If you take care, you will find those who have put their heart and affection into the perfection of the sciences not only have forgotten the sensuality of the flesh, but the most necessary things, like eating and drinking, for when the soul has this affection in its body the flesh remains as if insensible." Shakespeare's King Ferdinand also expects to fast and avoid sleep, sex, and all bodily pleasure. Oisille applies this to ideal love and tells how a true lover can burn himself in a real flame without pain because he is driven by the metaphorical fire of passion. The men are openly contemptuous, and Geburon comments, "If a girl let me endure that for her, I'd ask a big price, or I'd shift my imagination elsewhere."

In corroboration of this assertion of male fickleness Parlamente tells in the next tale, the sixty-fourth,[43] of a willful young woman who defers

42. Marguerite de Navarre, *Heptameron*, pp. 380–83.
43. Marguerite de Navarre, *Heptameron*, pp. 383–87.

her marriage to a young man thinking that her refusal for a time would serve her merely as a test of his good will. As she later writes to him:

> Pour ce qu'amour, s'il n'est bien esprouvé
> Ferme et loial, ne peut estre approuvé,
> J'ay bien voulu par le temps esprouver
> Ce que j'ay tant desiré de trouver:
> C'est un mari remply d'amour parfaict,
> Qui par le temps ne peut estre desfaict.
> Cela me feit requerir mes parents
> De retarder, pour ung ou pour deux ans
> Ce grand lien, qui jusqu'à la mort dure
> Qui à plusieurs engendre peyne dure. . . .
> Mais esperois te randre contanté
> Après t'avoir bien experimenté.

(Since love, if it is not well-proven firm and loyal, cannot be approved, I have much preferred by time to prove that which I have so much wished to find, which is a husband full of perfect love which cannot be undone by time; that made me oblige my family to defer for one or two years this great bond which lasts until death which causes great pain to many. . . . But I hoped to content you after having thoroughly tested you.)

In the event the young man commits himself to the hermit's life he has taken up in reaction and firmly rejects the woman's renewed interest in favor of the love of God. The pattern of compelled celibacy must have preoccupied Marguerite, and she presents a more extravagant version in the twenty-fourth[44] tale. There a sadistic queen traps an effusive courtier who seeks her love into seven years of exile from her to prove his devotion, saying: "When I shall have made this test for seven years, I shall have had time enough and will believe what your words cannot make me believe or understand." This lover also proves fickle, finally rejecting the service of his lady for that of God, like the other lover. But Parlamente, perhaps revealing Marguerite's own attitude, defends the queen: "It seems to me that she did him no harm at all in seeking to test for seven years if he loved her as much as he said;

---

44. Marguerite de Navarre, *Heptameron*, pp. 194–203.

for men are so accustomed to lie in such cases, that before trusting them much (if one must trust them) one cannot make too long a test."

These tales demonstrate the likely outcome of the analogous contracts with the ladies accepted by their suitors at the end of *Love's Labour's Lost*, which starts by showing the same asceticism in young men that motivates the recluses of the *Heptameron*. Marguerite's anthology reinforces our awareness of Shakespeare's stress on the pattern of contemptuous suspicion with which aristocratic Frenchwomen greet courtship, as shown in the play. Parlamente takes the lead so vigorously that another lady protests: "The result would be that the instant a man opens his mouth we'd have to say, no!—without knowing what he wanted." Parlamente explains: "To begin with a woman should never appear to understand what the man wants; nor yet, when he tells it, that she can believe it; but when he starts swearing great oaths, the most honorable thing for ladies is to leave him in this fine course rather than go downhill." One lady hastily says that this is un-Christian: "Is it not sin to judge one's neighbor?"[45] However, even Shakespeare's Juliet is smart enough to agree with Parlamente about extravagant protestations: "Do not swear at all," she warns Romeo (II.ii.112ff.).

The unfailing and unexpected contempt lavished on the lovers throughout *Love's Labour's Lost* fully realizes Parlamente's philosophy on rejecting oaths. Both Berowne the cynic and Longaville the idealist admit the poor precedents the play affords for trusting them. Berowne's poem concedes the point from the start in a minor gesture of honesty:

> If love make me forsworn, how shall I swear to love?
> Ah, never faith could hold, if not to beauty vowed!
> Though to myself forsworn, to thee I'll faithful prove.
>
> (IV.ii.101–103)

Sharing the cynicism of the philandering theologian in the seventy-second tale, Longaville is more sophisticated, insidious—and also Lutheran:

> Did not the heavenly rhetoric of thine eye
> 'Gainst whom the world cannot hold argument,
> Persuade my heart to this false perjury?

45. Marguerite de Navarre, *Heptameron*, p. 115.

> Vows for thee broke deserve not punishment.
> A woman I forswore, but I will prove,
>   Thou being a goddess, I forswore not thee.
> My vow was earthly, thou a heavenly love;
>   Thy grace, being gained, cures all disgrace
>   in me.
>
> (IV.iii.55–62)

Longaville's mistress shares with Donne's ladies the theological property, stressed by Luther and Calvin, of overriding lack of merit in her lover, by the impact of her "divine" good will on them. Given the character of the verses one tends to agree with the Princess when she says, "We are wise girls to mock our lovers so" (V.ii.58). Certainly that attitude would seem appropriate to the women in the *Heptameron* where, for a virtuous woman, "it would not be found bad to have suitors" if "she spoke to them in mockery rather than sympathy."[46]

Despite her religious mysticism Marguerite often parodies the extravagant metaphysics which contemporary neo-Petrarchan love poetry affected. There are close affinities between two of Donne's lyrics ("The Extasie" and "Aire and Angels") and the sentiments professed by Gabriel d'Albret, seigneur d'Avesnes, in trying to seduce his married mistress in the twenty-sixth story:

> Madame, remember your promise and understand that God, unknown to man except by faith, has deigned to take flesh like our sinful one in order that, in attracting our flesh to the love of his humanity, he should draw our spirit to the love of his divinity, and he wished to use visible means in order to make us love by faith the invisible ones. Also this virtue which I wish to love all my life is an invisible thing except by its external effects; therefore it is necessary that it take some body to make itself known among men, which is what it has done, clothing itself with your body as the most perfect it can find, whereby I recognize you and confess to you not only to be virtuous but Virtue itself, and I, who see it shine through the veil of the most perfect body

---

46. Marguerite de Navarre, *Heptameron*, p. 363.

which ever was, wish to serve and honor it all my life, leaving for its sake every other vain and vicious love.[47]

In "The Extasie" Donne expounds the need for overt sexual love by the same analogy of celestial materializations: "On man heavens influence workes not so, / But that it first imprints the ayre."[48] Only in more tangible forms is it possible that "weak men on love reveal'd may looke." The precedent in Marguerite is followed more fully in "Aire and Angels":

> since my soule, whose child love is,
> Takes limmes of flesh, and else could
> nothing doe,
> More subtile then the parent is
> Love must not be, but take a body too,
> And therefore what thou wert, and who,
> I bid Love aske, and now
> That it assume thy body, I allow,
> And fixe it selfe in thy lip, eye, and brow.[49]

In each poem, as with d'Avesnes, the Petrarchan commonplace of the woman as incarnating a heavenly ideal has been detached from the tradition of recession from the sensual (derived from the *Symposium*'s sense of seeking the universal in the particular). The allusion is now to the Christian model of the severe descent to the flesh through Incarnation and its parallel in angelology. If anything, the allusion is expressed more frankly and provocatively by the French aristocrat in the tale; Donne tends to avoid overt references to God such as d'Avesnes'. By Donne's time the risks of toying cynically with theology had become more evident, as the death sentence pronounced on Théophile de Viau for blasphemous verse was to illustrate.

Unlike Donne and Théophile, Marguerite shares Shakespeare's contempt for "metaphysical" seduction. Like Longaville, d'Avesnes may

47. Marguerite de Navarre, *Heptameron*, p. 214.
48. John Donne, *The Elegies and the Songs and Sonnets*, ed. Helen Gardner (Oxford: Clarendon Press, 1965), p. 61.
49. Donne, *Elegies and Songs and Sonnets*, p. 75.

use the Incarnation to exploit the Lutheran concern with the Fallen World, but the ploy evokes a no less doctrinal talent by means of which the lady successfully evades him:

> My lord, I will not undertake to refute your theology; but as one who fears ill more than trusting in the good, I would beg you to cease addressing me in terms which cause you to despise the women who believe them. I know very well that I am a woman not only like any other, but imperfect; and that Virtue would achieve a greater triumph in transforming me into herself, than in taking my form, unless she wished to conceal herself in the world; for in such a form as mine Virtue could not be known for what she is. So, my lord, because of my imperfection I can only offer you such affection as should a woman fearing God and her honor.[50]

Such are the subtleties of self-defence exacted of the sophisticated ladies of Marguerite's time in sexual matters. Yet this debate was clearly won by the lady to her own disadvantage, for the tale goes on to tell us that the strain of combatting her own desire for surrender to the subtle young man caused her in the end to die of a nervous fever. Her case was discussed throughout the century. As the tale mentions, the historical seigneur d'Avesnes died unmarried many years later. By his mixture of promiscuity and scholastic sophistry, he had provided a striking prototype for the kind of lover displayed in Donne's lyrics as well as in plays like *Love's Labour's Lost*, where Donne seems to have found his more immediate inspiration.[51] Donne did not invent wittily "metaphysical" courtship: the court of François I perfected it fifty years before his birth. Before we can estimate the achievement of the English amatory poets later in the century, we must recognize this court's social and intellectual climate. The types of personalities flourishing in it provided the models and patronage for the French Renaissance writers against whom English poets were to measure themselves from Wyatt to Milton. The *Heptameron* is one of the most vivid and accessible evocations of this milieu and the literary sources it afforded.

50. Marguerite de Navarre, *Heptameron*, p. 215.
51. See Hugh M. Richmond, "Donne's Master: The Young Shakespeare," *Criticism* 15 (1973), pp. 126–44.

Accounts of such ultrasophisticated seductions as d'Avesnes' surely imply that a comparably sophisticated audience for them must exist; more particularly there must be women to address who exact from their poets an art of such skeptical virtuosity. When we come to Catherine de' Medici's *escadron volant* we shall find such roles fully recognized, but the social model for this "light calvary" was mapped out for Catherine by her mentor in the *Heptameron*. For Marguerite did not hesitate to include from her own knowledge outrageous examples of female cynicism and exploitation of male sexual naiveté, of which the forty-ninth tale[52] is surely the most amusing and extravagant example (as well as apparently a true one). After a difficult courtship, a foreign countess at the court of Charles VIII secretly entertains one of his gentlemen called "Astillon" in her bedchamber:

> with which he was so satisfied that he was content to stay concealed in her wardrobe without leaving for five or six days, and lived on fortifying snacks. During the week he was hidden he saw one of his friends, called Durassier, pay court to the countess. She treated this suitor the same way as she did the first one, beginning with harsh and offensive words which each day became more gentle; and when the day came that she released the first prisoner, she put the next suitor in his place. And while that one was there, another friend of his named Valnebon underwent a similar ritual to the first two; and after them came two or three others, who in turn shared the sweet prison. This life lasted a long time and was handled so deftly that each of the men did not know what happened with the others. And as each had full experience of the love they felt for her, there was no one who thought he was not preferred alone in what he wanted, and each ridiculed in his own mind the man next to himself, whom he thought denied the final reward.

Astillon's complacency finally precipitates a mutual revelation among all the victims, who discover to their amusement and indignation their common servitude to the will of the countess. At Astillon's suggestion they decide to humiliate her by parading before her on the way to church as a chain gang, shackled neck to neck. But the countess, having

52. Marguerite de Navarre, *Heptameron*, pp. 318–23.

realized that they knew their misfortune, "didn't turn a hair, which so amazed them that they swallowed the affront they had thought to reciprocate."

Hircan, the tale's narrator, baits his wife Parlamente by drawing the moral that "a shameless woman is a hundred times more brazen and vicious than a man"—a truth about their ladies that only Berowne perceives among his fellows, warning: "be first advis'd, / In conflict that you get the sun of them," because "light wenches may prove plagues to men forsworn" (IV.iii.363–64, 380). The protracted comic sequence of overhearings and the ritual confessions of the tale offer parallels from real life to the famous unmasking of *Love's Labour's Lost* (IV.iii), with Berowne's initiative there being anticipated by "Astillon" (now known to be Charles VIII's chamberlain, Jacques de Chastillon; two of the others, like him known to Marguerite, are Germain de Bonneval as Valnebon and Jacques Gaillot d'Acier as Durassier; the countess, "unfortunately," has not yet been identified).[53]

In the *Heptameron*, Marguerite does not hesitate to show many similar examples of women "who will do the deed / Though Argus be her eunuch and her guard" (III.i.187–88). Such is the wife of the fifteenth story, whose husband, despite spying on her day and night, "did not know how to guard her well enough to prevent her from still speaking to her lover in an inaccessible and compromising spot, while conducting the affair so secretly that neither man nor woman could judge the truth."[54] She seems to be truly a woman, in Berowne's words,

> ever out of frame,
> And never going aright, being a watch,
> But being watched that it may still go right!
> (III.i.180–82)

However, to balance this particular verdict we might remind ourselves that Berowne (IV.iii.285ff.) also exploits the ideas at the conclusion of the *Heptameron*'s seventieth tale, where Dagoucin argues that women inspire men "to do a thousand worthy things," inviting Hircan sarcastically to inquire: "You mean that if there were no women, we

53. Marguerite de Navarre, *Heptameron*, pp. 484–85.
54. Marguerite de Navarre, *Heptameron*, p. 124.

would all be wicked?"[55] Such oscillations are as lively as the tales themselves, and in most of the dialogues in which the tales are embedded we feel the shifting tensions of the war of the sexes, since the *Heptameron* is essentially an encyclopedia of amatory case histories. Marguerite had no illusions at all about male loyalty and decorum either. The thirty-seventh tale ends with a comment anticipating Benedick's own "conclusion" in *Much Ado* that "man is a giddy thing" (V.iv.106–07): "I beg you, ladies, if God should give you such husbands that you don't in the least despair until you have persistently tried every means to overpower them, for there are twenty-four hours in the day, in each of which a man can change his opinion."[56] And all too many of the *Heptameron*'s stories show disconcertingly the volatility of the best men and women, who may turn corrupt without warning or logic.

Schücking and Rabkin have suggested[57] that drastic human inconsistency is a distinctive attribute of Shakespearean characterization, but we can see that the stress of such Reformation theologians as Luther and Calvin on human fallibility and the abrupt compensating effects of heavenly grace would ensure that far earlier sixteenth-century writers like Marguerite were equally conscious of the view that human corruptibility was so uniform that sooner or later even the best of men must fail as badly as the prior in the twenty-second tale. It is rewarding to juxtapose a possible source for *Othello* in Cinthio with similar precedents for the play in the *Heptameron*. The plot and rough outlines of the principal characters of Othello probably derive from the material covered by Cinthio, but Shakespeare tightened up the plot and achieved "a more rounded presentation of character," showing as usual a remarkably rich sense of the "local color" of Venice, Cyprus, and the Mediterranean generally. By all these characteristic heightening effects Shakespeare's genius moves his material away from the stark and hectic narrative of Cinthio by using the subtler psychology, intimate detail, and moral sophistication of Marguerite's narratives.

55. Marguerite de Navarre, *Heptameron*, p. 419.

56. Marguerite de Navarre, *Heptameron*, p. 268.

57. See Levin L. Schücking, *Character Problems in Shakespeare's Plays* (London: Harrap, 1922), and Norman Rabkin, *Shakespeare and the Common Understanding* (New York: Free Press, 1967).

Shakespeare would find in the *Heptameron* many psychological
subtleties to enrich Cinthio's harsh outline. In the thirteenth tale[58] a
beautiful young woman, devotedly married to a much older man, conforms to his tastes by the avoidance of company, dances, and other social sports. The husband proposes to go on a pilgrimage to Jerusalem,
and the wife insists on accompanying him. At this point they encounter
at the court a gentleman "who often had made war on the Turks and
sought to involve the French king in an expedition against one of their
towns from which could come profit to Christendom." The old man
seeks the captain's aid in his pilgrimage, and in his wife's company
"often spoke to the captain, who, paying more attention to her than
his words, was so amorous of her that often, in speaking to her of the
voyages he had made by sea, confused embarcations from Marseilles
and the Archipelago, and in wishing to speak of a ship spoke of a
horse, as if he was entranced and out of his wits." Often he meets the
couple in their bedchamber to speak of the pilgrimage, and while her
husband dozes his undressed wife talks to the captain of Jerusalem.
Fascinated by his tales the wife "begged him to tell her what life he had
led" as he recounts how "he had gone to sea to seek adventure and
done so much by his efforts that he had achieved honorable rank. . . .
All of his words pleased this lady." After leaving on his campaign
against the Turks the captain sends her a poem regretting that "instead
of telling her that he loved her, I spoke of the celestial zodiac and of
the seasons and of the Arctic and Antarctic." In the end, after a desperate and unsuccessful campaign against the Turks, the captain dies
without pressing his courtship, which the young wife conceals, to the
advantage of the captain's reputation and the well-being of his wife.
The impact of the exotic captain on this household resembles Othello's
on Brabantio's family, where the beautiful woman is also increasingly
compromised by her affection for the heroic warrior who is being en-
tertained by the aging master of the household. We too hear Othello's
answer to the lady's "prayer of earnest heart / That I would all my
pilgrimage dilate" (I.iii.153–54).

Some relevant Italian models for Othello's courtship via Cassio (and
for that of Claudio via Don Pedro in *Much Ado*) are sketched out in

58. Marguerite de Navarre, *Heptameron*, pp. 97–109.

the fifty-first tale, which deals with the son of the duke of Urbino.[59] Seeking to marry a woman of good family, this young aristocrat, "since he did not have access to speak to her as he wished, following the custom of the country, assisted himself by means of a gentleman who was in his service" who had access to the household because of a relationship with a young woman in it. Because this girl favored his son's affair the duke ruthlessly executed her, for "no pity could touch the heart of the duke, who knew no happiness than to revenge himself on those he hated." The listeners all agree "that the Italian temperament is to love things inordinately," one quoting how an Italian captain literally ate his enemy's heart, reminding us as much of Beatrice or Shylock as Iago. As for Othello's dignified sense of authority, Parlamente comments that Saint Paul knew pride in Italy firsthand, "all of those who think they surpass and overpower others in honor, prudence, and human reason, on which they depend so much that they fail to give God his due honor; for which the All Powerful, jealous of his honor, makes more insane than mad beasts those who have thought themselves possessed of more sense than all other men, making them show by works against nature how they are misguided." Othello's extraordinary transformation is thus entirely true to the Reformation psychology which Marguerite found in St. Paul.

The same extremism appears in the fiftieth tale,[60] set in Cremona, in which there occurs a romance as juvenile as Romeo's. After being refused by the girl the young man falls sick and is bled by the doctors but is cured through a pitying change of heart by the girl, who had thus, like Rosalind (III.ii.376ff.), cured a man of "a malady for which all the doctors could not find a remedy." Othello's jealousy is another such disease, according to Iago, for not "all the drowsy syrups of the world shall ever medicine" (III.iii.331-32) Othello's lost peace of mind. In the *Heptameron* story the revitalized lover approaches his girl's bed "with so extreme a contentment that it was bound to end soon, being unable to increase further"—which of course is what happens, since the surgeon's wound opens unnoticed in the midst of the passionate lovemaking, and he dies of loss of blood. The girl then kills herself with

59. Marguerite de Navarre, *Heptameron*, pp. 329–33.
60. Marguerite de Navarre, *Heptameron*, pp. 323–27.

her lover's sword, and in the morning the parents find her body lying on his. Everyone listening to the tale agrees on the stupidity of the affair —a comment relevant to *Romeo and Juliet*, and it also provides a sinister precedent for Othello's suicidal view of great pleasure as he approaches Desdemona on Cyprus:

> If it were now to die,
> 'Twere now to be most happy; for I fear
> My soul hath her content so absolute
> That not another comfort like to this
> Succeeds in unknown fate.
>
> (II.i.187–91)

The precedent for Iago in Cinthio is fairly well-developed, but the diabolic overtones of Shakespeare's villain seem quite likely to derive from Marguerite's far more theological frame. The *Heptameron* is full of warnings against pious men, "who think themselves to be something holy, and worthier than us . . . they are not only more merely men than others, but they have something diabolic in them above the common viciousness of men."[61] Moreover, anticipating Othello's description of Iago as a "demi-devil" (V.ii.301), Parlamente observes that: "The devil demi-angel is the most dangerous of all, for he knows so well how to transform himself into an angel of light that it becomes a fault of conscience to suspect them for what they are, and it seems to me the person who does not suspect them must be praised."[62] Oisille disagrees: "One should suspect the evil which can be avoided, above all if one has high office, for it is better to suspect evil where there is none than to fall by stupid credulity into the evil which exists." While such remarks helpfully define the contemporary moral considerations in a case like that of Othello and Iago, an exact illustration of Othello's problem occurs in the thirty-sixth tale,[63] about Geoffrey Carles, historically the president of the Parlement at Grenoble (and tutor of the

61. Marguerite de Navarre, *Heptameron*, p. 315.

62. Marguerite de Navarre, *Heptameron*, p. 310.

63. Marguerite de Navarre, *Heptameron*, p. 261–66; See Painter, vol. 2, pp. 101–3.

Reformist Renée, sister-in-law of Marguerite and protector, as duchess
of Ferrara, of refugees like Marot). An old and faithful retainer reports
that the president's wife is betraying him, and (in the words of Painter's
anthology, which Shakespeare used): "the President, which was a wise
man, would not beleue it vpon his light report, but sayde that he did
it of purpose to set discord betwene him and his wife, notwithstanding
if the thing were true as he had reported, he might let him see the
thing itselfe, whiche if he did not, he had good cause to thinke that he
had deuised a lye to breake and dissolue the love betwene them." One
recalls Othello's parallel reaction:

> Make me to see't; or at least so prove it
> That the probation bear no hinge nor loop
> To hang a doubt on, or woe unto thy life!
> (III.iii.364–66)

Unlike Iago, the servant undertakes to do so and is successful—but this
master is the absolute opposite of Othello (who accepts inadequate
proof), for he neatly falsifies the valid evidence, then dismisses the old
retainer as a "villain" (while providing for his future) and continues
a happily married man to all outward appearances, while achieving
complete control of all involved. Only after all is long past does the
president murder his wife, at leisure and quite undetected, thus preserving complete public decorum and earning praise for his "great
patience" from the teller of the tale; but others disagree, saying his
coldblooded vengeance proves his wickedness. Longarine says, "I would
have preferred that he had killed her in his rage, because theologians
say that such sin is pardonable since the first reactions are not within
human control, and therefore he could have been forgiven for it." Saffredent agrees with her:

> It gives me great pleasure to say that the theologians esteem such
> sins easy to forgive, for I agree with them ... that a man deeply
> in love whatever he does cannot sin except in a venial way, for
> I am sure that, if love holds him completely bound never will
> reason be heard either in his heart or in his understanding. And
> if we wish to speak the truth, there is none of us who has not

87

experienced this mad fury, which I think not only to be easily forgiven, but also I believe that God does not get angry over such sin, since it is only one remove from ascent to perfect love of him.

The tale thus illustrates an elegantly cynical solution to Othello's problem and yet specifically explains our feeling of the superior moral stature of the choice Othello blunders into, providing the ideal psychology for Shakespeare's hero. Shakespeare's own awareness was probably heightened by such a sympathetic discussion of wife-murder.

The women in the *Heptameron*, understandably, are made to sound a little nervous about these fine discriminations in killing one's wife, but we should see that this ingenious structuring of exacting situations, complex psychologies, and highly refined moral criteria is a format shared by the *Heptameron* and Shakespearean drama. Geoffrey Carles may be Othello's reverse—a kind of mirror image—but the cultural concerns, norms, and implications of the two accounts are almost identical and mutually clarifying. And indeed this elucidation is enhanced by the next tale, the thirty-seventh,[64] which raises the question of whether the victim of adultery is wise to be patient. The question of beating a nagging wife is raised first, and Parlamente declares her horror at any such idea, giving us a norm by which to judge Othello's striking of Desdemona (IV.i.250): "I do not believe any honorable woman should be so servile as to be beaten in anger." Longarine proves far more extreme in defense of women, saying that if her husband had committed adultery, "I loved him so much that I think I would have killed him and killed myself, for to die after such vengeance would please me more than to live loyally with my betrayer." This also provides a sympathetic approach to Othello's behavior, but it earns Hircan's immediate criticism because "you love your husbands only for your own sakes," a view which also touches Othello (IV.ii.47ff.). Longarine then hastily decides to tell a tale "in praise of the virtuous patience of ladies."

The *Heptameron* has other perverse sociological data affording possible sources for some of Iago's most insidious implications about Desdemona. The whole matter of evidence of sexual guilt, its proper pun-

64. Marguerite de Navarre, *Heptameron*, pp. 266–69.

ishment, and forgiveness for it recurs endlessly. Like Geoffrey Carles, the husband in the thirty-second story[65] is so in love with his wife "that I could not free myself from her until the point that the proof forced itself on my eyes, and I saw what I feared more than death." The assumption is that guilt can be definitive and made irreparable. One recalls Othello's "be sure thou prove my love a whore! / Be sure of it; give me the ocular proof" (III.iii.359–60). Yet the *Heptameron* falsifies even this kind of evidence by showing how "a woman can be unchaste without sin"[66] in the discussion after the forty-eighth tale, in which a wife who mistakes another man for her husband is held to be guiltless of adultery. Moreover, Iago's skeptical insinuation about the permissible excesses of "sophisticated" behavior at the start of Act IV receives some startling corroboration through the evidence about acceptable intimacies in the *Heptameron*. Iago questions the propriety of a wife and her lover "to kiss in private. . . . Or to be naked with her friend in bed / An hour or more, not meaning any harm." The inexpert Othello is astounded by the idea:

> Naked in bed, Iago, and not mean harm?
> It is hypocrisy against the Devil.
> They that mean virtuously, and yet do so,
> The Devil their virtue tempts and they
> tempt Heaven.
>
> (IV.i.5–8)

Yet Iago drily responds, "So they do nothing, 'tis a venial slip," and the *Heptameron* shows how this unlikely set of specifications could actually be achieved and is not just the malicious improvisation of Iago's diseased imagination.

In the eighteenth tale[67] the consummation of an affair between a pair of "perfect" young lovers is delayed by the woman's modesty and doubts, and "in order to test her suitor's patience, firmness, and love" she agrees to accept him as her lover only if he meets her "too difficult

65. Marguerite de Navarre, *Heptameron*, pp. 242–46.
66. Marguerite de Navarre, *Heptameron*, pp. 315–17.
67. Marguerite de Navarre, *Heptameron*, pp. 137–41.

demand," which is "that she was content to speak to him in bed both
lying only in their shirts, as long as he did not ask her for anything
more than words and kisses." This the young man did and continued
to do, and "the lady, as I think was more surprised than pleased with
this achievement." She decides he must have another mistress and tricks
him into bed with a naked girl from her household, a temptation which
he angrily rejects—almost breaking off the affair for good, until she
gives him the fullest bodily satisfaction herself. The story seems contrived to permit the courtly discussion afterwards about the difficulty
of the various tasks set the young men. However, the virtuoso "chastity" it illustrates offers an exact precedent for Iago's peculiar sugges-
tions.

We have not yet exhausted the *Heptameron*'s bizarre precedents
for the kind of strenuous virtue which might achieve the restraint to
defeat the temptations in Iago's perverse hypothesis. The mother of
the thirtieth tale,[68] who, hoping to stop her son's seduction of her chambermaid, takes her place in bed expecting to stop the consummation
if it proves in earnest, fails in her intention disastrously; but the discussion following this episode looks for further analogies to this "glorious
madwoman, who by some delusion inspired by talking to clergy thought
that she was so sanctified as to be impeccable." Oisille refuses to believe
anyone can be so madly complacent as this, but Longarine describes a
Milanese sect whose males prove their chastity by meeting, kissing, and
caressing the most beautiful women: "And when they have chastened
their flesh to the point of insensitivity . . . they come to trying the great
temptation, which is to lie together and embrace without any lust. But
for one who escapes from this, there are so many other inconveniences,
that the archbishop of Milan, where this religion was practiced, was
forced to separate them." A Milanese historian, Guiseppe Ripamonti,
offers a harsher conclusion, in a tale relating to the secret sect of
Saramita, who was burned by the archbishop with the bones of her
dead accomplice, Guglielmina.[69] Unlike this cruder historical version,
the *Heptameron*'s account shows that some sophisticated and idealistic

68. Marguerite de Navarre, *Heptameron*, pp. 229–35.
69. Marguerite de Navarre, *Heptameron*, p. 476.

Italian females were supposed to have met Iago's peculiar bedroom specifications and yet remained technically chaste. Thus in a very complex way Othello is shown to be unable to deal with the most eccentric and sophisticated questions of sex and morality: even if Desdemona had gone to bed with Cassio, she might still be virtuous and even excessively chaste! The more one knows about these social, psychological, and moral complexities of the period the more one understands the problems of the outsider, Othello, and sympathizes both with him and even more with Desdemona's innocence.

Whatever the emphasis in particular episodes, it is in portraying the most lively and autonomous sexual roles for women that Marguerite contributes most to later awareness. For example, Shakespeare shares her sense of French female initiative in characterizations as different as Queen Margaret in *Henry VI*, the Princess of *Love's Labour's Lost*, and the irrepressible Helena (alias Boccaccio's Gillette de Narbonne) of *All's Well That Ends Well*, not to mention the most dynamic, witty, and triumphant of all Shakespeare's comic heroines, who is also nominally French. Rosalind, like her model in Lodge's *Rosalynde*, is supposed to be a French princess, and both Lodge and Shakespeare endow her with a spirited personality of the kind Marguerite so often evokes. As Hircan wrily observes, "A subtle woman will know how to survive when everyone else will die of hunger."[70] And Simontault agrees: "They think it no little glory to be held subtler than their companions. And this word subtle [*fine*] which they have at others' expense makes suitors bolder to come and serve them. For one of the greater pleasures between those who love is to conduct their affair with subtlety." Later Hircan praises wives for similar talents, "for the wisest are those who take as much recreation in mocking the works of their husbands as the husbands secretly do in deceiving them."[71] Saffredent also observes that the "invention of a clever trick will be found more speedily and subtly by a woman than a man," and one of the early tales, the sixth, closely matches Chaucer's illustration of feminine wiles in the *Merchant's Tale*, for its adulterous wife tricks her one-eyed husband by

70. Marguerite de Navarre, *Heptameron*, p. 341.
71. Marguerite de Navarre, *Heptameron*, p. 397.

covering up his good eye when he risks seeing her with her lover, thus reducing him to conceding, "By God, wife, I'll never spy on you again: for in thinking to catch you out I got the subtlest trick ever invented. Let God reform you, for no man in this world can regulate the wickedness of women, unless he killed her off."[72]

This skeptical version of femininity is very much Rosalind's in Lodge's *Rosalynde* and in *As You Like It* in her famous speech in favor of female "giddiness" (IV.i.148ff.): "The wiser the waywarder. Make the doors upon a woman's wit and it will out at the casement; shut that and 'twill out at the keyhole; stop that, 'twill fly with the smoke out at the chimney." When Rosalind professes to defend such wives' adultery, Orlando asks in what way she could defend "a wife's wit going to your neighbor's bed." Rosalind replies, "Marry to say she came to seek you there. You shall never take her without her answer unless you take her without her tongue." In such passages we see just what is implied by the new concerns of the court over which Marguerite presided: "Conversation was developed," and "to talk wittily became the merit of sophisticated people."[73] In her poise, incisiveness, and skepticism Rosalind is a true sixteenth-century French princess, riding as spikily over her suitors' sentimentalities as was required by good breeding in Marguerite's style. She sweeps away Orlando's affections, like those of Troilus and Leander, with a puff of ridicule: "Men have died from time to time, and worms have eaten them, but not for love" (IV.i.96–98). She is echoing Saffredent: "I have heard so much of these frigid passions, but I have never seen anyone die of them," and Hircan agrees: "Die! Is there yet to be born a worthy gallant who would care to die for such an avowed reason?"[74] From such toughening debates is shaped the mind of a Marguerite, or an Anne Boleyn—or a Rosalind. Such skeptical verve was not for orthodox English princesses like Elizabeth of York or Mary Tudor. One sees why the more volatile personalities terrified the orthodox in both England and France: the "newfangledness" which Rosalind undertakes to profess (IV.i.138) not only frightens the

72. Marguerite de Navarre, *Heptameron*, p. 39.
73. Decrue de Stoutz, pp. 162, 165.
74. Marguerite de Navarre, *Heptameron*, pp. 49, 115.

fictional Orlando, it infuriated the historical Wyatt, denouncing his mistress for daring to "use new fangilnes" in "They flee from me";[75] and such manners probably helped more than one young English-woman trained at the French court to the block in the Tower.

However, the effects of the *Heptameron* should not be judged solely by such eccentricities. It is not in the least squeamish about sex, obscenity, morbidity, and downright viciousness, but these are balanced by a pragmatic moral candor which still seems remarkably fresh and modern. It is just this element which Painter and his successor strip from their excerpts by dropping the discussions of the tales but which Shakespeare probably recovered from the original text. Like some French clerics in the Sorbonne, most earlier sixteenth-century Englishmen were not yet ready for such dispassionate relativism as Shakespeare achieved under Marguerite's tutelage, and when they took up Clément Marot as a representative of the best in the French Renaissance they tended to emphasize his role as a proto-Huguenot and translator of the Psalms rather than as a skeptical wit. The two roles of Marot were in fact just as closely related in Marguerite's skeptical approach to orthodoxy, and Marot's verse gives us an excellent sense of the poetic models which French culture afforded to the English throughout the century. Before we can evaluate the character of Wyatt's verse we should see exactly what his French contemporaries were doing. The disparities may explain why Wyatt unexpectedly failed to do full justice to French literary models of his time, such as Scève and Mellin St. Gelais, while later the progressive assimilation of Marot's example (and of his Italian precedents) matches the flowering of the English Renaissance. But we must always remember that without Marguerite and her brother (as well as their "exiled" sister-in-law, Renée de Ferrare) as principal audience and protectors Marot's achievement would have been very different, even if he had survived long enough to print anything distinctive.

75. Thomas Wyatt, *Collected Poems*, ed. Kenneth Muir and Patricia Thomson (Liverpool: Liverpool University Press, 1969), p. 27. All later Wyatt references are based on this edition unless otherwise indicated.

5

"L'enfant sans souci": Clément Marot

In APRIL 1593 ONE JOHN ELIOT, "A TEACHER OF FRENCH AND COMPILER FOR the printer Wolfe of a London newsletter on French affairs," expressed his hostility to the professional competition offered by foreign refugees by publishing a conversation manual for students of French called *Ortho-Epia Gallica*. As with this book's modern analogues, one is not quite sure whether the illustrative dialogue is written for conscious comic effort or whether it simply records the eccentric usages and manners of its time. What is certain is that nowadays we find the brief scenes evoked by such textbooks' sample conversations often glow like Dutch interiors, evoking as vividly as Shakespeare's prose the texture of everyday life in London. Shakespeare himself may have depended on Eliot for information about France for a play with a contemporary setting like *Love's Labour's Lost* and for correct French usage in scenes like that between the French princess, Katherine, and her attendant in *Henry V*.[1] There is good evidence that at least one highly educated reader studied Eliot's treatise earnestly, for Gabriel Harvey's copy in the Huntington Library is heavily marked with his underlinings, asterisks, and brief exclamations—often so naively patriotic and partisan

1. Richard David, ed., *Love's Labour's Lost*, by William Shakespeare (London: Methuen, 1966), p. xxxix.

94

as to undermine any confidence in his sophistication. Various incidental references to English merits are approvingly marked; so also is
a discussion of fashionable French authors. In reply to the inquiry,
"Amongst the French, who are the most eloquent authors?" Eliot tells
us that there are "very many" but "first you have Clément Marot, that
was King Francis' Poet, who was admirable for his time." The naive
questioner observes, "He was the King's foole, for since his time they
call fooles and idiots in France Marots," but this is smartly corrected:
"You deceive your selfe greatly, he was the Poet Roiall, not a foole
royall: of whom the fine poesies shall be read and read again, as long
as Yea and Nay shall last among learned men. . . . They say that he
transported the Muses beyond the mountaines, and attyred them on
the French fashion. He hath done marvellous well in his beginnings
truly. Hold him of my word for a naturall Poet: when you shall understand French perfectly read me his bookes."[2] (See Plate 11.)

Twenty years earlier in *The French Schoolmaistr* Claude Holyband
had similar advice, and numerous other allusions indicate that sixteenth-century English educators favored Marot's works, often for reasons of religious sympathy, so that one modern scholar can even argue
"that Marot was perfectly well-known to the literate English public,
that his reputation was very great, and that in the end he probably exercised more influence on English literature than any other poet of the
French Renaissance."[3] Both Wyatt and Surrey not only knew Marot's
milieu firsthand (and could scarcely have missed encountering his
works at the French court) but were likely to have met Marot on these
visits. The familiarity with Marot's verse of these and later English
poets can be shown by various debts of a local and technical nature,
such as Surrey's use of a Marot rondeau, "Au temps passé . . . ," as a
source for his poem, "Yf he that erst . . . ," or Gascoigne's exploitation
of Marot's Alyx as a precedent for poetic obscenities, not to mention
E. K.'s avowal that Spenser's November eclogue "is made in imitation
of Marot his song which he made upon the death of Loys the frenche

2. John Eliot, *Ortho-epia Gallica* (London: Wolfe, 1592), pp. 32–33.
3. Dana Bentley-Cranch, "La réputation de Clément Marot en Angleterre,"
Studi Francesci 17 (1973), 201–21.

Queene" (even though, of course, "far passing his reache!").[4] Indeed, *The Mirror for Magistrates* blames Marot's vulgar model for the defeat of the English lyricists' efforts to rival the classics; so perhaps Pierre Villey is right in his exception to the estimate of the general failure of Marot's genius to travel abroad: "Only sixteenth-century England, which is schooled by France, affords Marot a favorable reception."[5]

In spite of this currency in England, Marot has rarely been fully recognized and understood even there, perhaps because his influence has been seen in so selective and technical a way as to ensure its exclusion from consideration in larger aesthetic terms.[6] For example, in judging foreign influences on Wyatt we find Kenneth Muir noting that Wyatt's greatest poems are not his translations but the lyrics for which no direct source has been discovered.[7] But the point of comparative studies does not lie in the demonstration of merely literal or mechanical use of sources, as Ian McFarlane warns: "We must not confuse literary archeology with critical appreciation."[8] And he goes on to point out that the study of demonstrable sources can be deeply misleading, since all Renaissance writers accepted the obligation to work within a recognized tradition: "The sixteenth century, for all its creative force, is a century which attaches the greatest importance to authority and tradition; and originality, in so far as it might involve a break with reputable tradition, was not therefore considered on that account to be recommendable. The word *invention* means originally the 'coming upon' (i.e. of something already there) and 'imagination' is not thought

4. See Prescott, pp. 1–36, for full details of Marot's reputation among lesser English authors. For some reason she ignores his relationship to Shakespeare and Milton entirely, and the chapter scarcely mentions Donne. This is partly offset by Richmond, *The School of Love*, which Prescott fails to notice.

5. Pierre Villey, *Marot et Rabelais* (Paris: Champion, 1923), p. 147.

6. In particular, there is a "vast" scholarship dealing with the influence of Marot on the European psalter, so that there is no need to recapitulate the exhaustive treatment of his translations of the Psalms and their religious influence. See bibliography in Prescott, p. 244, n. 27.

7. Thomas Wyatt, *Collected Poems*, ed. Kenneth Muir (Cambridge: Harvard University Press, 1949), p. xviii.

8. Ian D. McFarlane, ed., *The "Délie,"* by Maurice Scève (Cambridge: Cambridge University Press, 1966), p. 23.

to be a wholesome word until later."[9] In correlating Anglo-French literary traditions in the Renaissance we should remember that "the unity of the western world has not yet broken up, and it is not surprising that in a time of philosophic syncretism we should find some sort of analogue in the literary world as well."[10] This means that there are not only frequent local, mechanical, and technical interconnections between Renaissance literatures but a broader conformity of issues and attitudes. Professor McFarlane argues that "any personal poetry will be influenced in its presentation by the psychological assumptions on which it is based. . . . This *fonds commun* has to be distinguished from clear-cut borrowings for which precise sources can be cited. If we concern ourselves with this matter of undisputed obligations, we gain a very different picture"—and in a case like Scève's, for example, quite a misleading one.[11]

No mere listing of other poets' sources in Marot can do justice to the significance of his historical and literary personality. The understandable stress by scholars on his technical role as initiator of certain neoclassical genres and on the ecclesiastical impact of his translations of the Psalms also risks serious distortion of our sense of the nature of the man as a whole. He is not in the least like an English neoclassicist such as Milton, nor is he a religious poet like Spenser, even if his pastoral elegies influenced both of them in well-documented ways.[12] Eliot's naive questioner overstated the case in calling Marot the king's fool, but there is a strong Goliardic strain in Marot, as his devotion to Villon confirms. Villey notes that he haunted taverns and belonged to the sportive confraternity of "les Enfants sans souci," a kind of artist-intellectual group of medieval origins, associated with the analoguous Basoche or legal clerk's guild in all kinds of festivities and performances, many illustrating the societies' traditional anti-Establishment tone. This popular tradition was one necessary part of Marot's humane genius and ensured that, like St. Amant later, he was never stifled by the rigors of humanist pedantry, for "his semi-ignorance . . .

9. McFarlane, ed., p. 24.   10. McFarlane, ed., p. 29.
11. McFarlane, ed., p. 25.
12. See C. A. Patrides, *Milton's Lycides: The Tradition and the Poem* (New York: Holt, 1961)

was perhaps necessary for his originality."[13] One of Marot's friends, Boyssoné, denied not only that he had a knowledge of Greek but even that he knew any Latin in his earlier career, and Marot himself called the court his "schoolmistress."[14] When he joined the king's service Marot did not draw on classical traditions for his verse: "The novelty of this poetry was to be that above all Marot found material in his personal experience. His principal merit would be perhaps to substitute for the artificial subjects of the schools, the expression of his own opinions and feelings, and accounts of his mishaps. From earliest youth we note his tendency to talk about himself." This material suited the court, which did not care for erudition and elaborate allegories: "The courtiers wanted small, short, clear poems which required no effort. They also wanted to hear of opinion they shared and of things they knew."[15]

Such a personality was temperamentally at odds with the academic establishment in ways to which we are accustomed by the modern examples of Pound or Graves, and Marot did not hesitate to provoke his enemies by allusions to "the ignorant Sorbonne" with its "hatred of learning." Such quarrels confirm the view that Marot "was less a convinced Lutheran than an enemy of Catholicism," but his hatreds were "also of a humane kind, founded on the horror of cruelty, of tyranny, and of stupidity."[16] Marot shows no naive devotion to Luther in his verse:

> Luther pour moy des cieulx n'est descendu,
> Luther en croix n'a poinct esté pendu
> Pour mes pechés, et, tout bien advisé,
> Au nom de luy ne suys point baptizé.
> (*Epîtres* xxxvi.89–92)[17]

13. Villey, pp. 2, 12.

14. Clément Marot, *Les Epîtres*, ed. C. A. Mayer (London: Athlone Press, 1958), p. 241.

15. Villey, pp. 20, 13.

16. Marot, *Epîtres*, pp. 25, 197–98.

17. All further Marot quotations are based on the five volume edition of Clément Marot, *Les Épigrammes, Les Epîtres, Oeuvres diverses, Oeuvres lyriques, Oeuvres satyriques*, ed. C. A. Mayer (London: Athlone Press, 1958–70), and the references conform to its categories and format.

(Luther did not descend from heaven for my sake; Luther was not hung on the cross for my sins, and I am well aware that I was not baptized in his name.)

We find fervor more clearly in Marot's resentment of the effects of religious intransigence on "lovers of truth," who are religion's victims rather than its devotees:

> Les ungs souvant par poyne on persecute,
> D'aultres, helas! par mort on essecute,
> Les ungtz souvant chassés de leur pays,
> Les autres sont abhorrés et hays. . . .
> Mais la cher seulle endure ceste poyne,
> Car l'ame franche est de foy toute pleine,
> Et de liesse en se corps tant ravye
> Par ferme espoir de la segonde vie,
> Que les bruleurs, juges et deputés,
> Sont mille fois plus que eulx persecutés
> Par la collere ardante de laquelle
> Mettent à mort l'inocent sequelle
> Du grant Segneur, qui ça bas tout avise
> Et se rit d'eux et de leur entreprise.
>
> (*Epîtres* xxxv.7–10, 27–36)

(Often some will be persecuted by torture; others, alas, they put to death; often some are exiled; others are treated with revulsion and hate. . . . But the flesh alone suffers this pain, for the free soul is full of faith and so ravished with joy in this body because of sure hope of renewed life that the burners, judges, and deputies are, a thousand times more than they, the ones persecuted by the burning rage with which they put to death the innocent following of the great Lord, who sees all down there and laughs at them and their understanding.)

One recalls how a similar vision fires some of Shakespeare's verse in *Measure for Measure* when Angelo is starting his persecutions. Isabella exclaims:

99

> man, proud man,
> Dressed in a little brief authority,
> Most ignorant of what he's most assured,
> His glassy essence, like an angry ape,
> Plays such fantastic tricks before high Heaven
> As makes the angels weep—who, with
> our spleens,
> Would all themselves laugh mortal.
>
> (II.ii.117–23)

Obviously, awareness of the tragic consequences of Reformation controversy gave a deep seriousness to such passages in both writers, and it is significant that Marot, like Montaigne later, had enough firsthand experience of the sufferings in religious strife to speak out vehemently against the use of brutality and torture. If Marot's first imprisonment in 1526 was for eating bacon in Lent (a crime he may have partly "expiated" by living in a hostelry called L'Aigle, in Chartres), his second in 1527 resulted from his indignation at police brutality:

> Je suis bien fol: je me tourmente
> Le cueur et le corps d'un affaire
> Dont toy et moy n'avons que faire;
> Cela n'est que irriter les gens;
> Tellement que douze Sergens,
> Bien armez jusques au Collet,
> Battront bien ung homme seullet,
> Pourveu que point ne se deffende.
> (*Satiriques* VII.28–35)

(I'm really insane: I distress my heart and body with a business in which we have no interest; it just provokes people so much that twelve officers of the watch armed to the teeth will thoroughly beat a single man into helplessness.)

One cannot divine the rights and wrongs of this affair, but later Marot can be seen to show honorable resentment of unfair cruelty in another, more notorious case: the unjust execution of the "tresorier général" Semblancay in 1538 at the instigation of Louise de Savoie, whose greed he had dared to thwart. Voltaire himself picked out for praise Marot's acid reversal of public roles in an epigram describing the criminal aspect of the officer in charge of the execution and the victim's appearance as the epitome of judicial rectitude. An even more pathetic lament describes the old man's corpse swaying in the wind on the scaffold, washed by rain, dried by sun, and with its eyes picked out by carrion crows. Such tragic pictures show how Marot's feelings could intensify in the face of unjust suffering.[18]

His own troubles never reached this pitch; perhaps the hounding, imprisonment, and inquisitions to which he was subjected were just sufficient to challenge and temper a more resilient mind than that of Bonaventure des Périers, whose fears drove him to suicide. On his flight to seek sanctuary with Marguerite at Nérac in 1535, Marot was agile enough to escape even after capture by authorities in Bordeaux. And when her protection began to seem inadequate, his further flight to Renée of Ferrara had the paradoxical result of enriching his poetry with the Italian influences which later ensured its preeminence in France; so that, far from ruining his poetry, "the exile in Ferrara was one of the most fruitful periods in the poet's career."[19] There is thus a certain irony in Marot's deft exploitation of the analogy to Ovid's exile in the Crimea, even if Ferrara ultimately proved just as hostile to suspected heretics as France had. These persecutions in Ferrara led Marot to memorable expressions of sympathy for Renée's plight and, for himself, to an exciting visit to Venice, evoked with all the verve of *Othello* or *The Merchant of Venice*. The final vicissitudes of Marot's career, revulsion from Geneva and humble efforts at reassimilation into the French Establishment, served further to complicate and enrich his personality, just as the same process did with Théophile de Viau and St. Amant in the following century. Each adventure "obliged him to withdraw into himself to find there an echo of the great concerns of the age."[20] Nowhere can we find a better epitome of the creative effects on a sensitive mind of living through the moral tidal wave of the Reformation.

18. Marot, *Épigrammes* XLIII (and Introduction, p. 27); *Lyriques* V.
19. Marot, *Épîtres*, Introduction, p. 13.
20. Villey, p. 23.

The memorable intersection of poetic tradition and personal experience in *L'Enfer* is generally held to show the crystallizing of a modern, self-conscious personality. This subjective dimension also helps to make it a poem which insists on the practical and positive levels of value in literature, for "Marot perceived that in the Châtelet he had uncovered some of the tricks used by its judges [to incriminate prisoners], and that in reading *L'Enfer* to the King, he had invited the latter to reform the abuses of justice."[21] Marot allows us to see how the ecclesiastical inquisition builds up in the accused a unique awareness of his own identity, which it intends to suppress. The judge demands Marot's name, birth, and condition, but the poet affects jocularity:

> Mais puis qu'envie et ma fortune veulent
> Que congneu sois et saisy de tes laqs,
> Sçaiche de vray, puis que demandé l'as,
> Que mon droict nom je ne te veulx poinct taire,
> Si t'advertis qu'il est à toy contraire,
> Comme eaue liquide au plus sec element;
> Car tu es rude et mon nom est Clément.
>
> (*Satiriques* 1.342–48)

(But since envy and my fate wish that I should be known and held in your bonds, know the truth as you have asked for it, that my true name I won't at all suppress if I warn you that it is your opposite as flowing water is to the driest element, for you are harsh and my name is Clément.)

Buoyed up by his sense of royal protection Marot then confidently sketches out his career with a precision, rare for his time, which has proved invaluable to his biographers:

> Entends apres (quant au poinct de
>   mon estre)
> Que vers midy les haults Dieux m'ont
>   faict naistre,
> Où le Soleil non trop excessif est;
> Parquoy la terre avec honneur s'y vest
> De mille fruicts, de maincte fleur et plante;

21. Marot, *Satiriques*, Introduction, p. 6.

Bacchus aussi sa bonne vigne y plante
Par art subtil sur montaignes pierreuses
Rendants liqueurs fortes et savoureuses,
Maincte fontaine y murmure et undoye,
Et en touts temps le Laurier y verdoye. . . .
Le fleuve Lot coule son eaue peu claire,
Qui maints rochiers transverse et environne,
Pour s'aller joindre au droict fil de Garonne.
A brief parler, c'est Cahors en Quercy,
Que je laissay pour venir querre icy
Mille malheurs, ausquelz ma destinée
M'avoit submis. Car une matinée,
N'ayant dix ans, en France fus meiné;
Là où depuis me suis tant pourmeiné
Que j'oubliay ma langue maternelle,
Et grossement aprins la paternelle,
Langue Françoyse es grands Courts estimée,
Laquelle en fin quelcque peu s'est limée.
                          (*Satiriques* 1.377–404)

(Learn further, as to my derivation, that about midday the high
gods had me born where the sun was not too excessive, so that
the earth dresses itself worthily there with a thousand fruits and
many flowers and plants. Bacchus also plants the good vine there
with subtle art on the stony mountains to produce strong and
flavorful liquors. Many springs murmur and ripple there. . . .
The river Lot flows with its cloudy water, barred and bordered
by many rocks, to join the straight line of the Garonne. In brief,
it is Cahors in Quercy which I left to come seeking here a thousand misfortunes to which my fate submitted me. For one morning, being only ten years old, I was taken to France, where I have
since wandered so much that I have forgotten my maternal tongue
and clumsily learned the paternal French language esteemed in
great courts, in which in the end some small work has been
shaped.)

The combination of details here is extremely revealing. Just as his
patrons, François and Marguerite, conserved a vitality and idiosyn-

cracy deriving from a less than conventional background, so Marot is not initially part of the French intellectual mainstream, though perhaps John Berdan goes a little far in writing that "born in the provincial town of Cahors and brought up to speak the native dialect, his energy was absorbed in learning French: Greek and Latin went by the board."[22] Still one feels that Marot was as free of commitment to an aesthetic clique as Marguerite was of religious bigotry. In dedicating an anthology to Montmorency, Marot describes it as "ung Jardin garny de fleurs diverses" (a garden of varied flowers), one which is "sans arbre, ne grand fruict" (without trees or big fruit) and "il y a des orties" (there are nettles in it).[23] Elsewhere he concedes that he finds "ma plume trop rurale'" (my pen is too rustic) for great subjects, and he prefers "un bas stille et tendre" (a humble and soft style) such as love poetry will permit.[24] Thus one of his most successful veins is his series of witty *étrennes* praising court ladies, for "it is the simplicity of the *étrenne*, stripped of all affectation and of Petrarchan floweriness, which is its whole charm":[25]

> La Duchesse de Nevers
> Aux yeulx vertz,
> Pour l'esprit qui est en elle
> Aura louenge eternelle
> Par mes vers.
> (*Diverses* cxxxviii)

> (The Duchess of Never—
> Green-eyed fair—
> Since wit in her so plays,
> My verse shall sing her praise
> For ever.)

As for the rondeau, Marot's advice lays out the ground plan for the "strong" type of Elizabethan lyric:

22. John M. Berdan, *Early Tudor Poetry* (New York: Macmillan, 1920), p. 441.
23. Marot, *Epîtres* XXXII.
24. Marot, *Epîtres* III; *Lyriques* VI.
25. Marot, *Diverses*, Introduction, p. 30.

En ung Rondeau, sur le commencement,
Ung vocatif comme maistre Clément
Ne peult faillir rentrer par Huys ou Porte
Aux plus sçavans Poetes m'en rapporte
Qui d'en user se gardent sagement.

Bien inventer vous fault premierement;
L'invention deschiffrer proprement,
Si que Raison et Ryme ne soit morte
    En ung Rondeau.
Usez de motz receuz communement;
Rien superflu n'y soit aulcunement,
Et de la fin quelque bon propos sorte.
Clouez tout court; rentrez de bonne sorte!
Maistre passé serez certainment
    En ung Rondeau.

(Diverses 1)

(In a rondeau at the start, a vocative like "Mister Clément!" cannot fail to pass the gate or door; with the most learned poets, I agree on this, who wisely restrain its use. You must find some good material first; so rhyme and reason may not die in a rondeau, you must spell out the matter elegantly. Use familiar words; nothing there should be superfluous, and some epigram should emerge at the end. Nail it really close; return in good style! Then you'll be a past master in a rondeau.)

Marot himself illustrates the technique in an epigram which begins, "Tu dis, Prelat, Marot est paresseux" (You say, Bishop, that Marot is lazy), and also in an elegy starting with a question: "Qu'ai je mesfaict, dictes, ma chere Amye?" (What did I do wrong, tell me, my darling?).[26] Even in the middle of a poem such colloquial effects can be introduced:

Que dys je? où suys je? O noble Roy Françoys,
Pardonne moy, car allieurs je pensoys.

(Epîtres XXXVI.121–22)

(What am I saying? Where am I? O noble King François, forgive me, for I was absent-minded.)

26. Marot, Épigrammes CLIII, Lyriques LVIII.

To an extent the elegies, as a group, are among Marot's less successful work; most of them lack the vivifying personal touches which distinguish other genres exploited by Marot for intimate effects, like the verse epistle, which he made "marvelously supple and personal,"[27] a perfect model for the colloquial vigor so admired by the poets of the later English Renaissance like Jonson and Donne.

In fact, "Marot did not care much about determining the genre of a work"[28]—his approach to tradition was pragmatic and even casual, as the allegorical figure of Bon Espoir counsels him to be in an early epistle whose archaic format derives from his father's school of rhétoriqueurs:

> Et toy, Amy, croy moy, car guerdonneur
> Je te seray, si craintif ne te sens;
> Croy donc Mercure, emploie tes cinq sens,
> Cueur et esprit et fantasie toute,
> A composer nouveaulx motz et recens,
> En dechassant crainte, soucy et doubte.
> (*Epîtres* ii.115–20)

(And you, friend, believe me, for I will reward you if I feel you are not timid; believe Mercury therefore, use your five senses, heart, and mind, and all imagination to compose new words and fresh ones in dismissing fear, care, and doubt.)

It is not accidental that Marot anticipates Montaigne by calling his works "Coups d'essay" in the prologue to his "Adolescence."[29] Paradoxically Marot introduces alien genres into French in the very opposite of an antiquarian spirit. For example the first eclogue in French, his lament for Louise de Savoie, is a complex synthesis of effects borrowed from Theocritus, Moschos, and Virgil, not to mention Jean Lemaire, Jehan Molinet, and Jacopo Sannazaro.[30] Perhaps only Marot's headlong energy would have risked such an attempt. The same brisk energies were devoted to the conscious creation of a new vogue by a

27. Marot, *Epîtres*, Introduction, p. 33; *Lyriques*, Introduction, p. 33.
28. Marot, *Epîtres*, Introduction, p. 30.
29. Marot, *Satiriques* VI, 128.
30. Marot, *Lyriques*, Introduction, pp. 26–27.

poem on a pretty peasant girl's breast, which served other poets as a model for virtuoso praises of picturesque or intimate portions of female anatomy.[31]

Among the poems by Lyonnais poets whose efforts at such "blazons" competed for recognition with Marot's at the court of Renée de Ferrare, Maurice Scève's five pieces are more restrained and elegant, praising the Forehead, the Eyebrow, the Sigh, the Tear, and the Throat. Marot tells us that:

> du Sourcil la beauté bien chantée
> A tellement nostre Court contentée,
> Qu' à son Autheur nostre Princesse donne
> Pour ceste fois, de Laurier la Couronne.
> *(Epîtres* xxxix.21–24)

(the well-sung praises of the beauty of the eyebrow have so pleased our court that to their author our princess [Renée] gives on this occasion the laurel crown.)

It is amusing to find that Shakespeare ascribes knowledge of Scève's vein to Jaques, the affected French intellectual of *As You Like It*, whose "Seven Ages of Man" includes a parody of:

> the lover,
> Sighing like furnace, with a woeful ballad
> Made to his mistress' eyebrow.
> (ii.vii.147–49)

Scève's victorious poem on the Eyebrow matches the caricature, and his poem on the Sigh also asserts that the lover's sighs flow "ne plus ne moins qu'en estroicte fornaise / L'on voit la flamme yssir" (neither more nor less than one sees the flame gush from a narrow furnace). As usual, Shakespeare shows an infallible instinct for the apt allusion and a satiric approach to serious extravagance. Marot's view of the vein was nearer to Shakespeare's than Scève's, as we see when Marot tries to set up a counter-fashion to his own genre in satirical praise with his poem to a sagging bust, a model which inevitably proved less engaging

---

31. See "Blazons du corps féminin," in Albert-Marie Schmidt, ed., *Poetes du XVIᵉ siècle* (Paris: Gallimard, 1969), pp. 293–364.

to the ladies and hence to their poets. Luckily Marot's other satirical verse proves more significant, and "it is truly Marot who introduced Martial into French poetry."[32] Martial's wit, sophistication, and verve offered an excellent model for the expression of Marot's best talents in sprightly and charming or sarcastic investigations of social occasions of every kind. Whether or not Marot did translate the first sonnet into French, Martial rather than Petrarch is the best precedent for the verse of Marot which is now remembered.

However, if Marot can be as scurrilous as Martial and is known to have influenced English versifiers like Gascoigne by his obscene verses on Alix,[33] he also knows how to approach sex more seductively:

> Quand je voy Barbe en Habit bien duysant
> Qui l'Estomach blanc et poly descoeuvre,
> Je la compare au Dyamant luisant
> Fort bien taillé mis de mesmes en oeuvre.
> Mais quand je voy Jacquette qui se coeuvre
> Le dur Tetin, le corps de bonne prise,
> D'ung simple Gris Acoustrement de Frise
> Adonc je dy pour la beaulté d'icelle :
> Ton habit Gris est une Cendre Grise
> Couvrant ung Feu qui tousjours estincelle.
>
> (*Épigrammes* ii)

(When I see Barbe in a charming costume revealing her smooth white breast, I compare her to a shining diamond in a beautiful setting. But when I see Jacquette, who covers her firm breast and fine shape with a plain grey costume of frieze, then I say, because of that beauty, "Your grey costume is a grey ash covering a fire which still sparkles.")

And he writes just as directly of court ladies, one of whom he praises "d'estre blanche et en bon poinct / Sous le linge" (for being white and shapely underneath the linen).[34] Of another lady, called Mlle. de la Roue, he writes that she has supplanted in interest the theme of the

32. Marot, *Épigrammes*, Introduction, p. 28.
33. Marot, *Diverses*, pp. 227–28.
34. Marot, *Diverses*, p. 257.

Wheel of Fortune, for love has put his hand to this wheel, and any man would be happy to be sentenced to be broken on it.[35]

Perhaps his most elegant exercise in this kind of sensual flattery is devoted to Isabeau d'Albret, the sister of Marguerite d'Angoulême's second husband:

> Qui cuyderoit desguiser Ysabeau
> D'ung simple habit, ce seroit grand simplesse,
> Car au visage a ne sçay quoy de beau
> Qui faict juger tousjours qu'elle est Princesse,
> Soit en habit de chambriere ou maitresse,
> Soit en drap d'or entier ou decouppé,
> Soit son gent corps de toille enveloppé,
> Tousjours sera sa beauté maintenue,
> Mais il me semble (ou je suis bien trompé)
> Qu'elle seroit plus belle toute nue.
>
> (*Épigrammes* LXXIII)

A deft English poet translates this economically:

> My love in her attire doth show her wit,
>   It doth so well become her:
> For every season she hath dressings fit,
>   For winter, spring, and summer.
> No beauty she doth miss,
>   When all her robes are on:
> But Beauty's self she is,
>   When all her robes are gone.[36]

While the wit and elegance have been if anything heightened by this version, the sense of actual persons, the details of high fashion, and the fully evoked social milieu are lost with the fading of Marot's characteristic immediacy. Even in the *étrenne* Marot can paint a far more intimate, exact picture—as with Mlle. Macy, an androgynous charmer worthy of Shakespearean comedy:

35. Marot, *Épigrammes* XCIX, CIII.
36. A. H. Bullen, ed., *Speculum Amantis* (Oxford: Clarendon Press, 1889), p. 12.

Soubz vos attours bien fourniz,
D'or garniz,
A Venus vous ressemblez;
Soubz le bonnet me semblez
Adonis.

(*Diverses* CXLVIII)

Within, exquisite Miss,
A gilt dress,
You're like Venus, I deem;
Beneath a cap, you seem
Adonis.

Marot is capable of more complex sexual relationships in his work, and if Scève's *Délie* is the earliest French cycle of amatory lyrics in Petrarch's vein, Marot's scattered poems on Ysabeau plot an evolving relationship in harsher terms, anticipating Shakespearean skepticism of the elegant sentiments affected in the Petrarchan tradition. A. Alvarez has asserted that, "Compared with the Romance languages, English is extraordinarily non-rhetorical . . . in English, rhetoric is nearly always a substitute for intelligence."[37] But it is not hard to see in Marot's verse good precedents for the questioning of rhetorical poses which appears at times in Wyatt and Sidney and marks many of the most memorable poems of Shakespeare and Donne. Marot seems to have consciously created a disconcertingly realistic sequence about Ysabeau, making her comparable to Villon's treacherous mistress.[38] In 1538 Marot apparently inserted a fresh title, "A Ysabeau," over a poem praising constancy in love in terms as ambivalent as any of Donne's lyrics:

Ceste Vertu et ses Servans parfaicz
Portent le Noir qui ne se peult destaindre;
Et qui l'amour premiere laisse estaindre
Le noir Habit n'est digne de porter.

37. A. Alvarez, *The School of Donne* (London: Chatto and Windus, 1961), pp. 93–94.
38. Marot, *Diverses*, p. 132, n. 1; *Épigrammes*, p. 98, n. 1.

Tout Homme doibt ceste vertu attaindre;
Si Femme y fault, elle est à supporter.

(*Épigrammes* v)

(This virtue and its perfect servants wear the black which cannot fade, and who allows first love to be extinguished is not worthy to wear the black costume. All men must achieve this virtue; if woman fails in it, she must be endured.)

The irony of faithfulness to the inconstant Ysabeau is evoked by the new, specific title which replaces the originally more general "Le dixain de Fermeté." This new level of allusion implies complex attitudes like that of Shakespeare's Sonnet 116, which abstractly asserts that "love is not love / Which alters when it alteration finds," though the context indicates that the poet has been found wanting and seeks reconciliation.[39]

A different overtone can be detected in another epigram, which defends the poet for having named Ysabeau:

Quand j'escriroys que je t'ay bien aymée,
Et que m'as sur tous aultres aymé,
Tu n'en seroys femme desestimée,
Tant peu me sens homme desestimé.
Petrarque a bien sa maistresse nommée
Sans amoindrir sa bonne renommée. . . .

(*Épigrammes* lx)

(When I wrote that I loved you well and that you had loved me above all others, you would not have suffered thereby any loss of reputation, as I would not feel myself in disrepute. Petrarch had certainly named his mistress without diminishing her good repute.)

We sense here a forensic intent which exploits Petrarch as a cover for untraditional openness in sexual relations, in contrast to conventional courtship as visualized in the *Heptameron*, where concealment of ex-

39. For discussion of the dramatic context of the sentiment, see Hugh M. Richmond, *Shakespeare's Sexual Comedy* (Indianapolis: Bobbs-Merril, 1971), pp. 37–39.

tramarital love is axiomatic. Again, in a sonnet like 122, Shakespeare is concerned with the embarrassment of being "bold" enough to reveal details of a private relationship and defends his boldness by sophistry about its excellence.

In both poets the effect of writing on a particular occasion is to heighten the immediacy of the verse, and the expedient sophistry is less a defect than a device to use autobiography to achieve psychological verisimilitude. The next phase of Marot's relationship to Ysabeau is the one which achieves the most dramatic cadence while making a drastic revision of amatory stereotypes. "De l'inconstance de Ysabeau" repudiates the convention of devoted sacrifice to a woman who feels no more obligation to reciprocate this devotion than do many of the great ladies who mock their lovers in the *Heptameron*:

> Comme inconstante et de cueur faulse et lasche
> Elle me laisse. Or puis qu'ainsi me lasche,
> A vostre advis ne la doibs je lascher?
> Certes ouy, et aultrement fascher
> Je ne la veulx, combien qu'elle me fasche.
>
> Il luy fauldroit (au train qu'à mener tasche)
> Des Serviteurs a journée et à tasche;
> En trop de lieux veult son cueur attacher
>   Comme inconstante.
> Or, pour couvrir son grand vice et sa tache,
> Souvent ma plume à la louer s'attache;
> Mais à cela je ne veulx plus tascher,
> Car je ne puis son maulvais bruyt cacher
> Si seurement qu'elle ne se descache
>   Comme inconstante.
>
> *(Diverses* LXIII)

(She leaves me like a fickle woman with a false and vile heart. Now since she leaves me thus, in your opinion must I not leave her? Surely yes, and I do not wish to punish her otherwise, however much she provokes me. She would like, in the style she attempts, lovers by the day and for piecework; in too many places she fixes her heart, like a fickle woman. Now, to conceal her great vice and stain, often my pen occupied itself with her praise; but I no longer care to labor at this, for I cannot conceal her bad repute so surely that she won't betray her inconstancy.)

Perhaps nowhere else does Marot so exactly match the roughest tone of Wyatt's resentment at mistreatment by a mistress. At his most virile Wyatt too can break through conventional decorum in a salutary way which strikes a sympathetic chord to modern ears:

> Spyght askyth spight and changing change,
>   And falsyd faith must nedes be knowne;
> The faute so grett, the case so strange,
>   Of Right it must abrod be blown:
> Then sins that by thyn own desartte
> My soinges do tell how trew thou artt,
>   Blame not my lute.[40]

In both cases, instinctive resentment shatters refined decorum with brusqueness and candor, and each poet is conscious of an audience whose verdict carries a weight surpassing the traditional Courts of Love precisely because it reflects a truer consensus of literate opinion. Wyatt parallels Marot's question, "since she leaves me thus, in your opinion must I not leave her?" in the similar context of "They fle from me . . . ," with its pointed conclusion: "Syns that I so kyndely ame served, / I would fain know what she hath deserved" (or as it sometimes reads: "What think you bye this that she hat deserved?").[41]

There are many good reasons why Marot's poems about Ysabeau might have caught Wyatt's attention during or after May 1536 (when he was imprisoned about the time of the ruin of the Boleyns), for in a ballade published in 1534 Marot ascribes the incarceration which produced L'Enfer to the malice of Ysabeau after his censure of her fickleness:

> Ung jour rescripviz à m'Amye
> Son inconstance seulement;
> Mais elle ne fut endormie

40. Wyatt, ed. Muir and Thomson (1969), p. 213.
41. Wyatt, ed. Muir and Thomson (1969), p. 27.

A me le rendre chauldement.
Car des l'heure tint parlement
A je ne sçay quel Papelard
Et luy a dict tout bellement:
Prenez le, il a mangé le Lard!
                    (*Diverses* LXXX)

(One day I wrote to my girlfriend merely about her fickleness,
but she did not take it lying down and made it hot for me too.
For at once she talked to some Papist and said so sweetly to
him: "Arrest him, for he has eaten bacon in Lent!")

While the occasion of Marot's arrest appears bathetic in comparison to
Wyatt's potential trial for treason (which his supposed relations with
Anne might have invited), both poets risked execution, for Marot's
fast-breaking invited the opening up of the question of his supposed
Lutheranism. In fact both poets found their monarchs mercifully inclined, and Marot commemorated his release in a rondeau, following
the one about the inconstancy of Ysabeau, in which her involvement
in the imprisonment is also implied:

En liberté maintenant me pourmaine,
Mais en prison pour tant je fuz cloué.
Voyla comment Fortune me demaine!
C'est bien et mal. Dieu soit de tout loué.
Les Envieux ont dit que de Noé
N'en sortirois; que la Mort les emmaine!
Malgré leurs dentz, le neud est desnoué.
En liberté maintenant me pourmaine.
                    (*Diverses* LXIV)

(In liberty now I stroll, but in prison I was nailed up for so long:
that's how Fortune persecuted me. There's good and bad, God
be praised for everything. The envious said that by Christmas[42]
I would never get out of it, Death take them. In spite of their
teeth, the knot in untied. In liberty now I stroll.)

42. Schmidt, pp. 39, 1088. Differs from Marot, *Diverses*, ed. Mayer, pp. 133,
287, in following the sense.

Marot thinks his girlfriend was responsible, for he was jailed "aussi tost que fuz desadvoué / De celle là qui me fut tant humaine" (as soon as I broke with her who gave me her favors).

Wyatt surely experienced the same exultation at release. Whether or not a literal prison is involved in this lively poem associated with his verse, a refrain almost identical to Marot's is used, though the laughter may be borrowed from Serafino's "Fui serrato":

> Tanglid I was yn loves snare,
> Opprest with payne, tormente with care,
> Of grefe right sure, of Joye full bare,
> Clene in dispaire by crueltye;
> But ha, ha, ha, full well is me,
> For I am now at libretye. . . .
>
> Was never birde tanglid yn lyme,
> That brake awaye yn bettre tyme,
> Then I that rotten bowes ded clyme,
> And had no hurte, but scaped fre.
> Now ha, ha, ha, full well is me,
> For I am nowe at libretye.[43]

It is possible that the excitement here does not result merely from breaking off an affair but from the discounting of the charges against Wyatt which coincided with the final ruin of Anne Boleyn (the "rotten bowe"), events which would have doubly released Wyatt from entrapment. What is striking about the two poems is the plangent vehemence of the refrains, which are the very opposite of formal: they end in the reiteration of strong personal feeling, not in a musical recapitulation such as Spenser favors in his refrains.

Marot's other poems about Ysabeau intensify this acrid immediacy. One translates an epigram of Martial ascribing the gift of a hare from a girlfriend to a wish to improve her beloved's complexion (Pliny mentions this belief).[44] Each poet cruelly responds by asking, "If it's any use, why haven't you tried it yourself?" Another epigram sinks to crude

---

43. Wyatt, ed. Muir and Thomson (1969), pp. 227–28.
44. Marot, *Épigrammes* CLXX.

insult: Ysabeau is called "a fine stool pigeon" who is so cross-eyed that she would be better off stone-blind.[45] Perhaps Marot means "she can't see straight"—in the metaphorical sense of not understanding him or of seeing sins which are not there (that is, Lutheranism). At any event, the whole sequence of poems outlines economically a relationship as harsh as that reflected in Shakespeare's sonnets to his Dark Lady. As in Shakespeare, the cycle of sentiments is quite different from Petrarch's model. It evolves from a passionate and picturesque affair to the poet's gloating escape from the most embittering betrayal, precipitated by his own tactlessness and sexual resentment. Even without evidence to corroborate the historicity of the poems' subject matter, the poems have an intensity and dramatic verve which spring from the bitter entanglement of sex and ethical issues during the Reformation which notoriously tinctures most of Donne's verse. However, Marot's literal account of sensuality leading to religious persecution is as much an archetype of such sixteenth-century sexuality as Abelard's account of his affair with Eloise is of the stresses of sex and career for a medieval cleric. It illustrates grotesque and sinister interactions, epitomized in *Measure for Measure* at the end of the century, in which outrageousness verges disturbingly on the tragic.

Marot excelled in lighter deployments of literary devices to social ends, and a more relaxed and charming example of the interaction of religion and sexuality lies in his use of a topic at least as old as the *Song of Songs* (I.5): "Nigra sum sed formosa" (I am black but comely). Marot's dependence on women like Marguerite d'Angoulême and Renée de Ferrare ensured that he give full recognition to their feminine point of view in both psychological and physiological terms. One of his rondeaux praises the "three princesses" involved in the Treaty of Cambrai,[46] which ended the disastrous war between François and the emperor which had left François captured and almost dead with humiliation. Louise de Savoie, Marguerite d'Angoulême, and Marguerite d'Autriche are set higher than the Hellenistic divinities Hera, Athena, and Aphrodite because the pagan divinities had started a war over Paris' choice of Aphrodite as the most beautiful, while the Valois triad of contrasting beauties had achieved "La Paix des Dames." And

45. Marot, *Épigrammes* CCXXIII.   46. Marot, *Diverses* LVII.

in another poem, to the Queen of Hungary, Marot returns to the theme of the pacific goals of "cueurs feminins," compared with those of the kings.[47] Two of his elegies are written from the feminine point of view, following the model of the "Epître de Maguelonne," in which the youthful Marot had first imitated the *Heroides* of Ovid, thus setting important precedents for similar female personae in Surrey's lyrics and in Drayton's magnificent *England's Heroicall Epistles*.[48] However, a more physical consideration proves just as fertile: since all the Valois princesses were deep brunettes, it is hardly surprising that Marot turned his talents in occasional verse to exploiting every literary device to vindicate their dark complexions against the conventional ideal of blonde Hellenistic beauty, which was already causing difficulties for Ovid's girlfriend when she tried to compete with blonde Teutonic slave-women by using too powerful a bleach. Even in the sixteenth century, the first wife of Henri IV, Marguerite de Navarre, another brunette Valois princess, had resorted to blonde wigs to take advantage of the universal observation that "gentlemen prefer blondes."[49]

However, the cult of dark complexions becomes stronger in the Renaissance. No doubt Marot's praise of the dark Valois beauties did a great deal to establish the alternative feminine ideal, which may be more compatible with Reformation than Renaissance values. If we think of the English Renaissance tradition alone, we find that, from the "Lutheran" Anne Boleyn's affair with Wyatt onwards, English poets (if we except Spenser's archaism) show a marked capacity to recognize the superior individuality and poetic potentialities of a dark costume or complexion. They depart from the traditional norms of beauty in recognizing somber traits and, by implication as well as observed fact, they reject the associated Apollonian patterns of personality. If Surrey's Geraldine is a blonde, she yet vigorously exploits the paradoxical values of somber clothing: "I never saw you, madam, lay apart / Your cornet black."[50] The symbolism may be Petrarchan still,

---

47. Marot, *Lyriques* LXXXI.   48. Marot, *Lyriques* II, LXX, LXXI.

49. For a grotesque illustration of the antiquity of the prejudice, see Ovid, *Amores* I. xiv.

50. Gerald Bullett, ed., *Silver Poets of the Sixteenth Century* (London: Dent, 1947), p. 120.

but Sidney's Stella evokes a more intrinsic paradox: "Whereas black seems Beauty's contrary, / She even in black doth make all beauties flow."[51] An almost forensic skill in justifying dark beauty appears in Milton's puritanical praise of the dark goddess of Melancholy in "Il Penseroso." However, the most spectacular gallery of challengingly dark beauties is found in Shakespeare. Perhaps the supremely exacting one is Cleopatra—whom Marguerite de Navarre, "nouvelle Cléopatre,"[52] had consciously imitated on her barge trip upon the Meuse to seduce the great general Don John, victor over the Turks near Actium, at the battle of Lepanto.[53] The elaborate investigation of the sinister potentialities of the Dark Lady in the sonnets shows more intimately how relevant the Reformation sense of corrupt human values is to the theme, but in fact the earliest exploitation of the recurring Black Beauty theme in Shakespeare is made in the French context of Navarre's court in *Love's Labour's Lost*, where the dusky beauty of the sardonic Rosaline is analyzed exhaustively.[54] Shakespeare, as exactly as usual, is following up an existing literary mode particularly favored at the historical court of the king of Navarre, dominated as it was by a brunette Valois princess as frequently celebrated in such terms as her great aunt and namesake had been by Clément Marot. Marot's virtuosity and precision thus leads the way for many English explorations of "darker" feminine characters, and of course the color symbolism is readily transposed to masculine roles like Othello's.[55]

In building up his expedient case for brunettes, Marot cleverly resorts to the intensified interest in the Bible during the Reformation, drawing on both the Old and New Testaments. One lyric evokes the *Song of Songs*:

51. *Silver Poets*, p. 175.

52. Philippe Erlanger, *Henri III* (Paris: Gallimard, 1935), p. 116.

53. William Sterling-Maxwell, *Don John of Austria*, vol. 2 (London: Longmans, 1883), 233–40.

54. See *LLL* IV.iii.242–276; discussed further in Chapter 9.

55. See Hugh M. Richmond, "Love and Justice: *Othello*'s Shakespearean Context," in Waldo McNair and Thelma Greenfield, eds., *Pacific Coast Studies in Shakespeare* (Eugene: University of Oregon Press, 1966), pp. 148–72.

Pourtant, si je suis Brunette,
Amy, n'en prenez esmoy,
Aultant suis ferme et jeunette
Qu'une plus blanche que moy;
Le Blanc effacer je voy,
Couleur Noire est toujours une;
J'ayme mieulx donc estre Brune
Avecques ma fermeté,
Que Blanche comme la Lune
Tenant de legiereté.

(*Lyriques* xlv)

(However, if I am brunette, friend, don't be distressed. I'm just as firm and young as any whiter than I; I see white erased, black color is always the same; and I'd rather be dark with my firmness than white like the moon with its fluctuations.)

It is true that Marot next writes "Pour la Blanche," but this is tactfully less convincing—just as Milton's praise of black's beauty in "Il Penseroso" clearly outweighs the lighter complexions and spirits of "L'Allegro." The preference is reinforced in Marot's "Chant Royal de la Conception nostre Dame," where Mary's superior beauty is skillfully displayed as echoing the *Song of Songs*: "Brunette suis, mais belle en Cueur et Face" (I am dark, but beautiful in heart and face).[56] There is deftness in the implicit allusion to the same favor of God's approval bestowed on Marot's own brunette Queen Marguerite, who is both beautiful and God's true servant in the later age.

However, Marot is flexible enough to vary his technique, and in specifying the physical properties of the ideal bedmate he offers a list of attributes compatible with Marguerite's, including "pour durer, prenez la brunette" (to last, take the brunette).[57] Such unlocalized statements are applied overtly to one of the Valois princesses in the epithalamium on the marriage of Madeleine to King James V:

Maint Dyamant sur la teste reluit
De la Brunette, et, ainsi atournée,

56. Marot, *Diverses* LXXXIX.   57. Marot, *Lyriques* XXXIII.

Son tainct, pour vray, semble une clere Nuict
Quand elle est bien d'Estoilles couronnée.
Brunette elle est, mais pourtant elle est belle.
(*Lyriques* LXXXVI)

(Many a diamond shines on her brunette tresses, and thus at-
tired her complexion truly seems like a clear night when it is
richly crowned with stars. Dark she is, but still she is beautiful.)

The same overt praise for brunette beauty recurs in an *étrenne* flattering a Spanish *dame d'honneur*, Donna Leonora de la Chapelle, which
challenges any who miscall her ugly because she is dark,[58] and of course
it figures in several epigrams devoted to Anne d'Alençon, daughter
of the illegitimate brother of Marguerite's first husband, with whom
Marot conducted a sentimental relationship rather more in the Petrarchan vein. Even in this ethereal mode Marot achieves great charm
and intimacy in serenading "Anne, ma soeur," whose dark complexion
is explicitly noted with that concern to localize which marks Marot's
use of convention.[59] He manages to turn a Petrarchan conceit on the
occasion of her throwing of a snowball at him.[60] Marot never uses
stilted traditions of praise without such vitalizing detail, as in flattering
Anne d'Albret, sister-in-law of Marguerite:

Elle a tresbien ceste gorge d'Albastre,
Ce doulx parler, ce cler tainct, ces beaux yeux;
Mais en effect ce petit Ris follastre
C'est (à mon gré) ce qui luy sied le mieux.
(*Épigrammes* LI)

(She has indeed this alabaster breast, the soft speech, the clear
complexion, the fine eyes; but in fact this little frisky laugh is
what, to my taste, sits best upon her.)

In all these flatteries we see an epitome of the very feminine appearance and behavior on which the brunette Anne Boleyn carefully modelled herself. Wyatt even refers to his affair with "Brunet" in a line
(later cautiously rephrased) about "her that ded set our country in a

58. Marot, *Diverses* CLXI.   59. Marot, *Épigrammes* CXXII, CCIX.
60. Marot, *Épigrammes* XXIV.

rore."[61] Curiously enough Wyatt's attention may have been caught by another song of Marot's devoted to a brunette:

> Venons au poinct, au poinct qu'on n'ose dire.
> Belle Brunette à qui mon cueur souspire,
> Si me donnez ce bien (sans m'escondire)
> Te serviray; mais sçavez vous comment?
> De Nuict et Jour tresbien et loyaulment.
> Si ne voulez, je fuiray mon martyre.
>
> (Lyriques xxix)

(Let's get to the point, the point one dare not name, beautiful Brunette for whom my heart sighs; if you give me that blessing (without tricking me) I shall serve you; but do you know how? By night and day well and loyally. If you don't wish it, I shall flee my martyrdom.)

Wyatt's song is no less blunt and uncourtly:

> Madame, withouten many wordes,
>   Ons I am sure ye will or no:
> And if ye will, then leve your bordes,
>   And vse your wit and shew it so. . . .
>
> Yf it be yea, I shalbe fayne;
>   If it be nay, frendes as before;
> Ye shall an othre man obtain,
>   And I myn owne and yours no more.[62]

However, there is also another analogue, by Mellin de Saint-Gelais, which affords a parallel to the last lines:

> S'il ne vous plaist, amis comme devant,
> Un autre aurez, et moy ne pouvant estre,
> Servant de vous, de moy je seray maistre.[63]

61. Wyatt, ed. Muir and Thomson (1969), p. 78.
62. Wyatt, ed. Muir and Thomson (1969), p. 25.
63. See Hyder E. Rollins, ed., *Tottel's Miscellany*, vol. 2 (Cambridge: Harvard University Press, 1966), p. 171, and A. K. Foxwell, *A Study of Sir Thomas Wyatt's Poems* (London: London University Press, 1911), pp. 67–68.

(If it does not please you, friends as before, you will have another man, and I, unable to be your servant, will be master of myself.)

Amusingly enough, there is a smart rejoinder following Wyatt's verses in the Egerton manuscript ("Of few wourdes sir you seme to be")[64] which is written in another hand and which puts the woman's indignation at such crudeness as briskly as any sophisticated lady in the *Heptameron*. Only when Wyatt rises to such dramatic psychology and conversational directness are we conscious of close resemblances to Marot. They share a capacity for virile indignation at what they (rather egotistically) consider women's lack of good will, but Marot's remains the suppler personality and the wittier mind, as when he affects Martial's perverse delight in making love to a girl clever enough to affect refusal while accepting the embrace, a cynicism beyond Wyatt.[65]

Wyatt is less wittily aware of his own sensibility and thus more a victim of circumstances than Marot, who usually manages to turn the tables on hostile minds:

> Vous perdez temps de me dire mal d'elle,
> Gens qui voulez divertir mon entente;
> Plus la blasmez, plus je la trouve belle;
> S'esbahist on si tant je m'en contente? . . .
> Car mon Amour vaincra vostre mesdire;
> Tel en mesdit, qui pour soy la desire.
>
> (*Lyriques* XLIV)

(You're wasting time to slander her, you who wish to divert my choice; the more you censure her, the more I find her beautiful; why are you so shocked that she pleases me? . . . For my love will conquer your censure; who attacks her wants to get her himself.)

Marot shows here that he can write with a dramatic directness anticipating Donne's "Canonization" ("For Godsake hold your tongue, and let me love").[66] And the clever touch of rationalization in the ending shows an insight into human wilfulness worthy of the Shakespearean self-justifying psychology in Sonnet 70:

64. Bullett, ed., *Silver Poets*, p. 98.   65. Marot, *Épigrammes* LXVII.
66. Donne, *Elegies and Songs and Sonnets*, p. 73.

That thou art blamed shall not be thy defect
For slander's mark was ever yet the fair.

Wyatt's reactions to such ingenious sophistries are more gloomily traditional and repressive:

To fantasy pertaynys to chose;
All thys I knowe, for fantasy
Ffurst vnto love dyd me Induse
But yet I knowe as stedefastly
That yff love haue no faster knott,
So nyce a choyse slyppes sodenly.
Yt lasteth nott.[67]

Subjective moods do not offer Wyatt any satisfaction because of the
intrusion of traditional moral imperatives which he applies too cat-
egorically for his own peace of mind, while Marot's sprightly skepticism
always carries him clear of impending disaster.

This agility of Marot's mind also allows him to assimilate unexpected and paradoxical attitudes and ideas, coining "metaphysical" conceits as arresting as any in later English verse. When he writes that
"mes soubhaitz vont comme l'Escrevice, / Tout au rebours" (my wishes
move backward, like a crayfish) we may be reminded of Prufrock's
surrealistic desire to be "a pair of ragged claws / Scuttling across the
floors of silent seas."[68] Similarly Marot can catch the lover's ambivalence about having his way, just as Donne does in "The Prohibition":

Take heed of loving mee
At least remember, I forbade it thee.[69]

Donne argues that "so great Joy, our life at once outweares," and Marot
is similarly apprehensive:

Je l'ayme; mais trop je l'aymerois
Quand son Cueur au mien vouldroit joindre,
(*Épigrammes* cxl)

67. Wyatt, ed. Muir and Thomson (1969), p. 202.
68. Marot, *Diverses* X; T. S. Eliot, *Collected Poems, 1909–1935* (London: Faber,
1936), p. 13.
69. Donne, *Elegies and Songs and Sonnets*, p. 39.

(I love her; but I would love her too much if her heart wished to join mine.)

And indeed the lady precipitates a curious response when she shows interest:

> Me dit avec ung ris accoustumé
> Je croy qu'il fault qu'à t'aymer je parvienne.
> Je luy respondz: garde n'ay qu' il m'advienne
> Ung si grand bien, et si ose affermer
> Que je devroys craindre que cela vienne
> Car j'ayme trop quand on me veult aymer.
>
> (*Épigrammes* cxxxviii)

(She told me with her usual laugh, "I think that I'll have to fall in love with you." I replied to her: "May such a great good be averted from me; and if I dare avow it, I should fear that this happen, for I love too much when someone wishes to love me.")

In response the lady cuttingly withdraws her offer to so cowardly and unworthy a suitor, leading to a fairly sophisticated reply by Marot. Overall the effect is of a forensic investigation of sexual ambivalence not unlike Donne's alternation of attitudes in "The Prohibition," which uses the same dramatic mode of direct address to qualify a woman's affection, though using only one speaker.

This sense of the complex levels of an amatory relationship is one shared by Shakespeare. We have already seen how Sonnet 70 uses techniques of rationalization to discount censure of the beloved, techniques also used more than once by Marot:

> Et tant plus est la personne excellente
> Plus est subjecte a l'aigreur violente
> De telz assaultz.
>
> (*Lyriques* lxx)

(And the more a person is excellent the more he is subject to the violent bitterness of such attacks.)

In Sonnets 18 and 33 Shakespeare exploits the same conventional image of the sun besieged by clouds as was used by Marot:[70]

70. See also Marot, *Épigrammes* CCIX.

Tu me semblas le cler soleil des cieulx
Qui sa lumiere a long temps retenue;
Puis se faict veoir luysant et gracieux.
Mais ton depart me semble une grand'nue.
(*Épigrammes* xxxi)

(You seemed the clear sun of heaven which restrained its light
for a long time then let itself be seen shining and gracious, but
your departure is a great cloud.)

However, Shakespeare stresses the potential taint of the beloved by
heightening the sophistry in Sonnet 33:

Even so my sun one early morn did shine
With all-triumphant splendor on my brow.
But out, alack, he was but one hour mine,
The region cloud hath masked him from
me now.
Yet him for this my love no whit disdaineth;
Suns of the world may stain when heaven's
sun staineth.

Marot is quite capable of visualizing acceptance of a genuinely tainted
relationship like this, on occasion, as when he boasts that Hélène de
Tournon had told that she loves him best:

Vous me direz qu'il est assez notoire
Qu'elle se mocque et que je suis deceu.
Je le sçay bien, mais point ne le veulx croire;
Car je perdrois l'aise que j'ay receu.
(*Épigrammes* liv)

(You will tell me that it is notorious that she is a mocker and that
I am deceived. I know it well, but don't at all want to believe it,
for I would lose the comfort that I have received.)

This anticipates the cynical conventionality of love affected in Sonnet
138 to the mutual satisfaction of the lovers:

When my love swears that she is made of truth
I do believe her though I know she lies. . . .

> Oh love's best habit is in seeming trust . . .
> Therefore I lie with her and she with me,
> And in our faults by lies we flattered be.

Such suave skepticism about traditional emotions and ethics is probably a result of the religious conformity forced upon unorthodox personalities. Marot's ultimate efforts at reconciliation with the hierarchy were governed by expediency, and the oscillations of the French wars of religion later served to favor a kind of skeptical conformity of the kind epitomized by Henri IV's reacceptance of Catholicism. This "flexibility," which can accommodate seeming betrayal, is also what sustains the enduring love proclaimed so vehemently in Sonnet 116, where it is asserted that no impediment, even inconstancy, can be accepted as valid grounds for breaking a relationship:

> Love is not love
> Which alters when it alteration finds,
> Or bends with the remover to remove.

Shakespeare echoes the marriage service in his opening reference to "impediments" in order to point out that love is either an unbreakable commitment like Christian marriage or it is nothing. The plays themselves illustrate this exacting standard, for Helena's reconciliation to the contemptible Bertram in *All's Well* is often held to be as offensive as Mariana's reacceptance of the vicious Angelo of *Measure for Measure* (the behavior of Imogen and Hermione also comes to mind). The inevitability of human failure and the need to come to terms with it are, of course, central to Lutheran theology, and the offering of grace to the wholly unworthy was axiomatic in Calvinism.

Marot accepts this arduousness and fallibility as inevitable in true love, and one of his elegies anticipates the sentiment of the lovers in *A Midsummer Night's Dream* that "the course of true love never did run smooth" (I.i.134):

> Mais où sont ceulx qui ont eu leur desir
> En amytié sans quelcque desplaisir?
> Il n'en est point, certes, et n'en fut oncques,
> Et n'en sera.
>
> (*Lyriques* LXXII)

(But where are those who have had their desire in love without some displeasure? There are none whatsoever, certainly, and there never were and never will be.)

Much of the sentimental confusion which occupies the four young lovers in *A Midsummer Night's Dream* lacks a sure literary model, and this encourages one to argue that one of the earliest of Marot's elegies provided Shakespeare with a plausible model for the misunderstanding on which much of the comedy's action turns. This poem is modelled on Ovid's *Heroides*, particularly the tenth letter, sent by Ariadne to that same Theseus who appears in the play. Marot derives the outline of his plot from a medieval romance, *Pierre de Provence et la belle Maguelonne*. The poem purports to be a letter written by Maguelonne to her lover Pierre, who seems to have abandoned her in the middle of a frightening forest, and the missive is to be delivered magically, as the superscription indicates:

> Messaiger de Venus, prens ta haulte volleé,
> Cherche le seul Amant de ceste desolée,
>
> (*Lyriques* II.1–2)

(Messenger of Venus, take high flight, find the sole lover of this desolate woman.)

The plot starts with the problem that: "When the two young people have discovered their mutual love, Maguelonne declares herself ready to flee with Pierre, because her father [the King of Naples] will not let her marry him. He has in fact arranged another marriage for her."[71] This is of course the situation of Hermia, who loves Lysander, thus opposing her father's wish that she marry Demetrius (I.i.22–45). Maguelonne's letter describes the lover's flight:

> Vinsmes entrer seuletz, en desarroy,
> En ung grand boys, òu tu me descendis,
> Et ton manteau dessus l'herbe estendis,
> En me distant: m'amye Maguelonne,
> Reposons nous sur l'herbe qui fleuronne,
> Et escoutons du Rossignol le chant. . . .

71. Marot, *Lyriques*, p. 115.

Mais, en comptant ce qu'avions en pensée,
Sommeil me print, car j'estois bien lassée.
Finablement m'endormy pres de toy.
                    (*Lyriques* 11.26–31, 36–38)

(Alone and very confused we came into a great wood, where
you set me down from the horse and spread your cloak on the
grass saying to me: "My dear Maguelonne, let us rest on the
flowery grass, and listen to the song of the nightingale. . . ." But,
in telling what we had in mind, sleep took me for I was very
tired. Finally I fell asleep beside you.)

So far the situation is almost identical to the flight of Hermia and
Lysander (II.ii.35–36), but Pierre is more aggressive than Lysander:
Maguelonne later perceives that during her sleep he has partly undressed and embraced her, then sheltered her from the sun with branches
and left her (the romance source reveals that at this point he runs
after a bird who has stolen some jewels revealed when he removed
her clothes). Maguelonne awakens alone in "ce boys plein de bestes
inhumaines" (91, this wood full of wild beasts), and this scene ir-
resistibly evokes the name of Theseus for anyone knowing North's
Plutarch as Shakespeare did, since Marot's details are recognizably
based on the awakening of Ariadne after Theseus has similarly left her
(as well as on a version of the *Heroides* in André de la Vigne's *La
troizieme epistre de la belle Amazone*). In her fearful imagination
Maguelonne exclaims to the absent Pierre: "Te voys querant, comme
pleine de rage, / Parmy le boys"[72] (I see you hunting as if full of rage
through the wood)—which happens to be true of Lysander's furious
pursuit of Demetrius, who has by now become his rival for Helena's
love. The very name of Helen is also mentioned by Maguelonne, who
compares Helen's beauty to her own. As Hermia awakes she exclaims,
"Methought a serpent eat my heart away" (III.ii.149), and calls on
Lysander "to pluck this crawling serpent from my breast!" (III.ii.146).
The despairing Maguelonne wishes for death, as Hermia finally does,
and evokes the carnivorous snake:

72. Marot, *Lyriques* II.114.

> O fiers Lyons et venimeux Serpens,
> Crapaulx enflez et toutes aultres bestes,
> Courez vers moy et soyez toutes prestes
> De devorer ma jeune tendre chair.
> *(Lyriques* ii.140–43)

(O proud lions and venomous snakes, swollen toads and every other beast, run to me and be wholly ready to eat my young tender flesh.)

Maguelonne bitterly denounces Pierre's villainous trick and his cruel deception. She spends the whole night in the wood listening to the "hurlements des bestes dangereuses" (the howling of dangerous animals), commenting:

> je suis trescertaine
> Qu'oncques Thysbé, qui à la mort s'offrit
> Pour Piramus, tant de mal ne souffrit.
> *(Lyriques* ii.161–63)

(I am sure that Thisbe, who put herself to death for Pyramus, never suffered such misery.)

Here, of course, we can perceive another possible direct link, with the workmen's interlude about Pyramus and Thisbe at the end of Shakespeare's play, while the final role which Maguelonne visualizes for herself, as a nun, suggests the threat initially made to Hermia by Theseus if she disobeys her father. The whole story is told by Marot with a charming naiveté befitting its supposed narrator and matching the tone of Shakespeare's play, for which it offers some of the necessary but missing raw materials—for, as Arthur Quiller-Couch has said in his edition of the play: "No author, to be sure, can build *in vacuo*, fetching his bricks from nowhere."[73] The strange synthesis of allusions (which the range of Shakespeare's potential sources suggest that he could have acquired in Marot) includes the Greek setting, derived

---

73. Arthur Quiller-Couch, ed., *A Midsummer Night's Dream,* by William Shakespeare (Cambridge: Cambridge University Press, 1968), pp. xii–xiii. A further unrecognized source for the play appears in Cinthio's *Hecatommithi* II, vii.

from Marot's exploitation of Ariadne's letter to Theseus in the *Heroides*, which in turn invites the allusion to an Amazon such as Hippolyta, developed in André de la Vigne's similar verse epistle. Marot's references to Helen, Pyramus, and Thisbe may well have been instrumental in stimulating the introduction of the figures into the comedy.

Marot and Shakespeare share an eclectic use of identical raw materials. They show a similar range, lack of esthetic constraint, and bold power to improvise on incidental motifs. There is an exhilirating indifference to academic decorum and mechanical consistency in each piece, which has led one scholar to talk of Marot's "absurdity,"[74] though the dream world of Shakespeare's play has properly been allowed to permit the complex and unexpected juxtapositions he achieved. While the constricting format of Marot's love letter cannot provide the same variety in the rounding out of the romance, it is followed by a rondeau explaining that, because Maguelonne did not "feloniously" commit suicide like Dido, a divinity intercedes:

> celluy, qui toute puissance a,
> Renvoya cil qui au boys la laissa,
> Où elle estoit.
> (*Lyriques*, p. 124)

(he who is all-powerful returned him, who left her in the wood, to where she was.)

So the story ends happily as in Shakespeare, providing in its epigraph and postscript an account of those two magical and carefully unnamed identities, "the high flying messenger of Venus" and the providential *deux ex machina*, whom Shakespeare may have recast as Puck and Oberon. The close relationship of the two works, their resemblance in allusion, incident, personalities, and values provide a perfect example of that "literary syncretism" which Ian McFarlane sees as unifying the literary imagination of sixteenth-century Europe[75] and which is as much an inheritance of the Middle Ages as a symptom of the Renaissance. Shakespeare thus expands, enriches, and lightens Marot's prec-

74. Marot, *Lyriques*, Introduction p. 7.
75. See the start of Chapter 8.

edents for *A Midsummer Night's Dream*, which amply prefigure his skeptical view of human sexuality.

However, Marot's witty portrayal of courtship owes much more to the actual vivacious women of Renaissance courts as we see them in the *Heptameron* than to medieval romance, and a poem attributed to him illustrates just how vital a dramatic model the conversational virtuosity of the period provided. This little masterpiece takes the form of a lively dialogue between two lovers, one sexually entrapped by a mature woman and the other taking advantage of an adolescent girl of fourteen. The former liaison is evoked with a wry verve anticipating Berowne's relations with Rosaline or even Benedick's with Beatrice. The sophisticated lady dresses provocatively in the new fashion, with her bust openly displayed and her eyes sparkling and alert, flexing a lithe figure; but after a year's courtship, the suitor has had no pleasure or physical advantage. When his friend says he hears she's a "real lamb," the lover exclaims bitterly:

> Elle est le Diable.
> C'est par sa teste que j'endure;
> Elle est, par le corps bieu, plus dure
> Que n'est le pommeau d'une dague.
> (*Lyriques*, p. 373)

(She's the Devil. I have to endure her headstrong nature; she is, by the good body, as hard as the hilt of a dagger.)

When his complaisant friend assures him that firm flesh makes a good mistress, the lover is indignant:

> Voicy un mocqueur!
> J'entens dure parmy le cueur;
> Car, quand au corps, n'y touche mye.
> Des que je l'appelle m'amye:
> Vostre amye n'est pas si noire,
> Faict-elle. Vous ne scauriez croire
> Comme elle est prompte à me desdire
> Du tout. . . .
> Si tost que je la veux toucher,

Ou seulement m'en approcher,
C'est peine; je n'ay nul credit.
Et sçais tu bien qu'elle me dit?
Un fascheux et vous c'est tout un;
Vous estes le plus importun
Que jamais je vy!

(*Lyriques*, pp. 373–74)

(You're joking! I mean hard in heart, for as for her body I can't lay a finger on it. The moment I called her friend, "Your friend is not so black," she says. You wouldn't believe how quick she is to insult me in every way. . . . As soon as I try to touch her, or even get near her, there's trouble—I'm not trusted in the least. And do you really know what she said to me?—"A bore and you are one and the same—you're the biggest pest I ever saw!")

The lady's mood is identical to Rosaline's crushing manner on first encountering Berowne in *Love's Labour's Lost* (II.i.114–128), and Benedick makes an almost identical report of Beatrice to his friends in *Much Ado*: "She told me . . . that I was duller than a great thaw; huddling jest upon jest with such impossible conveyance that I stood like a man at a mark, with a whole army shooting at me. She speaks poinards, and every word stabs. . . . I would to God some scholar would conjure her; for certainly while she is here a man may live as quiet in Hell as in a sanctuary" (II.i.218ff.). Like Othello's mother (III.iv.56), Marot's lover even consults "the Egyptians" about his sexual problems, but he finds that aged magicians cannot exorcise his passion, for, like Benedick (I.i.191–95), the lover is as fascinated by her appearance as he is terrified by her personality. When his friend suggests she might succumb to cash he is admonished that she is "une femme d'honneur" (197), but the friend wryly observes that she is a Parisienne, and that a diamond set before her sparkling green eyes will knock her over backwards. As for the friend's girl, she is by contrast very obliging; the afflicted lover is quite suspicious of deception by "femmes fines" (232), but he realizes that a fourteen-year-old has a lot to learn, and a naive mistress seems preferable to his. The sprightliness of the dialogue is most amusing and attractive, foreshadowing the discussion of sexuality by Shakespeare's lovers, with which Marot's scene shares many turns of phrase. Above all it evokes the type of brilliant and skeptical female who proves so irresistible to her lovers and to her audiences while dominating the action in a whole series of Shakespearean comedies.

Other sardonic anticipations in Marot of Shakespearean effects are more clearly attributed to Reformation conflicts. Marot's third "Coq a l'asne" describes in detail his arrest in Bordeaux and argues forcefully that flight is better than protesting one's innocence in person, which would only get one roasted to a cinder. Falstaff echoes Marot's views about meeting the foe: "If I come in his way willingly, let him make a carbonado of me." Indeed Marot's hatred of war in this satirical poem matches Falstaff's "discretion":

> C'est assez d'un petit boullet,
> Qui poingt ung souldart au collet,
> Pour l'empescher de jamais boire.
> Fy, fy, de mourir pour la glorie,
> Ou, pour se faire grant seigneur,
> D'aller mourir au lict d'honneur. . . .
> Voila comment on se gouverne
> Dedans une bonne taverne.
> J'oseroys entrer hardyment,
> Mais où l'on frappe nullement.
> (*Satiriques* IX.201–06, 215–18)

(It only needs a little bullet hole in a soldier's neck to stop him drinking for good. Fie, fie, on dying for glory, or to become a great lord by going to death on the bed of honor. . . . See how one behaves in a good tavern, where I would enter boldly, but where there are no knocks.)

Falstaff's famous speech against honor in *Henry IV, Part 1* (V.i.128ff.) follows this model rather than Montaigne's essay on "gloire," for which Marot also affords a precedent; and Marot foreshadows Falstaff's prayer: "I could wish this tavern were my drum" (III.iii.230).

Marot is as capable of black humor as any Shakespearean cynic. Death asserts a paradox in the "Deploration de Florimont Robertet":

133

Brief, qui vouldra vivre au beau paradis,
Il fault premier que mourir je le face.
Confesse donc que je suis bienheureuse,
Puisque sans moy tu ne peuz estre heureux.
           (*Lyriques* VI.443–46)

(In brief, who wishes to live in glorious paradise must first be
killed by me. Confess then that I am fortunate, since without me
you cannot be happy.)

The same disconcerting argument greets Lady Anne when she denounces Richard of Gloucester for murdering Henry VI and sending
him to heaven, for Richard retorts at once:

Let him thank me that holp to send
           him thither;
For he was fitter for that place than earth.
           (1.ii.107–108)

Marot relishes such macabre strokes, but he is also capable of the
no less exotic moods of melancholy which we associate with Hamlet.
The exile to Ferrara and then to Venice induced great gloom in Marot:
he says of the Adriatic "ceste mer n'a point tant d'animaulx / Qu'en
moy d'ennuys" (this sea has not at all as many animals as there are
troubles in me), and he goes on:

Aucunefoys je dy: la nuict viendra,
Je dormiray, lors ne m'en sourviendra;
Le dormir est contre le soucy une
Grant medicine, à ung chascun commune.
Mais en dormant viennent m'espovanter
Songes divers et me representer
Aupres du vif de mon malheur l'ymaige,
Et mes espritz veillent à mon dommaige,
Si qu'advis m'est ou que huissiers ou sergens
De me chercher sont promptz et diligens,
Ou qu'enserré suis en murs et barreaux,
Ou qu'on me livre innocent aux bourreaux.
           (*Épîtres* XLVI.103–14)

(Sometimes I say: the night will come, I shall sleep, then I shall not remember it all; sleep is a great medicine for care, shared by all. But in sleeping various dreams come to frighten me and show me the lifelike image of my misfortune, and my mind keeps watch to my harm, so that I think that either the bailiffs or sergeants are quick and diligent in hunting me, or that I am locked up behind walls and bars, or that my innocence is handed over to the executioners.)

The same morbidity pervades Hamlet's thoughts in "To be or not to be . . . ," where the fear of threatening dreams extends to the sleep beyond death. One cannot help recalling also Hamlet's observation that "this fell sergeant Death / Is strict in his arrest" (V.ii.347–48). The chances are that Shakespeare did not see this epistle, as it was published from the manuscript at Chantilly, where it had been preserved, only in 1898; but the familiarity of Hamlet's mood among oppressed intellectuals during the Reformation is clearly established by it, and it is interesting to see that Marot lists as the proper grounds for exile, of which he is not guilty, several of which Hamlet is: unpremeditated murder, joining with pirates, and conspiracy against one's king. These are all faults which Marot asserts the truly virtuous can avoid, an interesting contemporary verdict on Hamlet's behavior which justifies Claudius to some extent.

Marot provides another useful perspective on Shakespeare's values in an account of Venice which affords the richness of texture so markedly missing in Cinthio's spare narrative prefiguring *Othello*. Marot is overpowered and shocked, as a relatively puritanical visitor from the north, by the exotic luxury and self-indulgence of this international trading center. He admits that the statesmen are "grands et saiges mondaines, / Meurs en conseil, d'executer soubdains"[76] (great and wise worldly men, ripe in counsel and swift in action), but he finds their morals very questionable:

> D'avoir le nom de chrestien ont prins cure,
> Puis sont vivans à la loy d'Epicure,
> Faisans yeulx, nez et oreilles jouyr

76. Marot, *Epîtres* XLIII.73–74.

De ce qu'on peult veoir, sentir et ouyr
Au gré des sens, et traictent ce corps comme
Si là gisoit le dernier bien de l'homme.
Mesmes parmy tant de plaisirs menus
Trop plus qu'ailleurs y triumphe Venus.
Venus y est certes plus reverée
Qu'au temps des Grecs, en l'isle Citherée;
Car mesme renc de reputacion,
De liberté et d'estimation,
Y tient la femme esventée et publicque
Comme la chaste, honnorable et pudicque.
Et sont enclins (ce disent) à aymer
Venuz, d'autant qu'elle est née de mer,
Et que sus mer ilz ont naissance prise,
Disent aussi qu'ilz ont basty Venize
En mer qui est de Venuz l'heritaige,
Et que pourtant ilz luy doivent hommaige,
Voila commant ce qui est deffendu
Est pardeça permys et espendu.
Et t'escriproys, Princesse, bien encores
Des Juifs, des Turcs, des Arabes et Mores
Qu'on veoit icy par trouppes chacun jour.
                        (*Epîtres* XLIII.79–103)

(They have taken great care to have the name of Christian, then live by the law of Epicurus, making eyes, nose, and ears enjoy what one can see, smell, and hear to the satisfaction of the senses, and they treat this body as if there lay the last good of mankind. Even among so many trivial pleasures too much more than anywhere else Venus triumphs there. Venus is more revered there than she was in the isle of Cyprus in Greek times, for the same rank of reputation, freedom, and esteem is held there by the promiscuous public woman as the chaste, honorable, and modest one. And they are inclined—they say this—to love Venus the more because she was born from the sea and that on the sea they took their birth. They also say they built Venice in the sea, which is an inheritance from Venus, and that therefore they must pay

136

her honor. There is how what is forbidden is thereby permitted and spread abroad. And I would like to write you, princess, yet more of the Jews, of the Turks, of the Arabs and Moors whom one sees here in crowds each day.)

This is how Venice looked to a northern European of Lutheran sympathies in the sixteenth century, and it is fascinating to see how the point of view anticipates Ascham's and can also reorient our anachronistic reactions to *Othello* and *The Merchant of Venice*, even if the specific text was not demonstrably available to most Englishmen at that time. One crucial point is that Venetian Christianity appears to Marot the merest affectation—which should encourage us to see that there is absolutely no compelling reason to expect any Englishman professionally associated with the Anglican establishment like Shakespeare to side with such fashionably shallow and insincere personalities as Marot describes, against deeper and more morally intense figures like Shylock and Othello. One can recognize that the phrasing of Othello's fury against the Venetian sensuality described by Iago closely parallels Marot's allusions to the organs of sense: "yeulx, nez et oreilles" match Othello's list of "noses, ears and lips" (IV.i.43). The dominant role of Venus in Marot's account of Venice is also a useful clue, for Venus surely presides over *Othello* as potently as over Racine's *Phédre*, even if she does not appear physically in either, as she does in the *Hippolytus* of Euripides. Her island is the setting for the ruin of Mars' champion, Othello, who closely resembles Diana's devotee Hippolytus in failing to cope successfully with the storms of sexual passion. With Marot's images in mind we can see that, like Antony at Actium, Othello is literally out of his element in most of Shakespeare's tragedy; the storm he travels through to Cyprus is raised in Venus' watery birthplace to prefigure the more fatal emotional storm she next arouses on her island itself. The sensuality and moral frivolity associated in minds like Marot's with the reputation of Venice is thus a crucial background to our understanding of Othello's behavior. We must see this Venice as a city more exotic but no less depraved than the Vienna of *Measure for Measure*. Only then can the irony of Desdemona's chastity be fully savored and the plausibility of Iago's cynicism about Venetian women appear irresistible. Marot's evocation of a powerful, opulent, and totally

137

amoral society establishes for us the largely ignored context of associations which Venice had for Europeans of the Reformation. It cannot be seen simply as a magical world to be taken at its own valuation
in either *Othello* or even in *The Merchant of Venice*, which has been
grossly sentimentalized by critics. Venice is subtle, sophisticated, and
hypnotic; but it is also morally decadent and intrinsically corrupt to
the extent that its finances and its armies must be handled by foreigners
who are treated in a spirit of cold expediency and then ruthlessly tricked,
trapped, and dismissed as soon as they have served their purpose. So
at least Marot sees the Venetians; he asserts

> qu'ilz n'eslevent leurs yeulx
> Plus haut ne loing que ces terrestres lieux,
> Et que jamays espoir ne les convye
> Au grand festin de l'eternelle vie.
> Advient aussi que de l'amour du proche
> Jamays leur cueur partial ne s'aproche.
> (Epîtres XLIII.17–22)

(that they do not lift their eyes higher or farther than earthly
places and that hope never bears them to the great festival of
eternal life. Also it happens that love of one's neighbor never
touches their selfish hearts.)

If Shakespeare's Venetian plays are correctly perceived to leave us questioning the values of the famous city as much as those of its victims,
they are then true to an earlier poet's vision of this effete civilization.
Moreover, the same puritanical dislike of Italian ostentation that Marot
shows for the Venetians' pagan temples of marble reverberates in later
English poems like Jonson's "To Penshurst" and Marvell's "Upon
Appleton House," not to mention the palace of Pandemonium built
by the devils in Hell at the end of Book I of *Paradise Lost*. Certainly
Jonson's moral vision of pagan Venice in *Volpone* is just as scathing as
Marot's, if less overtly theological.

The deep tension between Humanism and Reform which is at the
heart of Milton's career as a poet is in fact the best corroboration of
Marot's role as the archetypal illustration of the Reformist slant of much
successful poetry in the period. Neoclassicism proved ultimately incom-

patible with the most dynamic impulses of the age, whatever its incidental achievements at the hands of poets like the Pléiade and Jonson.[77] Initially the Humanists were the originators of the Reform, as Luther's intense preoccupation with textual analysis illustrates: "His study of the Greek New Testament led to the steady abandonment of the medieval method of exegesis and to a concern with the literal truth of the text, the *sensus literalis, grammaticus, historicus.* He was anxious to interpret the text accurately, readily abandoning an exposition which was grammatically untenable: 'in translating I always keep this rule: we must not contend against grammar.' He insisted on a good knowledge of the original language."[78] The emphases here match those of Erasmus, but in the long run "there was a basic divergence between Luther and the humanists. . . . Erasmus was the true scholar, the great Latin stylist, the friend of the great world, averse to enthusiasm and extremism, cool, almost sceptical in his attitude, tending to conceal the undercurrent of genuine sophistry which gave life to his personality. Whereas Luther, with a longer, richer and ultimately more fruitful experience of monastic life than Erasmus was almost exclusively concerned with religion."[79] This divergence was unavoidable, and in France it was becoming open by the end of Marot's life: "The end of the agreement between humanists and reformers was an event of outstanding importance," for "supports were . . . taken from the intellectual," and "the cleavage between literary production and religious enthusiasm was soon complete."[80] Humanism became elitist, backward looking, and conformist, while Reform became popular, radical, and iconoclastic.

The instincts of most dynamic writers like Marot and Marguerite were initially on the side of Reform: "The great poets are the most concerned to agree that there is a crowd of abuses in the Roman church, and they would willingly have rallied to Calvin's enterprise if it had responded to their wishes. We find in Ronsard sentiments of sympathy for Calvinism, in spite of its austerity, or rather because of its austerity,

77. See Hugh M. Richmond, *The Christian Revolutionary: John Milton* (Berkeley and Los Angeles: University of California Press, 1974), pp. 194–98.

78. Green, p. 48.   79. Green, p. 155.

80. F. C. Spooner in "The Reformation in Difficulties," *The New Cambridge Modern History*, vol. 2, *The Reformation*, pp. 218–19.

for if the illustrious poet complained too often of being oppressed in his pleasures by the puritanism of the sect, he could not prevent himself in the hours of calm reflection from recognizing the sound basis for an attempt to renovate Christian society."[81] This mood may be held the century's most creative, for "through the sensual graces of pagan art, Christian sentiment could reveal itself only in infusing a light and life wholly novel. This labour of transformation was to begin with 'militant' verse"—and "with militant works, it is an original and highly personal poetry which appears."[82] However, through events like the conversion of Henri IV in 1593, "the Roman party triumphed in France, and this victory truly seems to have resulted in French literary paganism." This is perhaps not the best moment to undertake a proof that later seventeenth-century literature suffered in proportion that it was neoclassical and conformist and that the spirit of Malherbe and the Académie française was necessarily sterilizing; but it is surely true that even Corneille has surprising affinities with the Calvinist Agrippa d'Aubigné and that the puritan spirit of Jansenism seems to have given Port Royal a remarkable literary fertility even if we only note the names of Racine and Pascal.

In these terms Marot's flight from Paris to Nérac and thereafter from Venice to Geneva has something classic about it—just as his final hesitant efforts at reconciliation with the French Establishment at the expense of protestant commitment may anticipate the current of the later French tradition. Certainly Marot's career shows how the personal drive toward a more authentic art inspired by Lutheran attitudes could work to give classicism a fresher, more meaningful character, while making it sacrifice scholarly decorum and religious conformism: "In stripping antiquity of its soft and sensual graces and keeping only its solid beauties and serious forms, protestantism could have given the French, following the agreeable sketches of du Bartas and Agrippa d'Aubigné, some finished masterpieces in the vein of Milton's *Paradise Lost*."[83] The current revival in interest in these two later Huguenot

81. F. Charbonnier, *La Poésie française et les guerres de religion (1560–1574)* (Paris: Revue des Oeuvres Nouvelles, 1919), p. 400.
82. Charbonnier, p. 438.   83. Charbonnier, p. 465.

writers is no doubt part of an increasing recognition of the modern value of French verse throughout the period of Reformation controversy, and we may see the strengthening of interest in Marot as part of this concern, which was certainly that felt by authors like Spenser and Milton.

The uneven classicism of Marot results in part from his subordination of neoclassical impulses to religious obligations in ways that look forward to the career of Milton. We may perceive analogies to Milton's religious lyrics in Marot's sequence of Ballades on Christmas, Lent, and the Passion. The Lenten poem illustrates well the triumph of religious impulse over classical effects:

> Cessez, Acteurs, d'escrire en eloquence
> D'armes, d'amours, de fables et sornettes!
> Venez dicter soubz piteuse loquence
> Livres plaintifz de tristes chansonettes!
> N'escripvez d'or, mais de couleurs brunettes,
> A celle fin que tout dueil y abonde;
> Car Jesuchrist, l'Aigneau tout pur et munde,
> Pour nous tirer des Enfers detestables,
> Endura mort horrible et furibunde
> En cez sainctz jours piteux et lamentables.
> Romps tes Flageolz, Dieu Pan, par violence,
> Et va gemir en champestres Logettes!
> Laissez les Boys, vous, Nymphes d'excellence
> Et vous rendez en Cavernes subjectes!
>
> (*Diverses* LXXVIII)

(Cease, authors, to write eloquently of wars, of love, of fables and flippancies! Come and write in pitiful style plaintive books of sad songs. Do not write of gold but dark colors, so that mourning wholly dominates it; for Jesus Christ, the wholly pure and clean lamb to rescue us from hateful Hell, will endure a horrible furious death in these pitiful and lamentable holy days. Break your pipes, god Pan, by violence, and go groan in meadow retreats! Leave the woods, you excellent nymphs, and make yourselves humble.)

141

This rejection of classical motifs is closely paralleled in the opening of Book IX of *Paradise Lost*, where Milton rejects the themes of the *Iliad*, *Odyssey*, and *Aeneid*, adding that he is:

> Not sedulous by Nature to indite
> Wars, hitherto the only Argument
> Heroic deem'd, chief maistry to dissect
> With long and tedious havoc fabl'd Knights
> In Battles feign'd; the better fortitude
> Of Patience and Heroic Martyrdom
> Unsung.
>
> (IX.27–33)

Similarly, in the "Nativity Ode" Milton visualizes the dismissal of the pagan Nymphs and *genius loci* from their customary retreats by the coming of Jesus, who supplants not only the classical pantheon but the whole range of pre-Christian divinities with their associated rites and performances. This subversion of the classical tradition by primitive Christianity reaches its drastic climax in Milton's *Paradise Regained* with Christ's repudiation first of Rome and then of Hellenistic literature both in subject and style:

> they loudest sing
> The vices of thir Deities, and thir own
> In Fable, Hymn, or Song, so personating
> Thir Gods ridiculous, and themselves
> past shame.
> Remove their swelling epithets thick laid
> As varnish on a Harlot's cheek, the rest
> Thin sown with aught of profit or delight,
> Will far be found unworthy to compare
> With Sion's songs, to all true tastes excelling,
> Where God is prais'd aright, and Godlike men.
>
> (IV.339–48)

Obviously, in his translations of the Psalms, Marot illustrated memorably a comparable point of view, producing popular, biblical poetry rather than sophisticated, neoclassical, pagan verse for the elite.

Neither Marot nor Milton were consistent in this preference, and much of their more formal verse shows that, if anything, the poets favored the classical option in their "official" writing rather than the biblical one. It is well known that Marot's experiments in the vein of the Virgilian eclogue (like the lament for Louise de Savoie) led the way for Spenser's *Shepheards Calendar* and for "Lycidas." However, Marot's lament for Florimont Robertet also affords a prototype for "Lycidas," even though Marot's poem fits perfectly with the late medieval conventions of the *rhétoriqueurs,* and one may make too radical a split, from hindsight, between late medieval and early Renaissance effects. The two poems share processions of allegorical mourners (such as the River Loire, the Church, the French State) and formal speeches with harsh moral censure of "l'avare pretrise" and the vanity of outward shows. The device of the naive interlocutor is also used in both poems to achieve a drastic psychological progression: from reluctant confrontation with untimely death, involving the sacrifice of delicious sexual entanglement, to a sense of the deeper personal application of the victim's fate:

> La fiere mort, sur le char sejournée,
> Sa face palle a devers moy tournée,
> Et à bien peu qu'elle ne m'a rué
> Le mesme dard dont elle avoit tué
> Celluy.
> *(Lyriques* vi.159–63)

(Proud Death, seated on the funeral wagon, has turned her pale face toward me and has come close to destroying me with the same dart with which she had killed this man.)

The core of Marot's poem is a powerful speech by Death evoking the images of the Dance of Death, so popular in the fifteenth century yet continuing in the woodcuts and engravings of Marot's contemporaries like Dürer and Holbein. Ronsard will also sustain the confrontation in his *Hymne de la Mort*; yet like Milton the two French poets achieve a sense of Christian apotheosis which transforms the pagan classical material and transcends even medieval stoicism through a Reformation

143

intensity of subjective faith, paradoxically put in Death's mouth by Marot:

> Ainsi celluy qui par vive foy voit
> La mort de Christ guerist de ma blesseure
> Et vit ailleurs plus qu'icy ne vyvoit.
> (*Lyriques* vi.401–03)

(Thus he who in living faith sees the death of Christ is healed of my wound and lives elsewhere more than here he lived.)

Marot's poem may serve to remind us that "Lycidas," for all its neo-classical surface texture, basically grafts a Reformation "solution" onto a late medieval theme.

In fact the deepest affinities between Marot and Milton lie less in humanist devices adjusted to medieval allegory than in the elementary hostility to institutional authority which they share with Luther. Marot clearly outlines the opposition to censorship of *Areopagitica* in one of his most vehement self-defences. He writes a verse letter to the king containing as contemptuous an attack on his enemies of the Sorbonne as Milton ever expressed against Oxbridge in *Of Education,* and he denies them any right to monitor his reading:

> Scavoir le mal est souvent proffitable,
> Mais en user est tousjours evitable.
> Et d'autre part, que me nuyst de tout lire?
> Le grand donneur m'a donné sens d'eslire
> En ces livretz tout cela qui accorde
> Aux saintz escriptz de grace et de concorde
> Et de jecter tout cela qui differe.
> (*Epîtres* xxxvi.143–49)

(To know evil is often advantageous, but to use it is always avoidable. Besides, how does it harm me to read anything? The great giver has given me the sense to choose in these books everything compatible with the holy writings in grace and harmony and to reject all that which differs.)

This poem was one which outraged conventional supporters of the Sorbonne and the Church:

Very obviously, before the freedom and boldness of the poet these champions of orthodoxy experienced real fury. That one condemned by the authorities, banished from the kingdom, sentenced to death for flight from trial, several of whose associates had just been burned to death, should dare to write to the king in his own defence and take an assured and ever proud tone, that he should dare to claim ambitiously the right of free investigation of all texts and a complete freedom in his reading, that he should dare to express compassion and pity for victims of religious persecution instead of applauding the punishment of heretics, that finally he should dare to justify himself by attacking the corruption of justice and the narrow-mindedness of the Sorbonne— these were excesses that the defenders of the established church could not endure. Truly the liberty, openness, and humanity that Marot manifests in this poem were exceptionally daring for his time.[84]

One need hardly stress how this account prefigures the role that Milton assumed. Any impression that *Areopagitica* initiated a new view of intellectual liberty fails to do justice to this far more daring exposition a century earlier.

It indicates the complexity of Marot's personality and influence that we can also find evidence for his compatibility with the Cavalier poets' point of view as well as with the Puritans'. For among the poems ascribed to Marot in early editions is the "Adieu aux Dames de Court," written on the occasion of the departure of the king and his followers to fight in Italy in 1537, and its sentiments closely parallel those of Richard Lovelace's "Going to the Warres":

> Adieu m'amye la derniere
> En vertuz et beauté premiere,
> Je vous pry me rendre à present
> Le cueur dont je vous feis present,
> Pour en la guerre ou il faut estre
> En faire service à mon maistre!
> Or quand de vous se souviendra,
> L'aiguillon d'honneur l'espoindra

84. Marot, *Epîtres*, p. 208, note.

Aux armes et vertueux faict;
Et s'il en sortoit quelque effect
Digne d'une louenge entiere,
Vous en seriez seul heritiere.

(Lyriques, p. 365)

(Farewell my last love, in virtue and beauty first, I pray you to
return to me for the moment the heart which I presented to you,
for it to serve my master in the war where it must go! Then when
it recalls you, the prick of honor will spur it to arms and virtuous
deeds; and if any effect emerges from it worthy of wholehearted
praise, you shall be the sole inheritor of it.)

The gallant pose is skilfully handled, and as with Lovelace it is the
power to achieve the right social tone and attitude for a public occasion which impresses. The question of sincerity is irrelevant, the achievement of true decorum paramount: like the Cavalier poets Marot understands perfectly how to phrase the sentiments propriety requires, and
in a post-Romantic world this tact may be granted the admiration it
deserves, as the now rising reputation of comparably poised English
poets like Thomas Carew and Edmund Waller seems to confirm.

Indeed the sociable poetry so confidently created by Ben Jonson and
his followers proves to develop the same attitudes as Marot:

Demain que Sol veult le jour dominer,
Vien, Boysonné, Villas et la Perriere,
Je vous convye avec moy à disner;
Ne rejectez ma semonce en arriere.
Car en disnant Phebus par la Verriere
(Sans la briser) viendra voir ses Suppostz
Et donnera faveur à nos propos
En les faisant dedans noz Bouches naistre.
Fy du repas qui en paix et repos
Ne sçait l'Esprit (avec le Corps) repaistre.

(Épigrammes CXXVI)

(Tomorrow, which the sun wishes to dominate, come, Boysonné,
Villas, and la Perriere, I invite you all to dine with me; do not
turn back my request on me, for while we dine Phoebus will

146

come through the window (without breaking it) to see his supporters and will show favor to our words in giving them birth
in our mouths. Fie on that meal which in silence and peace does
not know how to restore the mind as well as the body.)

The sense of intelligent conversation as a prime part of civilized hos-
pitality was one which Jonson shared, and a whole series of his pieces
match and expand on Marot's epigram: not only in his "Inviting a
friend to supper," but in his "leges conviviales" to apply "in the Apollo
of the Old Devil Tavern at Temple-Bar" rules such as: "3. Eruditi,
urbani, hilares, honesti, adsciscuntor" and "12. At fabulis magis quam
vino velitatio fiat":

> Let the learned and witty, the jovial and gay,
> The generous and honest, compose our
>> free state, . . .
> Let the contests be rather of books than
>> of wine.[85]

The same alert social awareness also governs "An Epistle answering to
one that asked to be Sealed of the Tribe of Ben."

Moreover, Marot's aesthetic impact on his peers was very similar to
Jonson's, for Boysonné has left us a poem describing the effect on other
poets of Marot's impending arrival in Toulouse:

> Puisque Marot, comme l'on dict, arrive
> Il nous fault mettre en la main nostre plume
> Et que chescung de son quartier escrive
> Forgeant ouvrage affiné sur l'enclume
> De purité. Sus, Villars, qu'on allume
> Tous les fourneaulx de Rhetorique fine,
> Et ces metaulx, sortant de rude myne,
> Quel'on les purge avant que presenter
> Au grand forgeur Marot; qu'on les affine
> Si nous voulons tel ouvrier contenter.
>> (*Épigrammes*, p. 196)

---

85. Ben Jonson, *Works*, ed. William Gifford (London: Routledge, 1869), pp.
726–27.

(Since they say Marot is arriving, we must get our pens in hand and each work in his home ground to forge a refined work on the anvil of purity. On, Villars, let them light the furnaces of fine rhetoric, and let them purge its metals coming from the crude mine, before they are presented to the great craftsman Marot; let them refine them if we are to content such a workman.)

These are the values of labored art to which Jonson was equally devoted, to the point of insisting on their application to the very different genius of Shakespeare:

> Who casts to write a living line, must sweat,
> (Such as thine are) and strike the second heat
> Upon the Muses anvile: turne the same,
> (And himselfe with it) that he thinkes
> to frame.[86]

In this at least Marot may well have been as true a neoclassicist as Jonson and the Cavaliers: he achieves an easy decorum by conscious effort. His art has the elegant simplicity which is the ultimate mark and achievement of self-conscious sophistication in any culture. Seen in this light, the whole Reformation's desire to recover the pristine simplicity of Christendom's origins makes it the natural climax of the High Middle Ages, just as the "primitive" pastoral is one of the favorite genres of any evolved metropolitan society like that of the European Renaissance. Marot, in progressing from the oversophisticated art of "rhétoriqueurs" like his father, thus proves to be unmistakably the last medieval French poet, just as he is the first modern one. Sixteenth-century English writers valued him correctly as both a radical and a restorer of ancient traditions in his art as in his beliefs. The fusion of Virgilian pastor and the Puritan sense of "the Good Shepherd" is very much his achievement, as the poems on this subject amply illustrate.[87]

86. Ben Jonson, *Poems*, ed. George B. Johnston (Cambridge: Harvard University Press, 1962), p. 287.

87. See "Du bon pastour et du maulvais" and "La complaincte d'un pastoureau chrestien" in Clément Marot, *Oeuvres complètes*, ed. Pierre Jannet, vol. 1 (Paris: Flammarion, 1868), pp. 74–86, 97–106.

6

Wyatt and French "Newfangledness"

WYATT RESTETH HERE, THAT QUICK COULD NEVER
rest;
Whose heavenly gifts increased by disdain;
And virtue sank the deeper in his breast:
Such profit he by envy could obtain.

(Surrey)[1]

Of the remarkably talented men by whom Henry VIII was served, only Sir Thomas More has proved more attractive to modern taste than Sir Thomas Wyatt, and the tremendous penalty paid by More for his commitment has earned him a truly sanctified status. Wyatt scarcely escaped unscathed either, and it demonstrates the complexity of literary values that the question of his involvement with Anne Boleyn has given an important extra dimension of interest to his verse, which helps to explain its current rating above the smoother, less enigmatic work of his equally talented junior, Surrey. The failure of Wyatt's relationship to so distinctive a personality as Anne is central to the aesthetic and psychological value of his work, because it shows the excitement and difficulty generated by the introduction into English society of the more autonomous, skeptical woman who had evolved in France and was so definitively reflected in the works and life of Marguerite d'Angoulême.

1. Bullett, ed., *Silver Poets*, p. 140.

Wyatt's verse is not valuable because it assimilated Petrarchanism; indeed it did not reflect Petrarch's values and style any more successfully than it mastered French fashions and models of behavior and lyricism. Wyatt's fascination for us lies in the struggle between a talented if fairly orthodox mind and an alien sophistication which eludes traditional expectations. Wyatt was not so much betrayed by Anne Boleyn as outmaneuvered, and his bewilderment, awkwardness, and resentment give fire to his verse, enflamed the more by the political harassment to which the liaison exposed him.

Surrey's testimony that the persecution of Wyatt enriched his personality and performance corroborates the pattern that we have seen in Marguerite and Marot: that talent may often have been tempered to genius in the turbulent waters of Reformation politics. For all his virtues and advantages, Wyatt's career is marked by misfortunes which were at least painful, though hardly crippling. They began with his bitter alienation from his adulterous wife Elizabeth Brooke and progressed to a climax through the ambiguous and risky relationship with Anne Boleyn, which led to various imprisonments and accusations resulting partly from the malicious hostility of the duke of Suffolk and the bishop of London. No doubt Wyatt's peace of mind was not helped by the enforced ending of his happy love affair with Elizabeth Darrell as a condition of his "pardon" in 1540, after one of these episodes, when it was required that he take back his rejected wife (whose sister became the mistress of Henry VIII about the time that this "penalty" was assigned). Other poets may achieve power more imaginatively, but such provocative experiences seem very relevant to Wyatt's achievements when we read praises like Frederick M. Padelford's:

> He breaks through the hypothetical world of fancy, with its artificial emotion and studied address, and with fine imagination realizes his experiences, and presents them in simple, fervent, and sincere language. At such times of penetrative insight, the nervous intensity of feeling calls up rare, subtle harmonies of sound and rich qualities of tone, so that the music of the verse seems inwrought with the emotion. These poems are like monologues snatched from intense situations. . . . The language is direct, fa-

miliar, and unadorned; a case left to stand or fall by the bare truth of it.[2]

This estimate echoes the wording in a poem which suggests Wyatt's tribulations:

> Mystrustfull mindes be moued
> > To haue me in suspect:
> The troth it shalbe proued,
> > Which times shall once detect.
>
> Though falshed go about
> > Of crime me to accuse,
> At length I do not doute
> > But truth shall me excuse.
>
> (254)[3]

But the process of introspection, often fostered by such political and social hostility (as it was in Marot's *L'Enfer* by more religious prosecution), appears more strikingly in another lyric associated with poems of Wyatt, whose repetitions have little of the musical refrain about them and a great deal of psychological assertion:

> I am as I am and so wil I be,
> But how that I am none knoith trulie;
> Be yt evill, be yt well, be I bonde, be I fre,
> I am as I am and so will I be.
>
> I lede my lif indifferentelye,
> I meane no thing but honestelie
> And thoughe folkis judge full dyverslye,
> I am as I am and so will I dye. . . .
>
> Yet sum therbe that take delyght
> To Judge folkes thowght by outward sight;

2. Wyatt, ed. Muir (1949), pp. xli–xlii.

3. All further Wyatt references follow Muir and Thomson (1969), giving its item number only. I have not explored the authorship controversy here: a Tudor poet wrote each of these poems.

But whether they Judge me wrong or Right,
I am as I am and soo doo I wright.

I pray ye all that this doo rede,
To truste as you doo your cred,
And thynck not that I wyll change my wede,
For I am as I am howe sooever I spede.

But how that ys I leue to you;
Judge as ye lyst, false or true;
Ye know no more then afore ye knew;
Yet I am as I am whatsoeuer insew. . . .

(140)

The result of censure, for such a resilient personality, is an intensifica-
tion of identity and a clarification of values. The appeal to a larger consensus of opinion, including posterity, is a natural recourse which Wyatt
characteristically exploits in most of his more original and memorable
poems. The same recourse is one often sought by Marot, as we have
seen; and the Wyatt lyric provides an important precedent for later
poems like Shakespeare's Sonnet 121 ("Tis better to be vile than vile
esteemed"), which also arises from indignation at humiliation to a
confident self-affirmation echoing Wyatt's:

why should others' false adulterate eyes
Give salutation to my sportive blood?
Which in their wills count bad what I think good?
No, I am that I am; and they that level
At my abuses reckon up their own.

It needs little explication to demonstrate that two of Wyatt's best-
known poems illustrate these patterns of self-vindication. "They flee
from me" (37) depends for its impact on the contrasting phases in the
evolution of the poet's status at court, from fashionable frequentation
by seductive females to the cautious avoidance likely at such moment as
Henry VIII's questioning of his relations with the now equally alienated
Anne. A more overt allusion to this sinister rhythm than its ultimate
Petrarchan model affords[4] is usually detected in the famous sonnet

4. See Richmond, *School of Love*, pp. 251-54.

"Whoso list to hunt" (7), with its account of a fickle mistress lost to "Caesar." A precise sense of context confirms even in such "Petrarchan" verse how much Wyatt is a court poet in Marot's sense, writing for an aristocratic audience in current, plain language about experiences which they can immediately recognize. These are the virtues for which he is still generally admired, and they rise directly from the tensions of a rapidly evolving society.

In fostering such highly social verse in the French vein, Anne Boleyn's influence was surely decisive, both in general and on Wyatt particularly. In the life of the court as a whole Kathleen Lambley judges that "with the advent of Queen Anne Boleyn, French acquired a powerful and enthusiastic patroness. Anne was entirely French by education and tastes." Moreover, "Camden asserts that Anne's French jollity first attracted her to the notice of Henry. At any rate the court-ship was largely carried on in French."[5] So we should visualize the advent of Anne as reinforcing that scandalous preoccupation with things French among the fashionable young at the court which had even at-tracted the censure of the council. Whatever Henry made of Anne at first, we do have a historical estimate of how she appeared to his cour-tiers' eyes, for Thomas Wyatt's initial reactions to the new arrival are outlined with some confidence (on testimony from contemporary wit-nesses) by his grandson George Wyatt in his life of Anne Boleyn. Be-cause of some official relations between their two families, biographers agree, "That they were childhood friends is possible," and this rein-forces George Wyatt's assertion of his grandfather's attraction to Anne:

> The knight, in the beginning, coming to behold the sudden ap-pearance of this new beauty, came to be holden and surprised somewhat with the sight thereof; after much more with her witty and graceful speech, his ear also had him chained to her, so as finally his heart seemed to say, 'I could gladly yield to be tied for ever with the kind of her love,' as somewhere in his verses hath been thought his meaning was to express. She, on the other part, finding him to be then married, and in the knot to have been tied then ten years, rejected all his speech of love; but yet in such sort at whatsoever tended to regard of her honour,

5. Lambley, p. 71.

153

she showed not to scorn, for the general favour and good will she perceived all men to have him, which might the rather occasion others to turn their looks to that which a man of his worth was brought to gaze at in her, as, indeed, after happened. The king is held to have taken his first apprehension of this love after such time as, upon the doubt in those treaties of marriage with his daughter Mary . . . by some of the learned of his own land, he had . . . been prayed to forsake that incestuous life by accompanying with his brother's wife.[6]

This account has been somewhat neglected, perhaps because of incidental inexactness. Almost certainly Wyatt's first sight of Anne was much earlier than the tenth year after his separation from his wife, even if Anne returned to France after the war with France which sent her back to England in 1521 (though it is likely that an important later phase of their relationship did occur at the time George Wyatt specifies, in 1530, as we shall see). Moreover, the poem alluded to ("A face that should content me") specifies blonde hair, unlike Anne's. Nevertheless, the psychological analysis of Anne offered is remarkably convincing in its exposition of her subtly calculated sexual exploitation of Wyatt. This technique of Machiavellian sexuality will soon be applied in France almost as if by a government department, with Catherine de' Medici's *escadron volant.* One can see prefigured in Anne's behavior their pattern of merciless sexual ingenuity, devoted to political and religious goals, which Shakespeare captures so vividly in his portrayal of historical French court ladies in *Love's Labour's Lost.* Such women have no naive delusions about sexual sentiments, and their lovers are treated with that diplomatic detachment preferred and illustrated by the most talented women in Marguerite's *Heptameron,* like the heroine of the fifty-eighth tale.

The same pattern of diplomatic finesse can be detected in an episode later in the sexual triangle of Wyatt, Anne, and Henry:

About this time, it is said that the knight entertaining talk with her as she was in earnest at work, in sporting wise caught from

6. George Wyatt, "The Life of . . . Queene Anne Boleigne," in George Cavendish, *The Life of Cardinal Wolsey,* vol. 2 (London: Harding, 1825), Appendix, pp. 183–85.

her a certain small jewel hanging by a lace out of her pocket, or otherwise loose, which he thrust into his bosom, neither with any earnest request could she obtain it of him again. He kept it, therefore, and wore it after about his neck, under his cassock, promising to himself either to have it with her favour or as an occasion to have talk with her, wherein he had singular delight, and she after seemed not to make much reckoning of it, either the thing not being worth much, or not worth much striving for. The noble prince having a watchful eye upon the Knight, noted him more to hover about the lady, and she the more to keep aloof of him; was whetted the more to discover to her his affection, so as rather he liked first to try of what temper the regard of her honour was, which he finding not any way to be tainted with those things his Kingly majesty and means could bring to the battery, he in the end fell to win her by treaty of marriage, and in this talk took from her a ring, and that wore upon his little finger; and yet all this with such secrecy was carried, and on her part so wisely, as none or very few esteemed this other than as ordinary course of dalliance. Within few days after, it happened that the King, sporting himself at bowls had in his company (as it falls out) divers noblemen and other courtiers of account amongst whom might be the Duke of Suffolk, Sir F. Brian, and Sir T. Wiat himself being more than ordinarily pleasantly disposed, and in his game taking an occasion to affirm a cast to be his that plainly appeared to be otherwise; those on the other side said, with his grace's leave they thought not, and yet still he pointing with his finger whereon he wore her ring replied often it was his, and specially to the knight he said, Wiat, I tell thee it is mine, smiling upon him withal. Sir Thomas, at the length, casting his eye upon the king's finger, perceived that the king meant the lady whose ring that was, which he well knew, and pausing a little, and finding the king bent to pleasure after the words repeated by the king, the knight replied, And if it may like your majesty to give me leave to measure it, I hope it will be mine; and withal took from his neck the lace whereat hung the tablet, and therewith stopped to measure the cast, which the king espying knew, and had seen her wear, and therewith spurned away the bowl, and said, It may be so, but then I am deceived; and so broke up the game. This thing thus carried was not perceived for all this of many, but of some few it was. Now, the king, resorting to his chamber, showing some discontentment in his countenance, found means to break this matter to the lady, who with good and evident proof how the knight came by the jewel, satisfied the king so effectually that this more confirmed the king's opinion of her truth than himself at the first could have expected. Shortly, upon the return of the cardinal [Wolsey], the matter of the dutchess [Marguerite d'Angoulême] cooling everyday more and more his credit also waned until it was utterly eclipsed.[7]

George Wyatt claims that his account is derived from two contemporary observers intimately associated with the events,[8] and one must recognize that whatever the reliability of individual details here the tactics of the lady are those required by her situation, while her role as sexual substitute for her earlier mistress, the author of the *Heptameron*, matches many of the subtler maneuvers in that work strikingly. The use of one relationship to advance another is a recurring motif in this novella cycle, which rarely leaves its victims unscathed emotionally or socially.

The question of Anne's culpability in the matter is still debated among scholars, and this reflects a puzzling ignorance of the principles of feminine decorum which served to maintain the social and diplomatic supremacy of the great ladies of the Valois courts: they welcomed and exploited attractive and talented suitors but eluded (at least overtly) the least surrender or compromising circumstance in order to preserve their public autonomy and status. Looked at in this light, Anne's treatment of Wyatt is completely intelligible, and most of the supposed "problems" in the history of the relationship evaporate—without affording any proof of satisfaction to Wyatt's sexual desires. Of course, it would be exhilarating for critics to find their favorite poet bedding the future queen of England and beating the egregious Henry VIII to the mark in the bargain, but the elementary facts of the situation will not fall plausibly into this pattern, any more than they will corroborate the charge of incest against Anne, which George Wyatt correctly describes

7. Wyatt, "Life of Anne Boleigne," pp. 185–87.
8. Wyatt, "Life of Anne Boleigne," p. 180.

as "incredible."[9] It seems more likely that Anne resembled the "lady of very lively wit who, by her good nature, worthiness, and pleasing conversation, had gained the heart of many suitors without dishonor, entertaining them so agreeably that they did not know what to make of her."[10] This is exactly how Shakespeare shows Anne at court in *Henry VIII* (I.iv).

William H. Wiatt, a scholar anxious to prove Wyatt and Anne successfully committed adultery and fornication respectively, concedes from the start that "the only evidence for an illicit connection between Wyatt and Anne comes from three late and pro-Catholic accounts of the reign of Henry VIII." These are from "an anonymous Spanish chronicle of 1550," "an Italian merchant" who retailed the story without evidence to Nicholas Harpsfield, and the notoriously malicious polemicist Nicholas Sanders.[11] None of these sources carries authority or specificity, and George Wyatt even argues that their stories relate to Sir Francis Brian and another lady entirely. Far more interesting is a letter dated 10 May 1530 to the Emperor Charles V from Chapuys, the imperial ambassador to England, who reported that the duke of Suffolk had been "exiled for some time owing to his having denounced to the King a criminal connection of the Lady [Anne] with a gentleman of the Court who had already been dismissed from Court on such suspicion. This time the gentleman had been sent away at the request of the Lady herself, who feigned to be very angry with him and it was the King who had to intercede for his return."[12] Chapuys admits that all this is only conjecture—but there is evidence in George Wyatt's account to confirm that his grandfather was involved as Chapuys suggests: "It is true also, that Sir Thomas was twice sifted and lifted at, and that nobleman [the duke of Suffolk] both times his most heavy adversary."[13] William

9. George Wyatt, *The Papers*, ed. D. M. Loader (London: Royal Historical Society, 1968), p. 187.

10. Marguerite de Navarre, *Heptameron*, p. 357.

11. William H. Wiatt, "Sir Thomas Wyatt and Anne Boleyn," *English Language Notes* 6 (1968), p. 94.

12. Richard C. Harrier, "Notes on Wyatt and Anne Boleyn," *Journal of English and Germanic Philology* 53 (1954), pp. 582–83; see also Wiatt, p. 96.

13. Wyatt, "Life of Anne Boleigne," p. 192.

H. Wiatt notes that the poet could have been involved in Henry's affair with Anne twice before her marriage, even though he served as marshal of Calais between 1528 and 1532, because there is evidence that he was back in England and no longer marshal in early 1530 but was then redesignated in that role later in the same year. William H. Wiatt plausibly conjectures that in 1530 the poet had been allowed to return after a diplomatic exile from the court, where he had been a seeming rival to the king for Anne's favors (as the jewel incident indicates).

However, on Wyatt's return the duke of Suffolk seems to have maliciously revived rumors such as might have circulated after the earlier incident, to Wyatt's disadvantage and Anne's. If Henry himself got rid of the inconvenient Wyatt on the earlier occasion, it seems likely from Chapuys' letter that Anne decided *her* reputation now required that Wyatt be shipped off a second time, to silence any trace of the gossip for which Suffolk was ostracized. When we consider that after Wyatt's second return from Calais in 1532 he was forced to go back there yet a third time in October of that year, in the train of Henry and his now openly avowed mistress on their state visit to meet François I, we can understand the bitterness of the Wyatt poem usually held to apply to this last humiliating excursion:

> Some tyme I fled the fyre that me brent,
> By see, by land, by water and by wynd;
> And now I folow the coles that be quent
> From Dovor to Calais against my mynde.
> Lo! how desire is boeth sprong and spent!
> And he may se that whilome was so blynde;
> And all his labor now he laugh to scorne,
> Mashed in the breers that erst was all to torne.
>
> (59)

The implication of self-exile in the opening lines may even suggest that Wyatt had himself exploited his diplomatic career to escape Anne's attractions before his Calais appointment. Certainly he had at least two more arduous experiences bearing on his love for Anne: his role in deputizing for his father as chief ewer at the coronation of Anne Boleyn and his arrest in 1536 when she and her associates were tried and executed (the other occasion on which George Wyatt indicates Suffolk may have unsuccessfully maligned him).

Whatever the exact permutation of options one favors in interpreting these details of Wyatt's relationship to Anne, it cannot be reasonably doubted that Wyatt was in love with her and that (whatever initial courtesies he received from her) he became progressively more dissatisfied with her elusive behavior.[14] While this involvement proved the major negative factor in his career as a courtier, it was also a crucial stimulus to the intensity and circumstantiality of his verse, the result of the associated persecution and hostility which his most vivid writings reflect.

These factors help us to evaluate Wyatt's poetry in relation to its social context and to weigh it against Marot's, whose work Wyatt found of definite interest. In "Yf it be so" Wyatt imitates a rondeau ("S'il est ainsi") that Marot's father Jean had derived from Serafino, and in the Egerton manuscript Wyatt includes a somewhat salacious, anticlerical epigram of Marot himself. Wyatt's sonnet "Like to these unmeasurable mountayns'" shares a contemporary source in Serafino with a sonnet possibly by Marot ("Voyant ces monts"). Sergio Baldi also notes two other minor debts of Wyatt to Marot, and no doubt others could be found.[15] The fact remains that Wyatt was much more impressed with the archaic Petrarchan love sonnet than was Marot, whose stay at Ferrara seems to have given him sufficient awareness of current Italian verse to ignore the increasingly old-fashioned Petrarchan sonnets which Wyatt translated, often rather uncouthly, according to most critical verdicts. While Wyatt and Surrey rehearsed this antique vein, it was largely ignored by Marot and (metrically at least) by Scève, so that the English lyricists may even have anticipated French exploitation of the Petrarchan sonnet which Ronsard took up after his long stay in Britain. Whether the sonnet form truly advanced the meaningfulness of either lyric tradition as much as modern critical attention has implied is one question raised by recognition of the significance of the Reformation. As much as half of Wyatt's poetry sustains the abstract, impersonal,

14. See Harrier, p. 584.

15. See Bentley-Cranch, p. 202; and also Patricia Thomson, *Sir Thomas Wyatt and His Background* (Stanford: Stanford University Press, 1964), pp. x, 54, 212.

and undramatic vein of courtly sentimentality of the archaic Petrarchan tradition, as reflected with elegant musicality in a poem like "O goodely hand" (86). Even the repudiation of sexuality in a poem like "Farewell Love" (13) conventionally echoes the stoic moralism (not to say misogyny) of medieval clerics. In such poems the attitudes are largely inaccessible to modern sympathy, for they lack both sophistication and intimacy, though the best do have a plainness and lucidity like that which Marot usually attains with his other virtues.

It is safe to say that if Wyatt had confined himself to this vein of stylized sentiment he would not have drawn much modern attention outside literary histories. The intersection of this stylization with two other types of harsher experience seems to have transformed the more autobiographical part of such verse: on the one hand, awareness of skeptical classical authors like Horace and Terence, if not Martial, and on the other, the disorientating impact of "newfangled" modes of unsentimental behavior like Anne Boleyn's, which shattered the meaningfulness of Petrarchan conventions. Consider the wry example of the following sonnet, which takes up the classical tag François scratched with his diamond on the windowpane of his bedroom at Chambord: "Souvent femme varie / Bien fol est qui sy fie" (Often women change, he's quite mad who trusts them).[16] With the aid of this cynical anti-Petrarchan sentiment, this poem associated with Wyatt achieves an urbane distancing, which paradoxically allows the author to recognize his own intimate experience more vividly:

> Dyvers dothe vse as I have hard and kno,
> Whan that to chaunge ther ladies do beginne,
> To morne and waile, and neuer for to lynne,
> Hoping therbye to pease ther painefull woe.
> And some thereby that whan it chansith soo
> That women change and hate where love hath
> bene,
> Thei call them fals and think with woordes to
> wynne
> The hartes of them wich otherwhere dothe gro.

16. Seward, p. 175.

> But as for me though that by chaunse indede
> Change hath outworne the favor that I had,
> I will not wayle, lament, nor yet be sad,
> Nor call her fals that falsely ded me fede,
> But let it passe and think it is of kinde,
> That often chaunge doth plese a womans minde.
>
> (217)

Here the poet's mind is at one with the skeptical yet urbane acceptance of human fallibility which Marguerite d'Angoulême shared with her brother and which the belief in Original Sin fostered by the Reformation ought to have widely disseminated (but often failed to, because of the self-righteousness of the Reformers themselves).

What Wyatt learned from maltreatment by his wife and Anne Boleyn was precisely the need not to be defeated by a situation if his mind and art were to continue to function humanely. One classic resource under such pressure is to shift the time frame, as Wyatt does in so many of his lyrics. In the Middle Ages this escape was accomplished by shifting drastically from the temporal to the eternal time scale, as at the end of *Troilus and Cryseyde*, where the dead Troilus in "the eighthe spere" is able to "lough right at the wo" and reject "al oure werk that foloweth so / The blynde lust, the which that may not laste" (V.1823-24).[17] Our age may find the eighth sphere a little inaccessible, and Marot illustrates the Reformation shift to something more subjective and individual, showing also Renaissance values compatible with our earthbound perspective:

J'ay contenté	(I have content
Ma voulenté	In my intent
Suffisamment	Sufficiently
Car j'ay esté	For I have been
D'amours traicté	In loving seen
Differemment.	Differently.
J'ay eu tourment,	I've had torment,
Bon traictment.	And good treatment.)

(*Lyriques* xxv)

17. Geoffrey Chaucer, *The Complete Poetry and Prose*, ed. John H. Fisher (New York: Holt, Rinehart, and Winston, 1977), p. 539.

Wyatt and his peers exploit the same distancing tactic in the face of persecution: at the end of "Spight hath no power," the poet consoles himself with the thought that "sins thou setst thie faithe so light, / Yt doth suffise that myne thou warte." The same subjective consolation lies at the core of "They flee from me," which has the richer texture of circumstantial detail of Wyatt's best love poems. It balances the pain of courtiers' current avoidance of the speaker by recalling his past popularity and more specifically evokes the maximum sexual satisfaction of earlier times: "Thancked be fortune, it hath ben othrewise / Twenty tymes better; but ons in speciall" (37). Nostalgia is a sedative in times of stress, and Wyatt has the psychological sophistication to perfect the technique in the second stanza of this poem. It is an evasion, of course, and Shakespeare ruefully recognizes its morbid potentialities in Sonnet 30 ("When to the sessions of sweet silent thought"), even while exploiting its consolations: "But if the while I think on thee, dear friend / All losses are restored."

Because of its escapism the resource may not be ultimately acceptable to a discriminating mind. But "They flee from me" does not conclude in mere voluptuous reverie as so many "dream" poems do. It ends in a challenge, implying moral superiority in the speaker. He has behaved with "gentilness," but has received "new fangilness" and "forsaking." If loyalty has earned such treatment, the question arises of "what she hath deserved." Marot is equally conscious of the psychological compensations of self-righteousness, for in one of his elegies, a woman expresses the same sentiments:

> Je l'ay receu de grace honnestement;
> De moy mesdit par tout injustement
> Et me blasonne.
> Helas, fault il qu'apres bon traictement
> Ung Serviteur blasme indiscretement
> Sa Dame bonne?
> Que feront ceulx qu'on chasse et abondonne
> Si ceux à qui le bon receuil on donne
> Vivent ainsi!
>
> (*Lyriques* LXIX.7–15)

(I received him with honest kindness, but he unjustly criticizes and mocks me everywhere. Alas, must a lover indiscreetly censure his kind mistress after good treatment? What will those do who are dismissed and abandoned if those who are well received do thus!)

In this elegy Marot also uses the consolation of a shifted frame of reference, in which his female speaker notes another of her lovers has been faithful—a stabilizing idea reminiscent of the young aristocrat who manages to avoid joining François in pursuing a bevy of seductive Parisiennes in the sixty-fourth tale of the *Heptameron* because he already has a loving wife—and a beautiful mistress. Amusingly enough, Wyatt did "console" himself for Anne Boleyn's rejection with the devotion of Elizabeth Darrell, as he seems to avow:

> sins I did refrayne
> Her that did set our country in a rore
> Th'unfayned chere of Phillis hath the place
> That Brunet had: she hath and ever shal.
> She from my self now hath me in her grace:
> She hath in hand my witt, my will, and all.
> (95)[18]

However, much more powerful negative options are available to the affronted lover, ones which reject Petrarchan courtliness and match the angry realism of a pagan like Horace, who feels no scruples about a cathartic outburst of hostility in his attack on Lydia:

> invicem moechos anus arrogantes
> flebis in solo levis angiportu,
> Thracio bacchante magis sub inter-
>   lunia vento,
> cum tibi flagrans amor et libido,
> quae solet matres furiare equorum,
> saeviet circa iecur ulcerosum,
>   non sine questu.

18. See Muir's footnote for the version cited (Wyatt, ed. Muir and Thomson [1969]).

laeta quod pubes hedera virenti
gaudeat pulla magis atque myrto,
aridas frondes hiemis sodali
    dedicet Euro.
      (*Odes* i.xxv.9–20)[19]

(Thy turn shall come, and thou, a hag forlorn in deserted alley, shalt weep over thy lovers' disdain, when on moonless nights the Thracian north wind rises in its fury, while burning love and passion, such as are wont to goad the stallions' dams, shall rage about thy wounded heart. Then shalt thou make moan that merry youths take more delight in ivy green and myrtle dark, consigning withered leaves to the east wind, winter's mate.)

Horace's anger seems more accessible to a secular modern mind than the stylized despair of a courtly lover reflected by such versions of Petrarch as Wyatt's "My galy charged with forgetfulness" (28), in which the poet's use of the ship image largely supplants the lover's situation and feelings as the focus of interest. But at his best Wyatt achieves a more virile (not to say classical) note much closer to Horace's candid outburst. There is nothing Petrarchan about the climax of "My lute awake!":

Vengeaunce shall fall on thy disdain
That makest but game on ernest pain;
Thinck not alone vnder the sonne
Vnquyt to cause thy lovers plain,
All tho my lute and I have done.

Perchaunce the lye wethered and old,
The wynter nightes that are so cold,
Playning in vain vnto the mone;
Thy wisshes then dare not be told;
Care then who lyst, for I have done.

And then may chaunce the to repent
The tyme that thou hast lost and spent

---

19. Horace, *The Odes and Epodes* (Cambridge: Harvard University Press, 1947), pp. 70–71.

To cause thy lovers sigh and swoune;
Then shalt thou knowe beaultie but lent,
And wisshe and want as I have done.

(66)

The effect is brutal but vivid, and Marot can be equally ungallant, as
we saw in his acrid attacks on Ysabeau and in his harsh admonitions
in "Aux Dames de Paris" (171–89); but neither poet could be said to
achieve eminence in such a vein, which is scarcely more true to Reformation ethics than Petrarchanism, and Horace remains definitive in
his epitome of the reactions of "l'homme moyen sensuel." If we are
looking for something worthy of the new and suppler sensibility, it
must reflect not merely neoclassical worldliness but a moral sophistication which transcends the involuntary pangs of crude sensuality.

Horace was conscious of the propaganda value of his art, and this
concern with the poet's power to confer fame or infamy was one of the
great themes of Renaissance verse.[20] Marot warns a fickle mistress in
one of his elegies:

Incontinent, desloyalle Fumelle,
Que j'auray, faict et escript ton Libelle
Entre les mains le mettray d'une femme
Qui appellée est Renommée ou Fame,
Et qui ne sert qu'à dire par le Monde
Le bien ou mal de ceulx où il abonde.

(*Lyriques* LXV.33–38)

(As soon, disloyal female, as I shall have made and written your
denunciation I shall put it into the hands of a woman called
Reputation or Fame, who serves only to tell through the World
the good or evil of those in whom it abounds.)

This subtler mode of revenge is sufficiently vivid and authentic to have
attracted poets at least as late as Carew, in poems such as "Ingrateful
beauty threatned." However, Wyatt manages to give it a distinctive
turn of phrase by grafting on a musical motif well illustrated by Mellin

20. See J. B. Leishman, *Themes and Variations in Shakespeare's Sonnets* (New
York: Harper and Row, 1966), pp. 27 ff.

de St. Gelais, who speaks of playing on his "luth qui respons à mes pensées" (lute which reflects my thoughts):

> Si ma main vient mal aux accords
> Iouant de ce luth bien monté
> Le coeur qui fait mouuoir le corps,
> Trouble son arc et sa bonté;
> Il est d'amour si surmonté,
> Si lié à si fausse corde,
> Que mon doigt lourd et mesconté,
> Discordant avec luys s'accorde.[21]

(If my hand goes ill in harmony playing the well-turned lute, the heart which made my body move troubles its chords and its virtue; this heart is so overpowered with love so bound to so false a string that my heavy, sad finger in discord harmonizes with it.)

Wyatt deftly takes up the topic of musical performance[22] and uses it to give specificity to a poetic denunciation of a fickle mistress which has the authentic moral intensity of Reformation ethics. The puritan preoccupation with "sin" is explicit:

> My lute and strynges may not deny
> But as I strike they must obay;
> Brake not them than soo wrongfully,
> But wryeke thy selffe some wyser way;
> And tho the songes whiche I endight
> Do quytt thy chainge with Rightfull spight,
>   Blame not my lute.
>
> Spyght askyth spight and changing change,
> And falsyd faith must nedes be knowne;
> The faute so grett, the case so strange,
> Of Right it must abrod be blown:
> Then sins that by thyn own desartte
> My soinges do tell how trew thou artt,
>   Blame not my lute.

(205)

21. Mellin de St. Gelais, *Oeuvres poetiques* (Lyon: Rigaud, 1582), p. 165.
22. Compare also "Sins you will nedes that I shall sing" (209).

166

The catalytic effect of betrayal on Wyatt's moral sensibility is obvious. One should notice how much play Wyatt makes with the objective ethical issue: his obligations in the interest of social order to publish a "case so strange." The concern to formalize amatory experience in new patterns shows that Wyatt shares Marguerite's desire to crystallize a sexual code relevant to Renaissance and Reformation mores via case histories of current behavior. We can hear the same note in the final question of "They flee from me" in which Wyatt asks: "I would fain knowe what she hath deserved" (37). There too Wyatt implies at least the quest for a norm to evaluate specific sexual conduct. Marot is less stiffly philosophical and moralistic, more subjective and ingenious, not to say skeptical and even whimsical. This lesser moral intensity makes him initially more lively and attractive but ultimately less compelling and profound than Wyatt or Marguerite.

The divergence in seriousness appears in juxtaposing some songs of Marot, on themes familiar enough in Wyatt, with the English poet's varied use of the same material. Marot starts emphatically from his private preferences, which stress a reciprocity alien to the Petrarchan tradition:

> Amour au cueur me poinct
> Quand bien aymé je suis;
> Mais aymer je ne puis
> Quant on ne m'ayme poinct.
>
> Chancun soit adverty
> De faire comme moy;
> Car d'aymer sans party,
> C'est ung trop grand esmoy.
> (*Lyriques* xxx)

(Love strikes my heart when I am well loved, but I cannot love when I am not in the least loved. Let everyone be advised to do as I, for love without return is too distressing.)

The medieval stress on absolutes, eternity, and impassivity has been replaced by Reformation immediacy, intensity, and subjective satisfaction. The sentiment accords with modern taste, but Marot makes little formal attempt to "convert" his hearers beyond asserting his own preference, and the same lack of forensic skill and moral intensity appears in a similar song which may appear to generalize on the fallibility of women and their suitors, but which is also a personal assertion:

> Qui veult entrer en grace
> Des Dames bien avant,
> En cautelle et fallace
> Fault estre bien sçavant.
> Car tout vray Poursuyvant
> La loyaulté suyvant
> Aujourd'huy est deceu,
> Et le plus decepvant
> Pour loyal est receu.
>   (*Lyriques* xxxi)

(Who wishes to enter fully into women's good will has to be well-versed in craft and fraud. For any true suitor following loyalty today is deceived, and the most deceptive is received as loyal.)

The cynicism is current, but the presentation lacks substance—its impersonality paradoxically reduces its view of women to an assertion without vividness, particularity, or systematic demonstration.

Wyatt can share exactly this kind of merely sententious cynicism:

> What vaileth trouth? or, by it, to take payn?
> To stryve, by stedfastness, for to attayne
> To be iuste, and true: and fle from dowbleness:
> Sythens all alike, where rueleth craftines
> Rewarded is boeth fals, and plain.
> Sonest he speedeth, that moost can fain;
> True meanyng hert is had in disdayn.
> Against deceipte and dowbleness
>   What vaileth trouth?

                                    (2)

The loss of ideals and a comprehensive moral system such as stabilized the worldview of the Middle Ages is reflected in both poets—for a modern lover there can be no recourse to a higher good or authority than a woman's individual will. But this earthbound focus is just as archaically pagan as the Petrarchan idealist is archaically medieval in the Reformation world. None of these facile songs have much resonance to a modern ear, and they add little to their precedents in quality of verse, feeling, or insight.

However, both poets can achieve a much subtler pattern in which one detects not only psychological insight but social and moral finesse of an admirable and amusing kind. Take this song of Marot on a similar theme:

> Ma Dame ne m'a pas vendu,
> Elle m'a seulement changé;
> Mais elle a au change perdu,
> Dont je me tiens pour bien vengé,
> Car ung loyal a estrangé
> Pour ung aultre qui la diffame.
> N'est elle pas legiere femme?
> (*Lyriques* xxiv)

(My lady did not sell me off, she turned me in for a new model; but she got a bad bargain, so that I feel properly revenged, for she alienated a loyal suitor for another one who slanders her. Is she not a flighty woman?)

One feels that the speaker has triumphed without viciousness and has vindicated his moral vision wittily rather than censoriously. This poem is more positive than and at least as civilized and sophisticated as Horace's sardonic attack on Barine (*Odes* II.viii). Horace's poem exploits a wittily agnostic attack on the gods who tolerate his lover's broken vows, while Marot's subtly vindicates a providential universe.

However, merely pious or complacent sentiments cannot achieve this greater dimension of awareness characteristic of the most refined Reformation sensibilities. One of Marot's elegies strikes a smugly moralistic pose:

> Si ma complaincte en vengeance estoit telle
> Comme tu es en abus et cautelle,
> Croy que ma Plume amoureuse, et qui t'a
> Tant faict d'honneur dont tresmal s'acquitta,

Croy qu'elle auroit desja jecté fumée
Du style ardant dont elle est allumée,
Pour du tout rendre aussi noir que Charbon
Le tien bon bruit (si tu en as de bon);
Mais pas ne suis assez vindicatif
Pour ung tel cueur, si faulx et deceptif;
Et neantmoins si me fault il changer
Mon naturel pour de toy me venger,
A celle fin que mon cueur se descharge
Du pesant fais dont ta ruse le charge;
Aussi affin de te faire sçavoir
Qu'à trop grand tort m'as voulu decepvoir,
Veu qu'en mon cueur ta basse qualité
N'a veu qu'Amour en Liberalité.

(*Lyriques* LXV.1–18)

(If my complaint was vengeful enough to match your mistreatment and craftiness, believe that my amorous pen—which has done you so much honor that has been very ill repaid—believe that it would have already flung the smoke of burning style with which it is alight in order to make your good fame, if you have any such, as black as coal; but I am not so vindictive as to match a heart so false and deceptive. Yet nevertheless I must still force my nature to revenge myself so that my heart may be lightened of the heavy deed with which your cunning has burdened it, also in order to make you realize that at too much cost you wished to deceive me, since in my heart your base nature has seen only Love and Generosity.)

The passage fails totally to assimilate Reformation awareness of humanity's "fallen" condition; it is vainglorious, canting, and self-contradictory: the speaker rates himself above revenge, yet rationalizes the bitter denunciation he affects to avoid. It is a conventional piece of hyprocrisy, and Wyatt shares its smugness:

Within my brest I neuer thought it gain,
Of gentle myndes the fredom for to lose.
Nor in my hart sanck neuer such disdain,
To be a forger, faultes for to disclose.

> Nor I can not endure the truth to glose,
> To set a glosse vpon an earnest pain.
> Nor I am not in nomber one of those,
> That list to blow retrete to euery train.
>
> (247)

The tone is that of complacent assertion, not of a compelling and witty demonstration. The pious sentiment is certainly not sustained by other lyrics of Wyatt, which are often resentful, malicious, and specific. We detect the attempt to set up a virtuous persona to compensate for a lover's implicit censure through rejection, though the details of this humiliating situation have been slyly suppressed. A Freudian (or, better still, an Adlerian) analysis of the technique and grounds for repression here might be salutary. If it were argued that this analysis would lack facts and substance, the relationship of Anne and Wyatt sketched out by the poet's grandson still affords many clues. While this poem may reflect a personality compatible with the verdicts of modern psychiatry, it also lacks the complexity, depth, and even authenticity by means of which great literature eludes or transcends such a pathology.

Such virtues can be found in a sonnet almost identical in theme but infinitely more exact, finely honed, and cruelly surgical. Here there is an ethical wit worthy of the Reformation:

> To Rayle or geste ye kno I vse yt not
> Though that such cause some tyme in folkes
>   I finde:
> And tho to chaung ye list to sett your minde,
> Love yt who liste, in faithe I like yt not.
> And if ye ware to me as ye are not,
> I would be lothe to see you so unkinde;
> But sins your faithe must nedes be so, be kinde,
> Tho I hate yt, I praye you leve yt not.
> Thinges of grete waight I never thought
>   to crave:
> This is but small—of right denye yt not.
> Your fayning wayis as yet forget them not,

171

But like rewarde let other lovers have:
That is to saye, for seruis true and faste,
To long delaies and changing at the last.

(211)

If ever a poem truly outmaneuvered an oversophisticated woman this would be it, and it fully corroborates any assertion that a woman who could dextrously manipulate Wyatt's interest while encouraging the king's involvement, as did Anne Boleyn, might be capable of anything. As a prophetic epitaph it seems remarkably apt in anticipating Anne's execution for adultery after the king's long courtship. The sense of the sonnet is antithetical to the elusive emotions reflected in Donne's witty ambivalence, even though it heralds his style by its paradoxical compression and surface ambiguity. A whole human relationship is crammed into these fourteen lines. The opening assertion of virtuous restraint is vindicated by the scarcely suppressed resentment of the second line and the almost involuntary candor of the fourth. The second quatrain displays a mind working with a malicious virtuosity which requires paraphrase: "And if you were to be truly loving to me, as you are not, this would distress me because it would be unlike you. But since your kind of loyalty requires that you be falsely loving, continue insincere love." The original irony lies in the pun: calling seeming goodwill "unkind," i.e., "uncharacteristic." Yet the real bite comes in the conclusion, in which the speaker wishes that by seeming equally gracious the woman will earn the resentment of other lovers—say of a Henry VIII, if it *were* Anne of whom the author writes. If this were so, then the ominous overtone of the basic request would be understandable: "I will not personally hurt you for your fickleness, but keep up this little game, and then perhaps you will get your just deserts in the end." The author has become as psychologically agile as any Valois court lady.

A Wyatt poem with less sinister power and a more gracious didacticism is another sonnet which achieves a memorable *tu quoque*:

Eche man me telleth I chaunge moost
    my devise.
And on my faith me thinck it goode reason

172

To chaunge propose like after the season,
Ffor in every cas to kepe still oon gyse
Ys mytt for theim that would be taken wyse,
And I ame not of suche maner condition,
But treted after a dyvers fasshion,
And therupon my dyversnes doeth rise.
But you that blame this dyversnes moost,
Chaunge you no more, but still after oon rate
Trete ye me well, and kepe ye in the same state;
And while with me doeth dwell this
    weried goost,
My word nor I shall not be variable,
But alwaies oon, your owne boeth ferme
   and stable.

       (10)

This poem makes an interesting contrast with Marot's song inviting others to share his preference for reciprocity in love. The opening here is subtly self-critical while affecting self-defense, only to spring the trap in the end: "Yes, I am fickle, and even defend it frankly—and you've only to stop being so yourself to cure me." The psychology is alert, and the self-awareness again prefigures that in Shakespeare, as in Sonnet 121 with its resentment that "others false adulterate eyes / Give salutation to my sportive blood" and with its similar verdict: "they that level / At my abuses reckon up their own." Shakespeare would have read Wyatt's sonnet in *Tottel's Miscellany*. Each poem dismisses both Petrarchan idealism and Horatian resentment in favor of recognition of the need to be generously reconciled to universal fallibility and to that of one's beloved. The ending implies reacceptance of each other by both failed partners.

It is through exposure to new and alien modes of behavior such as were mapped out in the *Heptameron* that Wyatt's mind painfully acquired that sense of the multilayered nature of human awareness now thought of as typically Shakespearean. His resulting complexity appears in another sonnet which precedes the one just discussed in Tottel's and most other editions. It begins by recognizing Caesar as, in

173

Shakespeare's words, one of those "that do not do the thing they most do show" (Sonnet 94) since he affects to weep on receiving Pompey's head, "covering his gladness." Hannibal likewise affects to laugh at misfortune:

> So chaunceth it oft that every passion
> The mynde hideth, by colour contrary,
> With fayned visage, now sad, now mery:
> Whereby, if I laught, any tyme, or season
> It is for bicause I have n'other way
> To cloke my care, but vnder sport and play.
>
> (3)

Wyatt has understood the witty decorum which is favored in the *Heptameron* and which is to be praised in Horatio by Hamlet (III.ii.68–79), but he can no more truly illustrate it consistently himself than can Petrarch, whom he is following here. And that leaves us acutely aware of the crucial difference between Marot and Wyatt—the latter never wholly loses his archaic sense of dignity and solemnity. This gives him more tragic force than Marot, but it minimizes his charm, his wit, and his sense of humor. And it limits his power to assimilate the potentialities of the Reformation.[23] Marot is thus a livelier, more original poet—but a less moving one. Perhaps nowhere better than in Wyatt can one see so vividly the shocked dawning of awareness of life's hostility in a complacent and talented mind (unless it be in the far more powerful and complacent mind of the youthful Milton).

For I have neglected one class of poems in which Wyatt and his peers also excel: precisely the notation of defeat. At their best such poets can record with neutral clarity and unique economy this exemplary experience. If ever a poem refutes the artistic superority of irony, ambivalence, and complexity, it is this:

23. If H. A. Mason finds "Protestantism in the Psalms" of Wyatt, he also says, "Wyatt was not a sectarian" and Joost Daalder agrees that "this was a time when the best and most earnest minds struggled with their religious and ethical problems in an independent way" (Thomas Wyatt, *Collected Poems*, ed. Joost Daalder [London: Oxford University Press, 1975], p. xix).

Wythe seruyng still
 This haue I wonne,
Ffor my good will
 To be vndonne.

And ffor redres
 Of all my payne
Disdaynffulnes
 I haue agayne.

And ffor Reward
 Of all my smart
Lo, thus vnhard
 I must departe.

Wherefore all ye
 That after shall
Bye ffortune be,
 As I am, thrall,

Exempell take
 What I have wonne,
Thus for her sake
 To be vndone.
   (174)

The poem contains sixty-two words, arranged in brief sentences, with only the faintest tinge of imagery. In its own terms the poem is fault-less—all one can object to is that its author has so obviously allowed himself to be entrapped in the role of victim.

One last pathetic example will epitomize this potential for defeat, which hangs over Wyatt from the moment when his marriage failed. In this case one must imagine a scene such as would have occurred when Wyatt accepted the order to abandon Elizabeth Darrell and take back the alienated wife, whose sister Henry VIII was about to debauch:

There was never nothing more me payned,
Nor nothing more me moved,

As when my swete hert her complayned
That ever she me loved.
                    Alas the while!

With pituous loke she saide and sighed
"Alas, what aileth me
To love and set my welth so light
On hymn that loveth not me?
                    Alas the while! . . .

"My restful nights and Joyfull daies
Syns I began to love
Be take from me; all thing decayes
Yet can I not remove.
                    Alas the while!" . . .

Her paynes tormented me so sore
That comfort had I none,
But cursed my fortune more and more
To se her sobbe and grone.
                    Alas the while!

                                        (38)

That the experience was not incidental is confirmed by its reappearance in almost identical terms in another lyric ("I lovve lovyd and so doithe she / And yet in love wee sufer still" [106]). In such poems one admires the candid economy and precision. Yet surely one also feels that the author is still largely a medieval figure, entrapped by an indifferent cosmic fate to which and against which the human will is quite insignificant and powerless. Wyatt's subtlest contemporaries were beginning to repudiate such gloomy determinism, either from the vainglory of Renaissance egotism or from the intense sense of a providential and personal God, fostered by the Reformation simultaneously with a sense of self-sufficient private identity.

Both these positive drives may be detected impressively in Anne Boleyn, and despite the ultimate tragic cost, she realized her goals fully: she encouraged a megalomaniac king to divorce his loyal wife, reject his church, dismiss his chief minister, and beget on her an heir who presided over one of England's greatest eras. It would be facile to weight the factors that produced these extraordinary results, but her autonomy was fostered by Lutheran resistance to conventional values. Certainly Wolsey's frustration of her romance with Harry Percy was part of the toughening process that helped turn her against the established church; equally her involvement in Reformation ethics and politics helped her to formulate her marital policies; but the flair and magnetism which she exercised were mostly the result of a tempering in the dazzling ambience of the French court, where apt and fluent speech, emotional poise and manipulative finesse, and the skillful exploitation of sophisticated manners all combined to produce women of a new and distinctive authority. Wyatt's encounter with such a woman may have been less intimate than is usually assumed without sufficient awareness of evidence, but it was nonetheless salutary to his art for all that. To Anne, Wyatt may never have seemed more than an agreeable diversion or a convenient social asset, but to the poet she presented a challenge which male-dominated literature has confronted ever since: how to relate its egotistical concerns to the talented female who rejects the conventional feminine posture of subservience. On balance it must be said that Anne's incompatibility with Wyatt's original archaic Petrarchan ethic and aesthetics forced a drastic and creative awareness of human unpredictability on the poet. Nevertheless, he shows little capacity to understand her type of mind and personality, with the result that his final hostile verdict on her is just as savage and partisan as the tribunal that sentenced her to death and the husband who ensured it would. Wyatt's own marriage, if less tragic, was scarcely happier.

Despite this crucial failure in empathy and sophistication, Wyatt is a memorable poet for exactly the opposite reason to that usually alleged: not because he imported Petrarch into England but because he showed the intrinsic irrelevance of Petrarchan conventions to the great amatory issues of his life and society, even if he remained himself largely trapped within that archaic frame. Marguerite d'Angoulême had a personality capable of a larger, less orthodox vision, and a poet like Marot necessarily had to share her comprehensiveness if he was to maintain her interest and protection. English society, as illustrated by Henry VIII and Wyatt, failed to understand the "newfangled"

French culture and its initiates during the earlier parts of the sixteenth century, even though fascinated by them; and this is demonstrated by the appalling list of judicial murders committed in England during this period against sophisticated women, often young, attractive, and educated in France, a list including the deaths of such queens as Anne Boleyn, Catherine Howard, Jane Grey, and even Mary Stuart later. Perhaps the best that can be said of their treatment is that they achieved parity with men: having developed a new autonomy and individuality, they received the same harsh penalties for political crimes and ethical errors which the male sex had traditionally received.

1. Marguerite d'Angoulême, queen of Navarre,
author of the *Heptameron*.
Sketch by Clouet
from the Musée de Condé,
Chantilly. (Giraudon)

2. Marguerite d'Angoulême, queen of Navarre.
From a portrait in the Bibliothèque Nationale.

3. Guillaume Gouffier
de Bonnivet, lover
of Marguerite d'Angoulême.
Drawing by Clouet
in the Musée de Condé,
Chantilly. (Giraudon)

4. Anne Boleyn.
Contemporary portrait in the
National Portrait Gallery, London.

5. Francis I.
Reproduction of a
contemporary medallion.

6. King Charles IX,
son of Catherine de' Medici,
perpetrator of the
St. Bartholomew Massacre.
Engraving in François de Mezeray,
Histoire de France
(1696).

7. Catherine de' Medici.
From a Clouet drawing in
the British Library.

8. Henri, king of Navarre,
later king of France,
and husband of Marguerite de Valois.
From a portrait (1582) in
the Bibliothèque Nationale.

9. Marguerite de Valois,
queen of Navarre,
daughter of
Catherine de' Medici.
Portrait in
the Bibliothèque
Nationale.

10. Henri de Lorraine,
duc de Guise,
leader of the Catholic
League, lover of
Marguerite de Valois.
Engraving by
Le Blond in
the British Library.

11. Clément Marot.
Engraving of a lost portrait
attributed to Holbein, in
the Bibliothèque Nationale.

12. Théophile de Viau.
Frontispiece of the
edition of his collected verse
of 1672.

13. Pierre de Ronsard.
Frontispiece in the
edition of his collected verse
of 1571.

14. Cassandre de Talcy,
a court lady
celebrated by Ronsard.
Portrait in his *Amours*
(1553).

15. The puritan poet
Agrippa d'Aubigné.
Portrait in the Musée
publique de Genève.
(F. Martin)

16. A lady and gentleman of
the Valois court.
Watercolor from the
Habits de France (1581) in
the Bibliothèque Nationale.

"Monseigneur Saint Ronsard"
The Pagan and the Heretics

Tu fais comme un joueur, à qui sur
      l'eschaffaut
Le polmon plein de vent, et le coeur ne defaut
Pour se monstrer hardy jouant son personnage,
Bien qu'au fait et au prendre il perdist
      le courage. . . .
Je veus tant seulement (puis que tu as envie
D'estre cognu de tous) discourir de ta vie,
Afin qu'apres ta mort on presche ton renom,
A jour que l'on fera feste de ton saint nom. . . .
Ceus-là qui à ce jour feront pelerinage
En ton temple sacré, verront un grand image
Au plus haute de l'autel, et au dessous à part
Escrit en lettres d'or, Monseigneur
      Saint Ronsard. . . .
La chappe qui sera esparse sur ton dos,
Sera bordée autour de verres et de pots, . . .
Et pour nous advertir, qu'il faut que
      ton tombeau
Soit orné quelque jour, pour urne,
      d'un tonneau. . . .
Les pauvres verolez te viendront faire offrande,

179

A celle fin d'avoir response à leur demande. . . .
Là rendant à Bacchus le deu de ton office,
D'un gros bouc tout barbu tu feras sacrifice,
Où tu appelleras avec tes alliez
Tous tes beau dieus bouquins et tes
        dieus chevrepieds,
Tu seras couronné d'un beau tortis
        de l'hierre. . . .
Et que doresnavant en tous tes beaus sermons,
On n'orra que prescher la gloire des demons.
           (Pineaux II.308–13)[1]

(You perform like an actor on the stage with lungs full of air and keen enough to play his role, although in fact he loses courage in the undertaking. . . . Since you wish to be known of all, I just want to discuss your life so that after your death they can preach your fame on the day which they will celebrate your saintly name. . . . Those who on that day will make a pilgrimage to your sacred temple will see a great statue at the altar's highest point, and below separately written in golden letters: his eminence Saint Ronsard. . . . The cope which shall be spread on your back will be bordered with glasses and wine pots. . . . And for our instruction some day your tomb must be ornamented with a wine cask for urn. . . . Poor victims of venereal disease will come to make offerings to you to have their wishes granted. . . . There, giving to Bacchus what your office requires, you will sacrifice a great bearded goat, or you and your confederates will call on your fine goatish gods and your goatfooted ones. You will be crowned with a fine ivy crown. . . . And henceforth in all your fine sermons one will only hear preached the glory of demons.)

One of the ironies of such literary malevolence as the above passage effects is that it often confers historical substance on some of its otherwise almost forgotten combatants. Lord Chesterfield may be best known for Dr. Johnson's savage parody of his role as non-patron of the Dictionary, and Pope unwittingly eternalized a horde of poetasters

---

1. Jacques Pineaux, ed., *La Polémique protestante contre Ronsard*, vol. 2 (Paris: Didier, 1973), pp. 308–13. See Plate 13.

and literary hacks in the *Dunciad*. The mutual abuse showered on Ronsard and his Protestant critics until the Court interfered now proves of less interest for the issues than for the vigor and vividness of Ronsard's self-defense in the *Response*, which is worthy of comparison to *L'Enfer*, and for the lively caricatures in the diatribes of his opponents. It is true that some of the abuse approaches fatuousness, as when Ronsard is accused of having surpassed Nero, Domitian, and Diocletian in their "bloody cruelties" or is abused as "atheist, madman, devil, deaf, and frenetic." We find that one modern term of abuse is predictably archaic, for Ronsard is called a "shameless pig" or "an Epicurean pig" and "brainless" into the bargain.[2] Such unsubtle libels were the base currency of Reformation pamphleteering, but others have a truer ring to them and have passed current in literary tradition, like the admirably brief and witty *Le Temple de Ronsard*, which was partly written by Florent Chrestien (the tutor of Henri de Navarre, later Henri IV), from which the extracts above have been quoted. The mock apotheosis of one's opponent is a subtle mode of attack, and among later writers the puritan Marvell chose to indict his own exotic temperament in similar atavistic terms to those used to attack Ronsard:

> Out of these scatter'd Sibyls Leaves
> Strange Prophecies my Phancy weaves: . . .
> The Oak-Leaves me embroyder all,
> Between which Caterpillars crawl:
> And Ivy, with familiar trails,
> Me licks, and clasps, and curles, and hales.
> Under this antick Cope I move
> Like some great Prelate of the Grove.
> (577–78, 587–92)[3]

It is most revealing that Marvell's persona in "Upon Appleton House" comes so close to falling victim to the same seductive paganism of which Ronsard is accused. Without assenting to the censoriousness of his enemies, one recognizes that Ronsard has genuine affinities with

2. Pineaux I. 145; II. 284, 288, 233, 238.
3. Andrew Marvell, *Poems and Letters*, ed. H. M. Margoliouth, vol. 1 (Oxford: Clarendon Press, 1927), p. 77.

classical animism and even with the cults of the Greek pantheon. There is an irony here, for it is because as a youth Ronsard lacked a full Humanist education and "was spared the least experience of sterile scholasticism" that "his worship of pagan antiquity gains from it an innocence and a naiveté, which will sometimes scandalise, because the choice between tradition and renewal had never posed itself to him." Not unlike Marot, from a scholarly point of view, Ronsard is "without deep intellectual roots"; yet this early "ignorance of books" will "explain in great measure the later enthusiasm for study which he felt. He will not have to correct a vicious training. He will have been spared college." The result is a spontaneity and eclecticism which must offend more rigorous minds. "Enthusiasm is one of the fundamental traits of his personality. Quickly excited, quickly depressed, flung from crest to abyss, he lives in spurts. His jumps in humor are frequent. . . . Inconstancy is his law, for he has more heart than head." As for his beliefs, "the religion of Pierre will always be more a structure of habits and rituals than an interior life and a spiritual need, a religion of vine-growers which accommodates much license and superstition."[4]

While such volatility produces inconsistencies, deplorable lapses in good judgment, and grotesque self-betrayals, it also implies the essential positives of his art: "There is in all of Ronsard a consistency . . . not of aspiration but of exuberant vitality. His more serious and longer poems surge with a glowing energy, a teeming plethora of ideas. . . . He could settle down to the corruscating flux of earthly affairs and feel no wish to rise above it. In this, and in the cultivation of the Self, the 'Moi,' Ronsard achieved a classically quiet heart; with a minimal aspiration towards the changeless and the immutable he was able to take root in mutability and to extract a vivid joy from flux." If this is true, then it is natural that "he excels at the poetry of the senses, the tactile, the here-and-now."[5] Such practical considerations bear on our response to his verse, as anyone who has explored the Vendômois with Ronsard in hand must know—just as the connoisseur of Rabelais still recognizes

4. Michel Dassonville, *Ronsard: Étude historique et litéraire*, vol. 1 (Geneva: Droz, 1968), pp. 27, 38, 61–62.

5. A. W. Sattersthwaite, *Spenser, Ronsard, and du Bellay* (Princeton: Princeton University Press, 1960), pp. 192, 231–39.

with delight familiar traits in the modern villages first mentioned in *Gargantua*. "*Paganus*, pleasant and pagan, Ronsard is already both unconsciously. The roses preserved within almost all the pages of his work are the roses of Val-de-Loire, and the vinous slopes he surveys in his Bacchic musings are the hills of Trôo. . . . In his work, as in that of Rabelais . . . walk shepherds and cowgirls, herdsmen and laborers, and a whole race of workmen who are not the artificial persons of pastorals but familiar, ordinary folk." It is for this reason that the mere demonstration of classical indebtedness does not detract from a freshness and insight denied to many neoclassicists: "His debt is without any doubt immense. But he knew the Bellerie spring before the Bandousian one. . . . Life for him preceded study, and no Arcadia ever supplanted in his heart the charms of his Vendômois."[6]

The Protestants were therefore correct in charging Ronsard with restoring currency to essentially pagan beliefs, which is why they seize with such bitterness on the enthusiastic Hellenism of the "Voyage d'Arcueil" and return again and again to the theme of the supposed ritual killing of a goat, a sacrifice mentioned approvingly in Ronsard's version of the Bandusia ode, which he redirected towards the Bellerie spring (*Odes* II.ix).[7] In their attacks on his sensuality, they frequently point out that he exceeds the bounds of decency set even by pagans such as Augustus and Plato, thus violating the very sources of his inspiration:[8]

> Mais les Muses, qui sont tant chastes et savantes
> T'ont elles enseigné, noble coeur et hautain,
> Sous titre de Maistresse avoir une Putain?
> (Pineaux II.291–92)

(But the Muses, who are so chaste and learned, have they taught you, noble and proud heart, to take a prostitute under the title of Mistress?)

Inevitably such critics censure pagan precedents provided by "the lying harp of Horace or Catullus" and attack the cult of "nouveauté" as bitterly as Wyatt. They even find Ronsard so brazen that he is capable of

6. Dassonville, pp. 11, 26–27.   7. Pineaux I.41, 81, 138, etc.
8. Pineaux I.111–12.

writing classical tragedy and of favoring democracy, while they are
loyal subjects of the king who feel that pagan poetry and medieval
romances are excrescences on the body politic which could profitably
be excised, favoring as they do the vainglory with which Ronsard is
so deeply infected that he seeks a bishopric, if not beatification. By contrast each Protestant critic carefully stresses his own limitations: "Je
ne suis pas grand chose, / Mon corps est bien petit" (I am nothing
great, my physique is very slight) murmurs one;[9] another makes the
Lutheran case:

> Et ne nous vantons point qu'on nous estime
> > et prise
> Comme mignons de Dieu, et qu'il nous favorise
> Comme le meritans, car nous luy confessons
> Que pour nos grans pechés sur nos
> > chefz amassons
> Les charbons de son ire.
>
> > (Pineaux 1.136)

(And we do not pride ourselves at all that we should be esteemed and held as God's darlings and that he favor us because
we merit it, for we confess to him that for our sins on our heads
we heap the coals of his wrath.)

A whole Reformist persona is being crystallized in such passages,
one which is to be unkindly stereotyped in the false humility of Tartuffe.
But one should be cautious about taking a merely contemptuous view
of such personalities, to whom Molière does less than justice in *Tartuffe*;
Alceste is nearer to a true portrait. One can hear many notes in the
attacks on Ronsard which will be echoed by Milton and even Shakespeare. It is crucial that we recognize how far Protestants were from
considering themselves modern revolutionaries; to most of them it was
rather the established church and sophisticated society which favored
"nouveauté," "newfangledness," and a revived but archaic paganism.
The characteristic Huguenot tone is not that of Shakespeare's "radical," Jack Cade, but of his Coriolanus, anxious to repudiate "modern"
usage founded on fashionable conventions:

9. Pineaux II.349, 496; I.75, 128, 153; II.277, 334.

> Custom calls me to't.
> What custom wills, in all things should
> we do't,
> The dust on antique time would be unswept
> And mountainous error be too highly heaped
> For truth t' o'erpeer. Rather than fool it so,
> Let the high office and the honour go.
>
> (II.iii.112–17)

The speech of Coriolanus echoes the phrases of one of the verse polemics against Ronsard written in part by Antoine de la Roche-Chandieu:

> Mais qu'est il de besoin recercher en l'histoire
> Les tableau plus poudreux, de l'antique
> memoire? . . .
> On doit donc rejetter tout homme qui presume
> Rendre la Verité serve de la Coustume
> Et celuy doit avoir poids et auctorité
> Qui la coustume met dessous la Verité.
>
> (Pineaux 1.39)

(But what is the need to hunt out in history the dustiest chronicles of antique memory? . . . One must therefore reject all men who presume to make truth subservient to custom, and that one must have weight and authority who sets custom beneath truth.)

With this context in mind one begins to recognize in Coriolanus yet another stern moralist like Angelo, Isabella, Brutus, Malvolio, Shylock, and Lear. The intense sense of ethical imperatives on which all these characters are founded derives as much from Shakespeare's awareness of the personality of the Protestant as from any historical or social context nominally involved in their plays.

In many ways the bitterness of religious schism provides the best models and sources for the great Shakespearean emotional storms. We have already seen that Marot's somewhat puritanical view of Venice provides a useful context in which to review *Othello*, and the even more tempestuous sentiments of *Lear* are prefigured in the savage moods of

185

the next generation of sectarian confrontation after Marot. Ronsard's aging fury is actually evoked by his opponents in terms identical to those applied to Lear. The meteorological correspondencies are exploited in a way indicating how closely Shakespeare conforms to Reformist formulas:

> Si la saison permet à cil qui souffre perte
> D'exercer sa cholere à pleine gorge ouverte,
> Oultrager sans propos, maugreer, despiter
> Et sortir hors de soy en voulant s'acquitter,
> On te doibt supporter, Ronsard, et place faire
> Au ver esguillonné qui picque ta cholere,
> Et ne trouver nouveau si ton poulmon rongé
> T'as si tost converty de fol en enragé,
> Veu la perte que fais par la cheute prochaine
> De celle qui nourrist gayement ta bedaine.
>
> (Pineaux 1.191)

(If the season allows him who suffers loss to express his anger with full throat, rage wordlessly, curse, spite, and go out of his mind in seeking self-justification, one must approve of you, Ronsard, and give place to the fanged snake which pricks your rage, and not find it strange if your rotted lung should have changed you so soon from folly to fury, in view of the ruin which you will suffer by the fall of her who has so cheerfully filled your belly.)

* * *

> En l'arriere-saison, qui fait les cheveux gris,
> A saige devenir tu serois mieux apris.
> Tu trompes nostre espoir, et vieillesse qui renge
> Ton corps comm' elle veut ton courage
> ne change. . . .
> A l'encontre du vent tu te prens à combatre.
>
> (Pineaux 1.85–86)

In the wintry fall which makes hair grey, you would be well schooled to become wise. You falsify our hope, and the age

which gnaws your body freely cannot change your courage. . . .
Buffeted by the wind you brace yourself for combat.)

* * *

Il a bien preveu la tempeste,
Neantmoins il a presenté
Aux coups nue sa rase teste,
Tant orgueilleux il a esté:
Fol est celluy qui prevoyant l'orage
Va s'exposer à l'evident naufrage.

(Pineaux II.404)

(He did foresee the storm well, but nevertheless he offered his
shaven head naked to its blows so proud he has been: he is mad
who foreseeing the storm exposes himself to certain wreck.)

The contrast to medieval allegories of Wrath is clear in the intensely
personal and individualized application of the imagery here: controversy narrows the moralist's focus down to single personalities.

Moreover, persecution presented individuals with highly subjective
choices carrying the weight of life or death as their outcome. The exact
evaluation of one's motivations becomes acutely important:

Il faut suivre par tout nostre vocation
Par la vie, et la mort, disette, et abondance,
Par travail, et repos, danger, et asseurance.
Comme c'est couardise à l'homme, d'avoir peur,
Et d'estre surmonté par lascheté de coeur,
Quand il faut endurer la mort tant honnorable,
Pour estre à Dieu Martyr, et tesmoing veritable
C'est aussi pour certain, grande temerité,
D'encourir le tourment où tu n'es invité.

(Pineaux I.87)

(We must always follow our vocation in life and death, in want
and prosperity, in work and rest, danger and safety. Just as it is
overruled by cowardice of heart when such honorable death is
required as to be God's martyr and true witness, it is also certainly
great recklessness to run toward the torment to which you were
not invited.)

187

With satirical deftness Shakespeare assigns unexpectedly similar puritan sentiments to Falstaff, who defends his defiance of the law to the Prince thus: "Why, Hal, 'tis my vocation, Hal. 'Tis no sin for a man to labor in his vocation" (*1HIV* I.ii.98–99). When the Prince advises him to accept honorable death on the battlefield, urging "thou owest God a death," Falstaff deftly picks up the theme of not forcing God's will: " 'Tis not due yet, I would be loath to pay Him before his day. What need I be so forward with him that calls not on me?" (*1HIV* V.i.126–30). Indeed, in his ecclesiastical history, Bourgoing provides a good precedent for Falstaff's notorious maxim: "The better part of valour is discretion, in the which better part I have saved my life" (*1HIV* V.iv.118–19). Bourgoing asserts that the Fathers of the Church "are not of the opinion that anyone should thrust themselves into suffering on their own initiative, or expose themselves to dangers. . . . And he who does not obey them is rash, reckless, and presumptuous, throwing himself heedlessly into manifest danger."[10] By Huguenot principles Falstaff's "discretion" would be highly Christian and Hotspur deeply vicious in his headlong pursuit of honor. Once again a detailed knowledge of Reformation ethics enriches our awareness of the sources and true nature of issues raised by Shakespearean characterization. Falstaff is neither buffoon nor vice but a true reflection of the moral sophistication of the times.

The most important precedent for Shakespeare in the pamphlets attacking Ronsard lies in the evocation of the horrors of civil war. Historians tell us that the Wars of the Roses which Shakespeare displays so horrifically in his *Henry VI* cycle were in fact rather superficial affairs, little more than aristocratic brawls, leaving the economic and cultural development of the country basically undamaged.[11] By contrast the wars in France during Shakespeare's lifetime rose to a climax of mass national brutality in the St. Bartholomew's Day massacre of 24 August 1572, which indelibly impressed the monstrosity of civil strife on the Elizabethan imagination. This outrage left the

10. Pineaux I.87.

11. See for example Charles Ross, *Edward IV* (Berkeley and Los Angeles: University of California Press, 1974), p. 368–70.

reputation of Catherine de' Medici irremediably stained and ensured chronic schism and disorder throughout France until the end of the century. The language and attitudes of French writers contemplating the disorders leading up to and following this appalling event not only afford models for Burgundy's magnificent plea for peace to heal sufferings of France itself at the end of *Henry V* (V.ii.23–67), they are also echoed in comments on the troubles in England under Henry IV. In fact the opening chords of *Henry IV, Part I* are those struck in the *Palinodies,* in which the author (probably Antoine de la Roche-Chandieu) affects the vein of a Ronsard supposedly converted to Lutheranism:

> Las! paouvre France, helas, la superstition
> De l'Antechrist Romaine brise ton union.
> Tes enfants qui devroyent t'engraisser
>   te travaillent,
> Et pour les estrangiers encontre toy bataillent,
> Et comme reprouvez d'un courage meschant,
> Contre ton estomach tournent le fer tranchant.
> N'avions-nous pas assez engressé la campagne
> De Flandres, de Piedmont, de Naples, et
>   d'Espagne
> En nostre propre sang sans tourner les cousteaux
> Contre toy nostre mere et tes propres
>   boyaux? . . .
> Las! faut il (ô bon Dieu) que le sceptre
>   Françoys,
> Que le fier Espagnol, l'Alemand, et l'Angloys
> N'ont jamais sceu dompter, tumbe soubz
>   la puissance
> Des Guysars, qui devroyent luy rendre
>   obeissance?
> Sceptre qui fut jadis tant craint de toutes partz,
> Qui jadis envoya outre mer ses soldartz
> Gagner la Palestine, et toute l'Indumée,
> Tyr, Sydon, Antioche, et la ville nommée

Du saint nom, où Jesus en la croix attaché
De son precieux sang lava nostre peché?
Sceptre qui fut jadis la terreur des barbares.
(Pineaux I.11–12)

(Alas, poor France, alas: the superstition of the Roman Anti-
christ breaks your unity. Your children, who should make you
plump, wear you out and fight for strangers against you and, like
outlaws, with vicious bravado turn the trenchant iron against
your breast. Have we not sufficiently enriched with our blood
the countryside of Flanders, Piedmont, Naples, and Spain without turning the knives against our mother and your own bowels?
. . . Alas! Good God, must the French sceptre, which the proud
Spaniard, the German, and the English have never been able to
tame, fall under the power of the Guysards, who should give it
obedience? Sceptre which was once so feared by all parts, which
once sent overseas soldiers to win Palestine and all Idumea,
Tyre, Sydon, Antioch, and the city bearing the holy name, where
Jesus nailed to the cross washed our sins away with his precious
blood? Sceptre which was once the terror of the barbarian.)

These are the kinds of pious sentiments which Shakespeare's Henry IV
affects in order to distract his subjects from civil war when he is newly
crowned, after contriving the deposition and conniving at the murder
of Richard II. He hopes to still the impending insubordination of the
Percys, a family as potent and contentious as the Guises, by reminding
his countrymen of their "higher" duty to conquer Palestine:

No more the thirsty entrance of this soil
Shall daub her lips with her own children's
   blood:
No more shall trenching war channel her fields,
Nor bruise her flow'rets with the armed
   hoofs. . . .
All of one nature, of one substance bred,
Did lately meet in the intestine shock
And furious close of civil butchery,
Shall now in mutual well-beseeming ranks
March all one way, and be no more opposed. . . .

> The edge of war, like an ill-sheathed knife,
> No more shall cut his master. Therefore, friends.
> As far as to the sepulchre of Christ . . .
> Forthwith a power of English shall we levy,
> Whose arms were moulded in their mother's
>   womb
> To chase those pagans in those holy fields
> Over whose acres walked those blessed feet
> Which fourteen hundred years ago were nailed
> For our advantage on the bitter cross.
>   (1.i.5ff.)

The imagery which Shakespeare shares with Roche-Chandieu applies very well to the French civil wars of religion but very little to the bloodless accession of Henry, which occurred without major warfare, with Parliamentary approval, and by popular consent. Shakespeare is seeing Henry's accession with hindsight through the haze of civic disturbance which came well after his triumph and in the context of horror based on fear of duplication in England of the vicious bigotry of the struggle in France, a bigotry like that which later would also alter German history when it spread to cause the Thirty Years' War. This larger historical context also invites us to make the same admonitory application of Shakespearean imagery to possible English troubles as that made retrospectively by Marvell to the English Civil War. Echoing John of Gaunt's speech in *Richard II* (II.i.31ff.), he asks:

> Oh Thou, that dear and happy Isle
> The Garden of the World ere while,
> Thou Paradise of four Seas,
> Which Heaven planted us to please,
> But, to exclude the World, did guard
> With watry if not flaming Sword;
> What luckless Apple did we tast,
> To make us Mortal, and The Wast?
>   (321–28)[12]

12. Marvell, ed. Margoliouth, vol. 1, p. 69.

Insofar as Shakespeare grafts on to medieval chronicles the sense of monstrousness which was fostered by the French religious wars, we may see that the context of *Henry IV* is not a euphoric nationalism of the kind reflected in Peele's *Edward I.* The author of *Henry IV*, *Richard III*, and *King John* has not a shred of illusion about English virtue. What he is concerned with is not recapitulation of any earlier "glories" but a desperate attempt to keep the bad contemporary omens clearly before the minds of his countrymen. And this fearful admonition surely is a primary concern of his contemporaries' works on France, in cases like Marlowe's *Massacre at Paris* and Chapman's *Bussy d'Ambois* and *Biron.* All these plays share with Montaigne a horror of the kind of egotistical public personality fostered by neoclassical models and the confusions resulting from religious extremism in France.

It is no accident that the theme of disorder so powerfully evoked by Ulysses in his speech in *Troilus and Cressida* (I.iii.75ff.) offers parallels to Burgundy's lament for devastated France at the end of *Henry V* and no less closely matches passages borrowed from Ronsard by his opponents:

> L'artisan par ce monstre a laissé sa boutique,
> Le pasteur ses brebis, l'Advocat sa pratique,
> Sa nef le Marinier, sa foyre le Marchant,
> Et par luy le preud'homme est devenu
> meschant.
> L'escolier se desbauche, et de sa faux tortue,
> Le laboureur faconne une dague pointue. . . .
> Morte est l'authorité, chacun vit à sa guyse,
> Au vice desreglé la license est permise,
> Le desir de blaspheme, et l'erreur insensé
> Ont sans dessus dessous le monde renversé. . . .
> Tout ainsi est la France en armes divisée,
> Depuis que la Raison n'est plus authorisée.
> Mais vous (Royne tressaige) en voyant
> ce discord,
> Pouvez par bon advis mettre le tout d'accord;
> Imitant le pasteur, qui voyant les armées,
> De ses mouches à miel fierement animées. . . .

Se percer, se piquer, se navrer, se tuer. . . .
Retenant des deux camps la fureur à son ayse,
Avec un plaisant son leurs querelles appaise.
Ainsi par bons editz, la seule dignité,
De vos enfants, de vous, de vostre authorité,
Que pour vostre vertu chaque estat vous accorde,
Pourra bien appaiser une telle discorde.

(Pineaux 1.24–26)

(Because of the monster [atheism] the craftsman has left his shop, the shepherd his flock, the lawyer his practice, the sailor his ship, the merchant his market, and by it the noble has become wicked. The student debauches himself and from his curved scythe the laborer makes a pointed dagger. . . . Authority is dead, everyone lives in his own way, license is given to uncontrolled vice; love of blasphemy and insane error have turned the world upside down without top or bottom. . . . Thus all France is divided by war since reason has no longer authority. But you, most wise queen [Catherine], in seeing this discord, can by good advice get all to agree: imitating the keeper who, seeing the armies of bees fiercely active . . . stabbing, stinging, agonizing, and killing themselves . . . holds back the rage of the two armies with ease, with a sweet sound calms their quarrels. So by good edicts, the dignity alone of your children, of yourself, and your authority . . . which every estate grants to your virtue, you will be able to pacify such discord.)

The strange thing about this passage is that the same lines are shared by both sides in the poetic conflict between Ronsard and his Huguenot opponents: the passage appears almost word for word in two ostensibly conflicting poems.[13] The sixteenth century is thus a period in which no one normally spoke up for complete freedom of conscience and individual autonomy. When Shakespeare's Ulysses speaks in favor of order in the community he is not routinely voicing political orthodoxy but expressing the corporate anxieties of all Shakespeare's contemporaries, in terms scarcely differing to those of either of the two parties who were battling in France during most of the century:

13. See Pineaux I. 24, n. 193.

193

The speciality of rule hath been neglected;
And look, how many Grecian tents do stand
Hollow upon this plain, so many hollow
   factions.
When that the general is not like the hive
To whom the foragers shall all repair,
What honey is expected? Degree being
   vizarded,
Th' unworthiest shows as fairly in the mask.
The heavens themselves, the planets, and
   this centre
Observe degree, priority, and place,
Insisture, course, proportion, season, form,
Office, and custom, in all line of order. . . .
   O, when degree is shaked,
Which is the ladder of all high designs,
The enterprise is sick. How could communities,
Degrees in schools and brotherhoods in cities,
Peaceful commerce from dividable shores,
The primogenity and due of birth,
Prerogative of age, crowns, sceptres, laurels,
But by degree, stand in authentic place?
Take but degree away, untune that string,
And hark what discord follows. . . .
Strength should be lord of imbecility,
And the rude son should strike his father dead;
Force should be right, or rather right
   and wrong . . .
Should lose their names, and so should
   justice too.
Then everything includes itself in power,
Power into will, will into appetite. . . .
This chaos, when degree is suffocate,
Follows the choking.

        (i.iii.78ff.)

194

Such shattering of complex Renaissance social structures could not be shown in the far simpler historical setting of the *Iliad* without anachronism, and it certainly did not occur in Elizabethan England—but it was happening under the last Valois kings of France and in the early years of the reign of Henri IV, when the League fought to impose its will on the nation.

Even a Puritan politician like Marvell could share these sentiments after the English Civil War, writing: "The cause was too good to be fought for; men ought to and might have trusted the King."[14] And it is perhaps significant that in describing the genesis of Death near the beginning of *Paradise Lost*, Milton matches the specific devices used by the anonymous French author to describe the genesis of this monster which is destroying France:

> On dit que Lucifer faché contre la race . . .
> Un jour tout depiteux, plein de forcenerie,
> Descendit aux plus creux des enfers, où s'amye
> Dame presomption, ayant ces nuits autour,
> Estoit en son obscur et horrible sejour,
> Elle tost decouvrit qu'il n'estoit à son ayse,
> Et se mit en devoir pour chasser ce malaise:
> Si le vint caresser, et le baisant, soudain
> L'atheisme conceut, peste du genre humain. . . .
> Il estoit si hydeux, et tant farcy d'erreur,
> Que mesme à ses parents il apportoit horreur. . . .
> Puis apres se glissa dedans les grands palais,
> Où la tourbe brouillarde assouvie à jamais
> Ne cesse d'attraper offices et chevance:
> Voyla ce qu'a permis Dieu par sa providence,
> Afin de les punir d'estre trop curieux,
> Et vouloir escheller comme Geants les cieux.
>   (Pineaux 1.21–23)

(They say that Lucifer, angry with the race . . . one day, all spite, full of frenzy, descended to the deepest hells where his love, Lady

14. Andrew Marvell, *The Rehearsal Transpros'd*, ed. D. I. B. Smith (Oxford: Clarendon Press, 1971), p. 135.

Pride, having these nights around, was in her dark and horrible setting. She quickly perceived that he was ill at ease and did her duty to dissipate this melancholy: so she began to caress him, and kissing him, suddenly conceived Atheism, plague of human kind. . . . He was so hideous and so full of error that he even gave horror to his parents. . . . Then afterwards he slid into great palaces where the glutted, foggy crowd never fails to catch at offices and goods: there is what God has permitted by his providence, so as to punish them for being too curious and for wishing to scale the heavens like the Titans.)

Satan's love affair with Sin in *Paradise Lost* (II.746ff.) produces an analogous monster, Death, who also provokes his father (Satan) against himself, the son of this incestuous union—and after her Minerva-like birth from Satin's brain in heaven Sin and her offspring are sunk like Satan to deepest hell. Yet both poets recognize the enigmatic ways of God in allowing such forces to escape and roam freely in the world:

> the will
> And high permission of all-ruling Heaven
> Left him at large to his own dark designs,
> That with reiterated crimes he might
> Heap on himself damnation.
>
> (1.211–15)

Clearly the allegories and interpretations of such Huguenot poets afford important precedents for parts of Spenser's and Milton's more artificially ambitious enterprises, but in fact the Huguenots' techniques were firmly based on the poet whom they were attacking, for such mythological passages are largely plagiarized, or at least modelled on, episodes in Ronsard, like the one in "Discours des Miseres de ce Temps" (127ff.), which itself may have inspired such English poets directly.

Above all it is in their authors' intensely subjective relationship to the divine will that the Huguenot polemicists lead the way for Milton. No doubt Milton's sonnet on his blindness is one of his most personal and moving:

> When I consider how my light is spent,
> Ere half my days, in this dark world and wide,

And that one Talent which is death to hide,
Lodg'd with me useless, though my Soul
      more bent
To serve therewith my Maker, and present
My true account, lest he returning chide;
"Doth God exact day-labor, light denied,"
I fondly ask; But patience to prevent
That murmur, soon replies, "God doth
      not need
Either man's work or his own gifts; who best
Bear his mild yoke, they serve him best;
      his State
Is Kingly. Thousands at his bidding speed
And post o'er Land and Ocean without rest:
They also serve who only stand and wait.[15]

Here the classic Puritan compulsion to effort is dextrously balanced against the Reformation's sense of the overpowering might of the Divinity, able at any moment to reverse obligation and legal penalties for the good of the individual. Nothing so elegant and complex can be found in the Huguenot poets, but the raw materials certainly can, as in a challenge made by la Roche-Chandieu to French poets in general and to Ronsard in particular:

Race du Souverain, que les haults cieux
      cherissent,
Et d'un tresor caché douent et enrichissent, . . .
Vous, ô Poëtes saincts, de qui le vers chanté
N'ha pour son argument que vertu et bonté, . . .
Ne cognoissez vous pas quelle est la violence
Du mal qui est couverte sous l'ombre du
      silence? . . .
Voila enquoy reluit le beau lustre du sage,
Qu'en usant bien du bien, l'applique à
      son usage. . . .
Ainsi quand les meschants tiennent enseveli

15. Milton, p. 168.

Le bien receu de Dieu, sous leur ingrat oubli, . . .
Tu sçaurois que des grands l'affection contraire,
Sans le congé de Dieu ne peut jamais
      rien faire. . . .
Ainsi que l'oeil du Ciel à l'heure qu'il nous luit,
Est semblable à obscur de quelque aveulge
      nuict, . . .
Tu sçaurois que de Dieu le service ne pend
A l'inconstant vouloir de celuy qui
      est grand. . . .
Tu tremblerois voyant tant de Romains Tyrans
Jetter les saincts en proye aus glaives devorans.
          (Pineaux 1.33–34)

(Chosen of God, whom the high heavens cherish and endow and enrich with a hidden treasure. . . . You holy poets whose chanted verse has for its theme only virtue and goodness. . . . Do you not understand the violence of evil which is covered by the shade of silence? . . . There is wherein shines the fine light of the wise, who, in using well what is good, fit it to its purpose. . . . While the wicked keep buried the good received of God beneath their ungrateful forgetfulness. . . . You know that the hostile wishes of the great can achieve nothing without the permission of God. . . . Just as the sun in heaven at the hour when it shines on us is like the darkness of some blind night. . . . You would know that the service of God does not depend on the inconsistent will of him who is great. . . . You would tremble seeing so many Roman tyrants throw the saints as prey to the devouring swords.)

Ronsard was stung by this attack on him because, as he paraphrased it, he "cachoit son talent dedans terre" (hid his talent in the earth [II. 571]). But he defends himself by arguing that he can ignore such challenges because "Dieu . . . sonde seul ma pensée" (God alone judges my thought). What is curious about the juxtaposition is to note that Milton's sonnet takes up the defensive position which is required of someone like Ronsard after this attack on his inertia by the Protestants. Their attacking role affords less opportunity for vivid self-definition, and it is revealing that, in the French literary battle, Ronsard's range of poems justifying himself proved of permanent poetic distinction, while his attackers now appeal mostly to antiquarian interests.

Similarly, we find "Lycidas" superior in poetic worth to these polemics against Ronsard precisely because it is basically geared to the author's search for his own identity and motivations, even while sharing many of the formal devices and ideas of the French polemicists. They had advised Ronsard contemptuously to revert to his amatory self-indulgence instead of concerning himself with political issues beyond his capacity:

> D'estre loué de tous il n'est pas desirable, . . .
> Non, ce n'est pas à toy de parler des miseres . . .
> Certes il valloit mieus rechanter ta Cassandre,
> Et remettre en papier les Pergames en cendre,
> Remaschant le laurier, que mettre par escrit
> Le discours de ce temps qui passe ton esprit.
> Il valloit mieus encor' remonter sur la croppe
> De Parnasse, et chanter les yeus de ta Sinope.
>
> (Pineaux II.390)

(To be praised by all is not desirable. . . . No, it is not for you to speak of sufferings. . . . Certainly it was better to sing again of your Cassandra and set on paper again the ashes of Pergamus, rechewing the laurel leaf, rather than setting down in writing discussions of this time which exceed your intelligence. It was better still to reclimb to the crest of Parnassus and sing of your Sinope's eyes.)

Again this is the kind of challenge which Milton treats defensively as an issue bearing on his own identity and career as a serious poet rather than as an accusation to be made against the more secular poets:

> Alas! What boots it with uncessant care
> To tend the homely slighted Shepherd's trade,
> And strictly meditate the thankless Muse?
> Were it not better done as others use

199

To sport with Amaryllis in the shade,
   Or with the tangles of Neaera's hair?
   Fame is the spur that the clear spirit doth raise,
   (That last infirmity of Noble mind).
                          (63–70)[16]

For all the poem's puritan, anti-establishment slant, it is Milton's
self-concern which these questions address and which unifies the poem,
for even the famous denunciations attributed to St. Peter acquire intensity from Milton's own angry sense of alienation from his intended
clerical career. However, this passage also conforms on the surface to
the models ironically afforded by both sides of the quarrel between
Ronsard and the Huguenots, for Ronsard does recognize the corruption of the clergy, and his lines are very closely followed in the Huguenot passages invoking biblical figures to indict the present corruption
of the Church:

                               de toute part
    Le revenue du paouvre au meschant se depart.
    Dont ne faut s'estonner (Chrestiens) si
            leur nacelle
    (Qu'ils mentent) de saint Pierre, ainsi par
            toute chancelle:
    Puis que les ignorans, les enfants de deux ans,
    Je ne sçay quels muguetz, je ne sçay quels
            plaisans
    Tiennent le gouvernail: Puis que les benefices
    Se vendent par argent, ainsi que les offices.
    Mais que diroit saint Paul, si'il revenoit icy,
    De ces jeunes prelatz qui n'ont point de soucy
    De leurs paouvres troupeaux? dont ils tirent
            la laine,
    La chair, sang et le cuyr, qui tous vivent sans
            peine. . . .
    Sans precher, sans prier, sons bon example d'eux.
                     (Pineaux 1.9–10)

16. Milton, p. 123.

(Everywhere revenue flows from the poor to the wicked, wherefore it should not surprise you, Christians, if their boat which they
lyingly derive from Saint Peter thus rocks every way. For the
ignorant, two-year-old children, some strange birds, and unknown jesters are the steersmen, because benefices are sold for
cash and so are official posts. But what would Saint Paul say if
he were to return here, of these youthful prelates who have no
care for their poor flocks? Of which they take the wool, the
flesh, blood, and hide, and all live comfortably themselves . . .
without preaching, without prayer, without themselves setting a
good example.)

While Milton uses almost identical material, he avoids the complacency of making these accusations in his own person. By dramatizing
the reactions of a returning saint such as those who are merely mentioned rhetorically in the French versions, Milton's "Lycidas" achieves
greater authority and objectivity than if he attacked the Church himself and thus exposed his own pretensions to censure:

> Last came, and last did go,
> The Pilot of the Galilean lake. . . .
> He shook his Mitred locks, and stern bespake:
> "How well could I have spar'd for thee,
>   young swain,
> Enough of such as for their bellies' sake,
> Creep and intrude and climb into the fold?
> Of other care they little reck'ning make,
> Than how to scramble at the shearers' feast,
> And shove away the worthy bidden quest;
> Blind mouths! that scarce themselves know
>   how to hold
> A Sheep-hook, or have learn'd aught else
>   the least,
> That to the faithful Herdsman's art belongs!
> What recks it them? What need they? They
>   are sped;
> And when they list, their lean and flashy songs

Grate on their scrannel Pipes of wretched straw.
The hungry Sheep look up, and are not fed."
$$(108-9, 112-25)^{17}$$

One is conscious of the same issues as the Huguenot poem's (and Ronsard's), but treated with an enormous increase in sophistication of manner and perspective. Milton is more deeply concerned with himself and yet continually exploits devices to distance himself from the surface texture and sentiments of his verse. The two attributes are surely related: the deepening of self-awareness requires the masks of the pastoral role and the dramatic speeches by alternative personae if the verse is to avoid stridency and the appearance of being a mere private resentment.

Most of the juxtapositions of this kind confirm the superior objectivity of tone of Milton's verse, which (unlike most of his polemical prose) seems always to rise to a kind of ritual authority even when dealing with the most disturbing subjects. Take the theme of vengeance for religious massacre; Ronsard's personal anger allows him to address his deity with aggressive imperiousness:

O Seigneur tout-puissant, qui as tousjours esté
Vers toutes nations plein de toute bonté,
Dequoy te sert là-haut le trait de ton tonnerre,
Si d'un esclat de feu tu n'en brusles la terre?
Es-tu dedans un throsne assis sans faire rien?
$$(\text{II}.573)^{18}$$

(O omnipotent Lord, who has always been full of bounty for all nations, what use is the dart of your thunder if you do not burn the earth with a flash of fire? Are you sitting on a throne doing nothing?)

This almost contemptuous call for violent reaction contrasts with the subtler, less dramatic approach of the Huguenots:

Mais quant aux temples saints, au Seigneur
consacrez,

17. Milton, p. 123.
18. Pierre de Ronsard, *Oeuvres complètes*, ed. Gustave Cohen (Paris: Gallimard, 1950), p. 573. All further references to Ronsard relate to this Pléiade edition.

Qui sont ceux qui les ont pillez et massacrez?
Qui ha commis, di moy, les lasches brigandages?
Brisé du Dieu vivant les vivantes images?
Qui ha lancé le feu, le feu di-je au millieu
De la maison, du temple, et l'Eglise de Dieu?
Tu ne peut pas nier, que le peuple fidele
(Qui est de l'Eternel son Eglise eternelle)
N'ait laschement esté par vos boureaux Prelats
Pillé, brullé, meurdri, estranglé de leur laz.
Le sang en est encor tout bouillant es bouteilles
Du juge souverain, dont les gouttes vermeilles
Luy crient la vengeance. O Dieu plein
      d'equitté
Venge le sang de ceux qui (de ta verité,
En tous endrois, portans bon et seur
      tesmoinage)
Ont esté des Tyrans faitz l'injuste carnage.
Mais venons maintenant descouvrir de Ronsard
La grande hypocrisie. . . .

              (Pineaux II.429)

(But as for holy temples consecrated to the Lord, who are those who have pillaged and massacred them? Tell me who has committed cowardly robbery? Broken the living statues of the living God? Who has spread fire, fire I say, in the middle of the house, of the temple, and of the church of God? You cannot deny that the faithful people who are the eternal Church of the eternal God have not been, by your prelatic executioners, in cowardly fashion pillaged, burned, murdered, and strangled by their cords. Their blood is still boiling in the phials of the sovereign judge, and its scarlet drops cry out to him for vengeance. O God full of justice, avenge the blood of those who (of your truth in every place bearing good and sure testimony) have been made the unjust carnage of tyrants. But let us now come to the discovery of Ronsard's great hypocrisy. . . .)

The argument is that, while Huguenots have only destroyed "graven images" from church walls, the Catholics have destroyed God's living image and living church by murdering Protestants. It is a powerful thrust, brushing aside mere poetic technique and assertion of private personality. But for all that, there is a partisan violence of attitude here which is almost as frightening as the issue itself, and this vehemence produces a stumbling, fragmenting, and repetitive manner which interferes with our clear recognition of the point of the argument, even if "these accents still move us."[19]

At first sight Milton seems merely to echo the effect of the French poets in his sonnet "On the Late Massacre in Piemont":

> Avenge, O Lord, thy slaughter'd Saints, whose
> bones
> Lie scattered on the Alpine mountains cold,
> Ev'n them who kept thy truth so pure of old
> When all our Fathers worship't Stocks and Stones,
> Forget not: in thy book record their groans
> Who were thy Sheep and in their ancient Fold
> Slain by the bloody Piemontese that roll'd
> Mother with Infant down the Rocks. Their moans
> The Vales redoubl'd to the Hills, and they
> To Heav'n. Their martyr'd blood and ashes sow
> O'er all th' Italian fields where still doth sway
> The triple Tyrant; that from these may grow
> A hundredfold, who having learnt thy way
> Early may fly the Babylonian woe.[20]

Most of the rhetorical effects here are shared by both poets. However, Milton is more exact in his evidence and references, more modest in his own context ("When all our Fathers worship't Stocks and Stones"), and subtler in his specification of penalties. He recognizes that (short of death and total genocide) orthodox persecution often defines and strengthens opposition in individuals and communities. Indeed repression usually proves the catalyst to decisive action by its victims.

Both the Huguenots and Milton are able to recognize this paradox, that evil is a catalyst of good, but it is often claimed that this positive note is not sounded enough by Milton in *Paradise Lost* and that there-

19. Pineaux, Introduction, I. xvii.   20. Milton, pp. 167–68.

fore it fails to achieve the residual affirmative impression which must be its goal. Certainly most Protestants belie their own doctrine of human fallibility if they express too much surprise at hostility, persecution, and their failure to achieve the New Jerusalem on earth. Moreover, the doctrine of Original Sin does not merely apply to one's opponents but also to oneself, so that excessive self-righteousness and contempt for others' failings may reflect adversely on one's own mental condition and serve to vindicate the virtues of an opponent. This is very much what the Huguenot poets accomplished in their more strident attacks on Ronsard.

Even their turns of phrase come curiously close to reversing the ostensible censure that is sought, for the allusions and motives suggest heroic insights:

> tu t'enrolle'
> Au nombre de Thamyre et d'Homere, et
>   de toy
> Miserable Everide, à qui la dure loy
> De la sage Deesse emporta la lumiere
> De ses yeux trop voyants sans que la
>   pouvre mere
> Compaigne de Pallas, Chariclo, peust devant
> Detourner le destin aus yeus de son enfant....
> Aussi tu pourrois bien avoir perdu l'ouye,
> Pour avoir à ton dam nostre doctrine ouye,
> Que Verité Deesse enfant de l'Eternel
> Ne communique pas à tout homme mortel.
>   (Pineaux II.356–58)

(You enroll yourself in the number of Thamyris, and of Homer, and of you, unhappy [Tiresias] son of Everes, from whom the severe law of the wise goddess Pallas Athena carried away the light of your eyes which saw too much without your poor mother Chariclo, companion of Pallas, being able to deflect destiny from the eyes of her child. . . . So you [Ronsard] could well have lost your hearing from having to your cost heard our doctrine which the goddess Truth, child of the eternal, does not communicate to all mortal men.)

Though the allusions to classical figures are turned deftly to the advantage of Protestanism, they scarcely discredit Ronsard and involuntarily reaffirm his own proud comparisons. Indeed the verses afford some precedent for one of Milton's most famous passages: the invocation of celestial light at the start of Book III of *Paradise Lost*. In his blindness Milton also remembers Thamyris, Homer, and Tiresias:

> Those other two equall'd with me in Fate,
> So were I equall'd with them in renown,
> Blind Thamyris and blind Maeonides,
> And Tiresias and Phineus Prophets old.
>   (III.33–36)

And matching the Protestant argument that such victims may have had compensatory experience of higher reality, the blind Milton prays:

> So much the rather thou Celestial light
> Shine inward, and the mind through all
>   her powers
> Irradiate, there plant eyes.
>   (III.51–53)

Here we have a striking illustration of how a theory of compensation would operate in favor of those who suffer adversity in either physical or social terms. It is not sufficient simply to say that great poets transcend adversity which happens to befall them. Adversity is either the cause, symptom, or result of their achievement and therefore an intrinsic part of the experience both for them and for us, if we wish to understand its artistic consequences fully.[21]

The Protestant attacks on Ronsard are an ideal illustration of this generative power of adversity. The effects of the religious debate on Ronsard's verse are marked, as "Ronsard was very closely associated with the propagation of Royal policies at this period . . . when he was called on to serve the government, and to transmit a message formu-

21. For a fuller application of this argument see "The Uses of Adversity" in Hugh M. Richmond, *The Christian Revolutionary: John Milton* (Berkeley and Los Angeles: University of California Press, 1974), pp. 122–54.

lated by others . . . the poet painter being replaced by the poet-orator.
. . . Gone are the *copia* of poetic efforts. . . . Instead we find a richness
of *invention* in the rhetorical sense, the amassing of a series of arguments in favour of a policy or attitude. . . . Ronsard is aware that he
is presenting a case not creating an image."[22] The impact of Calvinism
was also profound on many of Ronsard's friends, some of whom became
Calvinists, including Odet de Coligny, Jacques Grevin, and Loïs des
Masures,[23] while Ronsard himself confesses to "tasting" that doctrine
"when I was young" in the *Remonstrance au Peuple de France* (II.
578). In confronting the Calvinists Ronsard found he had to use their
weapons of simplicity, common speech, and unpretentious devotion to
the Biblical message. While expounding Catherine de' Medici's Galli-
canism, Ronsard concedes many points to those who sought ecclesiastical reform, and he freely criticizes the clergy and the papacy. But in his
great poems on religious issues he transcends the role of political advocate, and this gives unique interest to his two *Discours a la Royne*, his
Remonstrance, and the *Response aux injures*: "In the *Discours* cycle the
exposition of government attitudes is absorbed into a much more personal expression of feeling. Appeals to national unity, exposition of
Gallican policy, support for the queen mother, are channelled into the
poet's irrepressible urge to express his own fervent emotions—grief,
anger, hope, despair. The persona of the poet in these comparisons is
that of Pierre de Ronsard, ordinary Frenchman and patriot, not the
poet claiming divine inspiration, nor the spokesman granted an official
status. . . . The first person singular is omnipresent. . . . The use of
direct speech . . . gives Ronsard the framework within which to create
verse of unequalled fluidity and almost conversational ease."[24]

In many ways the *Response aux injures* is the climax and epitome
of this series, which has correctly been called "by far the most successful group of public poems composed by Ronsard" because of "the
mastery he shows of a popular, accessible verse form."[25] In the sequence Ronsard triumphantly meets the various challenges to his in-

22. Francis M. Higman, "Ronsard's Political and Polemical Poetry," in *Ronsard the Poet*, ed. Terence Cave (London: Methuen, 1973), pp. 248, 252.
23. Higman, p. 257.   24. Higman, p. 265.   25. Higman, p. 268.

tegrity, as a man, as a poet, and as a Christian, which had been levelled by a series of Calvinist assaults in verse and prose. Yet without the challenges Ronsard would hardly have formulated his own point of view with such force and precision. He sees himself as St. Paul's Christian gladiator: "Laborieux athlete et poudreux d'exercise" (toiling athlete, dusty with action [II.595]), like Milton's "warfaring Christian" who wins his laurels "not without dust and heat."[26] Ronsard's poise is nonchalant, and he sidesteps his naive opponent's cruder slashes with practiced ease: he asserts that his misfortune of deafness is no divine penalty but a badge of honor like the blindness of Thamyris, Tiresias, and Homer (II.600) and that the accusation of suffering from venereal disease merely shows the critic's own preoccupation (II.601). Ronsard parries the charge of being aged with Falstaffian complacency in his youthful physique (II.601), and he is almost as content that "chacun trouve a diviser de moy" (everyone finds how to be clever against me [II.608]) as Shakespeare's fat knight is that he is "not only witty in myself but the cause that wit is in other men" (2HIV I.ii.10–12). Indeed it is curious to note how Falstaff, affecting the puritan cant of persecution by the authorities, displays many of the same subtle techniques of self-vindication as Ronsard's poem. When Falstaff is censured by the Lord Chief Justice for being aged and having a cracked voice, he responds, "I was born about three of the clock in the afternoon, with a white head and something of a round belly. For my voice, I have lost it with hallooing and singing of anthems" (2HIV I.ii.177–80). If Ronsard firmly rejects the charge of being fat, he does admit "j'ay mauvaise vois" (I have a bad voice [II.608]), but asserts that "depuis le matin jusqu' au retour du soir / Nous chantons au Seigneur loüanges et cantiques" (from dawn until the return of evening we sing praises and hymns to the Lord). In many ways the liveliness of Ronsard's self-defense makes clear how much of Oldcastle-Falstaff's evasive wit is associated with his expertise in parrying malicious attacks on his character generated by his original lollardry, a situation given an authentic vividness by Shakespeare's borrowing of motifs from contemporary Reformation controversy, like those involving Marot and Ronsard. For example, Poins charges Falstaff with eating meat on Friday (1HIV

26. Milton, p. 728.

I.ii.127–29), a familiar accusation against heretics in sixteenth-century France, as we saw that Marot found to his cost.[27]

It is ironic that Protestant attacks on Ronsard generated in him something of the lively language and spontaneous self-awareness which orthodox persecutions had precipitated in many Huguenots and their sympathizers like Marot. But it is not the mere evading of crude insult that elevates Ronsard's *Response* to great verse, rather it is the poet's power to crystallize a vivid persona and ideology which carries conviction and attracts sympathy. One of the passages which has earned general approbation for its success in these terms in his "beautifully naive timetable of his day, in simple, unadorned language.":[28]

> Tu te plains d'autre part que ma vie est lascive,
> En delices, en jeux, en vices excessive;
> Tu mens meschantement : si tu m'avois suivy
> Deux mois, tu sçaurois bien en quel estat je vy;
> Or je veux que ma vie en escrit apparoisse,
> Afin que pour menteur un chacun te cognoisse.
> M'esveillant au matin, devant que faire rien
> J'invoque l'Eternel, le pere de tout bien,
> Le priant humblement de me donner sa grace
> Et que le jour naissant sans l'offenser se passe;
> Qu'il chasse toute secte et toute erreur de moy,
> Qu'il me vueille garder en ma premiere foy,
> Sans entreprendre rien qui blesse ma province,
> Tres-humble observateur des loix et de mon
>   Prince.
> Apres je sors du lict, et quand je suis vestu,
> Je me range à l'estude et apprens la vertu,
> Composant et lisant suivant ma destinée
> Qui s'est dés mon enfance aux Muses enclinée;
> Quatre ou cinq heures seul je m'arreste
>   enfermé;

27. For further discussion of this parallelism see Richmond, "Personal Identity and Literary Personae."

28. Higman, p. 271.

Puis, sentant mon esprit de trop lire assommé,
J'abandonne le livre et m'en vais à l'eglise;
Au retour, pour plaiser, une heure je devise;
De là je viens disner, faisant sobre repas,
Je rends graces à Dieu; au reste je m'esbas.
Car, si l'apres-disnée est plaisante et sereine,
Je m'en vais promener tantost parmy la plaine,
Tantost en un village, et tantost en un bois,
Et tantost par les lieux solitaires et cois:
J'aime fort les jardins qui sentent le sauvage,
J'aime le flot de l'eau qui gazouille au rivage.
Là, devisant sur l'herbe avec un mien amy,
Je me suis par les fleurs bien souvent endormy
A l'ombrage d'un saule, ou, lisant dans un
      livre,
J'ay cherché le moyen de me faire revivre,
Tout pur d'ambition et des soucis cuisans.

(II.606–7)

(You complain moreover that my life is licentious, overburdened with luxury, sport, and vices. You lie maliciously; if you had followed me for two months you would know well the state of my life, and now I intend to spell it out for you, so that everyone will know you are a liar. When I wake each morning, before I do anything, I say a prayer to the Eternal Father of all good, praying him humbly to give me his grace and that the day which is dawning should pass without offending him, that he expel all bigotry and all error from me, that he should seek to keep me in my pristine faith without undertaking anything which harms my native land, observing very modestly the laws of my prince. Then I get out of bed, and when I am clothed I devote myself to study and learn virtue, writing and reading as my vocation requires, which has been inclined to the Muses since my childhood. I stay closeted for four or five hours; then when too much reading wearies my spirit, I drop my book and go to the church. Returning I devote an hour to recreation, then dine soberly, saying grace; for the rest of the day I relax, for if the afternoon is fine and calm I go for a long walk now through the fields, then

in a village, or in a wood, or sometimes in truly lonely and obscure spots: I greatly love gardens that verge on wildernesses, I
love the rippling streams that brush their banks gently. There,
discussing on the grass with a friend, I often allow the flowers to
lull me to sleep in the shade of a willow, or browsing in a book
I strive to find means to restore my life free of ambition and
piercing anxieties.)

The evolution of tone in the extract is remarkable—from resentment
Ronsard rises swiftly to a prayerful repudiation of narrow sectarianism,
which is subtly transcended by the peacefulness of the diurnal rhythm
he evokes. The speciousness of the religiosity is redeemed by the authenticity of the poet's evocation of his innocent love of the unspoiled
countryside, which has made one of these lines the epitome of western
taste in horticulture, if not in landscape more generally.[29] One might
argue that our whole European view of nature is summed up in the
delicate balance of cultivation and spontaneity savored in the line:
"J'aime fort les jardins qui sentent le sauvage." It is this deeper resonance which is missing in the youthful Milton's duplication of Ronsard's self-defense against moral detraction; the self-congratulatory
technique is similar, but the self-discovery is minimal in Milton's account of his daily routine: "Up and stirring, in winter often ere the
sound of any bell awake men to labor, or to devotion; in summer as oft
with the bird that first rouses, or not much tardier, to read good authors,
or cause them to be read, till the attention be weary or memory have
its full fraught: then, with useful and generous labors preserving the
body's health and hardiness."[30]

If Milton's prose were all that could be compared to Ronsard's verse
we would have to recognize that his opponents had failed to precipitate
the same self-awareness as those of Ronsard. But the challenge of much
deeper threats, of ostracism and even execution after the Restoration,
creates in the persona of the narrator of *Paradise Lost* a power of self-
projection which is quite beyond Ronsard's relatively innocent values.

29. For a detailed discussion of this tradition, see Hugh M. Richmond, *Renaissance Landscapes: English Lyrics in a European Tradition* (Hague: Mouton, 1973),
pp. 55–129.
30. Milton, p. 691.

Nevertheless, we must recognize in Milton's magnificent prelude to Book III of *Paradise Lost* the natural evolution of that pattern of self-vindication in misfortune which we have seen as the necessary consequence of sectarian controversy such as Ronsard triumphed over in his *Response*:

> Hail holy Light, offspring of Heav'n
>   first-born . . .
> Thee I revisit now with bolder wing, . . .
> Taught by the heav'nly Muse to venture down
> The dark descent, and up to reascend,
> Though hard and rare: thee I revisit safe
> And feel thy sovran vital Lamp; but thou
> Revisit'st not these eyes, that roll in vain
> To find thy piercing ray, and find no dawn;
> So thick a drop serene hath quencht thir Orbs,
> Or dim suffusion veil'd. Yet not the more
> Cease I to wander where the Muses haunt
> Clear Spring, or shady Grove or Sunny Hill
> Smit with the love of sacred Song; but chief
> Thee Sion and the flow'ry Brooks beneath
> That wash thy hallow'd feet, and
>   warbling flow,
> Nightly I visit: nor sometimes forget
> Those other two equall'd with me in Fate,
> So were I equall'd with them in renown
> Blind Thamyris and blind Maeonides,
> And Tiresias and Phineus Prophets old. . . .
> Seasons return, but not to me returns
> Day, or the sweet approach of Ev'n or Morn . . .
> But cloud instead, and ever-during dark
> Surrounds me, from the cheerful ways of men
> Cut off, and for the Book of Knowledge fair
> Presented with a Universal blanc. . . .
> So much the rather thou Celestial Light

Shine inward, and the mind through all
      her powers
Irradiate, there plant eyes, all mist from thence
Purge and disperse, that I may see and tell
Of things invisible to mortal sight.

(III.1ff.)

If Ronsard illustrates the creative power of self-vindication, Milton evokes the principle of creative compensation itself. A hundred years of theological controversy have given system and structure to what was once honorable but still naive self-assertion.

This is not to diminish the scale of Ronsard's achievement, for in formulating a plausible identity and point of view under the pressure of circumstances Ronsard defined the core of modern personality and provided the aesthetic to frame it. We must be careful to avoid two mistakes which might confuse and diminish the value of this achievement—to assume either that Ronsard was a static Euclidean entity or that all his views and the works reflecting them are of equal interest and relevance to modern concerns. The period was after all one in which the Reformation restored psychological discontinuity as a proper approach to the human mind's propensity to failure and potentiality for unpredictable grace. In an assault on Ronsard entitled significantly "Conversion de Pierre de Ronsard," probably by Joachim du Chalard, the Protestants had offered Marot as a model for Ronsard's own mutation:

Marot fut bien en ses ans fort lascif
Voluptueux, en plaisirs excessif
Plus inconstant qu'arondelle qui volle:
Mais devestu de sa jeunesse folle
Aquant les ans repurgé son cerveau,
Il vint ainsy qu'un homme faict nouveau,
Laissant virlaiz, rondeaux, chansons lascives
Pour rechanter hymnes et chansons vives
Au hault Seigneur.

(Pineaux II.509)

213

(Marot was certainly in his time very lascivious, voluptuous, excessive in pleasure, more inconstant than the swallows in flight; but stripped of his mad youth, the years having purged his brain again, he became thus a new-made man, leaving virilais, rondeaux, and lascivious songs to re-sing hymns and living songs to the high Lord.)

Such an evolution actually occurred in Ronsard as a result of "the outbreak of the wars of religion in 1562, with the bitter polemic into which Ronsard was drawn, which marks the collapse of Ronsard's enthusiastic optimism."[31] In this experience Marot's reaction to the defeat of François at Pavia is a precedent:

> Ainsi diront leurs Victoires apertes,
> Et nous dirons nos malheureuses pertes.
> Les dire (helas) il vaut mieulx les taire!
> Il vaut trop mieulx en ung lieu solitaire,
> En Champs ou Boys pleins d'Arbres et de fleurs
> Aller dicter les plaisirs ou les pleurs
> Que l'on reçoit de sa Dame cherie;
> Puis, pour oster hors du cueur fascherie,
> Voller en Plaine, et chasser en Forest,
> Descoupler Chiens, tendre Toilles et Rhetz;
> Aulcunesfois, apres les longues Courses,
> Se venir seoir pres des Ruisseaux et Sources
> Et s'endormir au son de l'eau qui bruyt,
> Ou escouter la Musique et le bruyt
> Des Oyselletz painctz de couleurs estranges, . . .
> En ce plaisir le Temps nous passerons;
> Et n'en sera (ce croy je) offensé Dieu
> Puis que la Guerre a l'Amour donne lieu.
> *(Lyriques* LII.107–21, 124–26)

(Thus they will tell of their manifest victories and we of our sad losses. Tell them, alas!—it is better in a lonely spot, in fields or woods full of trees and flowers to go and speak of the pleasures

31. A. H. T. Levi, "The Role of Neoplatonism in Ronsard's Poetic Imagination," in Cave, pp. 134–35.

or the tears which one receives of one's beloved lady, then to clear
the heart of trouble to fly over the plain and hunt in the forest,
unleashing dogs and spreading nets and traps, sometimes after
long chases come to sit by brooks and springs and to sleep to the
sound of the water's murmur or listen to the music and sound
of birds painted in strange colors. . . . In this pleasure time will
pass us by and God will not, I believe, be offended by this since
war is replaced by love.)

The theme recurs in Marot's famous third eclogue, "by Marot to the
King under the names of Pan and Robin," where the aging Marot, ruefully "couché sur l'herb à la frescheur du vent" (lying on the grass in
the coolness of the wind), reviews his past failures and uncertain future.[32] Ronsard picked up the phrases here and Marot's reference to
"ma musette oysive" in his delightful ode to the Bellerie fountain on
whose bank he lies "Couché . . . osif à la fraischeur du vent" (I.498).

We must recognize that for many modern readers what gives current interest to the verse reflecting Ronsard's complex personality is
only a part of his extraordinarily diversified work. Much of the historical significance of his reform of French language and verse, above
all his neoclassicism, and his conventional amatory and court verse will
not reward non-scholarly tastes so much as the more authentic and personal verse, which the mood of revulsion from current affairs in part
encouraged him to write. If Marot's visions of rural retreat are fairly
conventional, Ronsard's are not: they reflect a recurrent return to sources
and instincts antecedent in his experience to the classical precedent
which authorized them. Ronsard is at his most interesting when he
rejects the specious coherence and stilted decorum which his Huguenot
critics preferred:

> Tu te mocques, cafart, dequoy ma Poësie
> Ne suit l'art miserable, ains va par fantaisie,
> Et dequoy ma fureur sans ordre se suivant
> Esparpille ses vers comme fueilles au vent: . . .
> Si tu avois les yeux aussi prompts et ouvers
> A desrober mon art qu'à desrober mes vers,

32. See Richmond, *Renaissance Landscapes,* pp. 55 ff.

Tu dirois que ma Muse est pleine d'artifice,
Et ma brusque vertu ne te seroit un vice.
En l'art de Poësie un art il ne faut pas
Tel qu'ont les predicans, qui suivent pas à pas
Leur sermon sceu par coeur, ou tel qu'il faut
        en prose,
Où tousjours l'orateur suit le fil d'une chose.
Les Poëtes gaillars ont artifice à part,
Ils ont un art caché qui ne semble pas art
Aux versificateurs, d'autant qu'il se promeine
D'une libre contrainte ou la Muse le meine.
                    (II.613–14)

(You mock, you humbug, at my poetry for not following a pathetic conventionality, but going by intuition, and at my inspiration for proceeding without sequence, scattering its verses like leaves in the wind. . . . If you had eyes as quick and open to steal my art as to steal my verses, you would say that my Muse is full of skill, and my blunt virtue would not be a vice to you. In the art of poetry there is no need of the art of preachers who plod through their memorized sermon point by point, or as is needed in prose, where the orator always follows the line of an argument. Lively poets have their own skill; they have a concealed art which does not seem art to versifiers, insofar as they stroll free of constraint as the muse leads them.)

This is no casual debating point, for Ronsard makes it again in prose in the preface to the reader of his *Odes* (1550): "I am of this opinion that no poetry should be praised for accomplished if it does not resemble nature, which was not held beautiful by the ancients unless it was uneven and varied in its perfection" (II.973).

This aesthetic is developed at length in the opening of the "Discours a Loys des Masures":

Comme celuy qui voit du faut d'une fenestre
Alentour de ses yeux une plaine champestre,
Differente de lieu, de forme et de façon:
Ici une riviere, un rocher, un buisson

Se presente à ses yeux, et là s'y represente
Un tertre, une prairie, un taillis, une sente,
Un verger, une vigne, un jardin bien dressé,
Un hallier, une espine, un chardon herissé,
Et la part que son oeil vagabond se transporte,
Il descouvre un païs de differente sorte,
De bon et de mauvais: Des Masures ainsi,
Celuy qui lit les vers que j'ay portraits ici,
Regarde d'un trait d'oeil mainte diverse chose,
Qui bonne, qui mauvaise, en mon papier
        enclose.
Dieu seul ne faut jamais, les hommes volontiers
Sont tousjours de nature imparfaits et fautiers.

                                        (II.570)

(Like him who sees around him from the opening of a window
a rural landscape varied in locale, in form, and use—here a river,
a rock, a bush present themselves to his eyes, and there is a hil-
lock, a grassland, a plantation, a path, an orchard, a vineyard, a
well-trimmed garden, a thicket, a thorn bush, a spiky thistle, and
each spot to which his straying eye moves he discovers a country
of a different kind, both good and bad: thus, Des Masures, he
who reads the verse I have written here sees at a glance of the
eye many different things, some good, some bad, enclosed in my
paper. God alone never makes mistakes, men are always readily
imperfect in nature and prone to error.)

The conventions of classical inspiration by the Muse are used as a defensive device to justify Ronsard's subjective tastes, as we see in his
rejection of court pressures in his 1564 preface, where he says that he
accepts commissions only if they "conform to my will" and insists that
"I not force my instincts" (II.985). What has most offended him in
putting the official position in his controversial verse "is that I have
not been able to enjoy the freedom of my mind" (II.989).

Very often we find Ronsard asserts that he cannot undertake great
formal enterprises: "J'ay experimenté / Qu'un pauvre ne sçauroit entreprendre un grand oeuvre" (I have proved a poor man cannot undertake
a great project [II.860]). Of his collection of elegies Ronsard asserts

that "if I had composed the greater part of these elegies to my own taste and not by express command of kings and princes, I would have been concerned for brevity" (II.647). His own taste is for "petits Sonets bien-faits, belles Chansons petites, / Petits Discours gentils" (little, well-made sonnets, brief pretty songs, small agreeable discussions [II.451]). His favored style is neither high nor coarse:

> Je n'ayme point ces vers qui rampent sur
> la terre,
> Ny ces vers empoulez, dont le rude tonnerre
> S'envole outre les airs: les uns font
> mal au coeur
> Des liseurs desgoutez, les autres leur font peur.
> Ny trop haut, ny trop bas, c'est le
> souverain style.
>
> (ii.947)

(I detest these verses which crawl along the earth and those inflated ones whose harsh thunder flies beyond the winds; the first nauseate their disgusted readers, and the second frighten them. Neither too high nor too low is the best style.)

As for content, Ronsard stresses that it must be personal and sustained. "Il faut du premier vers conter sa passion, / Et la suyvre tousjours" (One must from the first line present one's feeling and follow it consistently [II.647]): ornament may never take up more than a line or two, and the ending should be somewhat lively and epigrammatic.

The most accessible verse of Ronsard follows these patterns—it is subjective in content, dynamic in manner, and brusquely eccentric in attitude. Stylized amatory sentiments such as Petrarch's are often heartily ridiculed by Ronsard, and the cult of Neoplatonism is dismissed with an obscene gesture—Plato and his modern disciples like Leone Ebreo are consistently rejected in favor of an open sensuality which affords quite sufficient grounds for the indignation of the Huguenots.[33] He has no delusions in writing to his printer about his mistress Hélène de Surgères: "It is a great misfortune to serve a mistress who has neither

33. See Ronsard, ed. Cohen, vol. 1, pp. 94, 611; vol. 2, pp. 106, 236, 243, 499, 583, 674, 859.

judgment nor thought about our poetry, who does not understand poets. . . . I pray you, sir, not to trust Mlle. de Surgères in this matter. . . . Let her see this letter if you think it well" (II.1047). He is just as capable of expressing this severe view of her in his verse as in a prose letter:

> Chacun me dit: "Ronsard, ta Maitresse
> n'est telle
> Comme tu la descris." Certes je n'en sçay rien,
> Je suis devenu fol, mon esprit n'est plus mien,
> Je ne puis discerner la laide de la belle. . . .
> Et la fleur d'un chardon m'est une belle rose.
>
> (1.292)

(Everyone tells me: "Ronsard, your mistress is not as you describe her." True, I do not know anything about it; I have become so mad, my mind is no longer my own; I cannot tell the ugly from the beautiful. . . . And the flower of the thistle seems to me a beautiful rose.)

He does not hesitate to expand this ruthless exposition to his own eccentric personality in ways prefiguring Montaigne:

> Je suis tout aggravé de somme et de paresse,
> Inhabile, inutile; et, qui pis, je ne puis
> Arracher cest humeur dont esclave je suis.
> Je suis opiniastre, indiscret, fantastique,
> Farouche, soupçonneux, triste et melancolique,
> Content et non content, mal propre, et
> mal courtois;
> Au reste craignant Dieu, les princes, et les loix,
> Né d'assez bon esprit, de nature assez bonne,
> Qui pour rien ne voudroit avoir faché
> personne;
> Voilà mon naturel.
>
> (II.921–22)

(I am quite oppressed with sleep and laziness, unskillful, ineffective, and what is worse I cannot uproot this humor of which I am a slave. I am opiniated, indiscreet, whimsical, wild, suspicious, sad and melancholy, content and not content, messy, and discourteous; for the rest fearing God, princes, and the laws, born with quite good wit and good nature, who would not provoke anyone for nothing: that is my nature.)

Obviously this kind of acceptance of his own limitations makes him true to the sense of human fallibility reinforced by the Reformation, as he says: "Le naturel de l'homme est souvent de faillir" (It is man's nature to fail often [II.789]). Perhaps the most shocking illustration of his power to look at himself is one of his posthumous sonnets, in which he confronts his dying body as boldly as Donne did later in his own funeral preparations:

> Je n'ay plus que les os, un squelette je semble,
> Decharné, denervé, demusclé, depoulpé,
> Que le trait de la Mort sans pardon a frappé:
> Je n'ose voir mes bras que de peur je ne tremble.
>
> (II.634)

(I have no more than bones; I seem a skeleton, unfleshed, nerveless, unmuscled, depulped, which the dart of death has struck without reprieve: I dare not look at my arms for fear of trembling.)

Nor does he hesitate to record the most grotesque experiences and moods. His evocation of his hallucinations has an unnerving vividness —like the terrible visitation by the rotting corpse of his friend du Bellay or the nightmare encounter on the banks of the Loire.[34] Sometimes the eccentricities are more playful, as when he feels himself turning into a tree or a marigold by sheer empathy.[35] It is no accident that many of his most complex and valuable poems deal with the borders of human experience in ways which deeply disturb Reformation moralists, as with *Les Daimons*, *Des Estoilles*, *La Mort*. Perhaps no poet has caught so wide a range of elusive states of mind, from the most conventional

---

34. Ronsard, ed. Cohen, vol. 2, p. 571; Pierre de Ronsard, *Oeuvres complètes,* ed. Paul Laumonier, vol. 8 (Paris: Didier, 1966), pp. 134–35.

35. Ronsard, ed. Cohen, vol. 2, pp. 92, 365.

to the most bizarre. In the last resort Ronsard's neoclassicism and literary sophistication are only servants of this memorable survey of the full range of human psychology. This verse is based on an awareness for which the shocks and discontinuities of his life and times must be largely held responsible, as Michel Dassonville has so vigorously asserted in his literary biography of the poet.[36] To understand his impact in England, we must look carefully at the content and meaning of his works, not just at their allusions and style: "Classical mythology provided Ronsard with a medium through which he could explore and interconnect many different areas of experience."[37] Similarly, in other intellectual frames of reference, "he merely uses a convenient cosmological system, which he regards as semi-mythical, to probe into the meaning of human experience in the world."[38] To talk of Ronsard's concern for the reform of the French language or the revival of the classics is to note only some of the means he devoted to the greater end of mapping out the new range of psychological awareness in part opened by the shattering impact of the Reformation.

Indeed, it may be argued that the classical literary revival was no more crucial to the mature achievement of Ronsard than were the narrowly provincial antecedents which lend such vividness and precision to many of his best poems, like the Horatian odes to Gastine and Bellerie and the whole corpus of works evoking the Vendômois. As Michel Dassonville asserts, "The images of the Vendômois are always present and by a metamorphosis revealing his poetic gift, exterior objects become by degrees personal myths. . . . But if he passes from the exterior object to the personal myth he also discovers easily in ancient mythology certain rustic images which are familiar to him. . . . Mythology is thus clothed for him in rural charm. . . . One sees how slight his classical training still was and how vital and exciting were the impressions of his native country."[39] As a local poet Ronsard is a powerful precedent even for moderns like Hardy and Frost (not to mention Wordsworth):

36. Dassonville, pp. 9–17.
37. Terence Cave, "Ronsard's Mythological Universe," in Cave, p. 159.
38. Levi, p. 153.
39. Dassonville, pp. 173–74.

Quand je suis vingt ou trente mois
Sans retourner en Vendômois,
Plein de pensées vagabondes,
Plein d'un remors et d'un souci,
Aux rochers je me plains. . . .

(1.544)

(When I am twenty or thirty months without returning to the
Vendômois, full of wandering thoughts, full of regret and care
I complain to the rocks. . . .)

When death threatens him, his first thought is, "Il faut laisser maisons
et vergers et jardins / Vaisselles et vaiseaux que l'artizan burine" (One
must leave houses and orchards and gardens, tableware and jars en-
graved by craftsmen [II.637]) : the rhythm of rural life is identical to
his. Not only does he give to the classical motifs from Virgil and Horace
this fresh intimacy and authenticity, he writes of rural life with a technical precision and firsthand authority quite different from the faint
conventionalities of most Renaissance poets. In this Ronsard has more
in common with Hesiod, Aratus, and their even less fashionable Renaissance analogues, like Thomas Tusser or Michael Drayton, whose
Poly-Olbion is closest in English to Ronsard's vein of rural verse.[40]
Perhaps the traditional emphasis on Ronsard as above all a fashionable
court poet has deflected too much attention from his fascination for us
as a private, even a provincial writer. He withdrew from controversial
verses to more personal ones after receiving orders to stop the religious
confrontations in which he had been officially engaged up to the publication of the *Response* in 1563. All the evidence suggests that despite
the range of his writing it is as the recorder of psychological nuances,
private sensibility, and provincial particularities that Ronsard was most
stimulating and valuable as a model for the best English Renaissance
poets, not as the stylized courtier and supposedly Petrarchan sentimen-
talist. If Ronsard has been canonized by humane readers it is as the
prophet par excellence of subjective identity in verse, for which his
personal sufferings and confrontations were largely responsible.

40. Richmond, *Renaissance Landscapes, passim.*

Ronsard and
the English Poets

RENAISSANCE LYRICISM IN NORTHERN EUROPE USED TO BE MEASURED AGAINST
archaic "Petrarchan" conventions, which maintained their acceptability
there at least as late as Milton's sonnets.[1] The actual condition of Italian
poetry itself in the sixteenth century was far less rigidly conformist,
so that the "anti-Petrarchan" vein of Donne has turned out to be much
more conventional than English-speaking critics had once asserted.[2]
Even memorable metaphysical conceits such as his famous compass
image prove to have precedents in poets like Guarini or Tasso or Marino.[3] The more general characteristics of Donne's verse—his bravura
cynicism, colloquial style, and dramatic openings—have now been recognized as commonplace in European lyricism since the times of the
most ancient Greek poets.[4] In many ways this more informed view of
Donne has not been disadvantageous to our critical appreciation of his
work: instead of appearing an unheralded genius whose originality
eludes historical explanation, he can now be understood as a craftsman

1. See, for example, George Williamson, *The Donne Tradition* (New York:
Noonday, 1958), pp. 35, 75, etc.
2. See Guss, *John Donne, Petrarchist.*
3. Mario Praz, *Marinismo e Seicentismo in Inghilterra* (Firenze: La Voce,
1925).
4. Richmond, *The School of Love*, pp. 99–173.

who gave his own distinctive and intelligible twists to accumulated literary resources, without which his memorable effects would have been impossible.

Yet even if we study such writers of the *cinquecento* as Guarini, Berni, Serafino, Aretino, not to mention the minor works of Tasso, Ariosto, and others, we still find a discrepancy which leaves Donne and Jonson stylistically distinct from these models, indeed illustrating a temperament and social outlook at odds with the Italian tradition. Despite such traits as the savage anti-clericalism of Dante and Petrarch, the skeptical analysis by Machiavelli of ecclesiastical politics, and the dictatorial puritanism of a Savonarola, the leaders of the Italian Renaissance came too early to be deeply colored by Reformation values, and later Italian civilization was more deeply affected by the Counter-Reformation sponsored by the emperors and popes than were the northern Europeans among whom Protestantism struck its deepest roots. While minds like those of Castiglione and Machiavelli defined many of the social and political preoccupations of Elizabethans, Italians were seen by the English as remote and exotic figures readily transmuted into alien stereotypes or caricatures like the Machiavels of Marlowe and Shakespeare. As a result a representative Humanist such as Ascham could typify Italian influence in his notorious aphorism: "Inglese italianato e un diavolo incarnato" ("The italianate Englishman is a devil incarnate").[5]

The most accessible foreign sources for Elizabethan authors were often in French rather than Italian, as geography made inevitable. Tudor Englishmen often did not like France, but they emulated and copied her manners, fashions, and culture in ways most extravagantly illustrated in the Field of the Cloth of Gold.[6] And the increasing importance of the Huguenots in the second half of the century gave French political affairs a relevance to English commitment to Protestantism, which reached a climax in the sustained English support for the campaigns of Henri IV. Whether French poets sympathized with the mod-

5. Roger Ascham, *The Scholemaster*, ed. Edward Arber (London: Constable, 1927), p. 78.

6. See Charles Bastide, *The Anglo-French Entente in the Seventeenth Century* (London: Lane, 1914), p. 106.

erate Reformers as Marot seemed to, or with moderate Catholicism as
Ronsard found expedient, or even with the Calvinist faction who supported du Bartas and d'Aubigné, the French literary tradition normally responded to experiences which were directly accessible to English
minds, if not fully shared by them. However, in terms of sheer range
and verve Ronsard afforded the richest quarry, even for English poets
who did not share his views.

"Peter Ronsard, rich in the spoils of the Greeks and Latines, as his
Loues, his divers Poesies, his Odes, Elegies and Hymnes do testifie, in
the which we read all kind of verses, all kinds of Arguments in all
kind of styles"—these are the terms in which John Eliot justifies his
choice of Ronsard as one of the three major poets which every English
student of French must know (the others being Marot and du Bartas).[7]
It is the artistic comprehensiveness of Ronsard which commands Eliot's
respect: Ronsard as the great repository of poetical resources of his
time. Eliot's terms of reference confirm A. W. Sattersthwaite's estimate
that "without Ronsard and du Bellay on the Continent, neither Spenser
nor English poetry in the latter half of the sixteenth century could have
become what we know it to be."[8] Bearing in mind this role of Ronsard
as a basic reference for English Renaissance verse,[9] one can understand
the point of Sattersthwaite's assertion that "it cannot be too often repeated that the mere fact that [poets] present ideas which are Renaissance clichés, and which often seem identical both in conception and in
expression, is not sufficient reason for dismissing such parallels as having no significance." Ronsard is one of the most obvious sources for
such material, but just as important is the fact that his verse filters it
through a distinctive personality shaped by his provincial origins and
role in public controversy: "Ronsard in all his work was primarily
concerned with himself. . . . Ronsard is the centre of his own world."

7. John Eliot, p. 32.
8. Sattersthwaite, p. 252.
9. See the survey of Renaissance and academic comment on Ronsard's English
reputation in Prescott, *French Poets and the English Renaissance*, pp. 76–131. She
avoids "large conclusions" and the kind of discussion of questions of substantial
influence in my *The School of Love; Renaissance Landscapes*, Sidney Lee's *The
French Renaissance in England*, etc.; but many other current items are noted.

What English poets found in Ronsard was the European literary tradition refracted through the prism of a distinctive private sensibility:
given individuality, dramatic focus through "the cultivation of the Self,
the *Moi*." For "Ronsard is a man of the senses, of strong feelings . . .
his thoughts in his poetry take the form of feeling. His varying statements about poetry are as unpremeditated, as mercurial, and as assertive as his well-known statement about himself: 'Je suis, dis-je, Ronsard, et cela te suffise' " (I am, I say, Ronsard, and that's enough for you
[II.17]).[10]

How far Ronsard's years in Britain balance the debt English lyricism owes to him has never been fully determined, but he asserts himself
that he knew England well and Scotland even better: "En l'Escossoise
terre / Où trente mois je fus, et six en Angleterre" (In Scottish land,
where I was for thirty months, and six in England [II.80]). It is hard
to believe that Ronsard never glanced at a verse in English during such
a period, and surely at the time of the voyage with Madeleine, then
queen of Scotland, which began on 10 May 1537, one of the poets whom
Ronsard would recognize as among England's most fashionable would
be Sir Thomas Wyatt. Certainly the two often share a sardonic suspicion of "modern" sophistication and doubt about idealized love generally, as we see in comparing "They flee from me" with an elegy like
the third to Genévre; and both poets successfully transpose to a personal meaning Petrarch's "Una candida cerva"—Wyatt in "Whoso list
to hunt" and Ronsard in his sonnet "Franc de raison" (I.50). Still, the
obvious literary indebtedness overall flows from Ronsard to English
poets, though I intend to show that it is the major poets whom Ronsard
influenced after his death who used him most creatively.

We have already seen how Ronsard was forced to adopt the plain,
personal tone and forensic techniques of his Huguenot opponents, and
his wry account of the new sectarianism in the *Discours à G. Des-Autels*
is comparable in skeptical tone and moderate outlook to that in Donne's
Satire III—equally capable of censuring both slavish Catholic devotion
to an unreformed church and naive Protestant iconoclasm. In view of
his previous commitment to elegant neoclassicism, it is not surprising

10. Sattersthwaite, pp. 97, 111, 239, 249.

to find the mature Ronsard is a little defensive about his changes in style:

> Tyard, on me blasmoit, à mon commencement,
> De quoy j'estois obscur au simple populaire
> Mais on dit aujourd'huy que je suis
> > au contraire,
> Et que je me démens, parlant trop bassement.
>
> > > (1.116)

(Tyard, they used to criticize me when I began for being obscure to ordinary people, but nowadays they say I am the opposite and that I betray myself by writing too commonly.)

He even blames his rural girlfriend Marie because "m'avez tourné mon grave premier stile / Qui pour chanter si bas n'estoit point ordonné" (you have diverted my first serious manner which was not suited to sing of such low matters [I.160]), so that now "ma Muse est si basse et si rampante, / Qui souloit apporter aux François un effroy" (my muse is so low and groveling, which used to thrill the French), and all this, he complains, without setting a hand on her thighs! Interestingly enough, Ronsard often returns to the claim that it is not his dialogue with the Huguenots but his own sexual candor which has exacted this shift from earlier more stilted conventions, even though the love poetry could be just as provocative to his critics as his theological outlook:

> Car un homme est bien sot d'aimer, si on
> > ne l'aime,
> Or si quelqu'un apres me vient blasmer de quoy
> Je ne suis plus si grave en mes vers que j'estoy
> A mon commencement, quand l'humeur
> > Pindarique
> Enfloit empoulément ma bouche magnifique,
> Dy luy que les amours ne se souspirent pas
> D'un vers hautement grave, ains d'un beau
> > stile bas,
> Populaire et plaisant, ainsi qu'a fait Tibulle,

L'ingenieux Ovide, et le docte Catulle.
Le fils de Venus hait ces ostentations:
Il suffist qu'on luy chante au vray ses passions
Sans enflure ni fard, d'un mignard et doux stile.

(1.115)

(For a man is foolish to love without being loved back, so if someone comes in time to blame me for no longer being as serious in
my verse as I was at first when the Pindaric mood swelled with
exaggeration my magnificent mouth, tell him that love affairs
do not breathe out verse of high seriousness but a fine low style,
popular and agreeable, such as Tibullus made, or the witty Ovid
and the expert Catullus. The son of Venus hates these ostentations: it is enough that one sings to him truthfully one's passions, without swellings and cosmetics, in a dainty sweet style.)

There is some justification for the assertion of this lowering effect
of worldly sexuality on literary style, at least in Ronsard's less than
consistently sentimental love poetry. The *Sonnets pour Hélène* often
sink to subjects incompatible with Petrarch's attitude to Laura, as for
example in Ronsard's paradoxical address to a mosquito, which is almost as outrageous as Donne's "The Flea":

Cusin, monstre à double aile, au mufle
> elephantin,
Canal à tirer sang, qui voletant en presse
Sifles d'un son aigu, ne picque ma Maistresse,
Et la laisse dormir du soir jusqu'au matin.
Si ton corps d'un atome, et ton nez de mastin
Cherche tant à picquer la peau d'une Deesse,
En lieu d'elle, Cusin, la mienne je te laisse. . . .
Cusin, je m'en desdy: hume moy de la belle
Le sang, et m'en apporte une goutte nouvelle
Pour gouster. . . .

(1.251)

(Mosquito, double-winged monster with elephant's trunk as vessel to draw blood, which fluttering fiercely whistles with sharp
sound—do not bite my mistress, and let her sleep from evening

228

to morning. If your atom of a body and your mastiff's nose seek
so much to bite the skin of a goddess, instead of her, mosquito,
I offer you mine. . . . Mosquito, I retract that: suck up the
beauty's blood and bring me a fresh drop to taste. . . .)

One must admire the virtuosity of the ingenious opening ascription
of the outrageous epithet "elephantine," so unexpectedly applied to the
microscopic coiled proboscis of the mosquito. Obviously Ronsard can
justify this by accurate personal observation, as with his later, painfully valid reference to its mastiff's bite. The cannibalistic savoring of
the flavor of one's girlfriend's blood is more incidental, but if anything more grotesque, than Donne's provocative argument that his flea
achieves sexual consummation for the lovers by mixing their blood.
The defiance of decorum is self-evident in both poems.

Even in more serious matters Ronsard is capable of paradoxes in
Donne's vein. Donne concluded his holy sonnet "Death be not proud"
with the couplet:

> One short sleepe past, wee wake eternally,
> And death shall be no more, Death thou
> shalt die.[11]

Ronsard has already argued as wilfully that death is preferable to suffering in love:

> Douce est la mort d'autant plus qu'elle
> est bréve. . . .
> Pour me sauver il me plaist de mourir,
> Et de tuer la mort par la mort mesme.
>
> (1.7)

(Sweet is death even more since it is brief. . . . To save myself I
am happy to die and to kill death by death itself.)

In each sonnet the thought is governed primarily by the desire to achieve
the bizarre effect of its last line. However, Donne's poem is typical of
the "Holy Sonnets" in that, under the pressure of his religious anxieties
and divided ecclesiastical loyalties, he has transposed what had been

11. John Donne, *The Divine Poems*, ed. Helen Gardner (Oxford: Clarendon
Press, 1959), p. 9.

an amatory motif to more religious meaning—for the same ethical evolution seems to have occurred in the case of the infinitely more powerful and moving sonnet "Batter my heart." Through his intense concern with his own feelings in a confusing environment, Ronsard comes to recognize a deep ambivalence (which also gives to Donne's sonnet its religious desperation) when he addresses Cassandre (see Plate 14):

> Je veux brusler pour m'en-voler aux cieux,
> Tout l'imparfait de mon escorce humaine,
> M'éternisant comme le fils d'Alcmène,
> Qui tout en feu s'assit entre les Dieux.
> Ja mon esprit desireux de son mieux,
> Dedans ma chair, rebelle, se promeine . . .
> D'un feu divin, avienne que ton chaud
> Brusle si bien ma despouille connue,
> Que libre et nu je vole d'un plein saut
> Outre le ciel, pour adorer là haut
> L'autre beauté dont la tienne est venue.
>
> (1.75)

(I wish to burn the imperfection of my human exterior so I may fly to the heavens, becoming eternal like Alcmena's son [Hercules], who all in flames sits among the gods. Already my spirit, seeking its own good, paces rebelliously in my flesh. . . . With divine fire may your warmth burn so well my familiar remnants that free and naked I fly in a full leap beyond heaven to adore on high the other beauty from which yours came.)

This may not be the asceticism of Reformation theology, but it aspires to transcendence of sex in Plato's vein. The ambivalence toward sexuality recurs when Ronsard accuses his heart of treason in an ode full of military imagery generated by the turbulence of the times:

> Ce n'est pas moy, c'est toy, mon coeur,
> Qui pour allonger ma langueur,
> Desloyal envers moy te portes,
> Et pour faire un penser veinqueur,

De nuict tu luy ouvres mes portes . . .
Pour aller, traistre, secourir
L'ennemy de son Capitaine.

(1.543–44)

(This is not me, it is you my heart who, to prolong my distress, bear yourself disloyally to me and, to create a conquering thought, open my gates to it by night . . . to go, traitor, to the aid of the enemy of his commander.)

Again, his reason is no less treacherous to him than his heart in love, just as it proved in religion for many of his contemporaries whose faith fluctuated under the force of circumstances:

Je souspire la nuict, je me complains le jour,
Contre toy, ma Raison, qui mon fort
      abandonnes,
Et pleine de discours, confuse, tu t'estonnes
Dés le premier assaut, sans defendre ma tour.

(1.296)

(I sigh by night, and I lament by day against you, my reason, who abandon my fortress, and full of words, confused, wonder to yourself after the first assault, without defending my tower.)

Despite these specific precedents in Ronsard, we must recognize that the full power of the civil war motif in Donne's manner emerges best in another sonnet, which even accurately prefigures the seemingly distinctive opening of "Batter my heart":

Foudroye moy le corps, ainsi que Capanée,
O pere Jupiter, et de ton feu cruel
Esteins moy l'autre feu qu'Amour continuel
Tousjours m'allume au coeur d'une flame
      obstinée.
Il vaut mieux, ô grand Dieu, qu'une seule
      journée
Me despouille soudain de mon fardeau mortel
Que de souffrir tousjours en l'ame un
      torment tel

Que n'en souffre aux Enfers l'ame la
plus damnée . . .
Puis qu'autrement par soin, par peine et
par labeur,
Trahy de la raison, je ne me puis desfaire
D'Amour, qui maugré moy se campe dans
mon coeur.

(II.799)

(Blast my body as you did Capaneus, O father Jupiter, and with
your cruel fire extinguish in me the other fire which enduring
love keeps alight always in my heart with obstinate flame. It is
better, O great god, that a single day despoil me at once of my
mortal burden than always to suffer in one's soul a torment such
as the most damned soul suffers in Hell. . . . Since otherwise by
care, by suffering, and by labor, betrayed by reason, I cannot free
myself from love, which encamps in my heart in spite of me.)

Here is conclusive evidence that the deep emotional ambivalence, powerful language, and compressed imagery of Donne is quite traditional
—for the imagery of Donne's sonnet is clarified by Ronsard's reference to Capaneus: one of the Seven Champions led against Thebes by
Polynices when his brother Eteocles refused to surrender the throne
to him as required by their pact to rule the city in alternate years. The
fratricidal strife ended in both the brothers' deaths, while Capaneus
was struck dead by Zeus' thunderbolt for claiming that even Zeus could
not stop him climbing the walls of Thebes. The sense of human hubris
and of the resulting schisms reflected in these allusions helps to illuminate Donne's imagery vividly as he solicits direct revelation in the
Protestant vein to resolve his wavering allegiance:

Batter my heart three-person'd God; for, you
As yet but knocke, breathe, shine, and seeke
to mend;
That I may rise, and stand, o'erthrow mee,
'and bend
Your force, to breake, blowe, burn and make
me new.

232

I, like an usurpt towne, to'another due,
Labour to'admit you, but Oh, to no end,
Reason your viceroy in mee, mee should
      defend,
But is captiv'd, and proves weake or untrue,
Yet dearly'I love you, and would be
      lov'd faine,
But am betroth'd unto your enemie,
Divorce mee, 'untie, or breake that knot againe,
Take mee to you, imprison mee, for I
Except you 'enthrall mee, never shall be free,
Nor ever chast, except you ravish mee.[12]

There is an obvious relevance of the story of Thebes to "an usurpt towne, to another due," though Donne's opening seems to subordinate Capaneus' death to the apotheosis of Hercules in the other Ronsard sonnet. The sense of betrayal by one's own supporters, like reason, runs through all the poems, and the acute sense of sexual tension in Donne derives from the more emphatically amatory context of Ronsard's sonnets. The kinetic phrasing is also obviously prefigured in Ronsard's violent language: "foudroye," "esteins," "despoille," "souffrir," "torment," reinforced by the frequent massive alliteration, as in "corps ainsi que Capané" or "puis qu'autrement par soin, par peine et par labeur." One perceives two distinctive heightenings added by Donne: in reaction to the pagan divinity "Jupiter," who was also the Zeus of the original story, Donne has given his God the triple identity of the Christian trinity, overbidding the mere dualism of the Roman-Greek pantheons. The imagery of rape may arise naturally enough from the theme of sacking a city (as we may recall from the speech of Shakespeare's Henry V to the citizens of Harfleur [III.iii.1ff.]), but Donne gives it climactic shock value. Though Ronsard is quite deliberate in his provocative exploitation of sexuality, his various analogues do not quite achieve the same progression of emotion and argument as Donne, who tightens the structure and heightens the tone of his models. In both poems the tension is increased by a Reformation

12. Donne, *Divine Poems*, p. 11.

intensity of moral concern and by the ominous overtones of the allusions to military sieges.[13]

A similar process of synthesizing motifs in a dramatic psychological progression may be detected in the analogies between various Ronsard lyrics and Donne's "Aire and Angels." Donne's poem can be readily sited in the Reformation by its skeptical relation to scholastic angelology and its recognition of the evolution toward more practical values in contemporary theories about sexual relations among Neoplatonists like Leone Ebreo. However, it is disconcerting that so little recognition is given to Donne's poetic precedents; after all in an age of increasing theological controversy on the subject, Ronsard was particularly interested in spirits, demons, angels, and their psychological implications as alternatives for orthodox beliefs, though he was scarcely original in telling his mistress that "quelque Demon de ton corps s'est vestu" (some spirit has dressed itself in your body):

> A l'aller, au parler, au flamber de tex yeux,
> Je sens bien, je vois bien que tu es immortelle.
> La race des humains en essence n'est telle:
> Tu es quelque Demon ou quelque Ange
> des cieux.
>
> (1.248)

(At your going, speaking, and the flaming of your eyes, I feel sure, I see clearly that you are an immortal. The human race is not such in essence: you are some spirit or some angel from the heavens.)

As to the nature and function of such spirits, Ronsard agrees with the concepts reflected by "Aire and Angels" and "The Extasie" about those

> Legers Demons qui tenez de la terre,
> Et du haut ciel justement le milieu,
> Postes de l'air, divins postes de Dieu,
> Qui ses segrets nous apportez grand erre.
>
> (1.15)

13. This and other analogues were first noted in Hugh M. Richmond, "Donne and Ronsard," *Notes and Queries* 5 (1958), pp. 534–36.

(light spirits who hold the exact middle between earth and high heaven, postilions of the air, divine messengers of God, who swiftly bring us his secrets.)

The redeployment of the archaic terms of angelology also provides a novel sustaining pattern for a long Ronsard elegy, "Les Vers d'Eurymedon et de Callirée," in which, as unexpectedly as in "Aire and Angels," the lover is increasingly flattered by the analogies, and his mistress disadvantaged:

> Mon corps est plus leger que n'est l'esprit de ceux
> Qui vivent en aimant grossiers et paresseux. . . .
> Je ressemble au Démon qui ne se veut charger
> D'un corps, ou s'il a corps ce n'est qu'un air leger. . . .
> La matiere de l'homme est pesante, et ne peut
> Suivre l'esprit en hault, lors que l'esprit le veut,
> Si l'Amour, la purgeant de sa flamme estrangere,
> N'affine son mortel. Voilà, Dame pourquoy
> Je cognois par raison que n'aimez tant que moy:
> Si vous aimiez autant, vous seriez plus legere. . . .
> Vous estes paresseuse, et au Ciel je m'envole,
> Mais à moitié chemin je m'arreste et ne veux
> Passer outre sans vous.
>
> (1.194–95)

(My body is lighter than the spirit of those who live grossly and lazily in love. . . . I resemble the spirit who does not wish to burden himself with a body, or if he has a body it is only a light airy one. . . . The matter of man is heavy and cannot follow the spirit on high when the spirit wishes, if love does not refine his mortal parts, purging them with its strange flame. That is why, Lady, I know by reasoning that you do not love as much as I: if you did you would be lighter. . . . You are lazy and I fly to heaven, but half way I stop and do not wish to go beyond without you.)

Writing in a cynical vein acceptable in a world rejecting Catholic conventions, Donne is little more gracious to his mistress:

Then as an Angell, face, and wings
Of aire, not pure as it, yet pure doth weare,
So thy love may be my loves spheare;
Just such disparite
As is twixt Aire and Angells puritie,
'Twixt womens love, and mens will ever be.[14]

Yet like Donne, Ronsard is nervous about dismissing the senses wholly. The period turns to practical ethics not only in religion but in sexuality, and the result is often uncertainty and vacillation resembling the exploratory moods of "Aire and Angels":

Mon ame mille fois m'a predit mon dommage;
Mais la sotte qu'elle est, apres l'avoir predit,
Maintenant s'en repent, maintenant s'en desdit,
Et voyant ma Maistresse elle aime d'avantage.
Si l'ame, si l'esprit, qui sont de Dieu l'ouvrage,
Deviennent amoureux, à grant tort on mesdit
Du corps qui suit les Sens, non brutal comme on dit,
S'il se trouve esblouy des rais d'un beau visage....
Mais du premier assaut l'ame est toute esperdue.
                                                    (1.269)

(My soul a thousand times has predicted my harm, but fool that it is, after predicting this, now regrets it, now retracts it, and seeing my mistress, loves more than ever. If the soul, if the spirit, which are God's creation become amorous, one is greatly mistaken to censure the body which follows the senses, not brutal as they say, if it finds itself dazzled by the beams of a beautiful face.... But with the first assault the soul is completely overpowered.)

In so divided a mind, Ronsard often finds neither the metaphysical nor the physical dimensions of sexuality adequate to locate the source of amatory attraction. Donne also feels he must reject both pure theory and physiological excitement, writing that "not in nothing nor in things / Extreme and scatt'ring bright can love inhere," and Ronsard uses

14. Donne, *Elegies and Songs and Sonnets*, p. 76.

such terms to recognize the same need for mutuality with which Donne
concludes that "thy love may be my love's spheare":

> Amour est sans milieu, c'est une chose extréme
> Qui ne veut, je le sçay, de tiers ny de moitié:
> Il ne faut pas trencher en deux une amitié.
> Un est nombre parfait, imparfait le deuxiéme.
> J'aime de tout mon coeur, je veux aussi qu'on
>   m'aime.
> Le desir au desir d'un noeud ferme lié
> Par le temps ne s'oublie et n'est point oubliéé,
> Il est tousjours son tout, contenté de soy-mesme.
>
>   (1.239)

(Love is without place; it is an extreme thing which does not
want a third or a half, I know: one must not cut a love in half.
One is a perfect number, the second imperfect. I love with all
my heart; I wish also that I be loved. The desire with desire
bound in a firm knot does not forget itself with time nor is forgotten; it is always its whole self, content with itself.)

In the context of such passages conceptual poems like "Aire and
Angels" and "The Extasie" (as well as "The Good-morrow") appear
traditional not only in their allusions and systems but in tone and ar-
tistry.[15] The superiority of Donne lies primarily not in intellectualizing
sex but in a clearer sense of progression in the psychology of the lover.
Ronsard is merely discursive even if he uses almost identical ideas and
phrases to illuminate various states of mind, while in his two poems
Donne shows us how these attitudes may evolve: from mere unlocalized
passion, through an unfocused idealized attraction, to physical awareness, finally transcended by the discovery of some true mutuality by
the male lover's own initiative. None of these attitudes were invented
by Ronsard or Donne, though Ronsard is one of the best poets at catching and elaborating in dramatic phrases the psychological nuances of
sexuality, and Donne excels at giving them structure, coherence, and
progression. Most of the attitudes which Donne adopts, and which

15. See also Ronsard, ed. Cohen, vol. 1, p. 226; vol. 2, pp. 34, 663, 892 for
further precedents for Donne.

English readers often find excitingly "eccentric," are prefigured by prototypes in Ronsard or in his readings elsewhere. Neither poet would
have quite this way if the Reformation had not undercut the seriousness
of traditional metaphysics.

Even so curious a poem as "Negative Love," which describes the
state of mind of a man who is sexually excited yet lacks a mistress on
whom to focus his desires, is anticipated in one of Ronsard's most
whimsical poems explaining how he came to "aimer en l'air une chose
incognue" (to love something unknown in the air):

> L'homme est bien sot qui aime sans cognoistre.
> J'aime et jamais je ne vy ce qui j'aime: . . .
> L'oeil peut faillir, l'aureille fait de mesme,
> Mais nul des sens mon amour n'a fait naistre. . . .
> Ce qui m'offense à mes yeux est caché.
>
> (1.206)

(That man is really stupid who loves someone without knowing
[the beloved]. I love, and I have never seen what I love: . . . the
eye may err, and the ear equally, but none of the senses gave
birth to my love . . . what disturbs me is hidden from my eyes.)

Again the terms verge on the metaphysical, yet the subject is sexual
desire, and if anything Ronsard has achieved a more authentic documentation of an elusive mood than Donne, whose labored metaphysics
are more ingenious than dynamic. The concept is more technically
exact but less vividly expressed than Ronsard's phrasing:

> If that be simply perfectest
> Which can by no way be exprest
> But Negatives, my love is so.[16]

Donne' sexual ideal rejects the limitations of reality, but Ronsard makes
us feel the lover's resulting tension. In both cases, however, "a neopla-
tonic commonplace"[17] has acquired a dramatic immediacy which en-

16. Donne, *Elegies and Songs and Sonnets*, p. 56. The place of these poems
in a tradition is established by Hugh M. Richmond, "The Intangible Mistress,"
Modern Philology 56 (1959), pp. 217–23, which justifies Gardner's subsequent
reference on p. 178 of her edition (1965).

17. Donne, *Elegies and Songs and Sonnets*, p. 177.

ables us to recognize its application to sexual behavior. And if Donne has not advanced beyond Ronsard here, he surely does so when using the theme with masterly concision as a vivid starting point for the progression in "Aire and Angels":

> Twice or thrice had I lov'd thee,
> Before I knew thy face or name.[18]

The sardonic use of pre-Reformation concepts is a characteristic of Donne's best verse. Critics like Coleridge have found "The Canonization" one of Donne's more attractive poems[19] because it is more dramatic and less theoretical than "Aire and Angels" or "The Extasie" in achieving a similar progression of mind. The sequence is initiated with an even more startling emphasis on repudiation of orthodox values, whether religious or secular, in a way relevant to Donne's own inexpedient marriage:

> For Godsake hold your tongue, and let me love.
>   Or chide my palsie, or my gout,
>   My five gray haires, or ruin'd fortune flout,
>   With wealth your state, your minde with Arts
>   improve,
>   Take you a course, get you a place,
>   Observe his honour, or his grace,
>   And the King's reall, or his stamped face
>   Contemplate; what you will, approve,
>   So you will let me love.[20]

One may well believe the skeptical note is authentically biographical, for this is the lively personal vein which has justly earned Donne his reputation; but while admiring his success in catching a dramatic intonation, we should not suggest that he invented the self-assertive manner or even the immediate sexual application of it:

> Tu me fais mourir de me dire
> Qu'il ne faut sinon qu'une lyre

18. Donne, *Elegies and Songs and Sonnets*, p. 75.
19. Donne, *Elegies and Songs and Sonnets*, p. 203.
20. Donne, *Elegies and Songs and Sonnets*, p. 72.

Pour m'amuser, et que tousjours
Je ne veux chanter que d'amours.
Tu dis vray, je te le confesse, . . .
Car quand Amour un coup enflame
De son feu quelque gentille ame,
Impossible est de l'oublier . . .
Mais toy, Pasquier, en qui Minerve
A tant mis de bien en reserve
Qui as l'esprit ardent et vif,
Et nay pour n'estre point oisif,
Eleve au ciel par ton histoire
De nos Rois les faits et la gloire, . . .
Et desormais vivre me laisse
Sans gloire au sein de ma maistresse,
Et parmy ses ris et ses jeux
Laisse grisonner mes cheveux.

(1.573)

(You make me die to tell that all I need is a lyre to amuse me and that I always want to sing of love only. You speak truly, I admit it to you. . . . For when love strikes flame into some gentle soul it is impossible to forget. . . . But you, Pasquier, to whom Minerva has given so much potential, whose spirit is ardent and lively, and who have no need to be idle, lift up the doings and glory of our kings to heaven by your history. . . . And henceforth leave me to live without glory in the bosom of my mistress, and among her smiles and games let my hairs go grey.)

The controversial edge and defensiveness here are traits which theological debate reinforced in all expression. Elsewhere Ronsard repeats these unambitious sentiments to his mistress herself, wishing to die rather than to leave her "pour aller suivre le Roy" (to go and follow the king). Stressful public life is fostering an Epicurean retreat into private satisfaction, and the process will intensify in later periods.

Certainly we can detect the heightening of the tone from Ronsard's friendly rejection of good advice to Donne's overt resentment of any criticism, but the poems share the rejection of conformity through a dramatic mode of address and the evocation of the immediate social situation of each lover. It is also true that there are specific affectations in Ronsard's love poetry which are deftly satirized in Donne's second stanza:

> What merchant ships have my sighs drown'd?
> Who saies my teares have overflow'd his ground?
> When did my colds a forward spring remove?[21]

Though there is scarcely need for Ronsard's poem to be the specific cause of ridicule, these lines follow closely some of Ronsard's naive hyperboles, whose extravagance suggests the collapse of literary decorum in a period of emotional self-indulgence:

> D'une vapeur enclose sous la terre
> Ne s'est conceu un air si venteux,
> Ny de ses flô le Loir impetueux
> Perdant noz bleds, les campagnes n'enserre.
> Le Prince Eole en ces mois ne deterre
> L'esclave orgueil des vents tumultueux,
> Ny l'Ocean des flots tempestueux
> De sa grand clef les sources ne desserre.
> Seuls mes souspirs ont ce vent enfanté,
> Et de mes pleurs le Loir s'est augmenté.
>
> (1.91)

(From vapors locked beneath the earth such gusty air was not conceived; nor did the waves of the impetuous Loir grasp the countryside and drown our fields. Prince Eolus at this season did not release the enslaved pride of the tumultuous winds; nor did Ocean unlock with his great key the sources of the tempestuous waves. Only my sighs gave birth to this wind, and it is my tears which have swelled the Loir.)

Yet Donne's almost puritanical repudiation of grandiose memorials and "half-acre tombs" in favor of a sonnet or "a well-wrought urn" is a sentiment that the reclusive Ronsard had achieved earlier, not only in the universally admired "De l'election de son sépulchre" but also in a charming lament for Marguerite d'Angoulême herself:

21. Donne, *Elegies and Songs and Sonnets*, p. 74.

> Il ne faut point qu'on te face
> Un sepulchre qui embrasse
> Mille termes en un rond,
> Pompeux d'ouvrages antiques,
> Et braves en piliers Doriques
> Elevez à double front.
>
> (1.605)

(There is no need to make a sepulchre for you which includes a thousand statues in a circle, pompous with works of antiquity, and ostentatious with doric pillars raised in pairs.)

However, if he is content here to propose a simple rural inscription for Marguerite, earlier Ronsard had found the era of "new" religions suggested ways of being more ambitious for himself and Marie, and indeed Donne's own last stanza in "The Canonization" shows a sense of apotheosis similar to this blasphemous erection of oneself and one's lover into sacred beings:

> Si j'etois un grand Roy, pour eternel exemple
> De fidelle amitié, je bastirois un temple
> Desur le bord de Loire, et ce temple auroit nom
> Le temple de Ronsard et de sa Marion. . . .
> Vous tiendriez le haut bout de ce temple
>   honorable,
> Droict sur le sommet d'un pilier venerable.
> Et moy, d'autre costé assis au mesme lieu,
> Je serois remarkable en la forme d'un Dieu. . . .
> Ce temple frequenté de festes solennelles
> Passeroit en honneur celuy des Immortelles,
> Et par voeux nous serions invoquez tous les
>   jours,
> Comme les nouveaux Dieux des fidelles
>   amours.
>
> (1.175–76)

(If I were a great king, I would build a temple on the bank of the Loire as an eternal monument to faithful love, and this temple

would have the name of the temple of Ronsard and his Marie.
... You would stand at the high end of the worthy temple, right
on the top of an ancient column. And I sitting on the other side
of the same spot would be conspicuous in the shape of a god. ...
This temple, occupied by solemn festivals, would exceed in honor
that of the immortals, and by vows we would be invoked daily
as the new gods of faithful loves.)

This sense of creating a new religious sect devoted to a sanctified
yet unsublimated sexuality is distinctively Ronsard's individual resource among his peers. While there are numerous classical precedents
for the deification of mortals (as with the emperors and their spouses),
Ronsard initiates a uniquely modern pantheon, for those whose sexual
eminence earns them immortality. This verges on a parody of contemporary religious extravagances yet prefigures D. H. Lawrence's sexual
metaphysics. It is the sense of achieving the status of a cult figure which
also gives to some of Donne's serious love poems their unnerving hyperbole, not to say hubris, as at the end of "The Canonization"—though
there is more than a little irony in the version of sanctification of "The
Relique":

> Then, he that digges us up, will bring
> Us, to the Bishop, and the King,
>   To make us Reliques; then
> Thou shalt be'a Mary Magdalen, and I
>   A something else thereby;
> All women shall adore us, and some men.[22]

Despite the playfulness here, we must admit that both Ronsard and
Donne have proved correct in feeling that, like modern "prophets" of
sexuality, they may be beatified in some sense, for their love poems have
in the end achieved the ritual status of religious texts worthy of reverent
explication by modern clerics in classrooms throughout the world. Born
in an age of confusion and skepticism, these lyrics dare to compete with
the Bible as epitomes of human behavior for study and meditation and
continue to do so for serious students, which is close to what sanctifica-

22. Donne, *Elegies and Songs and Sonnets*, pp. 89–90.

tion implies. Because of the novelties and controversy about religious "love" in the Reformation, amatory poets readily dare to become innovators in secular love also.

This is not to say that either poet preserves decorum and aims merely at high seriousness in developing their new "cults." However suave the traditionally admired neoclassical poems of Ronsard such as "Mignonne, allons voir si la rose" may be, he emerges as a more than adequate model for Donne at his most jaded and cynical. Decorum and orthodoxy were no longer compelling literary virtues. There was no need for Donne to go back as far as Ovid for the opening claim of "The Indifferent" that "I can love both faire and browne." Ronsard had earlier defied puritanical propriety by flaunting his indifference to conventional morality:

> Maintenant je poursuy toute amour vagabonde:
> Ores j'aime le noire, ores j'aime la blonde,
> Et, sans amour certaine en mon coeur esprouver,
> Je cherche ma fortune où je la puis trouver.
>
> (II.17)

(Now I follow every wandering love: now I love the black; now I love the fair, and, without feeling sure love in my heart, I seek my fortune where I can find it.)

It is questionable for Ronsard to assert to Genévre that this cynical mood results from his betrayal by Marie, since earlier Ronsard had written to Marie in defense of inconstancy along the lines of the second stanza of "The Indifferent." Perhaps it is fair to see in this bluntness evidence of the subversion of conventional moral values in a disorderly and disoriented age:

> Marie, en me tançant vous me venez reprendre
> Que je suis trop leger, et me dites tousjours,
> Quand j'approche de vous, que j'aille à ma
>   Cassandre,
> Et tousjours m'appelez inconstant en amours.
> L'inconstance me plaist; les hommes sont bien
>   lours

Qui de nouvelle amour ne se laissent
    surprendre;
Qui veult opiniastre une seule pretendre
N'est digne que Venus luy face de bons tours.
(1.124)

(Marie, in reproaching me, you come to censure me because I
am too volatile and tell me every time I approach you that I
should go back to my Cassandre, and you are always calling me
fickle in love. Inconstancy pleases me; men are very dull who
won't allow a new love to surprise them; whoever stubbornly
wishes to claim one woman does not deserve that Venus do him
good turns.)

The Venus who concludes Donne's "The Indifferent" offers a view
similar to the fickle lover of a loyal mistress, even if the specific mistress fails to heed the advice on sexuality which Ronsard reiterates elsewhere, advising rejection of the moral restraints of conventional society:

La constance et l'honneur sont noms pleins
    d'imposture
Que vous alleguez tant, sottement inventez
De nos peres resveurs, par lesquels vous ostez
Et forcez les presens les meilleurs de Nature.
Vous trompez vostre sexe et luy faites injure;
D'un frein imaginé faussement vous domtez
Vos plaisirs, vos desirs, vous et vos volontez,
Vous servant de la Loy pour vaine couverture.
(1.296)

(Constancy and honor are names full of fraud which you are
always citing, stupidly invented by our dreaming fathers, by which
you eliminate or distort the best gifts of Nature. You betray your
sex and do it harm; with a fancied restraint you falsely tame your
pleasures, your desires, yourselves, and your will, using the Law
as a vain excuse.)

These are the values for which the Huguenots reproached not only
Ronsard but the Valois court as a whole.

    Another one of Ronsard's deliberately indecorous sonnets shows a

245

virtuosity in sexual role-playing at least as sophisticated as anything in Shakespeare, though rather less egocentric than in Donne. We can recognize a female psychology analogous to that often illustrated in the *Heptameron* and practiced on Ronsard himself by the *escadron volant*:

> Ma Dame en toute ruse a l'esprit bien appris,
> Qui tousjours cherche un autre apres qu'elle
>   m'as pris.
> Quand d'elle je bruslois, son feu devenoit
>   moindre.
> Mais ores que je feins n'estre plus enflamé,
> Elle brusle apres moy. Pour estre bien aimé,
> Il faut aimer bien peu, beaucoup promettre
>   et feindre.
>
> (1.297)

(My lady has a mind learned in every trick, for she always looks for another lover after she has taken me. When I burned for her, her fire became less. But now that I pretend that I am no longer on fire, she burns for me. To be well loved, one must love very little, promise and feign a lot.)

There is a trace of sociological detachment in the final generalization, matching the perspectives of Marguerite d'Angoulême and Brantôme. The urbane acceptance of the woman's skeptical point of view is unusually objective, and the whole sonnet shows a recognition of the volatility of sexual attitudes comparable to that admired in Drayton's study of quite different fluctuating moods in "Since there's no help, come let us kiss and part," where the supposedly hostile lover betrays his desire to continue the relationship after breaking it.

Ronsard's iconoclasm even overbids another well-known Donne effect in the insults lavished on "The Sunne Rising," which begins "Basie old foole, unruly Sunne." Ronsard is still more insolent, as well as classically exact:

> Jaloux Soleil contre Amour envieux
> Soleil masqué d'une face blesmie,
> Qui par trois jours as retenu m'amie
> Seule au logis par un temps pluvieux, . . .

Va te cacher, vieil pastoureau champestre,
Tu n'es pas digne au Ciel d'estre un flambeau,
Mais un bouvier qui meine les boeufs paistre.

(1.42)

(Jealous sun, envious of love, sun concealed by a blemished face, who have kept my girl at home alone for three days of rainy weather, . . . go and hide yourself, you old rustic herdsman; you are not worthy to be a torch in heaven but a cowherd who leads cattle to their grazing.)

On one level, the rhetoric is traditional, but it maintains the subversive spirit of the age. Both poets may have been competing with Ovid's insults to Aurora (*Amores* I.xiii), but the shift to attacking the sun is one which Ronsard experiments with sufficiently for us to think that he may have inspired Donne's second stanza, in which private feeling transcends objective reality. Conviction, or "faith," becomes the ultimate criterion of truth:

Looke, and to morrow late, tell mee,
Whether both the'India's of spice and Myne
Be where thou leftst them, or lie here with mee.[23]

Ronsard had rhetorically opened another poem with a challenge to the sun along these lines:

Ou soit, Soleil, que d'en-bas tu retournes
De l'Antipode, ou soit que tu sejournes
Sur nostre monde, hé! dy moy, grand flambeau,
Allant venant as-tu rien veu si beau,
Si valeureux, que ce corps? . . .

(II.511)

(Whether, sun, you return from below in the Antipodes, or if you stay above our world, well, tell me, great flame, going or coming have you seen anything so fine and brave as this body?)

Each poet takes up the defiant note later developed in the Marlovian "overreachers." Donne's hyperbole exceeds Ronsard's, but the rhetori-

23. Donne, *Elegies and Songs and Sonnets*, p. 73.

cal device is the same. Again it is the power of synthesis, not of invention in the modern sense, which makes Donne superior: he covers a greater range of motifs and attitudes than Ronsard's more diffuse and discursive manner usually permits, but the aggressive subjectivity is shared. For even the affected challenge to the sun's rays, "I could eclipse and cloud them with a wink,"[24] finds an analogy in the subjective power of the eyes of Ronsard's mistress: "D'un seul clin ils me peuvent defaire" (With a single blink they can undo me [II.813]). In private relationships such skepticism is more plausible and less costly than in the world of public controversy and sectarian bitterness.

However, we must recognize that Ronsard's unexpected wryness and sardonic wit reflect a mercurial personality which can revert to high sentiment and orthodox poses just as readily as Donne's. Seeing their continuity, Helen Gardner juxtaposes two of Donne's most sentimental poems, "Twickenham Garden" and "A Nocturnal upon S. Lucies Day, being the shortest day," and it is interesting to find both poems' correlated themes prefigured in a no less extravagant lament by Ronsard over the impending departure for her own kingdom of the newly widowed Mary Stuart, with whom he had close (but not amatory) associations:

> Nous perdons de la Court le beau Soleil qui luit
> Dont jamais la clarté n'a tiré vers la nuict,
> Mais tousjours, en monstrant sa splendeur
>   coustumiere,
> A fait contre le jour paroistre sa lumiere,
> Ne te souvient-il point des longues nuits d'hyver
> Où nulle estoile au ciel ne se daigne lever,
> Mais lente et paresseuse en son lict est cachée,
> Quant Tithon en ses bras tient sa femme
>   couchée,
> Et le monde languist, en tenebreux sejour,
> En horreur et en peur, pour l'absence du jour?
> Ainsi, amy L'Huillier, nostre Court sera telle,
> Veufve de la clarté d'une Royne si belle. . . .

24. Donne, *Elegies and Songs and Sonnets*, p. 72.

Le jour que je voirray son depart approcher,
Je veux, pour ne le voir, devenir un rocher,
Sourd, muet, insensible, et le long d'une plaine
Je me veux transformer en l'eau d'une fontaine,
Afin de la pleurer comme les Nymphes font
Quand les fleurs hors des prez par la bise s'en-vont,
Ou quand par un torrent les fontaines se souillent
Ou quand de leur verdeur les arbres se
      despouillent.

(II.299–300)

(We are losing from the court the fine sun which shines, whose brightness has never drawn toward night but always, in displaying its customary splendor, has shown its light against the day's. Do you not remember at all the long winter nights when no star deigns to rise in the sky but hides itself in bed slow and lazy while Tithonus holds his recumbent wife, and the world languishes in a shadowy phase in horror and fear at the absence of light? Thus, friend Huillier, our court will be so, widowed of the brightness of such a bright queen. . . . The day that I see her departure approach, I wish to avoid seeing it by becoming a deaf, silent, insensible rock, and along a plain I wish to become the water of a fountain, to weep like the nymphs when the flowers leave the fields in the north wind, or when by a torrent the fountains are stained or when the trees are stripped of their greenery.)

There is a memorable interaction of private emotion and public situation in the poem. Ronsard's sun image is conventional enough, but his protracted reference to the rigors of the winter solstice rises from his personal sensitivity to the seasons and his intimate sense of the threatening cycle of nature which leaves no human being secure, particularly in an age of uncertain religious faith. For all the references to Tithonus and the nymphs, nature is recognized in its own harsh terms by Ronsard, while Donne evokes rather the scholar's cabinet with his learned and esoteric allusions, which drive one at once to the footnotes: "The Sunne is spent, and now his flasks / Send forth light squibs" or "the generall balme th'hydroptique earth hath drunk."[25] Though very much

25. Donne, *Elegies and Songs and Sonnets*, p. 84.

shorter, Donne's two poems are nevertheless more complex and varied
—the motifs shared with Ronsard indeed provide the nominal subjects:
the shortest days of the year and the wintry feel of deprivation; but the
content of Donne's poems evokes a complex psychological interaction
of the lovers, which is their real point.

Similarly, when Ronsard exploits the contrast between the plaintive
lover and the natural cycle of spring's return on which "Twickenham
Garden" is founded, his lover, Polyphemus, is relatively conventional
in his rhetorical contrasts:

> Je voudrois me pouvoir en pierre transformer
> Pour ne sentir plus rien, comme chose inutile,
> Non plus que fait Niobe au rocher de Sipyle!
> O forests, que je porte envie à vostre bien!
> Et d'autant que tousjours vostre chef renouvelle
> De Printemps en Printemps sa perruque
> nouvelle;
> Mais je ne puis changer mon amoureux esmoy.
>
> (1.992)

(I would like to be able to transform myself into stone as some
useless thing in order to feel nothing any more, no more than did
Niobe at the rock of Sipyle! O forests, how I envy your good fortune! And as much because always your tops renew from spring
to spring their new headgear, but I cannot change my amorous
feelings.)

By comparison Donne turns the trees into a caricature, for, anticipating
a Disneyesque nightmare, he seeks to forbid

> These trees to laugh, and mocke mee to my face;
> But that I may not this disgrace
> Indure, nor leave this garden; Love let mee
> Some senslesse peece of this place bee;
> Make me a mandrake, so I may grow here,
> Or a stone fountaine weeping out my yeare.[26]

26. Donne, *Elegies and Songs and Sonnets*, pp. 83–84.

Nevertheless, if our local comparisons indicate that Ronsard is more discursive, less compressed and progressive, we must recognize that in this elegy he does manage to cover an emotional range at least as great as Donne's. For Ronsard's lover is not the suave, plaintive courtier that he seems: his complacent admiration of his single beautiful eye is calculated to achieve a grotesque shock effect in the midst of conventional wailings, and the amorous cyclops is driven to new levels of sophistication, concluding as wrily as Donne's "Twickenham Garden." Donne claims climactically that his mistress is not chaste, merely a sadist; Polyphemus decides in the end that he will do better to fantasize the effects of Galatea's love rather than bother to achieve it in reality:

> Car feindre d'estre aimé, puis que mieux on
> ne peut,
> Allege bien souvent l'amoureux qui se veut
> Soy-mesmes se tromper, se guarissant la playe
> Aussi bien par le faux que par la chose vraye.
>
> (1.996)

(For feigning to be loved, since one cannot do better, often cures the lover who himself decides to deceive himself, curing his wound as well by fantasy as by truth.)

So in the last resort the difference between Ronsard and Donne is not one of psychological or artistic range, simply one of compression. Donne is often as varied, yet also more economical, and therein, at least, a superior lyricist to Ronsard. But surely without comprehensive and provocative precedents like Ronsard's he could not have mastered and condensed his raw materials so effectively. If he scandalized the Huguenots, Ronsard provided new, livelier modes for wits and libertines of succeeding generations.

Curiously enough the more neoclassical poets of the English Renaissance, like Jonson, owe less to Ronsard's model than do the irregular minds of authors like Donne, Spenser, and Drayton, who found Ronsard's individualistic genius compatible with their own eccentric emphases. The obvious indebtedness of the sonnets and pastorals of Spenser and Drayton to French authors like Ronsard and du Bellay has been explored carefully and now occasions little surprise.[27] The less predictable relevance of Ronsard to the Puritan poets, Milton and Marvell, provides some indication of the enduring impact of Ronsard on the English tradition beyond his formulae for pastoral and amatory verse, which were so well recognized that even Ben Jonson gives tribute to the way "Ronsart prais'd / His new Cassandra, 'bove the old."[28] This is not to separate the Puritans from other Stuart poets who followed Jonson's leads. Perhaps we may see some bearing on Jonson's work of Ronsard's rhetorical mastery of the sustained oration when we juxtapose the "Hymne de l' or" and Volpone's opening paean to gold in *Volpone*, which shows a view of gold "comme un don sacré au temple" (like a heavenly gift in a shrine); but the topic necessarily invites shared references to "les corbeaux . . . et autres tels oiseaux" (crows . . . and other such birds [II.272]), which appear fit symbols of human venality to both poets.

A little less predictable is that Jonson and his followers share Ronsard's vindication of rural decorum and integrity, though this theme is at least as old as Martial's praise of Faustinus' Baian villa (not to discuss the palace of Alcinous in the *Odyssey*). Ronsard characteristically exploits the topic to justify his own delightful yet modest priory at St. Cosme, which still survives to vindicate his assertions:

> Bien que ceste maison ne vante son porphire,
> Son marbre ny son jaspe en oeuvre elabouré,
> Que son plancher ne soit lambrissé ny doré,
> Ny portrait de tableaux que le vulgaire admire,
> Toutefois, Amphion l'a bien daigné construire. . . .
> La bonté, la vertu, la justice et les lois
> Aiment mieux habiter les antres et les bois
> Que l'orgueil des Palais qui n'ont rien que
>   la pompe.
>
> (1.301)

27. See Sattersthwaite, Upham, Lee, Prescott, etc., *passim*.

28. Ben Johnson, *Poems*, ed. George B. Johnston (Cambridge: Harvard University Press, 1962), p. 156.

(Although this house does not flaunt its porphyry, its marble, nor its jasper in elaborate works, though its ceiling is neither paneled, nor gilded, nor has painted portraits at which the vulgar wonder, yet Amphion deigned to construct it. . . . Goodness, virtue, justice, and laws love best to inhabit the caves and woods instead of the pride of palaces which have only pomposity.)

Here we can see Ronsard's revulsion from the ostentation of the court and the Counter-Reformation. Jonson's praise of Penshurst is vindicated by the surviving building, to which he ascribes the same properties we can still also validate at Ronsard's priory of St. Cosme:

> Thou art not, Penshurst, built to envious show,
> Of touch, or marble; nor canst boast a row
> Of polish'd pillars, or a roofe of gold: . . .
> And these grudg'd at, art reverenc'd the while.
> Thou joy'st in better markes, of soyle, of ayre,
> Of wood, of water: therein thou art faire. . . .
> And though thy walls be of the countrey stone,
> They'are rear'd with no man's ruine, no man's grone,
> There's none, that dwell about them, wish
> them downe.[29]

Jonson's sentiments about ostentatious architecture are taken up by Herrick in his "Panegyric to Sir Lewis Pemberton" and by Marvell in "Upon Appleton House,"[30] but in both these authors we might look for more interesting analogues to Ronsard in their lightest pieces. Stuart lyricism, in these poets and similar ones like Carew, Stanley, Lovelace, and Suckling, openly shares the surface prettiness and partly sublimated sexuality of the French cleric, whose sensual interest in women offers some precedent for the tastes of those Anglican clergymen that we may easily forget Stuart poets like Herrick to have been. Ronsard, in one of his odes, also prefigures Crashawe's "Wishes to his

29. Jonson, *Poems*, pp. 76–77.
30. See William McClung, *The Country House in English Renaissance Poetry* (Berkeley and Los Angeles: University of California Press, 1977).

supposed mistress" and even the opening motif of Jonson's most famous
lyric:

> Drink to me, onely, with thine eyes,
>   And I will pledge with mine;
> Or leave a kiss but in the cup,
>   And Ile not look for wine.
> The thirst, that from the soule doth rise,
>   Doth aske a drinke divine.[31]

Ronsard had exploited the same mannered devices:

> J'avois, en regardent tes beaux yeux, enduré
> Tant de flammes au coeur, que plein de seicheresse
> Ma langue estoit reduite en extreme destresse ...
> Lors tu fis apporter en ton vase doré
> De l'eau froide d'un puits, et la soif qui me presse
> Me fist boire à l'endroit où tu bois, ma
>   Maistresse.
>
> (1.233)

(From looking into your fine eyes I had endured such flames in
my heart that my tongue was full of dryness and reduced to extreme distress ... when you had some cold water brought from
a well in your gold cup, and the thirst I felt made me drink at
the spot where you drink, my mistress.)

The next sonnet in Ronsard's sequence deals with a bouquet of flowers
sent by his mistress—the theme of Jonson's second stanza—but the
first stanza is also suggested by a recurrence of its motif a little later in
the cycle:

> Ma Dame beut a moy, puis me baillant sa tasse:
> "Beuvez, dit-ell', ce reste où mon coeur j'ay versé,"
> Et alors le vaisseau des lévres, je pressay,
> Qui comme un batelier son coeur dans le mien passe....
> Ce vase me lia sous les Sens dés le jour
> Que je beu de son vin, mais plus tost une
>   flamme.
>
> (1.255)

31. Jonson, *Poems*, p. 88.

(My lady drank to me, then passed me her cup: "Drink," she
said, "the rest where I have poured my heart in," and at once I
pressed my lips to the vessel which like a boatman carries her
heart into mine. . . . This cup bound me to the senses from the
day I drank its wine, but it was more like a flame.)

The motif is slight in the extreme, but the blend of a firm syntactical
order and a familiar sentimental occasion is something which the
Stuart poets could readily borrow from Ronsard's innumerable variations on this pattern. They too enjoyed flaunting their self-indulgent
sexuality in lyrics offending the staid English Puritans, as Ronsard had
offended Huguenots like d'Aubigné with his amatory trifling.

However, these rhetorical devices might just as easily be turned to
account in Reformation religious verse as in secular lyricism. We can
see why Herbert gave the title "Jordan" to two of his lyrics puritanically
attacking religious affectation if we look at another sonnet of Ronsard's,
which shows paradoxically how close some of his moods come to sharing
Huguenot hostility to courtly corruption:

> Laisse de Pharaon la terre Egyptienne,
> Terre de servitude, et vien sur le Jourdain;
> Laisse moy ceste Court et tout ce fard mondain, . . .
> Demeure en ta maison pour vivre toute tienne, . . .
> N'atten point que l'hyver sur les cheveux te vienne.
> Tu ne vois à ta Court que feintes et soupçons,
> Tu vois tourner une heure en cent mille façons,
> Tu vois la vertue fausse, et vraye la malice.
> Laisse ces honneurs pleins d'un soing ambitieux:
> Tu ne verras aux champs que Nymphes et que
> Dieux.

> (1.259)

(Leave Pharaoh's Egyptian earth, land of servitude, and come
to the Jordan; leave for me this court and all this worldly makeup . . . stay at home and live wholly your own way . . . do not
wait until winter comes to your hair. You see at your court only
affectations and suspicions; you see an hour twisted a hundred
thousand ways; you see false virtue and true malice. Leave these

255

honors full of ambitious care: you will see in the fields only nymphs or gods.)

Despite the pagan allusions, Ronsard's latent protestantism and anti-Establishment attitudes are recognizable. The reference to Pharaoh's Egypt and its equation with the affectations of contemporary courts helps to explain the allusions in Herbert's "Jordan I":

> Who says that fictions onely and false hair
> Become a verse? Is there in truth no beautie?
> Is all good structure in a winding stair?
> May no lines passe except they do their dutie
>   Not to a true, but painted chair? . . .
> Must all be vail'd, while he that reades, divines,
>   Catching the sense at two removes?
> Shepherds are honest people; let them sing. . . .[32]

As so often with the English poets, Herbert complicates and synthesizes the shared material—the allusion to Pharoah is no longer overt in Herbert's poem but is more tactfully implicit in its title, so that the religious dimension is only grasped (if at all) when the very end of the poem throws us back to the title by asserting the right to "plainly say *My God, My King*," a candid Christianity which Ronsard nominally avoids in his secular verse by making allusions to pagan gods. Under the pressure of their deliberate commitment to Anglicanism, the ethical and religious frames of Herbert and Donne are far more explicitly Christian in such lyrics than in the analogues and prototypes in the more secular verse of Ronsard—the aesthetic freshness lies often in just this unexpected synthesis of profane materials and religious explicitness.

We have already seen how Milton's "Lycidas" shares with Ronsard and his plagiarizing Huguenot detractors the denunciation of the depravity of the contemporary clergy, but much of the rest of "Lycidas" also shares motifs very familiar to Ronsard. The fact of premature death by disease or warfare was so universal in the Renaissance that

32. George Herbert, *The Works*, ed. F. E. Hutchinson (Oxford: Clarendon Press, 1964), pp. 56–57. See also note on title, p. 495.

the lament for gifted young men like Henry King necessarily follows highly standardized patterns. The "Epitaphe de Hugues de Sales" (translator of the *Iliad*) may exaggerate slightly in asserting that he died "au plus verd de ton âge" (at the greenest of your age), since he was forty-nine, but it is followed by another lyric epitaph whose sentiments Milton echoes:

> Que sert aus hommes de suivir
> Apollon et les neuf Pucelles,
> Et toute nuit pour les servir
> User tant d'huile et de chandelles,
> Et le jour, bien loing separé
> Du peuple, ou dans les antres vuides,
> Ou dedans un bois egaré,
> Béer apres les Pierides,
> Puis qu' Apollon n'est pas assés fort,
> Ni sa pauvre foiblette troupe,
> D'engarder que la fiere Mort
> La vie à ses mignons ne coupe?
> $$(\text{II.788})$$

(What use to men is it to follow Apollo and the nine Virgins and to burn so much oil and candles all night to serve them and gape after the Pierides during the day very far separated from people, either in empty caverns or wandering in a wood, since Apollo is not strong enough, nor his weak little flock, to prevent proud Death from cutting off the life of his darlings?)

The theme haunts Ronsard, whose religious faith often seems to sink almost to pagan nihilism, for on another melancholy walk he applies it to a third and even better known victim:

> Je blasmois Apollon, les Graces, et la Muse,
> Et le sage mestier qui ma folie amuse; . . .
> Je pleurois du Bellay qui estoit de mon âge,
> De mon art, de mes moeurs, et de mon
> parentage,
> Lequel, apres avoir d'une si docte vois

Tant de fois rechanté les Princes et les Rois,
Est mort pauvre, chetif, sans nulle recompense,
Sinon du fameux bruit que luy garde la France.
(1.866)

(I blamed Apollo, the Graces, and the Muse, and the wise profession which entertains my madness; . . . I wept for du Bellay
who was of my age, of my art, of my manners, and of my descent, who after having with such a learned voice so often sung
again of princes and kings has died poor, wretched, without any
recompense but the famous reputation which France preserves
of him.)

Ronsard continues in the rest of the poem to denounce "nos riches
Prelats" (our wealthy prelates) and their abuse of church resources,
but he has already, in the quoted lines, struck the same chord as Milton
will strike later in "Lycidas":

Alas! What boots it with uncessant care
To tend the homely slighted Shepherd's trade,
And strictly meditate the thankless Muse?
Were it not better done as others use,
To sport with Amaryllis in the shade . . .
Fame is the spur that the clear spirit
     doth raise . . .
But the fair Guerdon when we hope to find . . .
Comes the blind Fury with th'abhorred shears,
And slits the thin-spun life. "But not the praise,"
Phoebus repli'd, and touch'd my
     trembling ears;
"Fame is no plant that grows on mortal soil."[33]

And Ronsard, lamenting the death of yet another youth, attacks the
intervention of the same Fury:

Peu nous servent des ans les courses retournées;
Les vertus nous font l'âge et non pas les années. . . .
Or je reviens à toy, Parque qui n'as point d'yeux. . . .

33. Milton, p. 122.

Qui seule, sans merci, te plais à nous desplaire:
Tu devrois seulement tuer le populaire, ...
Ou, s'il est arresté que tout le monde passe,
Tu devrois pour le moins leur donner plus d'espace,
Et leur prester loisir, par un meilleur destin,
D'achever doucement, leurs cours jusqu'a à la fin,
Sans couper leur moisson avant qu'elle
        soit meure.

(II.476)

(The returning cycles of the years serve us little; virtues give us maturity and not years. . . . So I return to you, blind Atropos, . . . who alone without mercy please yourself by displeasing us: you should only kill the vulgar . . . or if it is required that all the world pass away, you should at least give them more time by a better fate to achieve their course smoothly to the end, without cutting the harvest before it is ripe.)

There is no necessary direct Miltonic debt to Ronsard, but these and the other precedents in Marot and the Huguenots confirm that "Lycidas" is a traditional work in almost all its details, distinguished like that of the other English poets we have encountered more by syncretic than inventive power. The English Renaissance poets found their best resource in transposing to their own needs the eccentric and intense distortions French poets had caused in the European tradition under pressure of their own country's religious and secular disorientation. Ronsard's skepticism (not to say his libertinism or Epicureanism) both prefigures Montaigne and looks forward to the cynicism of Théophile, St. Amant, and their circle. The use of pagan precedents as a cover for subjective vagaries is more marked in Ronsard than any earlier poet and is an important model for authors like Donne and Milton, both Anglican and Puritan.

Perhaps this derivation has always been obvious with a pastoral poem like "Lycidas," but far more idiosyncratic poems by Milton are also more traditional than their individual tones suggest. Nativity poems are not usually on the scale of the miniature epic achieved by Milton, yet Ronsard's "Hercule Chrestien" achieves a similar synthesis of pagan and biblical motifs, one that was notorious among Huguenots for the kind of bold syncretism of which *Paradise Lost* is the crowning example. The most incantatory lines of the "Nativity Ode" are probably those of the ending of the ancient cults:

> The Oracles are dumb
> No voice or hideous hum
>> Runs through the arched roof in words deceiving.
> Apollo from his shrine
> Can no more divine. . . .
> The lonely mountains o'er,
> And the resounding shore
>> A voice of weeping heard, and loud lament;
> From haunted spring and dale
> Edg'd with poplar pale,
>> The parting Genius is with sighing sent;
> With flow'r-inwov'n tresses torn
> The Nymphs in twilight shade of tangled
>> thickets mourn.[34]

The archaic pantheism is evoked here with a vividness, even nostalgia, which is very much Ronsard's own (and which reappears in the rural settings inspiring *Paradise Lost* III.26ff. and more ominously in *Paradise Regained* II.182ff.):

> A ton depart les gentilles Naiades,
> Faunes, Sylvains, Satyres et Dryades,
> Pans, Deitez de ces antres reclus,
> Sont disparus, et n'apparoissent plus.
> Loin de nos champs Flore s'en est allée,
> D'un habit noir Pomone s'est voilée,
> Et Apollon, qui fut jadis berger,
> Dedans nos champs ne daigne plus loger,
> Et le troupeau des neuf Muses compaignes
> Ainsi qu'en friche ont laissé nos montaignes . . .
> Bref, de nos bois toutes Deitez saintes,
> Cypris la belle et ses Graces desceintes,

34. Milton, p. 48.

Et nous laissant pour si piteux depart
La larme à l'oeil, habitent autre part.

(1.970)

(At your departure the gentle Naiads, Fauns, Sylvans, Satyrs and Dryads, Pans, Gods of remote caves have disappeared and no longer show themselves. Flora has gone far away from our fields; Pomona has veiled herself in a black costume, and Apollo, who was once a shepherd, does not deign to lodge in our fields any more, and the troop of nine companion Muses have left our mountains to become wildernesses. . . . In brief from all our woods the holy Deities, the beautiful Cypris and her uncinctured Graces live elsewhere, in tears leaving us for such a departure.)

It is typical of Ronsard's tactlessness that he ascribes to the departure of a princess consequences elsewhere ascribed to the coming of Christ. This is how Huguenot sensibilities were shocked into bitterness. Yet the deep empathy of Ronsard for the old order gives it a power recognized even in a Christian context when poets like Milton redeploy the same motifs to their own original ends.

One would expect that in using the increasingly archaic sonnet form Milton would find himself looking back to such classic models as Ronsard, and many of his sonnets do reflect this compatibility. We have already seen how Milton's sonnet on his blindness meets the charge of failing to turn his poetic skill to account in a reference used by Ronsard to meet similar criticisms of the Huguenots.[35] Ronsard had quoted his critics as accusing him of failing to use his proverbial talent, and Milton later applied the parable to his own inactivity:

Si Ronsard ne cachoit son talent dedans terre . . .
Et qu'il voulust du tout chanter de Jesus-Christ,
Il seroit tout parfait, car il a bon esprit.

(II.571)

(If Ronsard did not hide his talent in the earth . . . and if he wished wholly to sing of Jesus Christ, he would be quite perfect, for he has a good wit.)

35. See above, Chapter 7.

261

Milton justifies himself by asserting God's superiority to tribute. In defending himself from such charges to Henri III, Ronsard writes to the king in terms which risk further censure for blasphemous servility, for they apply this divine self-sufficiency to a mortal ruler:

> A vous qui avez tout, je ne sçaurois donner
> Present, tant soit-il grand, qui vous puisse estrener.
> Le terre est presque vostre, et dans le Ciel vous mettre,
> Je ne suis pas un Dieu, je ne puis le promettre. . . .
> Malin j'offenserois contre toute la France, . . .
> S'importun j'amusois vostre divin esprit . . .
> Dieu ne demande pas, car Dieu rien ne demande,
> Qu'on charge ses autels d'une pesante offrande:
> Il n'aime que le coeur, il regarde au vouloir,
> La seule volonté l'offrande fait valoir.
> Ainsi, suyvant de Dieu la divine nature,
> Vous prendrez mon vouloir, et non mon
>   escriture.
>
>   (1.800–804)

(To you who have all, I would not know how to give a present, however great which could hold you. The earth is almost yours, and I cannot promise to put you in heaven for I am not God. . . . Wretch, I would offend all France if I sought to distract your divine mind. . . . God does not ordain that we should load his altars with a weighty offering, for God does not ask for anything: he only loves the heart; he considers the willingness, the simple goodwill makes the offering worthy. Thus, following God's divine nature, you will accept my willingness, and not my writing.)

Ronsard characteristically deploys his enforced theological awareness as an apologist for courtly purposes, while Milton restores such metaphysical sophistication to its true subject of personal morality in his sonnet on his blindness, without forfeiting the intimacy and practical significance with which Ronsard's expediency had endowed it.

However, Milton also shares Ronsard's more Horatian moods when he advises Cyriack Skinner to make the best use of relaxation:

Today deep thoughts resolve with me to drench
In mirth, that after no repenting draws;
Let Euclid rest and Archimedes pause . . .
For other things mild Heav'n a time ordains,
And disapproves that care, though wise in show,
That with superfluous burden loads the day,
And when God sends a cheerful hour, refrains.[36]

The charmingly un-Puritan spirit of this piece provides a slightly more restrained analogue to Ronsard's typically energetic mood:

J'ay l'esprit tout ennuyé
D'avoir trop estudié
Les Phenomenes d'Arate:
Il est temps que je m'esbate,
Et que j'aille, aux champs jouer.
Bons Dieux! qui voudroit louer
Ceux qui collez sus un livre
N'ont jamais soucy de vivre?
(1.455)

(I have a mind quite wearied with too much study of Aratus' *Phaenomena*: it is time that I have some recreation and that I go to play in the fields. Good gods! Who would praise those that, stuck over a book, never have a desire to live?)

The language is delightfully direct and naturalistic, and again Ronsard is more authentically pagan-sounding; but his plans prove to be fairly modest: to enjoy a bottle of wine and some fresh fruit.

The same resemblance between the two poets appears if we juxtapose their two invitations to dinner, one to Maclou de la Haie and the other to Henry Lawrence:

Puis que d'ordre à son rang l'orage est revenu,
Si que le ciel voilé tout triste est devenu
Et la vefve forest branle son chef tout nu
    Sous le vent qui l'estonne,
C'est bien pour ce jourdhuy, ce me semble, raison,

36. Milton, p. 169.

Qui ne veut offenser la loy de la saison,
Prendre à gré les plaisirs que tousjours la maison
   En temps pluvieux donne.
Mais si j'augure bien, quand je voy pendre en bas
Les nuaux avallez, mardy ne sera pas
Si mouillé qu'aujourdhuy, nous prendrons le repas
   Tel jour nous deux ensemble.
Tandis chasse de toy tout le mordant souci. . . .
Du soin de l'advenir ton coeur ne soit
      espoint. . . .
Vien soul, car tu n'auras le festin ancien . . .
   Je hay tant de viandes.
Tu ne boiras aussi de ce Nectar divin
Que rend Anjou fameux; car volontiers le vin
Qui a senti l'humeur du terroir Angevin
   Suit les bouches friandes.

                 (1.508–9)

(Since the storm has duly returned, so that the clouded sky has become sad and the widowed forest shakes its naked head in the wind which startles it, it seems right to me today not to offend the rule of the season but to take willingly those pleasures which home offers in wet weather. But if I forecast correctly, when I see the low clouds hang down, Tuesday will not be so wet as today, and we shall take a meal together on that day. Meanwhile banish all care from you, . . . may your heart not be stabbed by care of the future. . . . Come having drunk well, for you will get no antique feast . . . I loathe so much food. You won't drink this divine nectar which makes Anjou famous either—for wine which has the savor of Angevin lands readily follows tasty morsels.)

Here Ronsard genuinely sounds like the urbane recluse which Petrarch also finally became at Arquà. It is a moment of total escape from controversy and brutality. However, we should recall he had also urged another friend not to be too consistently puritanical in such a retreat:

   Donq, pour attendre que le tour
   De ceste tempeste ennuyeuse
   Se change par le beau retour

D'une autre saison plus joyeuse . . .
Escri de main laborieuse
Des vers qui soyent dignes de toy . . .
Pesle-mesle dessus la table
Tibulle, Ovide soyent ouvers
Aupres de ton luth delectable,
Fidele compagnon des vers.
Dessus, par maints accords divers
Chasse de toy le souci grave . . .
Apres l'estude, il faut qu'on lave
L'esprit ja morne et perissant
D'un vin de reserve. . . .

(1.445–46)

(Therefore, to await the change of this wearisome tempest's visit
into the fine return of another more joyful season . . . write
verses worthy of you with careful hand . . . may Tibullus and
Ovid always lie open together on your table by your delicious
lute, the faithful companions of verse. Thereupon banish from
yourself heavy care with many varied harmonies. . . . After study
one must bathe the pale and fading spirit in a select wine. . . .)

We can see exactly how Milton follows the Humanist convention of
retreat from turbulent public involvement in politics and religious controversy. His delightfully hedonistic invitation to Lawrence avoids all
the intense issues of the time:

Now that the Fields are dank and ways are mire
Where shall we sometimes meet and by the fire
Help waste a sullen day, what may be won
From the hard Season gaining? Time will run
On smoother till Favonius re-inspire
The frozen earth, and clothe in fresh attire
The Lily and the Rose, that neither sow'd nor spun.
What neat repast shall feast us, light and choice,
Of Attic taste, with Wine, whence we may rise
To hear the Lute well toucht, or artful voice.[37]

37. Milton, pp. 168–69.

Typically the Puritan cannot resist the delicate biblical reference to Christ's parable of the beauty of the flowers—giving just that extra touch of moral intensity which marks so many English recensions of Ronsard's Epicurean effects. But otherwise the spirit of the two poets is in delightful harmony, equally superior to shallow prudishness and Puritan asceticism.

Even less predictable than this congruence of Catholic French cleric and Puritan recluse in elegant hedonism is a shared sober feminism which has been adequately recognized in neither. Ronsard unhesitatingly supported the role of Catherine de' Medici as effective ruler of France, recognizing "que le nom de femme, autrefois à mespris, / Par elle emporteroit sur les hommes de pris" (that the name of woman, hitherto despised, by her would win the prize over men [I.867]). He goes on to overbid even her worth by that of her mentor, Marguerite d'Angoulême, describing the consequences of the death of that benevolent mistress:

> Mais ainsi que Vesper la Cyprienne estoile
> De plus larges esclairs illumine la voile
> De la nuit tenebreuse, et sur tous les flambeaux
> Dont le Ciel est ardent, les siens sont les
> > plus beaux,
> Ainsi et la vertu, la grace et le merite
> De la sainte et divine et chaste Marguerite . . .
> Me semblerent, aux yeux sur les autres
> > reluire . . .
> Et comme vertueuse et d'honneur toute pleine,
> S'opposant à mon mal, charitable, mist peine
> D'avancer ma fortune, et fille et soeur d'un Roy
> Daigna bien, ô bonte! se souvenir de moy;
> Mais en perdant, helas! sa clairté coustumiere,
> Comme aveugle je suis demeuré sans lumiere.
> > (1.867–68)

(But just as Vesper, the evening star of Venus, with greater beams brightens the shadowy veil of night, and hers are finer than all the other flames burning in heaven, so the virtue, grace,

and merit of the saintly, divine, and chaste Marguerite . . . seemed
to my eyes to shine above others . . . and being virtuous and full
of honor, opposing my misfortune, charitably she took pains to
advance my fortune, and though she was daughter and sister
of a king she deigned, O goodness, to remember me; but when,
alas, I lost her customary brightness, like a blind man I have remained without light.)

The same pattern appears more literally in Milton's dream of his dead
wife, returning like the heroic Queen Alcestis, whose bravery exceeded
her husband's in laying down her life for him. His wife, it seems to
Milton:

> Came vested all in white, pure as her mind:
> Her face was veil'd, yet to my fancied sight,
> Love, sweetness, goodness, in her person shin'd
> So clear, as in no face with more delight.
> But O, as to embrace me she inclin'd,
> I wak'd, she fled, and day brought back my
> night.[38]

There is a startling heightened effect in Milton's conclusion, going far
beyond Ronsard's curiously parallel last couplet quoted, which reminds
us how Donne also took conventional motifs used by Ronsard and gave
them a new intensity. The skilled use of such a shocking and paradoxical conclusion may also remind us of Herbert's use of these motifs.

On the other hand, we tend to think of Milton's greater poems as
owing more to the Huguenot epic poets, like d'Aubigné and above all
du Bartas, than to Ronsard, whose *Franciade* seemed an aberration even
to himself. Yet Ronsard's dynamic neoclassicism endowed several of
his expository poems with qualities which prefigure *Paradise Lost* in
significant ways. It is true that Ronsard often vigorously rejected archaic
epic modes and topics in ways compatible with Huguenot contempt
for pagan motifs:[39]

> Qui pensez vous qui puisse escrire
> L'ardente ire
> D'Ajax, le fils de Telamon,

38. Milton, p. 171.   39. See McFarlane, pp. 331 ff.

Ou d'Hector rechanter la gloire,
   Ou l'histoire
De la race du vieil Emon? . . .
Adieu donc, enfants de la Terre,
   Qui la guerre
Entreprintes contre les Dieux,
Ce n'est pas moy qui vous raconte,
   Ne qui monte
Avecque vous jusques aux Cieux.
                    (II.714)

(Who do you think may write the fierce anger of Ajax, son of
Telamon, or sing again of Hector's glory, on the story of old
Emon's race? . . . Farewell then, sons of earth who made war
against the gods, it is not I who will narrate your story, nor
who will mount to the heavens with you.)

Yet this very motif of rejection of ambitious heroism is what Milton
uses to introduce the theme of the Fall, the climactic movement of
Paradise Lost, at the start of Book IX, which expresses the same contempt for classical swashbuckling as the French puritans felt in comparing it with modern moral concerns:

             Sad task, yet argument
Not less but more Heroic than the wrath
Of stern Achilles on his Foe pursu'd . . .
Wars, hitherto the only Argument
Heroic deem'd, chief maistry to dissect
With long and tedious havoc fabl'd Knights.
                    (IX.13ff.)

Even more striking is the opening of Ronsard's *Hymne de la Justice*
where he modestly tells the cardinal of Lorraine that he chooses not to
celebrate the bellicose virtues of traditional heroism—no doubt alienated
by contemporary analogues to its horrors:

Un plus scavant que moy, ou plus cheri des Cieux
Chantera les combas de tes nobles ayeux,
Dira de Godefroy l'aventureuse armée

Et la palme conquise en la terre Idumée
Et le cours du Jourdain qui fut si plein de morts
Que le sang infidele outre-couloit ses bords . . .
Il me suffist, Prelat, si chantant je puis dire
L'une de tes vertus dessus ma basse lyre.

(II.154-55)

(One more learned than I or more favored of the heavens will
sing the battles of your noble ancestors, will tell of Godefroy's
adventurous army and the palms conquered in Palestine and
the valley of the Jordan which was so full of dead that the in-
fidel's blood overflowed its banks. . . . It is enough for me, prel-
ate, if in singing I can speak of one of your virtues upon my
base lyre.)

The virtue Ronsard chooses is justice, and this sets up a pattern
which Miltonists will instantly recognize, for he surveys the history
of justice from the time of the Age of Gold, using the opening of
Ovid's *Metamorphoses* for his basic references, just as Milton does to
give depth and detail to enrich the spare biblical account of the Garden
of Eden on which he founded *Paradise Lost*. Ronsard follows Ovid's
account of the decline of mankind into sin which is outlined also in
the last books of *Paradise Lost*. Affronted Justice flees to Heaven,
where Ronsard's "Jupiter" again follows Ovid in staging a great council to decide how to deal with mankind's failure. The traditional holo-
caust by flood is determined, but at this point the intervention of Clemency strikes a note Milton favors later in his heavenly council:

"Pere, puis qu'il te plaist entre tes noms admettre
Le nom de tres-benin, il faut aussi permettre
A ta rigueur d'user des effects de ce nom;
Autrement tu serois en vain appellé bon.
Tu peux, si tu le veux, tous ce monde desfaire
Qu'en moin d'un seul clin d'oeil tu le pourras bien faire;
Ce qu'il ne faut, Seigneur, car la destruction
N'est pas seante à Dieu, mais generation. . . .
Si tu destruis le Monde, il faudra qu'il retiene
De son premier Chaos la figure ancienne; . . .

269

Il vaut mieux, ô Seigneur, que tu les espouvantes
Par songés, par Daimons, par Cometes volantes. . . .
Si tu frappes leur coeur, ils te voudront
      entendre."

(II.161–62)

(Father, since it pleases you to admit the title of most kindly
among your names, you must also permit your rigor to use the
effects of this name, otherwise you would be called good in
vain. You can, if you wish it, undo all this world, for in less
than the blink of an eye you can easily do it, but you should
not Lord, for destruction is not fitting for God, but creation.
. . . If you destroy this world, it must return to the ancient condition of primal chaos. . . . It is better, Lord, that you terrify
them with dreams and spirits, with flying comets. . . . If you
knock on their heart that they will seek to hear you.)

The same sentiments recur after Milton's Creation: "to create / Is
greater than created to destroy" (VII.606–7), but it is startling to discover that in Ronsard's council the final factor working for Clemency
lies in Themis' anticipation of a savior who will redeem human viciousness: a hero who is no other than "Henri second." Milton has at least
the advantage of keeping Jesus Christ at the core of the redemption,
under the guise of the Son, who adopts Clemency's role as well as that
of Themis, not to discuss Henri II. Again Ronsard's instinctive paganism and enforced submission to courtly pressures deflect him into a
superficiality of the kind which rightly earned him Huguenot censure.
The more rigorous ethical awareness and social isolation of the mature
Milton averts this kind of obtuseness.

    However, many of Milton's syncretic effects in *Paradise Lost* are
fully prefigured in Ronsard. The birth of Minerva from the head of
Zeus is frequently deployed to contemporary purposes by the French
poet, but where Ronsard uses it positively though politically (as when
describing the virtues of Marguerite de Savoie as similarly born of
the mind of François I), Milton degrades the myth deliberately by ad-
justing the pagan divinities to the roles of Satan's gestation of Sin (II.
752ff.). Even the hurling of Vulcan from heaven exploited by Milton
(I.740–51) is applied more tenderly by Ronsard to the fanciful fate of

the spirit of Winter, though many of the details of the day-long fall
are picked up by Milton, including "the setting sun":

> Il estoit rechigné, hergneux et solitaire;
> Et pource Jupiter, de tous les Dieux le pere,
> Prevoyant qu'il seroit quelque monstre odieux,
> Ainsi qu'il fist Vulcan, le renversa des cieux.
> Alors le pauvre Hyver, à teste renversée,
> Fut culbuté par l'air d'une cheute eslancée
> Roüant dés le matin jusqu'au Soleil
> couchant, . . .
> A la fin, en glissant par le travers les nuës,
> S'arresta, renversé, sur les rives chenuës
> De Strymon.
>
> (II.252–53)

(He was outcast, cantankerous, and solitary, and therefore Jupiter, father of all the gods, foreseeing that he would be some
odious monster, as he did to Vulcan, threw him out of the heavens. Then poor Winter was tumbled head over heels through the
air in a flying fall spinning from the morning to the sunset. . . .
In the end in gliding through the clouds he stopped, upended,
on the snowy banks of Strymon.)

Interestingly enough, the insult allows Boreas to encourage Winter
"d'entreprendre la guerre encontre Jupiter" (to undertake war against
Jupiter). One detects echoes of the subversive spirit rampant in the
Civil Wars:

> "Veux-tu souffrir, qu'on face au Ciel si peu
> d'estime
> De toy, jeune guerrier? et que tu sois fraudé . . .
> Quels sont tes alliéz? et quelle est ta puissance?
> Combien tu as de mains, de jambes et de bras,
> Pour renverser du Ciel ce Jupiter à bas?
> Il se vante d'avoir une maison ferrée . . .
> Et que seul, quand il veut, les Dieux peut
> surmonter. . . .
> Mais ce qui plus me fasche, et m'espoinçonne d'ire,

C'est qu'il avance au Ciel je ne sçay quel Satyre,
Une Mercure larron, un Mavors rioteux. . . .
Courage, la vertu n'est pas une fumée
Qui deça, qui delà s'esvanouyt en vain:
Elle veut l'action du coeur et de la main. . . .
Courage, compagnon, jouyis de ta contrée;
Quant à moy, je suis fils de l'Aurore et d'Astrée,
Et ne veux endurer que ce tort te soit fait;
Le magnanime coeur se cognoist à l'effet."

(II.253–54)

(Will you suffer that one make little of you in heaven, young
warrior, and that you be defrauded? . . . Who are your allies,
and what is your strength, how many heads, legs, and arms have
you to throw down from heaven this Jupiter? He boasts of
having an iron house . . . and that alone when he wishes he can
overcome the gods . . . but what most irritates me and provokes
my rage is that he promotes in heaven any unknown satyr, a
thieving Mercury, a riotous Mars. . . . Courage, virtue is not a
wraith which here and there fades to nothing; it seeks action
of heart and hand. . . . Courage, companion, enjoy your territory; as for me, I am son of Aurora and Astrea, and I will not
endure the harm that is done you; the magnanimous heart is
known by its results.)

The renewed rebellion evolves in a pattern fully prefiguring Milton's
Battle in Heaven, in which the envious Satan tries to overthrow the
new power of the Son, in its turn frequently echoing England's own
Civil War. The first muster of Winter's forces affords an epic picture
of the assembled Titans, on whom Ronsard projects traits of the Spanish
allies of the League and the German mercenaries who exploited the
French wars:

De la piste et du cry des chevaux hanissans
Et des soldars, chargez de harnois fremissans,
Du nombre d'estandars, du cliquetis des armes,
Dont les boucliers flamboient comme ces
    grands cheveux

> Des Cometes, qui sont envenimez de feux,
> Qui, deçà, qui delà, leurs grands rayons
> espandent.
>
> (II.255)

(of the trampling and cry of neighing steeds and the soldiers armed with vibrating harness, of the number of standards, of the clatter of weapons and an unfamiliar race of barbarous fighting men whose shields flash like the great tails of comets envenomed with fire which scatter their rays here and there.)

One recalls the imagery of the raising in Hell of Satan's "mighty standard":

> Th' Imperial Ensign, which full high advanc't
> Shone like a Meteor streaming to the Wind . . .
> Ten thousand Banners rise into the Air
> With Orient Colors waving: with them rose
> A Forest huge of Spears: and thronging Helms
> Appear'd, and serried Shields in thick array . . .
> Advanc't in view they stand, a horrid Front,
> Of dreadful length and dazzling Arms, in guise
> Of Warriors old with order'd Spear and Shield.
>
> (1.536ff.)

It is noteworthy that Milton defines Satan's domain as "the spacious North" (V.726) and compares the fallen angels to

> A multitude, like which the populous North
> Pour'd never from her frozen loins, to pass
> Rhene or the Danaw, when her barbarous Sons
> Came like a deluge.
>
> (1.351–54)

since, of course, the allies of Winter necessarily appear in exactly this northerly aspect in Ronsard. In fact among the Titans listed by him is "le fort Briarée" (the strong Briareus), and Milton also associates his fallen angels with these giants "of monstrous size, / Titanian, or Earth-born, that warr'd on Jove, /Briareos or Typhon" (I.197–99). At very least we may see in Ronsard a precedent for Milton's redeployment of Ovid's account of the rebellion against Jove (*Metamorphoses* X. 151ff.).

Ronsard's hymns on abstract virtues or themes, like justice or eternity, provide metaphysical precedents for Miltonic paeans heightening the text of *Paradise Lost,* and even allegorical effects like the discussion between Satan and Chaos (II.959ff.) find some precedent in the *Hyme de l'Eternité* (II.123). But we should recognize above all how immediately France affords images for the theme of the viciousness of civil war. It is self-evident that Ronsard's "La Harangue de . . . Duc de Guise aux soldats de Metz" might prove relevant to effects in Henry V's battle orations in Shakespeare like the savagery of the sack threatened in the speech before Harfleur and the superior recognition promised in the St. Crispin's Day speech (IV.iii.18–67) to bravery over mere rank if anyone is, as in Ronsard, "le premier sur la breche" (the first in the breach). It is more curious to find that for Milton, almost a hundred years later, the English Civil War has not basically disturbed the imagery of heroic warfare. Before the "harangue" Ronsard evokes the power-mad figure of the Holy Roman Emperor Charles:

> Empereur, qui se donne en songeant
> Tout l'Empire du monde, et qui se va rongeant
> D'une gloire affamée, et d'un soin d'entreprendre
> De vouloir, à son dam, contre nostre Roy prendre
> Les nouveaux murs François d'une foible cité,
> Où le Destin avoit son outre limité.
>
> (II.304)

(Emperor, who gives himself in a dream the empire of the world and who goes gnawn by hunger of glory and of care to undertake to his ruin a determination against our king of seizing the new French walls of a feeble city where destiny had set the limits of his extent.)

The campaign of "ce grand Empereur / Ne nous tient assiegez que par une fureur / Naissant de desespoir" (this great emperor held us besieged only by a madness born of despair [II.309]). Ironically, the Emperor's historical opponent, the duc de Guise, when described by Ronsard appears little less satanic, in Miltonic terms (see Plate 10):

Puis ils saisit apres sa merveilleuse targe,
Forte, massive, dure, en rondeur aussi large
Qu'est un Soleil couchant.
(II.305)

(Then he seized next his wonderful shield, strong, massive,
hard, in diameter as broad as is a setting sun.)

Milton describes Satan's equipment analogously, with the same classical models in mind:

> his ponderous shield
> Ethereal temper, massy, large and round
> Behind him cast; the broad circumference
> Hung on his shoulders like the Moon, whose Orb
> Through Optic Glass the Tuscan artist views.
> (1.284–88)

Each poet communicates negative overtones—Ronsard unconsciously,
Milton deliberately. Guise has suicidal sentiments like Hotspur's "Die
all, die merrily" (*1HIV* IV.i.134) when he exclaims, "Mouron, mouron, Amis, il vaut mieux" (die, die, friends, it is better [II.308]). Ronsard's final picture of the great Catholic captain unconsciously evokes
for us, with hindsight, the image of the archetypal fiend in Milton:

> Ainsi parla ton frere, inspirant au courage
> Des siens une prouësse, une horreur, une rage
> De combatre obstinez; son panache pendant
> Terriblement courbé, par ondes descendant
> Sur le dos escaillé, du haut de la terrace. . . .
> Comme un brandon de feu le rond de son
>   bouclair
> Escartoit parmi l'air un monstrueux esclair,
> Non autrement qu'on voit une rouge Cometé
> Enflamer tout le ciel d'une crineuse trette,
> Ou tout ainsi qu'on voit flamber le Sirien
> Aus plus chaud jour d'esté, quand la gueule
>   du Chien,

275

Allumant tout le Ciel d'une flameche forte,
Aux hommes et la soif et les fiévres apporte.

(II.310)

(Thus spoke your brother, inspiring a prowess in the courage
of his followers, an awed fear, a rage to fight obstinately; his
crest hung in a terrible sweep falling in waves on his scaly back
on the high terrace. . . . Like a flaming brand the round of his
shield shot through the air a monstrous flash just as one sees a
red comet inflame all heaven with a hairy train, or just as one sees
the star Sirius in the hottest of summer, when the dog's throat,
firing all heaven with a strong flaming coal, brings thirst and
fevers to men.)

While one understands the supposed virtue in a captain of striking
terror on the battlefield, Ronsard's "praise" verges on evoking a monster rather than a hero—if not exactly Satan, at least a Coriolanus. Moreover, Ronsard is as aware as Milton that sustained savagery ensures
damnation:

Mais Dieu, qui des malings n'a pitie ny mercy,
Comme au Roy Pharaon, a leur coeur endurcy,
A fin que tout d'un coup sa main puissante
          et haute
Les corrige en fureur et punisse leur faute.

(II.559)

(But God, who has neither pity nor mercy for the wicked as for
King Pharaoh, has hardened their heart so that suddenly his
strong and high hand may correct them furiously and punish
their fault.)

Both poets find "Busire" (II.558) or "Busiris" (I.306) the epitome of
such "perfidious hatred," and it may be felt that even in Ronsard (as
surely in Milton) there is not much to choose between the harshness
of either side in religious strife; Guise is not much preferable to the
Huguenots, even in Ronsard. The poet's retreat to rural life in part
reflects alienation from all political parties and religious sects.

Similar ironies lurk in the fact that the praise lavished on Mary
Stuart by Ronsard (II.294) proves equally suggestive of censure when

reapplied to Dalilah by Milton.[40] Nor, in an age of controversy, is either poet unaware of the difficulty of defining the narrow boundary between vice and virtue, in which only a slight shift of perspective is crucial. Milton had written memorably in *Areopagitica*: "As therefore the state of man now is, what wisdom can there be to choose, what continence to forbear without the knowledge of evil? He that can apprehend and consider vice with all her baits and seeming pleasures, and yet abstain, and yet distinguish, and yet prefer that which is truly better, he is the true warfaring Christian."[41] But many years before, Ronsard had advised on the education of the youthful King Charles IX:

> Car ce n'est pas le tout de sçavoir la vertu:
> Il faut cognoistre aussi le vice revestu
> D'un habit vertueux, qui d'autant plus offence,
> Qu'il se monstre honorable, et a belle apparence.
> De là vous apprendrez à vous cognoistre bien,
> Et en vous cognoissant vous ferez
> > tousjours bien.
> Le vray commencement pour en vertus accroistre
> C'est, disoit Apollon, soy-mesme se cognoistre:
> Celuy qui se cognoist est seul maistre de soy,
> Et, sans avoir Royaume, il est vrayment un Roy.
> Commencez donc ainsi; puis, si tost que par l'âge
> Vous serez homme fait de corps et de courage,
> Il faudra de vous-meme apprendre à
> > commander.
>
> > (II.562)

(For it is not the whole to know virtue; one must know also vice clothed in virtuous appearance, which is the more offensive in that it seems honorable and of fine appearance. Thereby you will learn to know yourself well, and in knowing yourself you will always do well. The true beginning of growth in virtues is to know yourself as Apollo said; he who knows himself is alone

---

40. See "Samson Agonistes," lines 710–25. The basic image is of a great ship in each case.

41. Milton, p. 728.

master of himself and, without having a kingdom, is truly a king. Begin thus therefore; then, as soon as age makes you man in body and spirit, you must learn to have command of yourself.)

All these sentiments have numerous antique and Renaissance precedents,[42] but it is worth noting that Milton returns to them throughout *Paradise Regained*, which in many phrases parallels Ronsard's program for the education of Charles IX as a ruler:

> Yet he who reigns within himself, and rules
> Passions, Desires, and Fears, is more a King;
> Which every wise and virtuous man attains:
> And who attains not, ill aspires to rule.
>
> (II.466–69)

Indeed, another address to the youthful king permits Ronsard to prefigure one of the most magnificent passages Milton ever wrote: the evocation of the glories of ancient Greece. A little ironically the role of Ronsard as adviser to the young king approximates that of Milton's Satan tempting Christ, for if Ronsard attacks "l'orgueil des grands Rois d'Assyrie" (the pride of the great kings of Assyria [I.821]), whom Milton's Christ repudiates, Ronsard also encourages Charles in emulation of Hercules as a naive reformer:

> Hercule alloit la terre tournoyant,
> De tous costez les monstres guerroyant;
> Et vous tournez vostre royaume, Sire,
> Pour sainctement nettoyer vostre Empire
> De toute erreur et de monstres qui vont
> Sans plus avoir la honte sur le front.
>
> (I.822)

(Hercules went round the world fighting monsters on every side, and you go around your kingdom, sire, to clean out religiously all error and monsters who go about without shame on their faces any longer.)

42. See Milton, pp. 476–77.

Milton's Christ refuses the Devil's simplistic invitation to do likewise and take over the Roman empire in order to "expel a brutish monster" (IV.128). This pessimism reflects the rueful sense of post-Restoration England that reform is less easy than it had seemed once. Even more antithetical is Milton's verdict on classical Greece. Ronsard had predicted that Charles IX,

> Comme Alexandre, aurez l'ame animée,
> Du chaud desir de conduire une armée
> Outre l'Europe, et d'assaults vehemens
> Oster le sceptre aux puissans Ottomans
> Qui sous leurs mains par armes ont saisie
> Tout le meilleur d'Europe et de l'Asie . . .
> Rompre leur Sceptre, et d'une foy meilleure
> Gaigner les coeurs des peuples Asiens . . .
> Là vous voirrez tant de villes hautaines,
> Fieres du nom de ces vieux Capitaines
> Alexandrie, Antioche, et aussi . . .
> De l'autre part la Grece, qui est telle
> Qu'onque en beauté terre ne fut plus belle,
> Qui a conceu tant de peuple guerriers,
> Et tant de fronts couronnez de Lauriers,
> Mere des Arts, des Philosophes mere,
> Dont l'ame vive, ingenieuse et clere
> Abandonna la terre, pesant lieu,
> Et d'un grand coeur s'en vola jusqu' à Dieu, . . .
> Sceut le Destin, et ce qu'on dit Fortune; . . .
> Bref, ceste Grece, oeil du monde habitable.
>
> (1.827–29)

(Like Alexander, you will have a soul fired by the hot desire to lead an army out of Europe and, with fierce attacks, to seize the sceptre from the fierce Ottomans, who beneath their hands by arms have gripped all the best of Europe and Asia, . . . to break their sceptre and with a better religion win the hearts of the Asian peoples. . . . There you will see so many haughty cities proud of names from these ancient captains, Alexandria, Anti-

279

och, and also . . . on the other hand Greece, which is such that
nothing else on earth has equalled it in beauty, which has conceived so many warlike people and so many heads crowned with
laurel, mother of arts, mother of philosophers whose lively soul,
ingenious and lucid, left the earth, heavy spot, and with great
heart flew away as far as God . . . knew destiny and what is called
fortune . . . in brief this Greece, eye of the habitable world.)

It seems Milton largely shared Ronsard's humanistic vision of Greece,
for the panegyric of Athens in Book IV of *Paradise Regained* echoes
such lines in detail:

> Be famous then
> By wisdom; as thy Empire must extend,
> So let extend thy mind o'er all the world,
> In knowledge, all things in it comprehend. . . .
> Westward, much nearer by Southwest, behold
> Where on the Aegean shore a City stands
> Built nobly, pure the air, and light the soil,
> Athens, the eye of Greece, Mother of Arts
> And Eloquence, native to famous wits . . .
> The schools of ancient Sages; his who bred
> Great Alexander to subdue the world. . . .
> Thence what the lofty grave Tragedians taught
> In Chorus or Iambic, teachers best . . .
> To sage Philosophy next lend thine ear.
>
> (IV.221ff.)

The parallels of phrase are perceptible: "Mere des Arts, des Philosophes
mere," "Grece, oeil du monde"—"Athens, the eye of Greece, Mother
of Arts . . . native to famous wits." Yet one's overpowering impression
remains that of the antithetical intent of the two evocations: written
before the worst of the Civil Wars in France, Ronsard's is designed
seriously to inspire the desire to reconquer Greece in a new crusade.
After a century of confusion, Milton puts the identical praise of Greece
into the mouth of a Satan seeking to inspire what now seem vicious
intellectual ambitions in Jesus. A hundred and fifty years of the Reformation have turned the sophistication of Greece from a positive

inspiration to aggressive heroism, into a diabolic resource for megalomania. To Milton, Ronsard's humanist counsels for the rearing of the young king in classical virtues approximate the voice of the devil incarnate, and without Ronsard as foil to Milton our sense of the triumph of Reformation over Renaissance values here would be less categorical.

Paradoxically we find Milton's fellow Puritan, Andrew Marvell, infinitely more sympathetic to the hedonism and volatile moods of the French poet, whose flight from public affairs into Epicurean retreat and rural meditation provides invaluable clues to this English poet's attitudes toward the elusive personae of his lyrics. Ronsard's verse fluctuates with his mood and momentary role: sometimes the pagan sensualist, sometimes the court's advocate, sometimes the ecstatic enthusiast, or alternately the stoic, the rural mystic, or the stern moralist. Ronsard's idiosyncracy matches the vicissitudes of his environment and is shared to a lesser degree by his contemporaries and his heirs, like St. Amant. Marvell's career passed through a similar spectrum of roles reflected in his verse from its lyric, idyllic phrases to its sardonically satirical ones. Marvell can affect as extravagant moods as Ronsard—indeed "The Definition of Love" is very much in the fantastical vein of a Ronsard sonnet "pour Astrée":

> Dois-je voler, emplumé d'esperance,
> Ou si je dois, forcé du desespoir,
> Du haut du Ciel en terre laisser choir
> Mon jeune amour avorté de naissance?
> Non, j'aime mieux, leger d'outrecuidance,
> Tomber d'en-haut et fol me decevoir. . . .
> Icare fit de sa cheute nommer,
> Pour trop oser, les ondes de la mer: . . .
> Ronsard voulant aux astres s'eslever
> Fut foudroyer par une belle Astrée.
>
> (1.205)

(Must I fly, plumed by hope, or should I, driven by despair from high heaven to earth, let fall my youthful love, abortive from birth? No, I would prefer, light with ambition, to fall from on high and madly deceive myself. . . . Icarus, by daring too much, by his fall gave a name to the sea waves: . . . Ronsard wishing to reach the stars was blasted by a beautiful Astrée.)

The wilfulness is explored self-consciously as well as wittily. It seems Marvell is conscious of working in the same vein when he writes, just as wilfully and ingeniously, of as virginal a mistress as the mythological Astrea, who withdrew from human vice to heaven:

> My Love is of a birth as rare
> As 'tis for object strange and high:
> It was begotten by despair
> Upon Impossibility.
>
> Magnanimous Despair alone
> Could show me so divine a thing,
> Where feeble Hope could ne'r have flown
> But vainly flapt its Tinsel Wing.[43]

One notes how any classical allusion of the kind which is always overt in Ronsard (to Icarus in this case) has faded away in the English version, with a consequent increase in the impression of originality and intellectual rigor. Moreover, the astronomical imagery derived from the name "Astrée" has become an extended conceit, as Marvell suggests the problem of the "Opposition of the Stars" can only be solved if "the giddy Heaven fall." Yet, in fact, Marvell's poem is not as unusual in its extravagant sentiments as New Critical approaches, hostile to arguments of historical context, imply. Marvell's cosmopolitan experience in literature and travel may have been undervalued, and inescapable models and precedents for idiosyncratic attitudes may also have been neglected. Ronsard can equal what Elizabeth Donno calls Marvell's "distinctive hyperbolical and paradoxical cast"[44] in his "Definition":

> vostre gentil esprit
> S'asseure que le Temps ny la Mort ny Fortune,
> Ny tout ce qui depend d'envie ou de rancune,

43. Marvell, ed. Margoliouth, vol. 1, pp. 36–37.
44. Andrew Marvell, *Complete Poems*, ed. Elizabeth S. Donno (Harmondsworth: Penguin, 1972), p. 232.

Ne scauroient empescher ny ce bien ny cest heur
Que je ne sois tousjours vostre humble
        serviteur, . . .
Car tant plus je verray mon fait desesperé,
Plus je verray mon coeur d'esperance asseuré,
Et feray fondement d'une perserverance,
Quand de plus esperer je perdray l'esperance.

(11.49–50)

(Your kind mind may assure itself that neither time nor death
nor fortune, nor anything based on envy or spite, would be able
to prevent this goodness or this happiness that I should be always your humble servant . . . for the more I see my act to be
despairing, the more I see my heart firm in hope, and I shall
establish perseverance when I lose the hope of further hope.)

Recalling that Marvell's love "was begotten by despair / Upon Impossibility," there seems little to choose in extravagance of sentiment
between the two poets; but on the other hand Marvell's development
of the astronomical imagery is far more technically exact, in using
words like "planisphere" and in the geometry of parallel lines which
concludes his poem.[45]

It may seem pointless to pursue the more popular genre affording
an infinite number of precedents for "To his Coy Mistress" (including Greek epigrams like one translated by Ronsard), but it is worth
noting that the most comparably famous *carpe diem* poem of the
Renaissance may well be Ronsard's "Mignonne, allons voir si la rose.
. . ." Moreover, since Marvell's forensic structure of "if . . . then . . . but
. . . therefore . . ." is still regarded as his unique contribution to the
topic, we should recognize the precedents in such poems as this:

Quand au temple nous serons
Agenouillez nous ferons
Les devots . . .
Mais quand au lict nous serons

45. This development is explored by Rosalie Colie, *My Echoing Song: Andrew
Marvell's Poetry of Criticism* (Princeton: Princeton University Press, 1970),
pp. 58–59.

Entrelassez, nous ferons
Les lascifs . . .
Pourquoy donc, quand je veux . . .
Ou baiser ta bouche aimée,
Ou toucher à ton beau sein,
Contrefais-tu la nonnain
Dedans un cloistre enfermée?
Pour qui gardes tu tes yeux
Et ton sein delicieux,
Ton front, ta lévre jumelle?
En veux-tu baiser Pluton
Là bas? . . .
Apres ton dernier trespas . . .
Ton test n'aura plus de peau . . .
Donque tandis que tu vis,
Change, Maistresse, d'avis. . . .

     (1.57–58)

(When we are kneeling in church we shall act religiously . . .
but when we are intertwined in bed we shall act lustfully. . . .
Why therefore, when I wish . . . either to kiss your beloved
mouth, or touch your beautiful breast do you pretend to be a
little nun enclosed in a cloister? For whom are you keeping your
eyes and your delicious breast, your forehead, your twinned
lip? Are you going to kiss Pluto with it down there? . . . After
your final end, your head will have no more skin. . . . Therefore,
while you are living, change your views, mistress. . . .)

The sense of a sardonic demonstration sequentially pursued may lack
some of the virtuoso detail of Marvell, but certainly it equals him in
coherence and in cynical sensuality, for the poem ends with a plea to
caress the woman's breasts and thighs.

Similarly shared commonplaces link a poem like Marvell's "Bermudas" with Ronsard's "Les Isles Fortunees." No less than the Puritan,
Ronsard is fleeing the horrors of religious bigotry, in mind at least, for
the idyllic western isles that have haunted the European imagination
from time immemorial:

Fuyon, fuyon quelque part où nos piez
Ou nos bateaux dextrement desliez
Nous conduiront . . . .
Pousson la nef à ce bord bien-heureux
Au port heureux des Isles bien-heurées,
Que l'Ocean de ses eaux azurées,
Loin de l'Europe, et loin des ses combas,
Pour nostre bande emmure de ses bras. . . .
Là, sans mentir, les arbres se jaunissent
D'autant de fruits que leurs boutons fleurissent;
Et sans faillir, en tous temps diaprez
De mille fleurs, s'y peinturent les prez. . . .
Avec grand bruit les pins on ne renverse
Pour aller voir d'une longue traverse
Quelqu' autre monde; ains jamais descouverts
On ne les voit de leurs ombrages verts
Par trop de chaud, ou par trop de froidure . . .
Loin des combats, loin des guerres mutines,
Loin des soucis, de soins et de remors, . . .
Aux bords divins des isles bien-heureuses,
Que Jupiter reserva pour les siens. . . .
La pauvre Europe! Europe que les Dieux
Ne daignent plus regarder de leurs yeux.

(II.410–14)

(Let us flee, flee somewhere that our feet or our dexterously un-
moored boats will carry us. . . . Push the ship to this happy coast
at the good port of the fortunate isles, which the ocean with its
azure waters walls round with its arms for our troop far from
Europe and far from its wars. . . . There, without lie, the trees
yellow with as many fruits as their buds flower, and without fail
at all times the dappled fields there are painted with a thousand
flowers. . . . With a great noise the pines are not cut down to go
to see by a long voyage some other world; thus one never sees
them stripped of their green shades by too much heat or too
much cold. . . . Far from fighting, far from mutinous wars, far
from anxieties, cares, and remorse . . . on the heavenly shores of

the fortunate isles which Jupiter reserved for his people. . . .
Poor Europe! Europe which the gods no longer deign to view
with their eyes.)

As usual Ronsard's elegy is an encyclopedia of classic motifs Marvell
could hardly avoid. We may recognize "les arbres jaunissant . . . de
fruits" and "leurs ombrages verts" as possible prototypes for the works
of Marvell's god:

> He hangs in shades the Orange bright,
> Like golden lamps in a green Night.[46]

Marvell's god is nearer the Old Testament Jehovah creating a new
Garden of Eden for his faithful, yet his peaceful blessings parallel those
of Ronsard's Jupiter. While avoiding Ronsard's stress on the ominous
European religious wars, Marvell otherwise observed all the conventions of the topic. However, Marvell dextrously substitutes overt biblical references for every allusion to the pagan classics in Ronsard's
vein, so that the effect is no less true to Reformation concerns.

This Puritanism differs more in surface than sentiment from Ronsard's distaste for modern Renaissance sophistication in comparison
with the rural dreams of his native Vendômois:

> Les chesnes ombrageux, que sans art la Nature
> Par les hautes forests nourrist à l'avanture,
> Sont plus doux aux troupeaux, et plus frais
>   aux bergers
> Que les arbres entez d'artifice és vergers;
> Des libres oiselets plus doux est le ramage
> Que n'est le chant contraint du rossignol en cage,
> Et la source d'une eau saillante d'un rocher
> Est plus douce au passant pour la soif estancher,
> Quand sans art elle coule en sa rive rustique,
> Que n'est une fontaine en marbre magnifique,
> Jallissant par effort en un tuyay doré
> Au milieu de la court d'un Palais honoré . . .
> Car tousjours la nature est meilleure que l'art.
>   (1.917–18)

46. Marvell, ed. Margoliouth, vol. 1, p. 17.

(Shady oaks, which nature has artlessly raised by chance in high forests, are sweeter to flocks and fresher to shepherds than the trees grafted artificially in orchards; free birds are sweeter in warbling than the constrained song of the caged nightingale, and the spring water leaping from a rock is sweeter to the passerby to assuage his thirst when it flows artlessly in its rustic banks than is a magnificent fountain in marble spouting strenuously by a gilded pipe in the middle of the courtyard of a noble palace . . . for nature is always better than art.)

Nor is this a pastoral affectation. In an intensely autobiographical address to Pierre Lescot, the architect of the Louvre, Ronsard insists that "il est mal-aisé de forcer la nature" (it is uncomfortable to force nature) because "la nature ne veut en rien estre forcée" (nature resists being forced in anything [II.424–25]). Hence Lescot is advised that he should have "franchement suivi ton naturel" (frankly followed his own nature). There is little doubt that Marvell's "Mower against Gardens" is following this model in his attack on "Luxurious Man" for turning the fields "where Nature was most plain and pure" into stagnant gardens full of vicious hybrids and paradoxical grafts:

> 'Tis all enforc'd; the Fountain and the Grot;
>   While the sweet Fields do lye forgot:
> Where willing Nature does to all dispence
>   A wild and fragrant Innocence.
> And Fauns and Faryes do the Meadows till
>   More by their presence than their skill.[47]

This is wholly in the pantheistic spirit of Ronsard serenading the tutelary genius of "la Forest de Gastine," where he lies "couché sous tes ombrages verts" (stretched beneath your green shade) and wishes its copses may always be full of satyrs, sylvans, and nymphs (II.452–53).[48]

In such "green shades" Ronsard undergoes strange vicissitudes: because his mistress is called Genévre he finds it easy to transport his passion to the shrub which bears the same name in French (the juniper):

47. Marvell, ed. Margoliouth, vol. 1, pp. 40–41.
48. See Richmond, *Renaissance Landscapes*, pp. 63 ff.

> Or-sus! embrasse moy, ou bien que je t'embrasse,
> Abaisse un peu ta cyme, afin que j'entrelasse
> Mes bras à tes rameaux, et que cent mille fois
> Je baise ton escorce, et embrasse ton bois. . . .
> Genévre bien-aimé, certes je te resemble,
> Avec toy le Destin sympathizant m'assemble.
> Ta cyme est toute verte, et mes pensers tous vers
> Ne meurissent jamais.
>
> (II.36–37)

(Now, at once, embrace me, or rather, so that I may embrace you,
lower a little your summit, so that I can interlace my arms in
your branches and that a hundred thousand times I kiss your
bark and hug your wood. . . . Beloved juniper, truly I resemble
you, and fate in sympathy assimilates me to you. Your top is
wholly green, and my wholly green thoughts may never die.)

The empathy is unique. Sexuality in Ronsard proves a means to another end: an unnerving transmutation of the human into the organic:

> Des mains d'Amour la racine plantée,
> En un moment devint si augmentée,
> Et le sommet de feuilles si couvert,
> Que tout mon coeur n'estoit qu'un arbre vert. . . .
> Sa vive humeur s'engendroit de mon pleur,
> Dont le genévre abondoit d'avantage,
> Me transformant moy-mesme en son ombrage.
>
> (II.92–93)

(The root planted by love became so massive in a moment, and
its crest so densely leaved, that my whole heart was just one
green tree. . . . Its living nature was born of my tears, with
which the juniper flourished still more, turning me into its own
shade.)

Such metamorphoses suggest how much Marvell's "Garden" owes to
the influence of the rural ecstasies of Ronsard, with "green thoughts,"
"green shades," and arboreal love affairs as his refuge from public strife.
Ronsard epitomizes the sublimation of sex into something more pantheistic and idiosyncratic: even if he provoked them by turning against

288

Protestanism, the Huguenots do seem justified in questioning his orthodoxy.

Of all Marvell's poems, that which comes nearest to establishing an idiosyncratic persona like Ronsard's is "Upon Appleton House," a poem until recently dismissed by many English scholars as eccentric and archaic. Yet in terms of psychological complexity and aesthetic range it achieves the status of a minor epic.[49] The interaction of subtle moods and public concerns which it displays rival anything in Ronsard. We have already seen on several occasions how Ronsard seems to find his own tastes and private life most compatible with a modest rural style of architecture such as that favored in Marvell's opening praise of the "sober Frame of" Appleton House. The rhetorical device of contemptuously juxtaposing extravagant baroque enterprises and humble but more serviceable natural shelters is shared by the two poets. Marvell asks:

> Why should of all things Man unrul'd
> Such unproportion'd dwellings build?
> The Beasts are by their Denns exprest:
> And Birds contrive an equal Nest;
> The low roof'd Tortoises do dwell
> In cases fit of Tortoise-shell.
>
> (11–16)[50]

Ronsard found exactly the same illustration:

> Autant en est de la tarde tortue
> Et du limas qui plus tard se remue,
> Porte-maisons, qui tousjours sur les dos
> Ont leur palais, leur lict et leur-repos,
> Lequel leur semble aussi bel edifice
> Qu'un grand chasteau basti par artifice. . . .
> Dieu qui tout peut, aux animaux permet
> De dire vray.
>
> (11.335)

49. See Richmond, *Renaissance Landscapes*, pp. 117 ff.
50. Marvell, ed. Margoliouth, vol. 1, p. 59.

(It is the same way with the slow tortoise and the snail which moves more slowly; they carry their houses and always have their palace on their own backs, with their bed and resting place, which seems to them as fine a building as a great palace built by contrivance. . . . God, who can do everything, allows the animals to tell the truth.)

This matter of divination through nature is another shared theme of great significance. Ronsard asserts flatly that "Dieu par tout en tout se communique" (God everywhere in everything reveals himself). Thus, rather slyly, Ronsard can compare his girlfriend's bosom to the entrails of animals examined by a classical augur:

> Tout ravy je humois et tirois à longs traicts
> De ton estomac sainct un millier de secrets,
> Par qui le Ciel en moy ses mysteres expose. . . .
> J'appris tous les secrets des Latins et des Grecs.
> Tu me fis un Oracle, et m'esveillant apres,
> Je devins un Démon scavant en toute chose.
>
> (1.225)

(Ravished away I drank and drew in deeply from your holy breast a thousand secrets by which heaven revealed its mysteries to me. . . . I learned all the secrets of the Latins and Greeks. You made me an oracle, and when I awoke again, I became a spirit learned in everything.)

A little less affectedly, Ronsard writes in his "Hymne des astres" of those who know how to read and interpret the "book of nature":

> philosophes grands, qui par longues estudes
> Ont fait un art certain de vos incertitudes;
> Ausquels avez donné puissance d'escouter
> Vos mysteres divins pour nous les raconter.
> Cestuy-cy cognoist bien des oiseaux le langage,
> Et sçait conjecturer des songes le presage;
> Il nous dit nostre vie, et d'un propos obscur,
> A qui l'enterrogue, annonce le futur. . . .
> Car vous estes de Dieu les sacrez characteres.
>
> (11.850–51)

(great philosophers, who by long studies have developed a sure skill from the uncertainties of you stars, to whom you have given the power to hear your divine secrets in order to tell us them. Such a man knows well the language of birds and knows how to divine the meaning of dreams; he predicts our lives and in obscure wording announces the future to a questioner. . . . For you are God's holy handwriting.)

One sees that the power to identify with nature is no poetical conceit for Ronsard, but a profound, not to say religious, initiation. It is with such more serious overtones that he writes playfully:

> je veux me transformer,
> Et mon corps fantastiq' de plumes enfermer,
> Un oeil sous chaque plume, et veut avoir en bouche
> Cent langues en parlant.
>
> (1.280)

(I wish to transform myself and enclose my fantastic body in feathers with an eye beneath each feather and have in my mouth the speech of a hundred languages.)

Ronsard here aspires to fuse the role of augury and augur, of which he writes so passionately in his weird poem "Le Chat," surely one of the strangest poems of the Renaissance:

> Dieu est par tout, par tout se mesle Dieu . . .
> Or, comme on voit qu'entre les hommes naissent
> Augurs, devins et prophetes qui laissent
> Un tesmoinage à la posterité . . .
> Et comme on voit naistre ici des Sibyles . . .
> Ainsi voit-on, prophetes de nos maux
> Et de nos biens, naistre des animaux,
> Qui le futur par signes nous predisent,
> Et les mortels enseignent et avisent.
> Ainsi le veut ce grand Pere de tous. . . .
> De là sortit l'escolle de l'Augure
> Merquant l'oiseau, qui par son vol figure
> De l'advenir le prompt evenement. . . .

Herbes et fleurs et les arbres qui croissent
En nos jardins prophetes apparoissent.

(II.331–33)

(God is everywhere, everything shares in God. . . . Now as one
sees augurers, diviners, and prophets born among men, who
leave us testimony about the future . . . and as one sees sibyls born
here . . . so one sees prophets of our ills and blessings born of
animals who predict the future for us by signs and instruct and
advise mortals. Thus the great Father of all wills it. . . . Thence
evolved the school of augury, studying the bird, which by its
flight prefigures the swift coming of the future. . . . Growing
plants and flowers and trees in our gardens prove to be prophets.)

If he is not as committed to the Bible as the Huguenots, still one sees
Ronsard practicing their exegetical skills rather than idly enjoying
nature when he writes of his rural contemplations:

Puis du livre ennuyé, je regardoit les fleurs,
Feuilles, tiges, rameaux, especes et couleurs,
Et l'entrecoupement de leurs formes diverses,
Peintes de cent façons, jaunes, rouges et perses,
Ne me pouvant saouler, ainsi qu'en un tableau,
D'admirer la Nature, et ce qu'elle a de beau,
Et de dire en parlant aux fleurettes escloses:
Celuy est presque Dieu qui cognoist toutes
    choses. . . .
Puis, alors que Vesper vient embrunir nos yeux,
Attaché dans le ciel je contemple les cieux,
En qui Dieu nous escrit en notes non obscures
Les sorts et les destins de toutes creatures.

(I.276–77)

(Then bored with the book I looked at the flowers, leaves, stems,
branches, species and colors, and the intersection of their various
forms, painted a hundred ways, yellow, red, and blue, unable to
satiate myself, as with a painting, with the admiration of Nature
and what she has of beauty; and to speak openly to the closed
flowers: such a one is almost God who knows all things. . . .
Then when Vesper comes to darken our eyes, drawn to heaven

I study the skies in which God writes for us quite clear notes about the futures and fates of all creatures.)

In this context one discovers that Marvell is also being more than flippant when he follows Ronsard's lead in writing of the superior theological values of nature to both the Bible and the pagan classics:

> Thus I, easie Philosopher,
> Among the Birds and Trees confer:
> And little now to make me, wants
> Or of the Fowles, or of the Plants.
> Give me but Wings as they, and I
> Streight floting on the Air shall fly:
> Or turn me but, and you shall see
> I was but an inverted tree.
> Already I begin to call
> In their most learned Original:
> And where I Language want, my Signs
> The Bird upon the Bough divines; . . .
> No Leaf does tremble in the Wind
> Which I returning cannot find.
> Out of these scatter'd Sybils Leaves
> Strange Prophecies my Phancy weaves:
> And in one History consumes,
> Like Mexique Paintings, all the Plumes.
> What Rome, Greece, Palestine, ere said
> I in this light Mosaick read.
> Thrice happy he who, not mistook,
> Hath read in Nature's mystick book. . . .
> The Oak-Leaves me embroyder all,
> Between which Caterpillars crawl
> And Ivy, with familiar trails,
> Me licks, and claspes, and curles, and hales.
> Under this antick Cope I move
> Like some great Prelate of the Grove.
>   (561ff.)[51]

51. Marvell, ed. Margoliouth, vol. 1, pp. 76–77.

Marvell implies a Druidical role, while Ronsard's persona is more classical; but both react adversely to Puritan severity and visualize a kind
of apostolate of nature which is far more exotic than might have been
expected of supposedly devout Christians, whether Catholic or Protestant. Marvell overbids Ronsard by claiming nature inspires in its devotee
not only the knowledge of Greece and Rome but even that of Palestine,
presumably in either Testament. Similarly Ronsard seems to exceed
the bounds of any Christian syncretism when he writes to solicit the
"Sainte fureur" (holy frenzy) of Bacchus and, "couvert de licrre" (covered in ivy), to be bound under his thyrsis (I.327–28). Even in death he
asks:

> De moy puisse la terre
> Engendrer une lierre
> M'embrassant en maint tour
>   Tout a l'entour.
>   (1.536)

(From me may the earth engender an ivy embracing me in many
curls all around.)

Ronsard's view of nature is thus profoundly religious and dynamic,
if pagan. He writes in thanks "a la forest de Gastine" for protecting
and inspiring him:

> Couché sous tes ombrages vers
>   Gastine, je te chante . . .
> Car, malin, celer je ne puis . . .
> De combien obligé je suis
>   A ta belle vendure:
> Toy, qui sous l'abry de tes bois
>   Ravy d'esprit m'amuses;
> Toy, qui fais qu'à toutes les fois
>   Me respondent les Muses;
> Toy, qui de ce mechant soin
>   Tout franc je me delivre.
>   (1.452–53)

(Lying under your green shades I hymn you, Gastine . . . for, darling, I cannot conceal how much I am indebted to your fine greenery: you who ravish my spirit with delight beneath the canopy of your woods, you who ensure that the Muses always respond to me, you who rescue me with complete freedom from this wretched care.)

The same genuine reverence is devoted to "la fontaine Bellerie," which might have expressed the feelings of some primitive animist:

> Escoute moy, Fontaine vive,
> En qui j'ay rebeu si souvent
> Couché tout plat dessur ta rive,
> Oisif à la fraischeur du vent;
> Quand l'Esté mesnager moissonne
> Le sein de Cerés dévestu,
> Et l'aire par compas resonne
> Gemissant sous le blé batu,
> Ainsi tousjours puisses-tu estre
> En devote religion.
>
> (1.498–99)

(Hear me, living spring, in whom I have so often drunk again, lying flat on your bank, lazy in the coolness of the wind, when the thrifty summer harvests the breast of cropped Ceres and the air resounds groaning under the wheat beaten with flails; may you always be worshipped thus.)

The mood of creative relaxation is that recreated almost as authentically in the grounds of Appleton House, in which it is hard to recognize a committed supporter of the Puritan Commonwealth:

> Then, languishing with ease, I toss
> On Pallets swoln of Velvet Moss;
> While the Wind, cooling through the Boughs,
> Flatters with Air my panting Brows.
> Thanks for my Rest ye Mossy Banks,
> And unto you cool Zephyr's Thanks,

> Who, as my Hair, my Thoughts too shed,
> And winnow from the Chaff my Head.
> How safe, methinks, and strong, behind
> These Trees have I incamp'd my Mind.
>   (593–602)[52]

Marvell dexterously interweaves Ronsard's imagery of the harvest threshing with his awareness of the inspirational effect of the landscape, but this subtle heightening and synthesis is the extent of his contribution to the topic here. Even the quaint devotion to the "Fair Trees" of "The Garden" does not exceed Ronsard's animistic love affairs, and the famous "green Thought in a green Shade" simply fits together two phrases coined by Ronsard, who also effectively epitomizes the whole classic pattern of rural inspiration recalled by Marvell:

> Here at the Fountains sliding foot,
> Or at some Fruit-trees mossy root,
> Casting the Bodies Vest aside,
> My Soul into the boughs does glide;
> There like a Bird it sits, and sings,
> Then whets and combs its silver Wings;
> And, till prepar'd for longer flight,
> Waves in its Plumes the various Light.[53]

Obviously Marvell's exotic moods and rural musings are not unique, nor are most of his ideas, images, and allusions. Above all in "Upon Appleton House" it is his skillful synthesis and heightening of these elements, prefigured in authors like Ronsard, which gives them a distinctive economy and coherence in the poem's progression toward choice of the active political life reflected in the poet's later career. Even this psychological progression is often anticipated in the best of Ronsard's odes. An exact estimate of Marvell's originality therefore requires recognition of Ronsard's genius, and the English poet's uniqueness may not be assumed without understanding the exotic moods resulting from Ronsard's revulsion from the Religious Wars.

52. Marvell, ed. Margoliouth, vol. 1, p. 77.
53. Marvell, ed. Margoliouth, vol. 1, p. 49.

Shakespeare's France

Shakespeare has been directly associated with many prominent Elizabethans having an intimate knowledge of French society and of the impact of the Reformation upon it. The earl of Southampton, to whom Shakespeare dedicated both his long narrative poems, is known to have traveled to Paris in January 1585 on an embassy which permitted him to establish "a friendship with the Biron family,"[1] one of whose scions largely dominates *Love's Labour's Lost*. Moreover, the fourth earl of Derby (who was the brother of Lord Strange, protector of Shakespeare's theater company) had led this same embassy with a suite of two hundred and fifty persons.[2] Derby lodged at the hotel of the Longueville family, whose son also figures prominently in *Love's Labour's Lost* with Biron. The English *Calendar of State Papers, Foreign* for the period indicates that religious sympathies also encouraged such visitors to attend the court of the king of Navarre, who is the central figure of this play. By the 1590s such sympathy had progressed to the level of enthusiastic participation in the English expeditionary forces sent to help establish the Protestant king of Navarre, now Henri IV, on the throne of France by fighting against the forces of the Catholic League, founded by the Guise family. The most prominent of these volunteers was Southampton's friend, the earl of Essex, who even com-

1. Clara Longworth de Chambrun, "Influences françaises dans la *Tempête* de Shakespeare," *Revue de Litterature Comparée* 5 (1929), p. 40.
2. Abel Lefranc, *À la Découverte de Shakespeare*, vol. 2 (Paris: Michel, 1950), p. 212.

manded the force at a time during which the London theaters were closed by plague and their staffs out of work. In the case of Essex "the French wars in particular exercised a peculiar spell over him; and the French King, battling for the Faith against overwhelming odds, was his *beau idéal* of knightly prowess. They were both men of romantic outlook on life, in whom latter-day chivalry found its best expression. To Henry IV Essex was *persona grata*: he confided in him, asked his advice, and regarded him as the one true friend of France in the English Council."[3]

Considering a society fascinated by the doings of such celebrities, one can understand why *Henry V* deals so convincingly with the experiences of English troops and generals fighting over the same terrain and with the same techniques and effects as in the French Civil Wars in northern France and in Normandy particularly.[4] Shakespeare shows such precise awareness of some of these military and diplomatic offensives that Abel Lefranc has even argued that the plays could only have been written by a well-traveled diplomat, such as the earl of Derby, with firsthand knowledge of the events shown.[5] However, it seems just as plausible to argue that Shakespeare might have acquired the precise and authentic knowledge of France shown in plays like *Love's Labour's Lost*, *Henry V*, *All's Well*, and even *As You Like It* either by travel there himself or by acquaintance with those around him who were intimately familiar with the country. Among these was certainly Richard Field, a contemporary of Shakespeare's from Stratford, whom he chose as printer of both his long poems. Field's role as Shakespeare's link with London's French community is likely as he had married a Frenchwoman, Jacqueline Vautrollier (the owner of a printing press and widow of his Huguenot master), and Samuel Schoenbaum suggests her advice encouraged Shakespeare later to live in Silver Street

3. John B. Black, *Elizabeth and Henry IV* (Oxford: Blackwell, 1914), p. 41.

4. Some of this detail seems to have been borrowed from the campaigns of Henri IV via Colynet, *The Civill Warres of France*. See Richmond, "Shakespeare's Navarre," pp. 193–216.

5. Lefranc, vol. 2, p. 197. However, many citizens of Nérac are convinced Shakespeare visited their city; see "Shakespeare a-t'il connu la Garenne," in Georges Caillou, *Nérac* (Nérac: Berceron, 1977), pp. 63–68.

for several years with a Huguenot family, the Mountjoys.[6] The delicious scenes in French involving Catherine de Valois with her lady in waiting and with Henry V merely make explicit a sensitivity to nuances of French language, life, and culture which scholarship can detect in plays as varied as *The Merry Wives of Windsor* and *King Lear*,[7] not to mention the numerous plays set largely in France. Whether or not Shakespeare crossed the Channel—and the possibility stops just short of probability—there is no doubt that he was intimately familiar with the culture and literature of France: we know that he read Marguerite de Navarre's lightly fictionalized accounts of the French court which Painter excerpted from the *Heptameron* in an anthology providing recognized sources of *All's Well* and *Romeo and Juliet*.[8] Shakespeare also shows an intimate familiarity with Ronsard in many of his more formal speeches. He makes Jaques allude appropriately to Marotisme.[9] Above all, editors of *Love's Labour's Lost* agree that "Shakespeare's play follows historical fact remarkably closely" and that, as a result, the problem that it "bristles with topical allusions has long been recognized."[10] Scholars like Abel Lefranc have clarified the French allusions, while Frances Yates has also proposed some English historical analogues.[11] Though both have overstated their cases, Lefranc's facts from French history are incontrovertible.

The fascination with things French is a permanent feature of British culture, scarcely affected by the open warfare that has often raged be-

6. Samuel Schoenbaum, *William Shakespeare: A Documentary Life* (Oxford: Clarendon Press, 1975), p. 208.

7. Clara Longworth de Chambrun, *Shakespeare, Actor-Poet* (New York: Appleton, 1927), pp. 59–60.

8. See Bullough, ed., *Narrative and Dramatic Sources*, vol. 1, pp. 179, 273; vol. 2, pp. 377–78.

9. See Maurice Scève, *Oeuvres Poétiques*, ed. Bertrand Guegan (Paris: Garnier 1927), p. x; and Hugh M. Richmond, " 'To his Mistress' Eyebrow,' " *Philological Quarterly* 40 (1961), pp. 157–58.

10. David, ed., *Love's Labour's Lost*, p. xxxii; John Dover Wilson, ed., *Love's Labour's Lost*, by William Shakespeare (Cambridge: Cambridge University Press, 1962), p. xi.

11. Frances A. Yates, *A Study of "Love's Labour's Lost."* (Cambridge: Cambridge University Press, 1936).

tween the two countries; and Shakespeare was in no way original in writing about contemporary French politics in *Love's Labour's Lost*. Seeing in Henri de Navarre a Protestant ruler seeking to establish something like the Tudor compromise in France, the English followed his career with intense interest and some military support. Henri became a "folk hero" to England in the early 1590s, and hundreds of pamphlets detailed his victories.[12] Around 1592 Marlowe had introduced many of their events and characters to Elizabethan audiences in *The Massacre at Paris*, in which we already find the King of Navarre; his wife, Marguerite de Navarre; her mother, Queen Catherine de' Medici; and even an aristocrat who is called Dumain (de Mayenne, one of the Guises). Exploiting the fashionable interest in Henri, the play ends with Navarre's fortunate elevation to the throne of France as Henri IV. Chapman deals extensively with the career of Bussy d'Amboise in two plays set in the same contemporary period, and he seems subsequently to have followed up the Elizabethan fascination with Shakespeare's Berowne by writing two plays about the later career and tragic execution of the duc de Biron as a traitor to Henry IV. These plays were so exact in their embarrasing allusions to the French court that the French ambassador protested against their insults to Henri's queen, and when the Biron plays were finally published they were so mangled by the resulting censorship that Chapman lamented the ruin of "these poor dismembered poems."[13] One sees why in printing *Love's Labour's Lost* a hasty effort seems to have been made to disguise the contemporary allusions by rechristening the King of Navarre "Ferdinand" in the opening stage directions of a text "newly corrected" according to the quarto's title page. As with the switching of the name Oldcastle to Falstaff in the same year, a somewhat flimsy effort is being made to prove that "this is not the man" (*2HIV* Epilogue 27) whom Shakespeare certainly had in mind throughout his composition.[14]

12. Arthur G. Dickens, "The Elizabethans and St. Bartholomew," in *International Archives of the History of Ideas* (Hague: Nighoff, 1975), p. 35.

13. George Chapman, *The Comedies and Tragedies*, vol. 2 (London: Pearson, 1873), p. 185.

14. Richmond, "Shakespeare's Navarre," p. 197. Much of the material in this

In fact the historical correspondencies are intrinsic to the texture and characterizations of the comedy. Frances Yates accepts K. M. Lea's plausible view that the device of four parallel love affairs has something in common with Italian Renaissance comedy,[15] but even this sexual multiplication derives from historical events during certain negotiations at Nérac in 1578 and later. Navarre originally bridged the Franco-Spanish border until Spain seized its southern zone, with its capital of Pamplona, and annexed it definitively in 1516. Over the centuries numerous negotiations about Aquitaine had occurred between the kings of Navarre and France, and precedents for the diplomatic matter of the play have been seen as early as 1422 or as late as 1586, when Catherine de' Medici grimly repeated once again her efforts to patch up a peace with the Huguenot Henri, whom the moderate Catholic government tried to keep subdued but strong enough to counterbalance the extreme Catholic League led by the Guises. However, there can be little doubt that the play deals with the happier negotiations begun in 1578 at Nérac,[16] the capital of French Navarre, which from the time of the earlier Marguerite de Navarre (originally d'Angoulême) had emerged as the focus for Huguenot sentiment and a refuge for fugitives from orthodoxy like Marot.

This Huguenot role of Nérac had been much intensified by Marguerite's daughter Jeanne d'Albret, whose son Henri was. She was a woman of such severity that d'Aubigné observes she was feminine only in physiology. She had Henri raised "without toys, jewelry, and fine clothes," sleeping on a palliasse of dry leaves, and trained by Calvinist tutors like Florent Chrestien.[17] The latter's impact may be gauged by the following harangue to his pupil:

> Consider, prince, the men around you. Once dead and rotting in the earth, what remains of these humans? Their carrion. But contemplate the earthly life of elect beings. They do not live, those, except in the spirit and for virtue. God has distinguished

chapter is reviewed in this article, and is reproduced by courtesy of the *Huntington Library Quarterly* (see also Plate 8).

15. Yates, p. 176.   16. See Bullough, vol. 1, pp. 429–30.

17. Jo Gerard, *Henri IV: Le plus vert des galants* (Paris: Dargaut, 1967), p. 33.

them and rewarded them to the point that their carcass scarcely counts during their passage on earth; it can become dust in turn, but these men will preserve their soul throughout eternity such as they have forged it in their lifetime.[18]

One recognizes at once the similarity to sentiments professed by Shakespeare's King of Navarre in desiring to make the members of his court the "heirs of all eternity" (I.i.7) through studious virtue and "war against your own affections." One of Henri's favorite sentences also parallels Ferdinand: "aut vincere aut mori" (win or die), and he is reported as expanding on such topics: "One must conquer by justice or die with glory"; "the most engaging power of royalty is to be able to do good"; "that prince who rules over the greatest states but who lets himself be tyrannized over by his passions is only a crowned slave."[19] Lefranc plausibly observes of the play that "the passion for austerity affected by the King of Navarre and his companions seems to relate somewhat to the prescriptions of the Protestant synod held at Sainte Foy in 1578 at which Turenne represented the king."[20] The vicomte Turenne was an intimate of the king at Nérac and asserts that when not employed at the court he "took up always some question of theology, of philosophy, of politics, of war, of how to speak and write well, or of politeness—having often several persons who were knowledgeable, this protected me from bad activities which attract lazy minds."[21] D'Aubigné even mentions a formal academy at Nérac attended by a dozen or more courtiers and civil servants, including the poet du Bartas, modeled no doubt on the one Henri attended with his wife Marguerite de Navarre at the Louvre under the superintendence of Guy du Faur du Pibrac.[22] The latter actually accompanied the

18. Gerard, p. 34.

19. Charles de Batz-Trenquelléon, *Henri IV en Gascogne* (Paris: Oudin, 1885), p. 27.

20. Abel Lefranc, *Les Éléments Français de "Peines d'Amour Perdues"* (Paris: *Revue Historique*, 1936), p. 13.

21. La Tour d'Auvergne, pp. 219–20.

22. See Jean H. Mariéjol, *A Daughter of the Medicis* (New York: Harper, 1930), p. 121 ff. Henri had already founded an internationally noted academy (with his mother, Jeanne d'Albret) at Orthez, according to Johan Stuck, *Carolus Magnus Redivivus, Hoc est Caroli Magni . . . cum Henrico M. Gallorum et*

queens on their visit to Nérac in 1578, and this is reflected in the character and functions of Boyet in the play—a fluent and ingenious diplomat who is more than a little in love with Marguerite de Navarre himself.[23] We find that the Protestant court at Nérac was known in England for its puritanical aspirations, since the English ambassador reported to Walsingham in 1583 that Navarre "has furnished his Court with principal gentlemen of the Religion, and reformed his house," so that already by the autumn of 1582 Marguerite de Navarre had written to her husband Henri: "If you are a man of honour you would give up agriculture and the spirit of Timon to come and live amongst men."[24] The general French enthusiasm for Platonic academies on the Italian model was well known in England, and the king of Navarre's heroical ambition and facility in high sentiments were particularly admired, though some of his numerous mistresses were rightly inclined to be a little skeptical when he avowed his loyalty as sentimentally as he did to "Corisande" for example: "Until the tomb to which I am perhaps closer than I know, I shall remain your faithful slave. . . . Dear soul take me under your care, and never entertain a doubt of my fidelity."[25]

Following the picturesque negotiations at Nérac, in the course of the skirmishes which have been romanticized by their context as "the Lover's War," Henri wrote rather more speciously in this vein to his wife, Marguerite de Navarre:

My dear, while we may still, you and I, be so united that our hearts and wills may be only the same thing and that I may not have anything so dear as the love that you bear me, in order to return the duties to which I feel obliged, I will beg that you will not find strange a resolution which I have made, forced by necessity without having spoken to you of it at all. But since you must

---

Navarorum . . . Comparatio, (Tigurino: Wolphium, 1592), p. 50v (sig. N2v); and later the Nérac Academy itself became a regular academic institution; see below, Chapter 10, "The Libertines."

23. He was ultimately ruined for openly professing his passion.

24. David, ed., p. xxix.

25. Duc de Lévis-Mirepoix, *Henri IV, roi de France et de Navarre* (Paris: Perrin, 1971), p. 172.

inevitably know of it, I can protest to you, my dear, that it is my extreme regret that instead of the contentment which I would wish to give you and to have you receive in this country, the opposite is needful, and that you have this dissatisfaction of seeing my condition reduced to such misfortune.[26]

Not to mention the shared power of obfuscation, Shakespeare's Ferdinand is just as ready with a similar excuse for changing his mind about his Princess: "We must of force dispense with this decree . . . on mere necessity" (I.i.146–47). Interestingly enough the same play also justifies irrationality in phrases matching the manuscript anthology of poetry to which Marguerite de Navarre added in Nérac:

> Contre ma volunté le destin necessaire
> Force ma liberté de s'i assubiectir.
> Ie congnoy mon erreur sans en pouvoir sortir.[27]

(Against my will, necessary fate forces my liberty to subject itself there. I know my error without being able to avert it.)

The conversational ploy must have been familiar enough at Nérac, and Shakespeare's Berowne is justified in his ridicule of it:

> Necessity will make us all forsworn
> Three thousand times within these three years'
>   space; . . .
> If I break faith, this word shall speak for me,
> I am forsworn 'on mere necessity.'
>
> (i.i.146ff.)

We find that Berowne's verdict is painfully relevant to the historical king of Navarre, for Jean Mariéjol judges that Henri was "amiable by nature, but brutally instinctive and, under the appearance of good grace, egotistical and imperious; he was all for present feeling, hot to satisfy it, irritated that one should deny him anything."[28] In his later

26. Philippe Lauzun, *Itinéraire raisonné de Marguerite de Valois en Gascogne* (Paris: Picard, 1902), p. 137.

27. Bibliothèque de la Société de l'Histoire du Protestanisme Français, MS 816[12], p. 65.

28. Jean H. Mariéjol, *La Vie de Marguerite de Valois* (Paris: Hachette, 1928), p. 182.

commercial squabble with the English, Henri "preferred *douce dissimulation* for the present but would lie in wait for an opportunity of extorting justice or revenge." Elizabeth wrote to him in 1598: "If one should wish to find one thing in worldly matters which marks the greatest iniquity and by which this earthly machine which we inhabit should be ruined it is in the lack of faith, the uncertainty of friendship and the lack of love where there is more reason."[29] The long line of debauched young women artfully courted, seduced, and abandoned by "le vert galant" should encourage us to recognize that beneath Henri's friendliness and good intentions lay a latent awareness of other pressures and expediencies which might abruptly surface at any time. Shakespeare's Princess is all too accurate in her verdict on him that "your grace is perjur'd much, / Full of dear guiltiness; and therefore this: . . . / Your oath I will not trust" (V.ii.782ff.). Like one or two young women, the duc de Biron in the end was to pay with his life for taking Henri at his word. Some of the king's followers, like d'Aubigné, never forgave him his abjuration of the Protestant faith for the second time to secure the French monarchy.

This is not to say that Henri was unjustified. The effects of the French civil wars of religion were as devastating morally as physically. After Catherine de' Medici had enforced a marriage of convenience upon the Protestant Henri de Navarre and her Catholic daughter Marguerite de Valois in 1572, Catherine also made the resulting assembly of notables the occasion for the Saint Bartholomew's Day Massacre, which literally soaked the new queen of Navarre's bed with a Huguenot's blood. No wonder the marriage from the start lacked intimacy, and Catherine found her daughter's notorious seductiveness was lost on her new husband. However, the queen mother never lacked varied resources to divert dangerous men from their potentialities. She had seduced Henri's own father from the Protestant cause and from his enraged wife, Jeanne d'Albret, with the aid of her "Flying Squadron," for "Catherine had extended the principle of François I's 'Petite Bande' from pleasure to politics and formed an 'Escadron Volant' of young beauties, mostly daughters of the smaller landed gentry, whom she could use to discover the secrets of her enemies." One of these girls,

29. Black, p. 137.

"La Belle Rouet," had "enslaved Antoine de Navarre so completely that he was willing to divorce Jeanne," Henri's mother.[30]

Such episodes corroborate historians' judgments of France in the early 1580s: "The condition of the country during these years offers a picture of demoralization hardly to be matched in the records of any period. . . . Duels and assassinations were matters of daily occurrence. The profligacy of the upper classes, as attested by unprejudiced witnesses, was appalling; nor was there much to choose in this respect between Catholics and Protestants."[31] In large measure the vacillating if usually pacific policy of Catherine was responsible for this: "She lacked any grasp of general principles, and was apt to see problems in terms of a palace intrigue . . . she was, in fact, a politician and not a statesman."[32] Having failed to entrap Henri de Navarre by his marriage with her own skillfully trained daughter, she succeeded in entangling him with another of her *escadron*, madame de Sauves, whose sexual proficiency (refreshed by systematic instruction from professional prostitutes) sufficed for a time to neutralize Henri as a moral and political force: "an early instance of that employment of affairs of gallantry as a political instrument which the queen mother was to develop into a fine art."[33]

Henri finally escaped from madame de Sauves' embraces and fled the court in order to be able to renounce his enforced Catholicism safely, sustaining a sequence of reversals of religious affiliation in which he must surely have our sympathy. Nevertheless, one can also sympathize with the baffled resentment of the English ambassador, Sir Amias Paulet, who wrote on 8 June 1578: "French doings are utterly uncertain and commonly fall out directly contrary to reason and good judgment." Even more bitterly he writes a paradox to Queen Elizabeth on 23 June: "The cunning dissimulation and subtle treachery of the French have served them to good purpose in time past to advance their trai-

30. Hugh R. Williamson, *Catherine de' Medici* (London: Joseph, 1973), p. 124.

31. A. W. Ward, ed., *Cambridge Modern History*, vol. 3, *The Wars of Religion*, (Cambridge: Cambridge University Press, 1904), pp. 36–37.

32. J. E. Neale, *The Age of Catherine de' Medici* (London: Capp, 1943), p. 41. See also Plate 7.

33. Gerard, p. 64.

torous practices; and now I think they reap no less profit of the opinion which is generally conceived of their faithless dealing. They pretend to do this or that, and because they so give it out, no man believes them, and by this means they do what they will before it is believed that they intend it."[34] The erratic behavior of the young men in *Love's Labour's Lost* has all too many good historical precedents in the uncertain allegiances of the Civil Wars.

One guesses the apprehensions of Henri de Navarre in late 1578 when the two queens bore down upon him at Nérac: both his formidable mother-in-law and her dazzling and "over-refined" daughter Marguerite, his legal but not actual wife and queen. The Calvinist cause to which he had recommitted himself was more truly threatened by Catherine's *escadron* than by the armies of the French king led by Marshal Biron, who was frightened of being too successful and unbalancing the Protestant forces weighed against the Catholic League. Before the meeting Paulet writes uneasily: "I think no man can tell what will come of this second marriage between the King of Navarre and his wife . . . she lacks no cunning to provide all dangers." Again he observes, "The Queen Mother goes with her daughter to the King of Navarre who shall have the wolf by the ears whether he accept or refuse her."[35] Most historians agree about Catherine's goals and methods both before and at Nérac: "What did she wish but to occupy the princes, to distract them so much and more to prevent them from warfare against each other. . . . Catherine organizes pleasures and deploys her whole troop of ravishing girls, some naive, others more mature, some without nobility but not without charms."[36] One recalls Berowne's rueful reaction to the lowly nature of his mistress, Rosaline: "Some men must love my lady, some Joan" (III.i.200).

Perhaps we need to recognize just how hypnotic this team of sexual Machiavels seemed to contemporaries. They were supposedly quite without prudery or inhibitions: after crises like the St. Bartholomew's Day Massacre they distracted Catherine by dancing before her naked, and to celebrate the royal victory at La Charité, they served a sumptu-

34. A. J. Butler, ed., *Calendar of State Papers, Foreign Series, of the Reign of Elizabeth, 1577–78* (London: Eyre and Spottiswood, 1901), pp. 5, 27.

35. Ibid., p. 471.   36. Gerard, p. 60. See also Plate 16.

ous meal naked but for a wisp of material around their hips, while the king himself reports that the "Maîtresses d'hôtel" for the dinner, the irresistible madame de Sauves and the duchesse de Retz, wore nothing at all. The feast reached its climax after a troup of naked dryads sprang on the guests from the shrubbery. On the other hand, to celebrate the same victory, Catherine organized another party in which men were dressed as women, and the "Amazons of the *escadron volant*" appeared in green male costumes.[37] The symbolism was apt, for even in feminine costume these women displayed youthful, martial aggressiveness. Pierre Lestoile notes their militant sexuality: "Women and girls seem to have learned the manner of warriors nowadays, who parade to show off their gleaming, gilded torsos when they are off to do monstrous things, and the women achieve the same impact with their breastworks, with their exposed busts and shoulders in perpetual movement, which these fine ladies swing rhythmically like a pendulum, or to be more exact like the pulsing of bellows, for they are stoking fires to serve their furnace."[38] In more strictly diplomatic terms Catherine's ladies had significant impact, for the duchesse de Retz, who could readily triumph by traditional feminine wiles, easily outmaneuvered one of the Huguenot leaders, Damville, in 1577, and turned him to the royal party.[39] English theatrical circles would be likely to hear of these various extravagancies of the French court because of the great interest in its concerns, particularly Italian drama, loved by the queen mother and her women, and the subject of much gossip in England. Plays and performances of all kinds were prominently featured at royal festivities in France, and the Italian stage conventions of the *commedia dell'arte* reflected in Shakespeare's comedies, gained great currency in Paris from the patronage which Catherine de' Medici and her son Henri III extended to the Venetian troupe of actors, called "I Gelosi," from 1577, which marks the beginning of the direct influence of the Italian theater. Moreover, the extravagant costumes (or lack of them) at such festivities soon spread beyond the court and even crossed the Channel and were em-

37. Gerard, p. 42 (see also Brantôme, *Lives*, pp. 190, 506); and Erlanger, *Henri III*, pp. 104–05.

38. Lestoile, p. 87. Compare this passage with Plate 14.

39. Erlanger, *Henri III*, p. 104.

ulated by fashionable ladies' costumes at the English court, of which later evidence remains in the exposed busts in many of Inigo Jones' designs for court masques. Women everywhere rejoiced in a new sexual freedom by the early years of the seventeenth century: "There is today scarcely the most insignificant coquette who does not flaunt her breasts following the example of Queen Marguerite." The bust of Henri IV's queen was so much admired that one Carmelite preacher risked a Donnesque comparison between it and the breasts of the Virgin Mary.[40]

Such were the sophisticated social and diplomatic resources with which Catherine de' Medici set out to pacify the rebellious provinces of southern France in 1577. Knowing Henri's sensual susceptibilities, it was inevitable that at Nérac Catherine was surrounded by

> a swarm of beauties dressed in fantastic costumes. The older ones, like the duchesse d'Uzès or the duchesse de Retz, shone by their erudition, their gaiety, their high daring, and above all by their deliberately mocking, sometimes murderous wit. . . . The juniors formed the flying squadron to whom was left an intelligence role which was more valuable to the queen mother than the victories of her army. These ravishing persons with hair covered in violet powder, outrageously exposed breasts, glittering with gold and jewels, were not mean with their favors but never granted them without the queen's permission and used them to trick and immobilize enemies.[41]

Contemporary sources covering this campaign even ascribe to one ambitious demoiselle, Anne d'Aquaviva, the single-handed capture of the strategic fortress of La Réole, which still dominates the Garonne, by fostering a slavish passion in its senile commander the baron d'Ussac and entrapping him into switching his fortress from the Protestant to the Catholic cause.

Brantôme describes the women as making the court "a true paradise" where "they had the time of their lives" since they were completely free to do whatever they wanted as long as they were nice to strangers and did not get pregnant. Brantôme wryly comments: "He was happy who

40. Tallemant des Réaux, *Historiettes*, vol. I (Paris: Pléiade, 1960–61), p. 739.
41. Philippe Erlanger, *La Reine Margot* (Paris: Perrin, 1972), p. 32.

could fall in love with such ladies, and just as happy if he could escape from their love."[42] There could be no doubt of the aggressive self-confidence of such women, for Brantôme observes that "as a rule such great ladies, when involved in affairs of state, always go one better than the usual behavior of ordinary people."[43] In his memoirs as the duc de Bouillon, Turenne grimly observes that "love got mixed up with everything else, which usually caused most of the troubles at court, and little or nothing went on which the women had no hand in, and mostly caused infinite trouble to those who loved them."[44] However, Turenne also proves the women's fascination by describing how he became "platonically" involved with one of these young ladies, Catherine de Bourbon, who was present at the Nérac negotiations and was in fact Henri de Navarre's own sister.[45] Indeed, it proves plausible that she is the very Katherine who figures in Shakespeare's play. Marguerite de Navarre mentions her as close friend at this time, and Abel Lefranc assures us that Katherine "was closely involved in all the details of the queen's journey; she was present from the start to the end of all the feasts and ceremonies which took place at the court of Navarre. Obviously Shakespeare intended to identify her when he called her 'the heir of Alençon' (*L.L.L.*, II.i.194), a term perfectly precise since she was the granddaughter of Marguerite d'Angoulême, sister of François I and duchesse d'Alençon."[46] Moreover, Shakespeare is very careful to reinforce this identification since he makes Katherine assert that she first saw Dumain "at the Duke of Alençon's" (II.i.61). It is equally more than accidental that Shakespeare's Longueville should be attracted to a "Maria," since in fact Marie de Nevers, twice widowed, did marry the relevant Léonor d'Orleans, duc de Longueville, who also did indeed have those estates "in Normandy" where Maria claims to have met him (II.i.43).[47] As for Rosaline, an attendant on Marguerite de Navarre, she would normally have accompanied the queen on her subversive mission to "Brabant" the previous year, where she claims to have met

42. Brantôme, *Oeuvres complètes*, ed. Ludovic Lalanne, vol. 1 (Paris: Renouard, 1873), pp. 377, 396.

43. Brantôme, *Lives*, p. 473. 44. La Tour d'Auvergne, p. 101.

45. Ibid., pp. 221–22. 46. Lefranc, *À la Découverte*, vol. 2, p. 205.

47. Ibid., p. 209.

Berowne—who incidentally alludes (III.i.185) to the famous clocks which caught visiting Frenchmen's attention, as Marguerite de Navarre herself tells us in her *Memoirs*.[48]

I have found no certain identification for Rosaline, though there was a Rose de Montal in the *escadron* who was closely associated with Marguerite de Navarre and was married to the grand sénéchal de Guienne, who signed one of the documents at the Nérac meeting in 1578. Brantôme devotes a sonnet to her wit and fascination, which he compares to the force of an attacking army.[49] However, the aggressive vivacity of ladies like Anne d'Aquaviva, not to mention the more sardonic phases of Marguerite herself, provides sufficient precedents for Rosaline's dark wit. The other uncertain identification among the lovers is Dumain, who cannot properly be the duc de Mayenne, as often is asserted,[50] since, as the leader of the Catholic Guise faction against Henri, he was universally known and hated in England, as Marlowe shows in *The Massacre at Paris*. However, in many letters during the 1590s we find three names frequently recurring in reports sent to England about the king's military councils: Biron, Longueville, and d'Aumont. The latter was so stylish and fluent that he handled much of the diplomatic correspondence with England: he frequently wrote elegant letters to Queen Elizabeth herself on Henri's behalf and was personally known to Shakespeare's patron, Essex. He is thus a plausible candidate to explain the genesis of "Dumain," as E. K. Chambers concludes;[51] and, if so, it seems that the intimate association of d'Aumont, Longueville, and Biron with the cause of Henri IV in the 1590s has been pushed back, without much evidence, to the earlier period of the Nérac Conference. This places the play's source of information in the later period, not (as Lefranc thought, in assigning the play to Derby) soon after the Conference. Shakespeare would have gathered all of it himself by a little research and careful questioning of his own friends and contemporaries.

However, the role of Berowne at Nérac is quite plausible historically.

48. Ibid., p. 204.   49. Brantôme, *Oeuvres*, vol. 10, p. 427.

50. E.g., Bullough, ed., vol. 1, p. 429.

51. E. K. Chambers, *William Shakespeare* vol. 1 (Oxford: Clarendon Press, 1930), p. 338.

There were in fact at least two Birons involved with the king of Navarre at that time. Born in 1524, Armand de Gontaut, baron de Biron, was originally attached to the court of the first Marguerite de Navarre (or d'Angoulême) as a page and never wholly lost his indirect associations with the reformed religion, so that he narrowly escaped death on St. Bartholomew's Day. However, he was a cynical and expert soldier, used to leading the armies of Henri III in order to keep the Huguenots off balance without actually destroying them. On the whole he trod this tightrope skillfully, though "the negotiations and intrigues in which Biron was engaged in this period are bewildering in their complexity. ... Early in 1577, Biron was sent to Henry of Navarre and the Huguenots to persuade them 'that they must again place themselves in obedience' to the King of France. Secretly, however, Biron's mission seems to have been 'rather to discover [Navarre's] forces, sound his devices, and to corrupt such as are about. ...' Biron, with an eye on the future, remained on good terms with Navarre."[52] Armand had a son, Charles de Gontaut, born in 1562, who was precociously involved in these political complexities: "A victim of this disastrous period where religious faith served mostly as a pretext for partisan politics, by the age of sixteen he had already changed his religion twice."[53] Inevitably "he quickly made himself noted by his total indifference to both of the Christian sects which were then causing such cruel wars."[54] Thus Charles de Biron emerges as even more equivocal, egotistical, and skeptical than his father, whom "in 1577 he accompanied to Guyenne when the negotiations which opened between Henri III and the king of Navarre led to the Peace of Bergerac. ... It is in this province, center of the activities of the Protestant party, that Biron could initiate his son into the secrets of politics, now in fact at war, now negotiating with the dashing court at Nérac."[55] Thus throughout the period covered by the

52. Armand de Gontaut, *Letters and Documents*, ed. James W. Thompson, vol. 1 (Berkeley and Los Angeles: University of California Press, 1936), pp. xxiii–xxiv.

53. Charles de Montigny, *Le Maréchal de Biron, sa vie, son procés, sa mort, 1562–1602* (Paris: Hachette, 1861), p. 9.

54. *Nouvelle Biographie Universelle*, vol. 5 (Paris: Firmin Didot, 1853), p. 129.

55. Montigny, p. 9.

play both Birons were deeply involved with the king of Navarre, mostly on diplomatic terms, but not yet ultimately committed to his cause as they were on his accession to the French throne in 1589.

This ambivalence is reflected in the distinctive role in the play of Berowne, whose reluctant outward conformity to the court's manners scarcely masks his skepticism and contemptuous detachment from its values. In fact both Birons were always held to lack naive commitment to any cause: at the victory of Ivry, when his son sought assistance to complete the rout of the Leaguers, " 'What,' roared the Marshall at his son, 'would you send us back to plant cabbages at Biron?' "[56] Both knew that as professional soldiers they stood to preserve their status as long as hostilities were protracted, and they were often rumored to have acted as if they "feared Henri IV's success" even after they became his generals. However, in 1578 they were still supposed to keep him in check and act as representatives of Henri III. Thus, as Mayor of Bordeaux, the elder Biron officially presided over that city's welcome to Catherine and her daughter during their trip to Nérac, and it is clear that sumptuous festivities were arranged, for Biron's own costume included a robe of crimson velvet, with masses of lace and cloth of silver, and the rest of the participants' costumes were comparable. So historically there really was a Biron directly involved in a performance to honor Marguerite de Navarre in 1578 (Catherine, her mother, tactfully gave her precedence in a territory of which the daughter was technically the queen).

Old Biron was a "character" who took continuous notes in "tablets" (like Hamlet) of all the intrigues that went on around him, and he was capable of brusque eruptions of prejudice. One of his sardonic *mots* was that "promises are feminine, while actions are masculine."[57] He did not like the English, and Roger Williams complained that he "demoralized" their troops and "chased me out of the army because I was a little better acquainted with his knavery."[58] Though often accused of Huguenot sympathies, the elder Biron harassed the king of Navarre maliciously, not only before negotiations of the treaty at Bergerac, but even after the Conference at Nérac in 1578. Marguerite had settled down at Nérac near her husband and, as the French king's sister, was promised

56. Gontaut, p. xl.　　57. Gontaut, p. xxix.　　58. Gontaut, p. xxxiii.

suspension of skirmishing in the area and an undisturbed residence as long as her husband kept away from the place. However, as soon as Biron got wind of one of Henri's amorous visits he craftily lobbed a few cannonballs across the town near them. Biron was later forced to apologize humbly for the dangerous trick, even though he had technically caught out the king of Navarre in a covert amatory excursion, against the terms of the truce, as Biron had proclaimed publicly by a herald at the time.[59] The historical Birons thoroughly enjoyed making Henri look silly like this, if they could get away with it.

This somewhat supercilious view of the king was quite understandable, since the Gontaut family was (and is) one of the most ancient and heroic in France. They had ruled the country around Biron since the eleventh century, suffering many vicissitudes over the centuries, particularly at the hands of the English in the Hundred Years' War. These disruptions are reflected in the current complicated architecture of their imposing château, which still stands (a little precariously) on a hill dominating Périgord for a radius of twenty kilometers around. It is said locally that the name Biron comes from a dialect word, "biroun," meaning windmill, perhaps from one which stood a thousand years ago on the same hill—but it is also an etymology altogether appropriate for the voluble Berowne of Shakespeare and his historical model in the younger Biron, Charles de Gontaut, who is described as "of a boiling character, of unbridled energies, brilliant in the court and on the battlefield; prodigal, magnificent, without any moral principles, vain, flighty, opinionated, presumptuous and unwilling to spare even Henri IV in his witticism."[60] Abel Lefranc unhesitatingly and correctly identifies Charles as Shakespeare's Berowne and recognizes that among the king's companions in the play he at least was with his father at Nérac during the negotiations, but unlike his father, Charles de Biron became one of Henri de Navarre's most intimate friends. Nevertheless, Lefranc is content to observe merely that "there is a resemblance between Charles

59. Marguerite de Valois, *Mémoires et lettres*, ed. M. F. Guissard (Paris: Renouard, 1842), p. 169.

60. Hugh J. Rose, ed., *A New General Biographical Dictionary*, vol. 4 (London: Fellowes, 1847), p. 253.

de Gontaut's character and that of Berowne."[61] No one has investigated this resemblance.

In fact, Shakespeare's extravagant portrait is largely taken from life: it is simply too improbable for fiction. The younger Biron's whole life was a paradox: "a person of great intrepidity; but all the good in him had so powerful an alloy of evil that made it of little value. He was vain, fickle, and treacherous."[62] Such a summary is typical and is based on the hindsight of his tragic execution for treason—but as an approach to Shakespeare's characterization it is profoundly inadequate. One might equally well stress the definitive military success Biron brought to the cause of Henri IV, of which Charles characteristically quipped: "Without me the king would have only a crown of thorns."[63] In such ways Biron helped to create a modern France unified under the Bourbons. This is how Charles de Biron appears from a more comprehensive and balanced point of view:

> Of medium build, well made in body but just a little stout, which gives some softness to his movements, Biron had fine black eyes, flashing with very warrior-like energy; his nose was well-shaped; as for his face, already lined with honorable scars, it inspired respect. Like all natures fitted for action, his hair and beard were strongly planted in his skull with such thickness as to ward off terrible blows. His proud and contemptuous mouth alone warned that the marshall was conscious of his own worth. The overall impression recalled the image of a master race. An iron man in the camp, he had endured without complaint the most cruel privations; a courtier when it was needful, he was more alert than any other captain of his time to bend to the demands of etiquette. None knew better than he how to give fire to the soldier in the field of battle; none knew better how to fill the delicate duties of ambassador. At ease in the vernacular of the barrackroom, he became as mannered in his expression as an old courtier when at

61. Lefranc, À la découverte, vol. 2, p. 59.

62. Hoeffer, ed., Nouvelle Biographie Générale, vol. 5 (Paris: Didot, 1866), p. 127.

63. M. Prévost, ed., Dictionnaire Biographie Française, vol. 6 (Paris: Letouzey, 1954), p. 522.

the pompous and literary English court. A gambler as was then the fashion, he knew how to lose vast sums like a great lord. And a rare thing in those times, he was learned.[64]

On the last point a contemporary, the duc d'Épernon, informs us, "Those who believed he was only capable of brutal behaviour did not know his nature. . . . He was learned to the point of reading Greek and Latin literature, and when he chose to exploit his superiority of wit, either in negotiations or councils of war or in routine business, he revealed extraordinary talents."

Ironically, the good nature of Henri de Navarre meshed perfectly on the surface with such a genius, for Henri was remarkably informal and unaffected. Sir Edward Stafford wrote on 3 July 1584 to Walsingham of the "great familiarity" with which Henri had greeted the duc d'Épernon and his companions: "He set himself down at the midst of the board, made them all sit down . . . and would not suffer anyone of them that came with him to serve him."[65] While this casualness was one of Henri's greatest charms it could also be one of his political weaknesses—indeed it was precisely what lost him La Réole through Anne d'Aquaviva, according to the king's biography by Hardouin de Péréfixe:

> Henri also lost La Réole by another youthful indiscretion. He had given command of the fortress to an old Huguenot captain called Ussac, who had a horribly deformed face. His ugliness did not prevent him from becoming enamored of one of the queen mother's girls, for she had many of the most seductive kind to excite everyone. The vicomte Turenne, later duc de Bouillon, then aged twenty-one or two, sought to mock the aged lover with one or two other young men. Instead of reducing them to silence, as he should have done, our Henri joined in the sport, and as he had much wit, helped them to launch shafts of mockery against the old lover. No passion renders a heart more sensitive than that. Ussac could not bear the mockery of his very

64. Montigny, p. 20.
65. Sophie C. Lomas, ed., *Calendar of State Papers, Foreign Series, of the Reign of Elizabeth, July, 1583–July, 1584* (London: His Majesty's Stationery Office, 1914), p. 582.

own master, and at the expense of his honor and his religion, he
withdrew and surrendered La Réole to Duras

who was another friend of Henri's alienated to the royal faction. It is
true that Henri "always seemed to be mocking others and himself,"
for "he adored witticisms," like his pun on his return to the ladies after
a dusty victory at Dreux: "Mesdames, vous me voyez tout cendreux,
mais non sans Dreux." His mistress Corisande reproached him for this
facility: "Be more restrained in speaking of your plans than you have
been hitherto."[66]

There was at bottom a streak of cruelty in all this: "His volatile
humor [was] aggravated by the absence of meaningful, deep feelings,
by the lack of moral discipline, and above all by an egotism the more
tyrannical in that, lacking awareness of himself, he never felt embar-
rassed."[67] Stafford's letter to Walsingham confirms this in noting that
"all the help they have to make his good usage evil-thought-of is that
they say the king of Navarre is a cunning and corrupt Béarnais, and
that what fair face soever he show, there is no trust in him."[68] Under
pressure of circumstances Henri certainly could not be trusted, as Biron
finally found, but the king's intuitive power was unmistakable, as he
proved to everyone when in 1579 by force of sheer personal example he
captured Cahors, a part of Aquitaine denied from his wife's dowry
negotiated at Nérac and the sole gain of "la guerre des amoureux." In
many ways, Biron was directly competing with his master in the 1590s
as appears at the seige of Amiens, where at the key moment "the king
arrived in the army to the great displeasure of the marshal [Biron],
who vehemently protested that the deployment had been completed before the king's arrival."[69] Furious at losing command at the moment
of victory, Biron exclaimed that the only useful thing the king brought
to the army was his girlfriend, Gabrielle d'Estrées. One sees here exactly
the contemptuous competitiveness with which Shakespeare's Berowne
treats the amorousness of his sovereign:

66. Hardouin de Péréfixe, *Histoire da Roy Henry le Grand* (Amsterdam:
Elzevir, 1664), p. 55. Raymond Ritter, *Henry IV lui-même, l'homme* (Paris:
Michel, 1944), pp. 80, 77.
67. Ritter, p. 167.   68. Lomas, ed., p. 584.   69. Montigny, p. 22.

Now step I forth to whip hypocricy.
Ah, good my liege, I pray thee pardon me.
Good heart, what grace hast thou, thus to reprove
These worms for loving, that art most in love? ...
You'll not be perjured, 'tis a hateful thing ...
But are you not ashamed? Nay, are you not, ...
To see a king transformed to a gnat;
To see a great Hercules whipping a gig,
And profound Solomon to tune a jig, ...
I am that honest, I that hold it sin
To break the vow I am engaged in,
I am betrayed by keeping company
With men like you, men of inconstancy.

(iv.iii.146ff.)

Well might Shakespeare's king exclaim, "Too bitter is thy jest," for this was very much the reaction of the historical king too: "Although Henri IV affected to pay no attention to Biron's bragging, these violent outbursts were at bottom very disagreeable," and when the duc de Savoie praised the Birons, Henri responded that he had difficulty in restraining the father's drunkenness and the son's effrontery.[70] Nevertheless for much of his career Henri clearly liked and accepted Charles de Biron and told his minister Sully: "I know all the marshall's ways of talking, and one should not always take all his bragging, threats, exclamations, and pretentions too literally, but put up with them as from a man who can't stop insulting everyone and praising himself excessively for doing well when he finds opportunities seated in the saddle, sword in hand; for I have seen him do an infinite number of good actions in the middle of the grossest spitefulness, recriminations, and threats."[71] There was at bottom on both sides a deep respect and affection masked by a surface competitiveness: at the battle of Fontaine-Française the king could not be restrained from personally rescuing Biron, whose adventurousness had got him into difficulties as usual. The king justified the risk to himself and to his incredulous advisers by saying that "it is true, but if I don't rush in the marshall will never

70. Ibid., pp. 22, 36.   71. Ibid., p. 60.

318

let me live it down as long as he lives."[72] And they were always squab-
bling over just how fairly Biron was rewarded: when he received the
rank of marshall Biron crudely riposted that "he would willingly have
given up the marshall's commission for a good hack worth fifty silver
pieces."[73]

For all Biron's outrageousness the king almost to the end trusted
him with the most significant and exacting responsibilities while discounting even such charges as the attempted murder of the king, trea-
sonous negotiations with Savoy, and a plot to marry into its royal
family against the king's wishes—much of which Biron frankly con-
fessed to Henri in private at Lyons and for which he was informally
forgiven. On embassies to Switzerland, Flanders, and England toward
the end of his career, Épernon testifies that Biron "showed great skill,"
and "we must not be surprised by this, for he only sought recognition
for his brutal valor to fit the coarseness of his age, when valor was less
esteemed when it was subjected to considered judgment; but at bottom
he had both aptitude and application, for one day the king inquired of
some legal dignities the meaning of a Greek inscription, which eluded
them, and Biron threw his explication back over his shoulder as he left
the room, seeming ashamed of revealing his knowledge."[74]

That Charles de Biron should have ultimately paid with his life for
his obtuseness should also occasion no surprise. He had privately indicated to Henri his temptation to share a dismembered France with
Savoy, but when the details resurfaced publicly Biron rejected repeated
opportunities to endure correspondingly public avowals of his guilt, for
which Henri IV afforded him opportunity. This proud refusal to re-
apply for a forgiveness which he held that the king had already granted
definitively at Lyon was the occasion for his final repudiation by Henri,
leading inevitably to a public trial in which the unofficial personal pardon was not accepted as relevant. To his great incredulity and indignation Biron found himself doomed to execution for offenses for which
he believed the king had already excused him. That he had plotted
against the state is certain; that none of his plots were actually realized
is equally certain, and it is probable that the king chose to let formal
justice be done by waiving his previous unofficial pardon entirely be-

72. Ibid., p. 19.   73. Ibid., pp. 16–17.   74. Ibid., p. 20.

cause Biron refused to humiliate himself anew before the world and thus end any sense of their parity in honor, which Biron had so much affected. It was an appropriately weird end to an extraordinary career, and Biron's last moments were as grotesque as any: he threatened attendants at the execution when they tried to secure him: "By God's death if I had my sword I'd cut out the guts of the lot of you," and then he turned on the executioner: "Get on, get on, finish me off quickly." Some modern historians think the whole affair was a cunning and successful plot of the Spanish to destroy the French king's best general, and Biron's own opinion confirms this: "How helpful the king is today to the king of Spain by ridding him of such a great enemy as me."[75]

Just how interested the English were by this extraordinary career appears in Chapman's two plays, which are protracted studies in hubris. The analogues to the fate of Biron's friend Essex are so obvious that it is often suggested that Biron was sent on an embassy to Elizabeth in 1601 just after the execution of Essex so that she could make clear to him the penalties for excessive ambition, for Elizabeth even pointed out Essex's head to him at the Tower to stress the lesson.[76] One of the more bizarre possibilities about this trip is that as *Love's Labour's Lost* was successful enough for it to continue to be performed, Biron could have seen or at least read advantageously of his own supposed exploits as detailed in the quarto edition of 1598.[77] There he could have read in Act IV of his concealed involvement with a lady, which is uncovered when an underling betrays to the king a letter containing "some certain treason" (IV.iii.185). This puts all Berowne's pretentions to virtue and superiority to rout as he is forced unwillingly to concede: "Guilty, my lord, guilty! I confess; I confess" (V.iii.200), and he admits for all who have thus betrayed their oath to the king: "We deserve to die" (IV.iii.204). Ironically, only a few years later than 1598, the uncovering by a double agent of a secret document bearing on Biron's planned marriage to the daughter of the duc de Savoie actually did prove Biron's

75. Ibid., pp. 45, 143.

76. Hardouin de Péréfixe, *Histoire du roy Henry le grand* (Amsterdam: Anthoine Michiels, 1662), p. 279.

77. The play was performed at least as late as 1604–5 according to E. K. Chambers, *William Shakespeare*, vol. 2, p. 331.

final ruin and caused his execution. Berowne's comic downfall immediately after refusing to confess his sexual betrayal of the court's code disconcertingly prefigures his actual tragic fall for concealing a plotted political marriage against French policy. We may ascribe prophetic insight into Biron's character on the part of Berowne's creator, of the kind suggested in a contemporary epitaph:

> Passant, qu'il ne te prenne envie
> De scavoir de Biron le sort,
> Car ceux qui auront sceu sa vie
> Ne s'etonneront de sa Mort.
>
> On vit le grand Biron desfaire
> L'An six cens et deux en Juillet.
> Pour le mal qu'il pretendoit faire
> Non pour celui qu'il avoit fait.[78]

(Passerby, don't seek to know Biron's fate, for those who have known his life will not be surprised by his death. We saw great Biron destroyed in July 1602 for the evil he intended to do, not for that he had done.)

Of course the English had every opportunity to observe Biron's nature during their active service with him often under his command, and we detect a mutual admiration between the English troops and the dashing commander. In more than one skirmish we find Henri and Biron dependent on a handful of bold English, as often as not headed by Roger Williams. The mutual awareness was such that we find it noted at one point that "the English were placed under Biron at his request."[79] At Yvetot in 1592 Henri was crafty enough to unite several nationalities under Biron's command, rather as we see in *Henry V*, so that national competitiveness would help carry the day. The English had therefore opportunity to observe the demeanor of the king and his friends under every kind of condition. Of course the king

---

78. Bibliothèque Nationale, Fonds français, MS 12666, p. 36.

79. Richard B. Wernham, ed., *List and Analysis of State Papers, Foreign Series, Elizabeth I, Preserved in the Public Record Office, vol. I, August 1589–June 1590* (London: Her Majesty's Stationery Office, 1964), p. 332.

and the other figures like young Biron, Longueville, and d'Aumont were hardened campaigners by now; and, as the English enthusiastically followed Henri's protracted conquest of his own kingdom, Shakespeare must have shared the great interest in studying the nature of this Protestant hero and his companions. There was an immense increase in newsletters about Henri and his campaign around 1589, indeed "in English publications the king continued to figure as Henry the Great around the time of his assassination."[80] This English preoccupation establishes the context of *Love's Labour's Lost*, which attempts to take advantage of fashionable contemporary political concerns in terms of a political biography covering the youthful escapades of the hero. The protracted battles and skirmishes of the period were seemingly less glamorous as a stage subject than a subtler biographical approach: as with his later studies of Henry V and Octavius, Shakespeare decided to seek historical answers to such questions as "who are these heroes of the Protestant cause? where did they come from? and how did they become the men that are so admired?" The representation of the brilliant assembly at Nérac for the Conference was an eminently theatrical occasion by means of which to enrich one's sense of the formative years of personalities now figuring on a bigger stage.

To understand what Shakespeare made of this diplomatic event it is first necessary to understand exactly what it was originally. In 1578 "Catherine de' Medici set out on her last great undertaking—a journey of pacification in the south. . . . She visited Guienne and Languedoc, Provence and Dauphiny, even Navarre itself. Frequently she found the towns and chateaux of the lesser nobility had shut their gates against her, but she pitched her camp wherever she could find a suitable site, . . . summoned the important men of the district and addressed and argued with them."[81] Hitherto Henri had proved just as reluctant, and at first he refused to accommodate or even meet Marguerite. However, the case of Henri de Navarre was to receive distinctive treatment since he had become the leader of the Protestant party after he had literally escaped from the clutches of madame de Sauve. The Peace of

80. Dickens, "Elizabethans and St. Bartholomew, p. 57.
81. Williamson, p. 260.

Bergerac of 1577 was slowly disintegrating in warlike skirmishes, and Catherine planned to restore it by negotiation and to follow this up by imposing a fresh influence on Henri. From the start she planned to secure the diplomatic initiative by dazzling and disorienting the Huguenot leaders with the brilliance of her own court and (after she left) through the power of a small detachment of the *escadron volant*, led by her own daughter, who was nominally Henri's wife: "Employing the methods of her mother, Marguerite was attended by thirty-three maids of honor to soften up the crude officers of her husband."[82] Shakespeare perfectly catches the ruthlessly destructive attitude of the band of young women toward their diplomatic male opponents. Their startling manipulative view of sexual psychology is therefore not so much Shakespeare's invention but an essentially historical record of Marguerite's impact on the court at Nérac, as planned and superintended personally at first by the queen mother and her army of Amazons. The ladies were very thorough in their preparations, holding "secret and merry councils of war." At these they trained themselves, in preparation for dealing with the Huguenot diplomats, "under the lead of that little clown mademoiselle d'Atri in what they called 'consistorial language': phrases like 'to approve the counsel of Gamaliel,' to say that 'the feet of those who bring peace are beautiful,' to call the King 'the Anointed of the Lord,' to ejaculate often 'God be judge between me and you.' They called this 'the language of Canaan' and practised it with bursts of laughter while the Queen was going to bed."[83] Shakespeare's Princess catches the authentic tongue-in-cheek cadence of these sessions in *Love's Labour's Lost* when she exploits Calvinist cliché:

> See, see—my beauty will be saved by merit.
> O heresy in fair, fit for these days,
> A giving hand, though foul, shall have fair
>   praise.
>
> (IV.i.21–23)

82. Erlanger, *La Reine Margot*, p. 20.
83. Paul Van Dyke, *Catherine de Médicis*, vol. 2 (New York: Scribners, 1922), p. 252.

The ladies' puritanical opponents were all too often outwitted, in history as in the play, by such virtuosity of expression combined with sexual vitality. Albert Savine confirms this in *La Vraie reine Margot*:

> It was there at Nérac that the queen mother had determined to wage a real battle of diplomacy and gallantry against the king of Navarre and his supporters in order to tame Huguenot independence. She claimed that the slowness of the negotiations was caused only by the desire to see more of her ladies. All the young protestant lords were driven frantic by these enticing tamers of hearts who were free to follow devotion to Diana or Venus as they wished, according to Brantôme. Sully says: "Love, still young, learned to dance in the school of Catherine de Bourbon; love had become the most serious thing for all the courtiers. The mixing of the two courts . . . produced the result that one might expect. All gave themselves up to pleasure, to festivals and courtly festivities, amusing ourselves only with laughter, dancing, and games."[84]

Catherine's initial success was all that she could have wished.

Marguerite herself was a well-endowed captain to lead the van, and after the treaty she could safely be left behind to consolidate any victory. She is "the modern woman," when compared to the stiffer manners of her father's wife, Catherine, and even of his mistress, Diane de Poitiers, whose views can be epitomized as: "I was born without the doctrine of conviction of sin, and I hate the Reformation." Marguerite was infinitely more fluent and unpredictable: she "wrote in her own individual style, created forms of her own with a freedom far from the days of the court of her mother."[85] As the play shows in the scene with the Forester quoted (IV.i), she could be overpowering even when hunting wild animals, for already at the age of thirteen she had been "an intrepid huntress more concerned with her horses [chevaux] than her hair [cheveux]," capable of "the harsh ways of the huntswoman," as the poor Forester at first discovers. Later, however, her physical talents developed in ways permitting other prey: she had "a sensual mouth, a

84. Albert Savine, *La Vraie reine Margot* (Paris: Michaud, 1908), p. 98.
85. Edith Sichel, *Catherine de' Medici and the French Reformation* (London: Constable, 1905), pp. 67–68.

sparkling complexion, a sly eye, and black curly hair which she often hid under a blond wig" (hence the possible role of the brunette Rosaline as the queen's *alter ego*).[86] Brantôme describes her impact on a Polish embassy: "She seemed to them so beautiful, so proudly and richly dressed, and furnished with such great majesty and grace that everyone stood stunned by her beauty."[87] Don John of Austria was heard to observe ominously: "However much the beauty of this queen may seem more divine than human, she is more fitted to ruin and damn men than to save them." And Brantôme goes on characteristically to note that "her beautiful costumes and pretty finery never dared to risk covering her beautiful throat and fine breast, fearing to spoil the world's view which fed on so fine a sight, for there was never seen one so pretty and while so full and tender, which she showed so openly displayed that most courtiers were overpowered." In fact Marguerite literally stood out in the court because of her robust figure (whose seductiveness suggests why Brantôme asserts that "love is better made with big, tall women").[88] She was powerful and athletic enough to sustain the crushing physical demands of her public roles, bearing easily robes "whose weight would have crushed another woman, but which her large and ample figure supports so well."[89] Her mother-in-law's frailer build required that she be carried to her first wedding because she could not sustain the massive accoutrements of her regal costume. Marguerite's Amazonian stature unexpectedly validates the historical accuracy of Costard's recognition of her as "the greatest lady, the highest. . . . The thickest and the tallest" in Shakespeare's play (IV.i.46–48). She did become quite stout in middle age, about the time the play was written; but in 1577 she was to be compared to Cleopatra as she sailed in her ornate barge on the Meuze attended by her elegant ladies to dine with her Antony: the victor of Lepanto (near Actium), Don John of Austria.

Tallemant des Reaux records[90] an unnerving example of the ruth-

---

86. Erlanger, *La Reine Margot*, pp. 44–45. See also Plate 9.

87. Brantôme, *Oeuvres*, vol. 8, pp. 25–26.

88. Brantôme, *Lives of Gallant Ladies*, p. 19.

89. Saint-Amand, *Women of the Valois Court*, p. 131.

90. Des Réaux, vol. 1, p. 62.

lessness with which Marguerite humbled the kind of pompous gentlemen with whom she had to deal at Nérac. One of them was related to
Biron—Jean de Gontaut, baron de Salignac. Compulsively attracted to
Marguerite's charms he insistently protested his limitless devotion.
"What would you do to testify to your love?" she asked. "There is
nothing I would not do!" "Would you be willing to take poison?" "Yes,
if you were to allow me to die at your feet!" "I want you to do so!"
Thereupon she prepared the potion, which he willingly consumed, and
she left him for it to take effect, with promise of her return before
death ensued. In fact, she had prepared a healthy but powerful laxative,
with predictable results in reducing her admirer's aggressiveness. With
such methods and resources Marguerite disorientated the rude Protestants of the Nérac court. Usually her procedures were more positive:
"Following the same techniques that she had often seen her mother
practice she instructed her ladies-in-waiting to entangle all the gallants
around her husband in their nets."[91] D'Aubigné glumly recalls that
"the court of the king of Navarre began to flourish in proud nobles
and excellent ladies, so well that in all kinds of unborn and acquired
talents it was no less esteemed than that of France. Relaxation brought
in vice, as heat does snakes. The queen of Navarre pretty soon polished
up everyone's wits while their weaponry got rusty. She taught the king
her husband that a gallant was without soul when he was not in love."[92]
The protestant poet du Bartas rose to the occasion with an elaborate
masque of muses to welcome Marguerite, and we find the court records
include expenses such as: "For the king, twelve ounces of sugar for the
maids of the queen mother to make sweet water; marzipan for them
after the ball." The summer of 1579 proved to be "the golden age of the
little court of Nérac."[93] Marguerite herself writes of the

> happiness which lasted for me during four or five years that I
> was in Gascony with the king of Navarre, passing most of that
> stay at Nérac, where our court was so fine and pleasant that we

91. François E. de Mezeray, *Histoire de France* (Paris: Bureau Central, 1839),
p. 498.
92. Agrippa d'Aubigné, *Histoire Universelle*, ed. Alphonse d'Aubigné, vol. 9
(Paris: Renouard, 1891), pp. 381–82.
93. Lauzun, pp. 64, 115.

did not envy even the French court, having there madame la
princesse de Navarre the king's sister . . . and myself being followed by a fine troop of lords and gentlemen, as worthy as the
most gallant that I have ever seen at the court, and there was
nothing to regret about them except that they were Huguenots.
But this diversity of religion was not heard spoken of at all: the
king my husband and madame la princesse his sister going on
the one hand to their sermon and I and my train to the mass in
a chapel which is in the park, whence as I came out we would
all gather to walk together, either in a very pretty garden which
has very long avenues of laurels and cypresses, or in the park
which I had caused to be made along the river, and the rest of the
day was spent in all kinds of honorable pleasures, dancing taking
place usually after dinner in the evening.[94]

The long line of this delightful park still survives on the left bank of
the River Baise opposite the town, and of course it is this setting, favored by Marguerite, which Shakespeare stresses as the more "natural"
environment preferred by his princess to the cloistered sophistication
of the Huguenot court in the palace on the opposite side of the river.

However, as to the innocence of the recreation fostered by Marguerite, there is some room for doubt: "Marguerite was not obsessed by
love. Since power eluded her she chose to rule minds, and in this
domain she succeeded perfectly."[95] It was at this period that historians
note the king of Navarre's "passion for gay entertainment showed in
all its brilliance."[96] Historians recognize that Henri sustained the fes-
tive extravagances of Catherine de' Medici: "Masques were then composed of troupes of masked persons, clothed in bizarre costumes of
diverse kinds, who executed dances accompanied by songs more or less
grotesque and appropriate to the subjects which the dances and costumes claimed to represent. They were brilliant under Henry IV."[97]
Shakespeare shows us the mode in *Love's Labour's Lost*, and as usual
his choice of detail is remarkably apt. We need not refer to Russian

94. La Tour d'Auvergne, p. 164.
95. Erlanger, *La Reine Margot*, p. 212.
96. G. B. de Lagrèze, *Henri IV* (Paris: Fermin Didot, 1885), p. 224.
97. Paul Durand-Lapie, *Un Académicien du XVIIᵉ siècle: Saint-Amant* (Paris:
Delagrave, 1898), p. 37.

missions to England in the 1580s or the Polish affiliations of Henri III to discover the Slavic symbolism. Again and again at the Nérac conferences such allusions are exploited. Catherine de' Medici stresses the "Muscovites'" devotion to their duke as a model for Protestant submission to Henri III, asking: "Are we worse than Persians, Turks, Muscovites, and barbarians?"[98] Figeac brusquely responds: "What's the use of all these examples if not to turn us into Mohammedans, Muscovites, barbarians, and pagans? We cannot be other than good Frenchmen and good Christians." In the play the young men make the same claim against the Princess and her court:

> Your beauty, ladies,
> Hath much deformed us, fashioning our humors
> Even to the opposed end of our intents; . . .
> Full of straying shapes, of habits and of forms.
>
> (v.ii.746–48, 753)

In other words, the ladies' hostility has turned them from civilized Frenchmen into "Muscovites," or barbarians. However, in turn, the ladies' hostility is a negative response to this aggressive disguise and to the repudiation of candor and true character involved in usurping such an exotic identity. We have already seen that in the sixteenth century wearing a mask always risked the accusation of concealing sexual corruption and insincerity (as even Castiglione recognized).[99]

These corrupt overtones of the Nérac entertainments derive from Henri's earlier stay at the court of France, where similar diversions organized by Catherine de' Medici had masked the seductive operations of madame de Sauves:

Henri had acquired at the French court some libertine habits of which not even age would cure him. He fell, more than once, into the traps sets for his weakness by the followers of Catherine and Marguerite: to the story of his liaisons with madame de Sauves and mademoiselle de Tignonville were added the scandalous chronicle of his dalliance with mademoiselle Dayelle, mademoiselle de Fosseuse-Montmorency, and mademoiselle le

98. D'Aubigné, *Histoire Universelle*, vol. 9, p. 365.
99. See above, Chapter 3.

Rebours. . . . The friends and officers of the king also paid their tribute to the Italianate machinations of the queen mother: one saw Turenne, Roquelaure, Béthune tamed in their turn, and Rosny, who would later become the solemn minister of a great king, fell like the rest. It must be added that after the departure of Catherine and her dangerous "squadron" gallantry did not cease at Nérac as long as it was held by the beautiful queen of Navarre at least. These passions or fashionable flirtations involved distressing political consequences. Catherine sowed a divisive spirit and fostered defections. When she left Gascony twenty treasons were on the eve of revealing themselves, and they weakened the Huguenot party: Lavardin, Gramont, and Duras among others became Henri's enemies. We will only mention the rivalries, quarrels, and duels: Condé and Turenne, themselves entangled by the counterstroke of the queen mother, managed to cross swords, and the viscount nearly died some time later in an encounter at Agen with Durfort de Rauzan.[100]

Turenne seems to have been as much Marguerite's victim as the impregnated Fosseuse was Henri's: "To her first lovers (for their number I regret my incapacity to list them accurately) there followed at various times others such as that great bore the vicomte de Turenne, who like the earlier ones she soon turned away, finding his physique somewhat lacking in a certain place, comparing him to an empty cloud which has only outward show; with which the sad lover, in despair and after a farewell full of tears, went on his way to lose himself in some remote spot."[101] The outcome was less gross but perhaps even more humiliating for Turenne than the laxative administered to Jean de Gontaut, though he turns it to the pursuit of solitary glory in his memoirs.

One begins to see just what lies behind the malicious games and switched identities with which Shakespeare's young women afflict their lovers. These are not Shakespeare's improvisations but transcriptions of the sexual virtuosity of Marguerite's female shock troops. Around the time Lady Cobham reported that women like the *escadron volant* had staged "a very gallant masque" of armed men and women, and "in

100. Batz-Trenquelléon, p. 132.   101. Mariéjol, *Vie le Marguerite*, p. 176.

the end the women overcame the men."[102] This is obviously how the *escadron* saw its Gascony campaign climaxing at Nérac, and Huguenot testimony of Henri's defeat there in uniform, for "who arriving at Nérac, would have believed it to be the capital of the Puritan party?"[103] Protestant ministers raged against "cosmetics, pleated garments, coiffures, hairpins, gilded hairpieces, exposed breasts, farthingales." Marguerite's personal commonplace book filled up with sentimental poems on "l'immortel subject de vostre déité" (the immortal theme of your godhead). The poems labor over her favorite themes of stars, suns, and eyes: "Je veois dedans tes yeux / Le soleil de mon ame" (I see in your eyes the sun of my soul). No doubt the verse reflects the required reading of Marguerite's suitors, who must "employ their time in reading Equicola, Leon Hebreo, or Marcillio Ficino" according to their Muse. And for their pains these amateur poets received stringent criticism from the metropolitan ladies: "Do we have to be imprisoned in this cursed Gascony for the sake of three or four rusty sworders serving the heretics?"[104] Quaintly enough we find this surly divinity affords a precedent for du Bartas to hand on to Milton. For du Bartas devoted to Marguerite, as fitting tribute, his *L'Uranie, ou Muse celeste*, on which Milton modeled the magnificent hymn which introduces the second half of *Paradise Lost*, at the start of Book VII.

The Platonic readings advocated by Marguerite favored idealizing types of amatory verse for the most part, some of it not unlike the more sentimental poems of Donne:

> Ces grossieres amours, par ces grossieres ames,
> Ne peuvent alumer jamais de claires flammes,
> Il n'en sort que fumee, ainsy que d'un bois vert,
> C'este fumee rend les yeux couvers de larmes;
> La belle amour sans pleurs, brusle les belles ames,
> Le corps est plus tost mort que l'amour decouvert.
> Avant que d'avoir veu quelque chose parfaicte

102. A. J. Butler, ed., *Calendar of State Papers Foreign 1579–80* (London: His Majesty's Stationery Office, 1903), p. 175.

103. Erlanger, *La Reine Margot*, p. 210.

104. Eugénie Droz, *La Reine Marguerite de Navarre et la vie littéraire à la cour de Nérac (1579–1582)* (Bordeaux: Taffard, 1964), pp. 31–36.

La belle ame, souvent quelque chose souhaitte,
Mais se sont soubaitz qui ne la peynent pas.[105]

(These crude lovers, by such gross souls, can never be fired by
clear flames; there comes from them only smoke as from green
wood; this is the smoke which fills the eyes with tears; fine love
without tears fires fine souls; the body dies rather than reveal
love. Before having seen something perfect the fine soul often
wishes for something, but these desires never oppress it.)

The sentiment favoring love's impassivity is that advocated in "The
Valediction: forbidding mourning," where surface emotion is repudiated as a sign of baseness. However, as so often in sophisticated amorousness, the refinement readily becomes perverse in a servile poem
written by Salomon Certon to Marguerite, after some minor lapse in
etiquette had offended her:

J'ay aveugle autrefois seruy une maistresse
Et puis une autre encore honteux ie le confesse
Et ie confesse auoir failly bien lourdement,
Mais se n'est estre Ingrat de les auoir laissees
Pour vous donner mon cueur mes desirs mes pensees
Vous que le meritez et elles nullement.

Pensez ie vous suply que leur peu de merite
Et le pauure subiect de leur beauté petite
Ne m'obligoient en rien a leur estre asseuré
Je n'ay point faict appuy de leur peu de puissance
Ie n'ay point fait serment soulz leur obeissance
Se retirer est libre a qu n'a point iuré

Ie n'ay donc point failly m'ostant de leur puissance
Qui ne meritoit rien de mon obeissance
Mais ie suis revenu plustot a mon debuoir. . . .

Le ciel m'a destine a vous seule Madame
Qui propice et benin fait capable mon ame
Pour comprendre le bien de vostre dignité
Tournant mes voluntez plus sainctes et plus saines
Vers le divin obiect de voz graces hautaynes.[106]

105. MS 816[12], p. 307.   106. MS 816[12], pp. 47-48.

(Earlier I served a mistress, and then another, I confess it with shame, and I confess to having failed very seriously; but it is no betrayal to leave them to give you my heart, my desires, and my thoughts, you who merit it while they don't in the least. Think, I beg you, that their lack of merit and the poor matter of their slight beauty did not require me in the least to support their weakness. I have given no oath at all to their obedience: withdrawal is free to one who has not sworn. I have thus not failed in leaving their authority, which does not justify my service in the least; but rather I have returned to my duty. . . . The heaven destined me to you alone, madame, who, propitious and benign, make my soul capable of understanding your worth, turning my holier and healthier will toward the divine object of your high graces.)

Shakespeare duplicates this servility with more "metaphysical" wit in Longueville's analogous sophistry to excuse his volatile behavior:

> Did not the heavenly rhetoric of thine eye,
>   'Gainst whom the world cannot hold argument,
> Persuade my heart to this false perjury?
>   Vows for thee broke deserve not punishment.
> A woman I forswore, but I will prove,
>   Thou being a goddess, I forswore not thee.
> My vow was earthly, thou a heavenly love;
>   Thy grace, being gained, cures all disgrace in me.
>   (IV.iii.55–62)

Even Berowne's notorious justification of volatility finds a remarkably close precedent in Marguerite's Nérac manuscript anthology, where we find a forensic exercise called "Pour la legerete" (in defense of lightness) written by Jean de Rivason, "avocat de Sarlat":

> Vuide de tout ennuy qui tenaille les coeurs,
> Ennemy du soucy des antiques censeurs,
> Veuf de la grauite que le vulgaire loue
> Deliure du repos qui me tient arresté
> Ie me veux enfoncer dans la legereté. . . .

332

Deesse qui soustiens dans ta puissant main
De tout cest uniuers le sceptre souverain
Qui auec noz esprits t'esiouis et t'esgayes
Tu traines apres toy tant de menuz plaisirs
Que lors qu'amour m'obstine a ses plus chauds desirs
Ie ne pourroy sans toy, medeciner mes playes. . . .

Tu presides au ciel qui se suit et se fuit,
Et sans aucun arrest tout chose produit,
Et bien qu'il semble auoir quelque peu
        d'asseurance
A son tour et retour sa vite fermeté
Autre base ne prend que la legereté
N'estant en rien constant qu'en sa seule
        inconstance. . . .

La nature a voulu que sur tout element
Le plus leger auroit entier commandement
Tant elle se delecte a ce qui est agile
Le feu commande a l'air qu'il abisme soubz soy
Et l'air a l'ocean superbe faict la loy
Et l'ocean venteux a la terre immobile. . . .

Puis donc qu'un corps leger a tout
        commandement,
Et que le corps pesant obeit seulement,
Et le commandement montre quelque excellence,
Que retardons nous plus changer il conuient
En leger le pesant qui assopis nous tient
Si nous voulons auoir quelque preeminence. . . .

Les espritz plus legers sont les plus excellens,
Les espritz plus legers sont les plus inconstans,
La gravité ne vient d'ailleurs que de lourdise,
On dit que les veillardz ont plus de gravité
Que les ieunes qui sont plus pleins de viuacité
Aussi sont ils plus lourds et chacun les
        mesprise. . . .

333

Si comprendre beaucoup est le seul argument
Par lequel on cognoit vn grand entendrement . . .
Certes de tous espritz celuy est le meilleur
Qui sur diuers subiectz, non sur vn seul se
      iette. . . .

Le sage sur le temps conforme ses desseins,
Le temps les authorise ou les faict trouver vains,
Si le temps inconstant a toute heure varie
Luy qui se scait tourner a toutes actions
Varie en volontés et en affections
Estimés vous cela de petite industrie?

Arriere donc dicy stoiques forcenés
Qui a tout accident constans vous obstines
Ce n'est ainsi qu'il faut vser de la constance. . . .[107]

(Empty of all the fear which tears up hearts, enemy of the concerns of antique censors, widowed of the gravity which is praised by the vulgar, free of rest which holds me fixed, I wish to commit myself to lightness. . . . Goddess, who bear in your powerful hand the sovereign sceptre of all this universe, you who play and delight yourself with our wits, you draw after you so many light pleasures that when love subjects me to its hottest desires I shall not be able to cure my wounds without you. . . . You rule in the heaven, which goes and comes and produces everything without faltering, and although it seems to have a little certainty in its turn and return in quick firmness, it has no other basis but lightness, being in nothing constant but only in its inconstancy. . . . Nature has wished that above every element the lightest should have entire authority, so much she is delighted by what is lively: fire rules air, which it precipitates below it, and air gives orders to the proud ocean, and the windy ocean to the immobile earth. . . . Since then a light body has complete mastery, and that a heavy body merely obeys, and since authority shows some excellence, why do we hesitate any more: we should change to lightness the heaviness which holds us stupefied if we wish any distinction. . . . The lightest spirits are the most ex-

107. MS 816[12], pp. 5–11.

cellent; the lightest spirits are the most inconstant; gravity comes from nowhere but from heaviness: they say that old men have more gravity than the young who are more full of vivacity, and they are also heavier, and everyone despises them. . . . If to understand much is the only argument by which one knows a great understanding . . . truly of all minds that is best which commits itself to various subjects not to one alone. . . . The wise man adapts his plans to the time; the time validates them or makes them prove futile. If inconstant time fluctuates every moment, the one who knows how to twist himself to every action varies in will and in affections—do you think that a little effort? Back then you fanatic stoics who resist constantly every accident, that is not the way to express constancy. . . .)

If this is the kind of poem valued by Marguerite de Navarre, it is clear that Berowne's cynical rationalization of sexual indulgence is delivered in exactly the sophisticated mood Marguerite wished to foster in order to discredit the bellicose Puritanism of the Huguenot party. It is historically true to character that Berowne should dismantle the religious fervor and moral commitment of his ascetic friends in a way destructive to fanaticism:

> keeping what is sworn, you will prove fools.
> For wisdom's sake, a word that all men love . . .
> Let us once lose our oaths to find ourselves,
> Or else we lose ourselves to keep our oaths.
> It is religion to be thus forsworn.
>
> (IV.iii.351ff.)

Shakespeare accurately shows that Catherine's policy of sexual diplomacy successfully disoriented the most prominent figures of the Huguenot opposition, just the men whose vitality and enterprise make them most susceptible to deflection from abstractions by emotional baits. Shakespeare has history to back his gracefully graceless narrative.

There are some other details which illustrate how little improvisation is involved in the play. It is not perhaps necessary to labor the way in which the names of even minor characters, not merely Boyet, but Moth and Mercade, are derived from contemporary figures. Nor is it important to exhaust numerous details from the data preserved from the period which show that Shakespeare's texture is largely filled in from historical incidents: details like the king's quaint habit of saving paper by writing in every direction on every corner of each page of his letter (V.ii.7–8), a technique which the surviving letters of Henri IV frequently illustrate; or his flamboyant presents to the ladies at Nérac (V.ii.1–4), which are documented in the accounts of the day; or his aggressive riding style (IV.i.1–2), which was noted when he fought alongside English troops; or even his penchant for extravagant Spaniards. Since Navarre had recently included parts of northern Spain, Henri was very susceptible to the seductive bombast of Spanish captains whose fantasies suggested the charms of past glories and the hope of future ones. D'Aubigné describes one of these pompous flatterers in detail: Captain Loro who "began with a harangue of compliments on his reputation, notable services, experience of difficult enterprises, great trust, and power with his master." The captain's sinister fascination overpowered Henri, who disregarded his minister's advice to the contrary and frequently interviewed this hypocritical adventurer at great risk to himself, since it finally proved that Loro intended to assassinate the king. Yet only the killing of the Spaniard ended the king's involvement.[108] D'Aubigné mentions another, more heroic Iberian, whose amatory sensibilities were trailed ostentatiously before the court, and the atmosphere of the times is heady with male sexuality fanned yet frustrated by the calculated deployments of the female diplomats trained by Catherine.[109]

Since the purpose of the ladies' enterprise was to keep the potentially bellicose leaders of Protestantism permanently off balance, the campaign was supposed to continue indefinitely, but two events indicate the progressive disintegration of the policy. One was the ill will generated in 1581 when the erratic Henri made Marguerite's maid, La Fosseuse, pregnant and tactlessly forced his resulting problems on his affronted wife: for once Marguerite seems to have lacked the cynical flexibility of her mother, allowing her resentment to show so openly that Henri in turn became alienated. The most obvious and final change of mood occurred much later, in June 1584, in a way closely

108. D'Aubigné, *Histoire universelle*, vol. 10, p. 183.
109. Ibid., vol. 10, p. 460.

resembling the shock effect of the death of the Princess's father which terminates the play's gaiety. Marguerite's brother, François de Valois, duc d'Anjou, died unexpectedly, and Marguerite, who had worked arduously to promote his interests, was deeply shocked. She went into heavy mourning "and wished to hear no more of festivals and receptions."[110] Pibrac (whom Boyet represents in the play) also died at exactly the same time, after a fearful and humiliating quarrel in which Marguerite had repudiated a declaration of love by him with the utmost savagery. The winter of 1584–85 at Nérac was a melancholy and hopeless end to the enterprise of merry seduction, for Henri made good his escape from Marguerite and her ladies as finally as he had from madame de Sauves. When Henri met Catherine de' Medici at Saint Bris in 1586, the goal was quite different, which is why the play's tone does not accord well with the later conference. Marguerite was not present, and indeed one of the participants' principal conclusions was not to negotiate reconciliation but to authorize her final divorce from Henri, hardly a topic compatible with the amorous mood of Shakespeare's play. Henri was now a politician whom Catherine could no longer dominate by sexual or any other means: after years of being manipulated, the hero had begun his progress to power as an autonomous personality.

We are now able to judge what drew the young and ambitious Shakespeare to this material and how it bears on his work as a whole. In the first instance *Love's Labour's Lost* is a work of popular "journalism" exploiting current interest in a fashionable hero of the kind familiar since Alcibiades and Alexander, or even Theseus, and including men like Julius Caesar, Mark Antony, Octavius Caesar, and Henry V. Indeed the more we study the congruence of Henry V and Henri IV the more we see how the playwright's view of the latter prefigures the investigation of the former in the second English tetralogy. In each we find the immature hero presented at a formative moment, confronted by classic temptations which deflect him from conventional decorum, with the reinforcement of a friend whose maturer mind at first operates as an *advocatus diaboli*: for Berowne behaves like a youthful Falstaff in his cynical sophistication, and both of them are humiliated climactically by the dramatist. It is an even more sinister fact that each youthful

110. Lauzun, p. 289.

hero effectively consented to the execution of his historical friend: Henry V reluctantly allowed Oldcastle to be burnt at the stake as Henri allowed Biron to be beheaded at the Bastille. Typically, in neither case does Shakespeare show us this horror (indeed, with Biron, the predictable event still lies in the future), but that Shakespeare senses this sinister correlation appears in Fluellen's comparison: "As Alexander killed his friend Cleitus . . . so also Harry Monmouth . . . turned away the fat knight" (IV.vii.47ff.).

To complete the related triad of the *Sonnets* with the young aristocrat and his witty friend, we require the skeptical mistress, whether she proves to be the Dark Lady, Marguerite de Navarre, or the other French princess at whose feet Henry V lays his trophies: Catherine de Valois. All these women are as skeptical as the young heroes' friends: in learning English, Henry V's future wife anticipates the sexual conquest implied by English victories in a scene which is riddled with nuances, susceptible to Freudian analysis (III.iv), of which the French aristocrats show themselves bitterly aware:

> Our madams mock at us and plainly say
> Our mettle is bred out, and they will give
> Their bodies to the lust of English youth
> To new-store France with bastard warriors.
>
> (III.v.27–30)

This sentiment for bastardy is one cited by Brantôme and Ronsard,[111] bred out of the sexual cynicism of the *escadron volant*, not from any fifteenth-century court lady. With their power to twist young men around their fingers, the women in *Love's Labour's Lost* are prototypes of Shakespeare's virtuoso heroines in his mature comedies, but the earlier female characters are no less surely modeled on historical French maids of honor than Berowne is based on the bravura of Charles de Gontaut, duc de Biron. Truth exceeds the scope of fiction, and it is Shakespeare's genius to have copied, not invented, such psychologies.

In all this we must recognize the cultural impact of figures like Marguerite d'Angoulême, Catherine de' Medici, and Marguerite de Navarre as intrinsic to Shakespeare's achievement in many of his most

111. See *Ronsard*, ed. Cohen, vol. 2, p. 235.

striking characterizations, understanding that their originals' virtuosity derived in part from their attempts to cope ingeniously with the tremendous internal pressures tearing France apart in the sixteenth century. Fortunately I can call on the testimony of a connoisseur to confirm that it was during the Valois dynasty's perilous rule that Frenchwomen achieved the supremacy of sophistication which they have never wholly forfeited since. Brantôme was writing about the time of the accession of Henry IV in 1589, or later, when he observed:

> As for our beautiful Frenchwomen, they used to look fairly crude in past times and to be content to display primitive manners, but for the last fifty years in these matters they have learned from other nations such charm, daintiness, attractions and virtues, costuming, fine airs, activities, in which they are so well studied to shape themselves that now we must say that they surpass all others in every way, and as I have heard say even by strangers they excell all others greatly, so that the French language of sexuality is more scxy, exciting, and better sounding in the mouth than any others. From this fine French freedom which is more admirable than other, it comes that our ladies are more desirable, approachable, kindly, and more current than any.[112]

Brantôme is in fact no shallow sensualist: he stresses that "when a beautiful woman is equally full of fine speech she contents doubly." He indicates that it was above all at the Valois courts that this intellectual value was stressed, for there even very beautiful women would be rejected by the gentlemen if they were "naive, unspiritual, without wit and verbal fluency." In all these ways, he says, "Frenchwomen surpass all, but they owe great thanks to the queen of Navarre," that is to say, Marguerite d'Angoulême.[113] In this context we may doubly ascribe to French prototypes both Beatrice and Benedick, who recreate the moods of Berowne and Rosaline, in a format probably borrowed from the *Heptameron* as we have seen. Shakespeare's ideal of the ruthlessly witty courtship, resting on a hearty good sense, is one he learned from the French, whether in France or London.

112. Brantôme, *Memories*, vol. 1 (Leyden: Jean Sambix, 1699), p. 224.
113. Ibid., vol. 1, pp. 294–95, 298, 353.

10

Puritans and Libertines: D'Aubigné and Théophile de Viau

D'Aubigné

As we have seen, Lucien Febvre detects "abrupt swings of feeling in sixteenth-century people."[1] Febvre goes on to deny that this can be explained by our contemporary psychiatry, psychology, or even our historians. No doubt the paradoxical nature of such historical personalities whom we recognize as compelling and influential explains the fascination of Renaissance works like *Love's Labour's Lost* which reflect them directly and without straining after the modern defect of formal consistency which even literary criticism seeks to impose, in the vein of Schücking's quaint censures of Shakespeare's "inconsistent" psychology in his *Character Problems of Shakespeare's Plays*. In denying the plausibility of erratic characters like Cleopatra, Schücking ignores the documentation of such paradoxes as her contemporary analogue, Marguerite de Navarre, illustrated in the Renaissance memoirs noted by Febvre. Again, E. R. Chamberlain may find it "wholly impossible"[2] that the hermit-like idealism of Shakespeare's King of Navarre should have any bearing on the lecherous figure of the actual "Vert Galant." Yet in

1. Febvre p. 281; see opening of Chapter 1.
2. E. R. Chamberlain, *Marguerite of Navarre* (New York: Dial, 1974), p. 209.

one of the most convincing modern accounts of Henri de Navarre, Raymond Ritter provides documentation of exactly such a trait: "If he had
the option, he would have changed his manner of life, and retired into
a solitude, for there alone he would at least have found a complete
spiritual serenity—'Nothing is lacking there,' he exclaimed . . . 'manna
falls there, the crows bring bread from heaven there.' "[3] Anyone knowing the rural charm of such refuges as Henri's "moulin de Barbaste"
must recognize the authenticity of such a reclusive mood. And his
paradoxical nature can be summarized in his own frank avowal to
his mistress, Corisande: "Si je n'étais Huguenot, je me ferais Turc."[4]
A philandering Calvinist, with Mohammedan instincts, who became
a committed Catholic—such a figure epitomizes the psychological mul-
tifariousness of his era. When Eliot praised Renaissance writers like
Donne so highly for possessing "a mechanism of sensibility which could
devour any kind of experience,"[5] he implied that this was a uniquely
literary resource, but it was shared by and often derived from their
contemporaries of every class and profession.

Almost all these eccentricities and paradoxes of behavior seem to
derive from the pressures of religious conflict or the disorders resulting
from them. Nevertheless, such tensions are largely missing from the
best-known literary model for Renaissance English writers emulating
France, the Huguenot du Bartas, who seems to have been principally
favored because his laborious and discursive biblical epics were so complacently in the Protestant vein. Though he was intimately associated
with the court of Navarre, which he served as soldier and diplomat, he
does not greatly reflect the lively characteristics of his native Gascony
or of his patron the king of Navarre. His encyclopedic influence on such
poets as Drayton or Milton, while well-documented,[6] favors the development of the more laborious, descriptive phases of a work like
Paradise Lost, whose account of Creation is superior in wit and vividness to its precedent in *La Semaine ou création du monde* yet still may
fail to compel the attention of many modern readers. Modern French
taste largely discounts du Bartas as a poet, and the study of his impact
on English verse risks antiquarianism, even if we find many echoes

3. Ritter, p. 140.   4. Ritter, p. 236.   5. T. S. Eliot, *Selected Essays*, p. 247.
6. See Prescott, *French Poets and the English Renaissance*, pp. 167–234.

and parallels from Spenser to Milton. Though du Bartas wrote more charming verse in the Gascon dialect, he does not even seem true to the Béarnese tradition, for "the local poetry of Béarn has preserved a distinction, a polished elegance which has a courtly rather than a rustic air." We can see this sardonically witty vein in another of Henri's Béarnese protégés when Guillaume Adler writes:

> Nou sies d'aquets qu'espousaran ue More,
> Un arrebec, mes qu'age force argent
> Si n'as mouillé de quanque bonne gent,
> L'argent s'en ba, è la bestie demore.[7]

(Don't be of those who would marry a dark woman, a misbirth, just because she's got lots of money—if you don't have a woman of good breeding, the money goes, and the beast is left.)

There is a wry affinity here with the witty debate over the limitations of Berowne's swarthy mistress, Rosaline, in *Love's Labour's Lost* (IV. iii.242–72). Despite the respect Protestants accorded to the biblical works of du Bartas, one understands why the more sophisticated members of the court of Marguerite de Navarre at Nérac might share d'Aubigné's mockery of the provincial solemnity and awkwardness of his work.

D'Aubigné is a better illustration of the dynamic literary results of the religious tensions of the time (see Plate 15). His personality is nearer to the paradoxical norm established by Febvre: a passionate Calvinist, he yet conformed for a time to the sensual sophistication of Valois courts, and even reluctantly accompanied their armies against his fellow Protestants. His courtly lyrics flattered the tastes of Marguerite and her ladies, even if his distaste for her family's behavior soon brought him into perilous disfavor. His epic about the collapse of the Valois dynasty, *Les Tragiques*, reveals this loathing in a poem increasingly recognized as the true epic statement of Protestant attitudes which du Bartas had once seemed to epitomize. His writing has recently been praised for its "truth of sentiment, intensity of realistic detail" and displays a "fevered rhythm, broken, tortured; the accumulation of the maximum of strong words in the minimum of rhythmic space, some-

7. Adolphe van Beuer, *Les Poetes du terroir du xv^e siecle au xx^e siecle*, vol. 1 (Paris: Delagrave, 1909–41), p. 124.

times at the expense of grammar."[8] Dealing with the agonizing first-hand experiences of the poet and his patron, Henri, by 1589 this work had already achieved currency at his court,[9] though not published in complete, printed form until 1616. With a dramatic verve perhaps learned from the playwright Jodelle, d'Aubigné led the way, in his savage caricature of the downfall of the Valois, for Marlowe in his *Massacre at Paris* and for the score of similar plays dealing with contemporary French examples of hubris, like Biron and Bussy d'Amboise, which followed.

How relevant d'Aubigné is to the themes, psychology, and style of the Elizabethan theater can be gauged by some unexpected juxtapositions between its masterpieces and his epic. For example, Geoffrey Bullough notes that the sinister temperament of Lady Macbeth has marked affinities with the Protestants' black vision of Catherine de' Medici, whose use of witchcraft was notorious. One current story which he quotes describes a magician's conjuration of a vision for her of the succession of the French monarchy which she breaks off in despair when the circling years of her sons' reigns are succeeded by the longer cycles of Henri of Navarre. The resemblance to Macbeth's vision of the Scottish succession may be traced through several extant Elizabethan accounts of this episode. More significant is Catherine's infamous role in spurring on the blood lust of Charles IX on the eve of the St. Bartholomew's Day Massacre, as reported by de Thou: "The Queen, fearing lest the King, whom she thought she did observe, still wavering and staggering at the horridness of the enterprize, should change his mind, comes into his bed chamber at midnight." The king was "upbraided by his Mother, that by delaying he would let slip a fair occasion offered him by God, of subduing his enemies. By which speech the King, finding himself accused of Cowardise, and being of himself of a fierce nature gave command to put the thing in execution," and Catherine then ordered the bell to be rung which started the murders.[10]

The parallelism is suggestive, but Bullough fails to follow up in detail the breakdown of the two protagonists' personalities thereafter,

8. Agrippa d'Aubigné, *Oeuvres*, ed. Henri Weber (Paris: Gallimard, Pléiade, 1969), pp. xxi–xxii.

9. D'Aubigné, *Oeuvres*, p. xxiv.   10. Bullough, ed., vol. 8, pp. 443–46.

which is fully described in other contemporary accounts, but nowhere more vividly than in d'Aubigné's use of Henri de Navarre's testimony in *Les Tragiques*. The disintegration of Charles IX's mind, which Henri personally observed, provides a central passage of the work, some details of which may well have been known to Shakespeare. After St. Bartholomew's Day the nearly lunatic king was on the verge of executing the two young princes who had headed the Huguenot faction, Henri de Navarre and the prince de Condé:

> Charles tournoit en peur par des regards
>   semblables
> De nos princes captifs les regrets lamentables,
> Tuoit l'espoir en eux, en leur faisant sentir
> Que le front qui menace est loin du repentir.
> Aux yeux des prisonniers le fier changea de face,
> Oubliant le desdain de sa fiere grimace,
> Quand, apres la semaine, il sauta de son lict,
> Esveilla tous les siens pour entendre à minuit
> L'air abayant de voix, de tel esclat de plaintes
> Que le tyran cuydant les fureurs non esteintes. . . .
> Il depescha par tout inutiles deffenses:
> Il void que l'air seul est l'echo de ses offenses,
> Il tremble, . . .
> Du Roy, jusqu' à la mort, la conscience immonde
> Le ronge sur le soir, toute la nuict lui gronde,
> Le jour siffle en serpent; sa propre ame lui nuit,
> Elle mesme se craint, elle d'elle s'enfuit.
> Toy, Prince prisonnier, tesmoin de ces merveilles,
> Tu as de tels discours enseigné nos oreilles;
> On a veu à la table, en public, tes cheveux
> Herisser en contant tels accidens affreux.
>   (v.1001ff.)[11]

(Charles by such looks turned to fear the woeful lamentations of the captive princes, killed the hope in them, by making them understand that the face which threatens is far from repentance.

11. All later references are to Weber's Pléiade edition. See also Plate 6.

A week later the proud man changed face before the eyes of the prisoners, forgetting the disdain of his proud grimace, when the king jumped from his bed, woke all his people to hear at midnight the air baying with voices, with such an outbreak of laments that the tyrant, thinking the furies not extinguished, . . . sent everywhere useless defenses. . . . He sees that the air alone is the echo of his crimes; he trembles. . . . The foul conscience of the king until death gnaws on him at evening, all night scolds him; the day hisses like a snake; his own soul harms him; it fears itself; it flees from itself. You, imprisoned prince, witness of these marvels, have instructed our ears with this account— one has seen your hair stand on end, telling these horrible events at table in public.)

That Shakespeare seems to know the episode appears in the additions he makes to the sources for *Richard III*, also dealing with two young princes more than threatened by a tyrant. Richard's nightmare before Bosworth leads to the distinctive schizoid reaction shared by Charles:

> O coward conscience, how thou dost afflict me!
> The lights burn blue. It is now dead midnight.
> Cold fearful drops stand on my trembling flesh.
> What do I fear? Myself? There's none else by. . . .
> Then fly. What, from myself? Great reason why—
> Lest I revenge. What, myself upon myself?
> (v.iii.180–83, 186–87)

The paradoxical pattern of self-hatred is phrased similarly in *Les Tragiques* and *Richard III* but appears in none of the play's earlier sources —ignoring as they must these psychologically divisive effects of Reformation schism. We can see the new mental world further emancipating itself from medieval behaviorist psychology in Pierre de L'Estoile's account of Charles IX's decline:

The Friday before the Sunday when King Charles died, at two in the afternoon, having called Mazille, his principal doctor, and complaining of the great pains he suffered, the king asked him if it was not possible that he and so many other great doctors that there were in his kingdom could give him some easing of

his ill; "for I am," he said, "horribly and cruelly tormented."
To which Mazille replied that all which belonged to their art
they had done . . . but that to speak truly of it, God was the
great and sovereign doctor in such sickness, to whom one must
have recourse.[12]

One recalls Macbeth's similar, fruitless request of his wife's doctor, who
reports her to be "not so sick" but "troubled with thick-coming fancies
/ That keep her from her rest" (V.iii.38–39). Macbeth exclaims:

> Cure her of that!
> Canst thou not minister to a mind diseased,
> Pluck out from the memory a rooted sorrow?
> (v.iii.39–41)

The doctor replies in Protestant vein: "Therein the patient / Must minister to himself."

A similar psychological sophistication is shown in d'Aubigné's historical account of the "terrifying death" of the cardinal of Lorraine,
once reputedly Catherine's lover. Again Henri de Navarre is the source
for a description anticipating *Macbeth*:

> Ta voix a temoigné qu'au poinct que cet esprit
> S'en fuyoit en son lieu, tu vis saillir du lict
> Cette Royne en frayeur qui te monstroit la place
> Où le cardinal mort l'acostoit face à face
> Pour prendre son congé: eHe bouschoit ses yeux
> Et sa frayeur te fit herisser les cheveux.
> (1.1023–28)

(Your voice has testified that, at the moment this soul fled its
place, you saw this queen rise from her bed in fear, who showed
you the place where the dead cardinal met her face to face to say
farewell: she hid her eyes, and her fear made your hair rise.)

"Tels malheureux cerveaux" (such unfortunate brains) as Catherine's
so encouraged the populace to evil that it "trempa dedans le sang des

12. Pierre de L'Estoile, *Mémoires*, ed. Petitot (Paris: Foucault, 1825), vol. 1,
pp. 85–86.

vieillards les couteaux" (soaked knives in old men's blood [I.1029–39]). Many of Catherine's diabolic moods and seances are also described by d'Aubigné in detailed terms like those of Lady Macbeth and the witches (*Les Tragiques* I.699–979).

The relevance to *Macbeth* of these episodes in Catherine's career is strengthened by L'Estoile's version of her haunting by the dead cardinal, which reminds one of Banquo's ghost at the dinner: "This day, the queen mother, sitting down at table, said, 'We shall now have peace, since the cardinal of Lorraine is dead,' who was the one who prevented it, so they said. . . . Then having asked for drink, when they had given her the glass, she began to tremble so much that they thought she would drop it, and she cried 'Jesus! there is my lord the cardinal of Lorraine whom I see.' Finally, being a little reassured, she said, 'This is a great example of fear' " (I.109). Still she could not sleep or remain alone for a month and imagined all the time he beckoned her to follow him. A servant tells that the cardinal was once seen going to visit the queen, wearing only a nightgown, and that "if he ever spoke of what he had seen, he would lose his life" (I.110). One recalls Lady Macbeth's Doctor: "Go to, go to! You have known what you should not," and "I think, but dare not speak" (V.i.43, 74). The medieval setting of the original *Macbeth* has almost nothing so psychologically sophisticated as these episodes of neurotically disturbed conscience thrown up by the newly subjective tensions of the Reformation, with its terrible side-effects.

Before leaving *Les Tragiques* one should note the inevitability of other precedents or analogues in it for authors like Shakespeare and Milton, particularly in the scenes of warfare, in which "le courage Anglais" was often revealed, thanks to "heureuse Elizabeth" (III.953). Bullough recognizes Tacitus as the ultimate source for Henry V's review of his army in disguise before Agincourt but admits that there Germanicus does not speak to his men and only overhears good things of himself. However, in d'Aubigné's grimmer version of Tacitus, the French Calvinist rejects the praise of kings, saying that modern princes will find a less flattering outcome to such spying expeditions, rather as Henry hears from Williams (IV.i.127–38, 186–91):

347

Le prince, defardé du lustre de son vent,
Trouvera tant de honte et d'ire en se trouvant
Tyran, lasche, ignorant, indigne de louange
Du tiers état.

(II.359–62)

(The prince, stripped of the luster of his fame, will find much shame and anger in finding himself tyrant, cowardly, ignorant, and unworthy of praise by the lower orders.)

It may not be Shakespeare who first turned Tacitus' account of Germanicus "to very different ends," as Bullough suggests, but d'Aubigné. In a similarly hostile vein, d'Aubigné provides Milton with a precedent for his diabolic army at the start of *Paradise Lost*, for God sees the proud Spanish army advance to conquer France from a "funeste chateâu . . . l'abregé d'enfer" (a funereal castle . . . the epitome of Hell [III.529, 536]):

Apres, Dieu vid marcher, de contenances graves,
Ces guerriers hazardeux dessus leur mules braves,
Les trompettes devant: quelque plus vieil soldart
Porte dans le milieu l'infernal estendart . . .
Cet oriflan superbe en ce poinct arboré
Est du peuple tremblant à genoux adoré;
Puis au fond de la troupe à l'orgeuil equippee,
Entre quatre herauts, porte un comte l'espee.
Ainsi fleurit le choix des artisans cruels, . . .
Nourris à exercer l'astorge dureté,
A voir d'un front tetric la tendre humanité. . . .
Dieu vid non sans fureur ces triomphes nouveaux
Des pourvoyeurs d'enfer, magnifiques
                    bourreaux.

(III.561ff.)

(Afterwards, God saw the march with serious faces of these daring warriors on their gallant mules, trumpets leading; some older soldier carries in the center the infernal standard . . . this proud banner planted at this point is worshipped on bended knee by the trembling people; then at the end of the troop, equipped with

348

pride, a count carries the sword between four heralds. Thus flowers the choicest of cruel craftsmen ... bred to exercise insensible harshness, to view humanity with a sinister expression. ... God saw not without fury these triumps of hell's agents, magnificent executioners.)

The aggressive images resemble the Satanic host in *Paradise Lost*:

> Then straight commands that at the warlike sound
> Of Trumpets loud and Clarions be uprear'd
> His mighty Standard; that proud honor claim'd
> Azazel as his right, a Cherub tall:
> Who forthwith from the glittering Staff unfurl'd
> Th' Imperial Ensign, which full high advanc't
> Shone like a Meteor streaming in the Wind,
> With Gems and Golden lustre rich imblaz'd.
>
> (1.531–38)

In his parallel account of this procession in his *Histoire universelle* d'Aubigné also stresses "the great red standard of the Inquisition, carrying on one side embroidered the name, the portrait, and the arms of the Pope Sixtus IV and on the other the pictures and arms of Ferdinand and Isabella, as those due the honor of the Inquisition."[13] Milton's account of the army of Fallen Angels thus shares the format of the armies of the Catholic League and its allies in France. And d'Aubigné is very conscious of the possibilities of such parallelism:

> les plus subtils esprits
> A deguiser le mal ont finement apris
> A nos princes fardez la trompeuse maniere
> De revestir le Diable en Ange de lumiere.
>
> (11.949–52)

(the subtlest spirits have taught our princes cunningly to conceal evil, disguised by deceptive manners, and reclothing the Devil as an angel of light.)

The French epic carefully evokes contrasting, candid examples of suffering and endurance by Protestant martyrs, English as well as

13. D'Aubigné, *Oeuvres*, p. 973.

French, which help to explain its interest for Puritan poets like Milton. The subjective awareness of d'Aubigné contrasts with the institutionalized brutality of church and state, opposing their hierarchies with a Protestant stress on the individual's direct rapport with God. D'Aubigné is as bold as Milton in personalizing his divinity with scenes in Heaven between God, the Son, and Satan. But some of the most memorable precedents for *Paradise Lost* lie in the author's own words to the divinity:

> Ame de tout, Soleil qui aux astres esclair . . .
> Ravi-nous de la terre au beau pourpris des cieux,
> Commençant de donner autre vie, autres yeux
> A l'aveugle mortel: car sa masse mortelle
> Ne pourrait vivre et voir une lumiere telle.
>
> . . . .
>
> Les apostres ravis en l'esclair de la nuë
> Ne jettoyent plus ça bas ni memoire ni veüe; . . .
> Nul secret ne leur peut estre lors secret, pource
> Qu'ils puisoyent la lumiere à sa premiere source:
> Ils avoyent pour miroir l'oeil qui fait voir tout oeil
> Ils avoyent pour flambeau le soleil du soleil. . . .
> Ainsi dedans la vie immortelle et seconde
> Nous aurons bien les sens que nous eumes au monde . . .
> Purs en subjects trés purs, en Dieu ils iront prendre
> Le voir, l'odeur, le goust, le toucher et l'entendre. . . .
> Chetif, je ne puis plus approcher de mon oeil
> L'oeil du ciel; je ne puis supporter le soleil.
> Encor tout esblouï, en raison je me fonde
> Pour de mon ame voir la grand'ame du monde,
> Sçavoir ce qu'on ne sçait et qu'on n'a peut sçavoir,
> Ce que n'a ouï l'oreille et que l'oeil n'a
>   peu voir.
>   (VI.2ff.; VII.1159ff.)

(Soul of all, sun who shines to the stars, ravish us from earth to the fine purple of the heavens, beginning by giving other life, other eyes to the blind mortal: for his mortal mass cannot live

350

and see such a light. . . . The apostles ravished in the cloud's brightness no longer throw down there either their memory or sight, . . . no secret then can remain secret to them, for they draw light from its first source: they have as a mirror the eye which gives sight to all eyes, they have for torch the sun of the sun. . . . Thus in the immortal second life, we shall have fully the senses we had in the world . . . pure in seeing very pure things, in God they will take sight, smell, taste, touch, and hearing. . . . Wretch, I can no more approach my eye to the eye of heaven; I cannot bear the sun. Yet all dazzled, in reason I trust my soul to see the great soul of the world, to know what is not known and cannot be known, what neither ear can hear, nor eye can see.)

One sees how important a precedent these sentiments and images afford to the blind Milton in his great hymn to light as he turns his mind from Hell to Heaven at the start of Book III of *Paradise Lost*—dexterously integrating the shift from hellish despair to divine assurance with his own progression from worldly blindness to mystical insight. If he is literally d'Aubigné's "blind mortal," he shares the expectations of recovered and enhanced sight:

> So much the rather thou Celestial Light
> Shine inward, and the mind through all her powers
> Irradiate, there plant eyes, all mist from thence
> Purge and disperse, that I may see and tell
> Of things invisible to mortal sight.

(III.51–55)

What for d'Aubigné is rhetoric, symbolism, and imagery has become for Milton literal experience and intense autobiography: the allusions to "light," "sight," and "blindness" have a fresh urgency, even though the ideas and attitudes are shared with the French Huguenot.

Poets of all faiths in seventeenth-century England and France increasingly move toward the rejection of public achievement in favor of such stoic acceptance and private insights. Montaigne's skepticism is only an example or symptom of this shift in values, not a unique precedent. The loyal Calvinist, d'Aubigné, shares Hamlet's suspicion of commitment and zeal in preferring a "man that is not passion's slave" (III.ii.69):

Ceux-là regnent vraiment, ceux-là sont de vrais Rois
Qui sur leurs passions establissent des loix,
Qui regnent sur eux mesme, et d'une ame constante
Domptent l'ambition volage et impuissante.

(II.663–66)

(Those truly reign, those are true kings, who establish laws over
their passions, who reign over themselves, and with firm soul
tame fickle and impotent ambition.)

This stoic commonplace[14] is also attributed to Milton's Jesus in his rejection of Satan's offer of temporal rule in *Paradise Regained*:

Yet he who reigns within himself, and rules
Passions, Desires, and Fears, is more a King;
Which every wise and virtuous man attains:
And who attains not, ill aspires to rule.

(II.466–69)

While the idea is not novel, it is of interest to see that all these passages
reject the virtue of zeal or high feeling as a guide to true achievement.
The affinities with Montaigne's repudiation of enthusiasm and public
roles illustrate a major shift of outlook in the later Renaissance, away
from the ideal of flamboyant virtuosity in the public eye toward a quiet-
istic, private skepticism. This new, subtler form of egotism seeks to
avert the civic penalties of religious schism by withdrawal into subjectivity, and it marks the last stage of the impact of the Reformation
on what we tend to consider to be "Renaissance" literature. This is the
rueful mood of Hamlet lamenting that "the time is out of joint" and
regretting the awareness that he "was born to set it right" (I.v.188–89).

The Libertines

Reformation strife was largely ended by the skeptical authoritarian-
ism justified in the political philosophy of Jean Bodin and realized in
the Peace of Westphalia in 1648, and it was followed by the century of
Enlightened Despotism. This era and its Erastian values were prefigured

14. See D'Aubigné, *Oeuvres*, p. 942.

in the abjuration of his Calvinism by Henri IV, the necessary prelude to his coronation as king of France—an act which scandalized many of his Protestant followers, not least d'Aubigné. The act has been variously interpreted as cynical, expedient, well-meant, or genuine and sincere. There can be no final verdict. Henri's own tendency was to find such embarrassing shifts of loyalty simply "necessary." Certainly it marked the end of major challenges to his sovereignty; it founded the fortunes of the Bourbon dynasty, and it permitted the Protestants to gain from the monarchy most of what they wanted, in the Edict of Nantes. The superior claim of such public pragmatism to the compulsion of personal commitment is the key to a major literary strain in the earlier seventeenth century, associated with the names of poets like Théophile de Viau and his friend, Girard de Saint-Amant, who were widely known and admired in England.[15]

In fact both visited England, and their families were closely associated with the Protestant cause in France, though their careers matched Henri IV's in formal rejection of their inherited affiliations with the Huguenots. Their families were deeply involved in the religious wars: Saint-Amant's father even commanded one of Queen Elizabeth's naval squadrons for twenty-two years, returning to France on her death. The family of Théophile de Viau was no less intimately associated both with the Huguenot party and with the Kingdom of Navarre, which provided one of its safest strongholds. An ancestor of Théophile had been "secretary to Marguerite de Navarre";[16] his uncle had been made governor of Tournon in reward for his services to Henri IV, and his father's Huguenot sympathies had forced him from Bordeaux to the minor family property of Boussières near Clairac in the Agenais, where the poet's brother took a leading role in asserting Protestant causes in the first half of the seventeenth century.

Théophile himself studied in the new Huguenot college at Nérac and later at other Protestant institutions such as the academy at Saumur

---

15. Marvell's borrowings in "Upon Appleton House," for example, result from the Fairfax family's interest in such authors. See G. Wolledge, "St. Amand, Fairfax, and Marvell," *Modern Language Review* 25 (1930), p. 481.

16. Antoine Adam, *Théophile de Viau et la libre pensée française en 1620* (Geneva: Slatkine, 1965), p. 10.

and the University of Leyden, where he encountered the Dutch hostility to Catholic Europe, and Spain in particular, as well as hearing the rationalistic and libertarian views of scholars like Arminius and Vorstius. Though for a time associated with an actor's troup, Théophile found himself involved later in the Protestant revolt led by his patron, Candale, who had renounced Catholicism for love of the duchesse de Rohan, a Protestant analogue to the successes of the *escadron volant*. Thereafter, increasingly, Théophile found the Huguenots inadequate allies, and his scandalous reputation as a profligate exposed him to pressures (such as temporary banishment) which forced him to serve the king's favorite, Charles, duc de Luynes, and to become a spokesman (and even a soldier) for the Establishment. In this role he had great success as well as a more covert fashionable following for his cynical private life. Like Saint-Amant,[17] Théophile waited until his father's death to become a Catholic—and then perhaps chiefly to avert the censure and persecution for his scandalous behavior which ultimately led to his arrest, long imprisonment, and trial, ending in a sentence of banishment. This persecution was instigated by ecclesiastical authorities who were offended by pirated publications supposedly revealing Théophile's private attitudes. (See Plate 12.)

In his evolution from Protestant self-assertion and resistance to orthodoxy, through self-indulgence vindicated by rational skepticism, to a final conformity to the outward requirements of church and state, Théophile may serve as an epitome of the model afforded to England by French culture under the early Bourbons. What makes him distinctive is his power to express with vivid precision the often destructive religious forces which defined his nature and career even more absolutely than they did those of Clément Marot, who had followed a similar progression. Experience of what the religious conflicts had done to ruin France was also to be the ultimate driving force behind Cardinal Richelieu's ruthless determination to stabilize and standardize French society, and, in a variety of ways, many of the artists of the time shared and supported the cardinal's goals and methods, as the triumph of Malherbe's decorum and the discipline of the Académie française confirm.

17. Van Beuer, vol. 3, 442.

A skepticism like Montaigne's was increasingly shared by Protestants and Catholics alike, and there was a reasonable desire "to oppose to points of dogma which divided men the worship of a supreme being who united them."[18] Skeptical rationalists and freethinkers like la Mothe le Vayer worked for Cardinal Richelieu, and Gabriel Naudé worked for Cardinal Mazarin, just as Théophile did for Luynes. All three were governed by the same sense of expediency or "necessity" that had been reflected in Henry IV's own archetypal conversion to orthodoxy. With such a model, a Hobbesian sense of determinism extended from politics to religion and morals, fostering stoic dutifulness in public and an Epicurean satisfaction of private rewards and pleasures. Man was seen as a largely passive part of the natural order rather than its pivot. We can be sure of the historical awareness of these values because they were the basis of the persecutions to which Théophile was exposed by the published attacks of the Jesuit François Garasse. Garasse asserted that, among the sentiments professed by libertines like Théophile in their private life and in some of their published works, were such views as that "all things are conducted and governed by destiny, which is irrevocable, infallible, immovable, necessary, eternal, and inevitable to all men, whatever they can do." More specifically, "There is no other divinity or sovereign power in the world but Nature, which one must satisfy in all things without refusing to our bodies and our senses what they desire of us in the exercise of their natural power and faculties."[19]

Such ideas had been pushed to the point of overt atheism by an Italian thinker, Lucilio Vanini, who paid the price for his proselytizing in 1619, being burnt at the stake in Toulouse. Théophile's known verse is rarely so outrageous, but that of some of his friends, like Jacques Vallée des Barreaux, comes close to nihilism:

> Estoudions-nous plus à jouir qu'à connoistre,
> Et nous servons des sens plusque de la raison. . . .
> J'entre dans le néant quand je sors de la vie.

18. Antoine Adam, *Les Libertins au XVIIᵉ siècle* (Paris: Buchet-Chastel, 1964), p. 9.

19. Adam, *Les Libertins*, p. 42.

(Let us study more to enjoy than to know and to use the senses more than reason. . . . I enter nothingness when I leave life.)

* * * * *

Il faut prendre pendant la vie
Tout le plaisir qu'on peut avoir,
La clarté que Dieu nous fait voir
D'une longue nuit est suivie.

(During life one must take all the pleasure one can have. The light God allows us to see is followed by a long night.)

* * * * *

Je renonce au bon sens, je hay l'intelligence.
D'autant plus que l'esprit s'élève en
connoissance,
Mieux voit-il le sujet de son affliction.[20]

(I reject good sense; I hate intelligence. The extent to which the spirit achieves knowledge reveals to it more clearly the subject of its misery.)

Marvell attributes these gloomy sentiments to the Body in his wry dialogue between it and the Soul. The Body rejects the "sorrow . . . / Which Knowledge forces me to know," for

So Architects do square and hew
Green Trees that in the Forest grew.[21]

Such an outlook also explains the renewed intensity of the *carpe diem* argument epitomized by "To his Coy Mistress," which is a dramatic monologue in the persona of a figure like des Barreaux (who launched Marion de l'Orme on her amorous career, after a protracted siege of her virtue). For des Barreaux had written to such a beauty:

Prenons tous les plaisirs que permet la Nature,
Pendant que nous voyons la lumiere du jour.

20. Adam, *Les Libertins,* p. 195.
21. Marvell, ed. Margoliouth, vol. 1, p. 21.

> On ne boit point là-bas, on ne fait point d'amour,
> Dans cette longue nuit qui suit la sépulture.[22]

(Let us take all the pleasures that Nature permits while we see the daylight. No one drinks down there; no one makes love at all in this long night which follows the tomb.)

Inevitably these skeptics were "obsessed with death":

> De toutes ces beautez célestes,
> Voyez les misérables restes,
> Dan le lit commun des humains,
> Où Dieu veut que tousjours on dorme;
> Ces beaux yeux et ces belles mains
> N'ont plus ny mouvement ny forme.[23]

(Of all these heavenly beauties, you see the wretched remains in the common bed of humanity, where God wishes one should sleep forever; these beautiful eyes and fine hands have no longer movement or shape.)

The poets' contemporaries shared this desire to savor fleeting joys: Yiveteaux wished "posséder le présent en pleine confiance"[24] (to possess the present with full confidence). Moreover, once the senses begin to decline one should make the most of one's remaining options, as Blot cynically avows:

> Enfin puisqu'il faut que je quitte
> Ce beau titre de debauché,
> Je veux devenir hypocrite—
> Peur qu'il ne me manque un Peché;
> Et quoi que tard je m'en avise,
> Je pretens qu'on me canonise.[25]

(At last, since I must surrender this fine title of debauchee, I wish to become a hypocrite, for fear of missing out a sin, and, though I noticed this late, I claim to be canonized.)

22. Frederic Lachèvre, *Le Prince des libertins du XVIIe siècle: Jacques Vallée des Barreaux* (Paris: Leclerc, 1907), p. 166.

23. Lachèvre, p. 170.   24. Adam, *Les Libertins*, p. 203.

25. Bibliothèque Nationale, Fonds français, MS 12666, p. 205.

Garasse comes close to this in his sarcastic summary of Théophile's belief that "it is true that to live happily one must extinguish and drown
all our scruples but not appear impious and abandoned."

Such minds were cited by Garasse for being equally skeptical of pagan and Christian beliefs: "It is true that this book they call the Bible
or Holy Scripture is a nice book which contains lots of good things.
But that a good mind must believe everything in it on pain of damnation, down to the tail of Toby's dog, is only affectation."[26] Again we
find corroboration for such beliefs' existence as Blot invites his friends:
"Moquons nous des dieux de la Fable"[27] (Let us mock the gods of
fable), and blasphemous comparativism was a customary party game
for such versifiers:

> Qu'une Colombe à tire d'aile
> Ait obombrée une Pucelle,
> Je ne crois rien de tout cela:
> On en dit autant en Phrygie—
> Et le beau Cigne de Leda
> Vaut bien le Pigeon de Marie.[28]

(That a dove with a flap of its wing should impregnate a Virgin,
I don't believe all that at all: they tell as much in Phrygia—and
Leda's fine swan is as likely as Mary's pigeon.)

With such models close to hand, one can see how even a Puritan like
Marvell can be quite flippant about Christian allusions in "Upon Appleton House," as when the nuns tempt Isabel by inviting her to:

> Each Night among us to your side
> Appoint a fresh and Virgin Bride.[29]
> (185–86)

Of course, Donne is quite in the vein:

26. Adam, *Les Libertins*, p. 42.
27. MS 12666, p. 274. Blot's authorship is conjectural.
28. MS 12666, p. 275. Blot's authorship is conjectural.
29. Marvell, ed. Margoliouth, vol. 1, p. 64; later parentheses refer to this
edition.

> Thou shalt be'a Mary Magdalen, and I
> A something else thereby.[30]

Donne's own "Canonization" as a lover comes close to Blot's as a re-formed debauchee.

These then are the kind of witty extravagances favored in Thé-ophile's milieu which allowed his enemies to incarcerate him for two years during his trial for blasphemy, ensuring the ruined health that soon after killed him. Though Théophile's own published verse largely avoids these more extravagant effects, which he surely savored in pri-vate, it still discreetly shares their philosophical point of view. His iconoclastic tone is scarcely less harsh than theirs:

> La sotte antiquité nous a laissé des fables
> Qu'on homme de bon sens ne croit point
> recevables.[31]

(Idiotic antiquity left us fables that no man of good sense would believe in the least acceptable.)

In his "novel" he announces a style based on rejection of archaism: "Writing should be firm, its meaning natural and easy, the language exact and intelligible: affectations are only softness and artifice, which are never found without effort and confusion. These thefts, which one calls imitation of ancient authors, must be called ornaments which are not in our mode. One must write like a modern." As for what such a modern style may require, he avows: "I let my fancy lead me, and, whatever thought offers itself, I do not keep my pen from it: I conduct here a varied and discontinuous conversation and not a specific class or orderly oration." Behind the manner lies a deterministic view of human personality: "The climate affects my mood; whatever the expression opposed to this necessity, the temperament of the body compels the movements of the mind: when it rains, I am drowsy and almost mis-

---

30. Donne, *Elegies and Songs and Sonnets*, p. 90.

31. Théophile de Viau, *Oeuvres poétiques*, ed. Jeanne Streicher, vol. 1 (Geneva: Droz, 1951), p. 80. All future page references are to this edition unless otherwise indicated.

erable; when it is fine I find everything delightful: trees, buildings, rivers. . . ."[32]

Obviously Théophile will have intense awareness of his environment and a skeptical view of human motivation, particularly if it does not recognize its own nature and limitations. He warns Candale that his love affair makes him "serf de tes passions" (slave to your passions [I.67]), so that "il sembla que tes fers estoient ta liberté" (it seemed your shackles were like liberty [I.68]). However, to resist such feelings is unwise: "Si tu veux resister, l'amour te sera pire" (If you wish to resist, love will be worse for you [I.87]):

> Je croy que les destins ne font venir personne
> En l'estre des mortels qui n'ait l'ame assez bonne, . . .
> Je pense que chacun auroit assez d'esprit,
> Suivant le libre train que Nature prescrit.
>
> (1.88–89)

(I believe destiny never brings humans a being without a good enough soul . . . I think each should have enough wit by following the free course prescribed by Nature.)

More aphoristically, Théophile announces: "J'approuve qu'un chacun suive en tout la nature" (I approve that each should follow nature entirely [I.85]), and as a literary corollary he admits:

> La reigle me desplait, j'escris confusément:
> Jamais un bon esprit ne faict rien qu'aisément.
>
> (1.11)

(Regulation displeases me; I write confusedly: a good wit never did anything but easily.)

How relevant to Stuart verse such a model may have been can be conjectured from Pope's comment about the cynical "mob of gentlemen who wrote with ease," including authors like Suckling, Sedley, Rochester, and the rest of the Cavaliers. But even a Puritan like Marvell shares Théophile's skeptical determinism, in his "Horatian Ode" on Cromwell:

32. Théophile de Viau, Les Oeuvres, vol. 2 (Lyon: Cellier, 1677), p. 3.

'Tis madness to resist or blame
The force of angry Heaven's flame.
(1.88)

Marvell later said Charles should not have been challenged by Parliament; yet when the king was overthrown by irresistible forces, Marvell implies the king was right calmly to accept execution, "though Justice against Fate complain." Like the French intellectuals, Marvell tends, reluctantly, to accept and advocate existing authority's claims, whether it is monarchic or dictatorial. A similar discreet passivity governs the lover in "The Definition of Love." Like Candale in Théophile's elegy on his unconsummated love affair with an honorable social inferior, this lover accepts the fated nature of his passion and the impossibility of bringing it to a climax.

Moreover, the remarkable inconsistency in the personae of speakers in Marvell's various lyrics is compatible with Théophile's acceptance of his own volatility of mind: the stoic lover of "The Definition of Love" alternates with the Epicurean of "To his Coy Mistress," who in turn contrasts with the mystical speaker in "The Garden" or the Puritan of "The Bermudas." We can even recognize in the seemingly inconsecutive phases of "Upon Appleton House" the characteristic associative progression of Théophile's longer meditative poems, which prefigure a Rousseau-esque type of reverie:

> Je veux faire des vers qui ne soient pas contraincts,
> Promener mon esprit par de petits dessains,
> Chercher des lieux secrets où rien ne me deplaise,
> Mediter à loisir, resver tout à mon aise,
> Employer toute une heure à me mirer dans l'eau,
> Ouyr comme en songeant la course d'un ruisseau,
> Escrire dans les bois, m'interrompre, me taire,
> Composer un quatrain sans songer à le faire.
> Apres m'estre esgayé par ceste douce erreur,
> Je veux qu'un grand dessain reschauffe ma fureur,
> Qu'un oeuvre de dix ans me tienne à la
>   contraincte.
>   (1.12)

(I wish to write verse which is not forced, to promenade my spirit in small projects, seek out secret places where nothing displeases me, meditating at leisure, dreaming at my ease, employing a whole hour in admiring myself in the water, to hear the flow of a stream as if in a dream, to write in the woods, break off, fall silent, compose a quatrain without thinking about it. After having delighted myself with this sweet wandering, I wish that a great project may heat my ecstasy, so that a work holds me fixed for ten years.)

The last mood is that of "The Garden" also, when Marvell meditates a "longer flight"—perhaps "Upon Appleton House" itself. When Théophile was driven from the court he found consolations similar to those of Marvell, ensconced in the Fairfax retreat at Appleton House:

> Le plus superbe ameublement
> Dont le sejour des Rois esclatte, . . .
> N'eurent jamais rien de pareil . . .
> Ce cabinet tousjours couvert
> D'une large et haute tenture,
> Prend son ameublement tout verd
> Des propres mains de la Nature.
> (II.167)

(The proudest furnishings which give glitter to a king's stay . . . have nothing equal . . . this arbor always covered with a large, high tent gets its wholly green decor from Nature's own hands.)

Théophile savors the same sensuous seductions as Marvell's garden affords:

> Je verray ces bois verdissants
> Où nos Isles et l'herbe fraische
> Servent aux troupeaux mugissants . . .
> Je verray l'eau qui les abreuve . . .
> Je paistray ma dent et mes yeux
> Du rouge esclat de la Pavie,
> Encor ce brignon muscat
> Dont le pourpre est plus delicat. . . .
> Je cueilleray ces Abricots,

Les fraises a couleur de flames, ...
Et ces figues et ces Melons ...
Je verray sur nos Grenadiers
Leur rouges pommes entrouvertes. ...
Je verray fleurir nos prez,
Je leur verray couper les herbes;
Je verray quelque temps apres
Le paysan couché sur les gerbes,
Et comme ce climat divin
Nous est tres-liberal de vin,
Apres avoir remply la grange,
Je verray du matin au soir.
Comme les flots de la vendage
Escumeront dans le pressoir.

(II.192–94)

(I shall see these green woods where our isles and the fresh grass
serve the mooing herds. . . . I shall see the water that satisfies
their thirst; I shall feed my mouth and eyes with the red burst
of the Pavian peach and moreover this muscat nectarine whose
purple is more delicate . . . I shall pick these apricots, the flame-
colored strawberries, and these figs and these melons. . . . I shall
see on our pomegranates their half-opened red apples. I shall see
our fields flower; I shall see the grass cut; I shall see some time
later the peasant lying on the sheafs; and as this divine climate
is very generous to us with wine, having filled the barn, I shall
see from morning to evening how the floods of the wine harvest
foam in the press.)

The close affinities between these last lines and Keats' "Ode to Autumn"
amply confirm Rémy de Gourmont's assertion that Théophile's intense
awareness of the detail of the countryside prefigures the Romantics.
However, we also should recognize the French poem's even closer resemblance to Marvell's stanza:

What wond'rous Life in this I lead!
Ripe Apples drop about my head;
The Luscious Clusters of the Vine
Upon my Mouth do crush their Wine;

The Nectaren, and curious Peach,
Into my hands themselves do reach;
Stumbling on Melons, as I pass,
Insnar'd with Flow'rs, I fall on Grass.

(I.49)

It is true that Marvell here may owe something to Jonson's earlier trans-
positions to Penshurst of Martial's praise of Faustinus' Baiain villa—
but those nectarines and specially bred peaches in "The Garden" be-
long in the Agenais, not Kent.

If there is Puritan reservation about the sensual snares of nature in
Marvell's "Garden," yet there is also a religious mysticism in the French
poet's awareness of landscape:

Que ces arbres sont bien ornez!
Je suis ravy quand je contemple
Que ses promenoirs sont bornez
Des sacrez murs d'un petit Temple.
Icy loge le Roy des Roys: . . .
Il a fait le Tout du néant, . . .
Il fait au corps de L'Univers
Et le sexe et l'aage divers;
Devant luy c'est une peinture
Que le Ciel et chaque Element,
Il peut d'un trait d'oeil seulement
Effacer toute la Nature. . . .
Son Esprit par tout espandu
Jusqu'en nos ames descendu,
Voit naistre toutes nos pensees:
Mesme en dormant nos visions
N'ont jamais eu d'illusions
Qu'il n'ait auparavant tracees.

(II.182–83)

(How well planted are these trees! I am ravished when I con-
template how these walks are bounded by the holy walls of a
little church: here dwells the King of Kings: . . . He has made
all of nothing, . . . he makes the body of the universe and the

varieties of sex and age; before him this is a painting of sky and each element, of which he can erase the whole Nature by a single glance. . . . His spirit, spread everywhere, descending down into our souls, sees all our thoughts: even in sleeping our dreams have no illusions that he has not traced before.)

One recognizes a mood akin to Marvell's "withdrawal" into metaphysical speculation "annihilating all that's made / To a green Thought."

During his ghastly imprisonment in Paris such moods of Théophile's acquire a hallucinatory vividness which reminds us of Romanticism. His nightingale ode disconcertingly prefigures the famous synesthesia of Keats's ode:

> I cannot see what flowers are at my feet,
> 　Nor what soft incense hangs upon the boughs,
> But, in embalmed darkness, guess each sweet
> 　Wherewith the seasonable month endows
> The grass, the thicket, and the fruit tree wild.[33]

Théophile, imprisoned deep in the Conciergerie, writes of the evening far away at Chantilly, evoked by his "esprit voluptueux":

> Au travers de ma noire tour,
> Mon ame a des rayons qui percent
> Dans ce Parc, que les yeux du jour
> Si difficilement traversent,
> Mes sens en ont tout le tableau,
> Je sens les fleurs au bord de l'eau,
> Je prendre le frais qui les humecte, . . .
> Les oyseaux n'y font plus de bruit.
> Le seul Roy de leur harmonie . . .
> Demeure en nostre compagnie: . . .
> Il concerte si sagement
> Qu'il semble que le jugement
> Luy forme des airs de la sorte.
> 　　　　　　　(II.175)

33. John Keats, *Poetical Works*, ed. H. Buxton Forman (London: Oxford University Press, 1946), p. 231.

(Through my black tower, my soul has rays which pierce into this park, which the eyes of day cross with so much difficulty; my senses have the whole picture; I detect the flowers at the water's edge; I breathe the fresh air which moistens them. . . . The birds make no more sound there, only the king of their choir stays in our company: . . . he harmonizes so skillfully that it seems that deliberate choice forms such songs for him.)

The same kind of studious nightingale "does here make choice / To sing the Tryals of her Voice" in the woods of Appleton House. Marvell's nightingales tend to be perfectionists:

> The Nightingale does sit so late,
> And studying all the Summer-night,
> Her matchless Songs does meditate.
>
> (1.44)

Théophile's birds are no less anthropomorphic:

> Leur vaine gloire s'estudie
> A reciter quelques leçons
> De leur plus douce melodie.
>
> (ii.169)

(Their vainglory studies to recite some variations upon their softest melody.)

Such picturesque effects are grouped around the duchesse de Montmorency, in the setting of Chantilly, by Théophile's famous sequence of poems called "La Maison de Silvie." This protracted series of lyrics in octosyllabic couplets, some occasional, others reminiscences refracted through the dark prism of his imprisonment, provides a conspicuous precedent for Marvell's "Upon Appleton House," with its dark themes derived from the Fairfax experience of the Civil War and its analogous local female "divinity," in the person of Mary Fairfax. Each woman defines and stabilizes her environment by her mere presence:

> Je sçay que ces miroirs flotants
> Où l'objet change tant de place,
> Pour elle devenus constans
> Auront une fidele glace. . . .

Ces Elements si furieux
Pour le respect de ses beaux yeux
Interrompirent leur querelle.
(II.141–42)

(I know that these floating mirrors where the object is always
shifting will become steady for her and will provide a faithful
glass. . . . These so furious elements will interrupt their quarrel
out of respect for her fine eyes.)

Marvell shares these hyperbolic effects and innumerable others:

The gellying Stream compacts below,
If it might fix her shadow so . . .
'Tis not, what once it was, the World;
But a rude heap together hurle'd;
All negligently overthrown, . . .
But in more decent Order tame.
(675–76, 761–63, 766)

In a less extravagant vein, similar passages appear in Théophile's boat-
ing poem, "Les Nautonniers" ("The Boatmen"), which are transposed
to flattery of the divinity by the rowers in Marvell's "The Bermudas,"
in which the amorous navigators become Puritan refugees from Europe.

If the persecutions and tumults of civil and religious strife drive both
Théophile and Marvell into effective seclusion amid the delights of
rural nature, neither lacks the sexual sophistication of the courtier in
thus conforming, once again, to the model of Henri IV. In gentle mockery of conventional attitudes, both poets recognize the calculated charm
of feminine mourning:

Vous meslez dans ce dueil tant d'agreables charmes
Que c'est estre insensé que luy donner des larmes . . .
Je mourrois de regret de ne l'avoir suivie.
J'ay creu que la tristesse estoit pleine de maux, . . .
Mais vous faictes le dueil avecques tant d'appas
Que j'aime la rigueur, combien que je l'accuse,
Et trouve du plaisir a craindre le trespas.
(I.118–19)

(You mix so many agreeable charms in mourning that it seems insane to give tears to the dead. . . . I would die of regret not to follow the same course. I have thought that sorrow was full of evils, . . . but you make mourning so full of charms that I love suffering, even as I censure it, and find pleasure in fearing death.)

Marvell is no less delicately sardonic in "Mourning":

> Yet some affirm, pretending Art,
> Her eyes have so her Bosome drown'd,
> Only to soften near her Heart
> A place to fix another Wound. . . .
> Not that she payes, while she survives,
> To her dead Love this Tribute due;
> But casts abroad these Donatives,
> At the installing of a new.
>
> (1.32)

However, both poets test love against death and find the latter the more powerful: Marvell's "To his Coy Mistress" needs no repetition here, but its compeling practicality is excellently prefigured in Théophile's tough-minded elegy to Chloris:

> Chacun s'ayme un peu mieux tousjours que son amy,
> On les suit rarement dedans la sépulture, . . .
> Ceux qui jurent d'avoir l'ame encore assez forte
> Pour vivre dans les yeux d'une Maistresse morte,
> N'one pas pris le loisir de voir tous les efforts
> Que fait la mort hideuse à consumer un corps,
> Quand les sens pervertis sortent de leur usage,
> Qu'une laideur visible efface le visage.
>
> (II.27–28)

(Each person loves himself a little better than his love; one rarely follows them into the grave. . . . Those who swear still to have the spirit to live in the eyes of a dead mistress have not taken the time to see the efforts of hideous death in consuming a body, when the distorted senses leave their functions and visible ugliness destroys the face . . .)

Théophile develops these horrors to discredit sexual ecstasy, and thereby he skillfully emancipates himself from love and commitments.

In such pessimistic arguments Théophile provides Carew and the other Cavalier amorists with lively models for cynical sexual attitudes (I.130, 133). Both poets affect Horatian satisfaction at the impending ruin of a hostile beauty, and both censure a calculated neutrality in women, yet themselves invent sophistries to avoid commitment. However, as the seducer and then the victim of Marion de l'Orme, we must note that Théophile's friend des Barreaux deserves credit for illustrating the most subtle sexual sophistries that the Cavaliers were to achieve. When des Barreaux attempts to rationalize himself out of love for his fickle mistress he affords a prototype followed by Waller, Stanley, Cotton, and other Stuart amorists:

> Je ne te connois plus, tu n'es plus qu'un image
> Q'un portrait effacé de ce divin visage.
> Tes laches cruautez, tes crimes ont éteint,
> Et l'éclat de tes yeux et celuy de ton teint.[34]

(I cannot recognize you; you are no more than a copy, a smudged portrait of that divine face. Your vile cruelties, your crimes, have extinguished the brightness of your eyes and that of your complexion.)

Charles Cotton echoes the motif in writing:

> Methinks thou'rt blemished in each part, . . .
> Those eyes grown hollow as thy heart.[35]

Meanwhile Waller, with characteristic urbanity, softens the effect:

> Silvia the fair, while she was kind,
> As if her frowns impaired her brow,
> Seems only not unhandsome now.[36]

34. Lachèvre, p. 142.

35. Charles Cotton, *Poems*, ed. John Beresford (London: Cobden-Sanderson, 1923), p. 117.

36. Edmund Waller, *The Poems*, ed. Thorn Drury, vol. 1 (London: Routledge, 1895), p. 97.

Still, it is of Marvell's amorist one thinks first in reading des Barreaux's basic argument:

> Prenons tous les plaisirs que permet la Nature,
> Pendant que nous voyons la lumière du jour.
> On ne boit point là bas, on ne fait point d'amour,
> Dans cette longue nuit qui suit la sépulture.[37]

(Let us take all the pleasures Nature permits while we see the light of day. One does not drink at all down there; one cannot make love in the least in this long night which follows the sepulchre.)

It must be said, however, that des Barreaux's suppleness lacks intellectual depth and intensity, despite vicissitudes as painful but less heroic than Théophile's—to which indeed des Barreaux abandoned him unkindly. Théophile's intelligence avoids the mere hedonism of his friend and rises to the level of analysis and demonstration for which the Metaphysicals have been praised:

> La Nature est inimitable
> Et dans sa beauté veritable
> Elle esclate si vivement
> Que l'art gaste tous ses ouvrages. . . .
> L'art ennemy de la franchise,
> Ne veut point estre recogneu. . . .
> (II.42–43)

(Nature is inimitable, and in her true beauty she bursts out so vividly that art spoils all her works. . . . Art, enemy of openness, does not want to be recognized.)

Théophile consistently develops this love of the spontaneous and unconstrained in ways duplicated in Marvell's "Mower against Gardens." His own persecution fosters in Théophile a sense of subjective self-justification and demonstration which poets like Marvell, Lovelace, and Suckling share with Donne as well.

Finally, the paradoxical juxtaposition of private Epicureanism and public decorum in Théophile must be stressed. However Huguenot his origins and hedonistic his personal life, his ultimate support of the

37. Lachèvre, p. 166.

Establishment is remarkably emphatic, despite his own misfortunes. His persecution by civic powers did not shake a ruthless support of authority, which became axiomatic in Hobbes and was shared by Marvell in his Horatian ode when he writes to Cromwell, threatened by radical sects:

> Still keep thy Sword erect:
> Beside the force it has to fright
> The Spirits of the shady Night,
> The same Arts that did gain
> A Pow'r must it maintain.
>
> (1.90)

Théophile had admonished Louis XIII in identical terms in warning of the threat from the most rebellious radicals:

> Usez moins de vostre amitié,
> Vous perdrez ce titre de Juste
> Si vous usez trop de pitié. . . .
> Je pense que les coups d'espée
> Sont un salutaire appareil.
> L'honneur d'un juste Potentat,
> Est de faire qu'en son estat
> La paix ayt des racines fermes:
> Par là se doit-il maintenir . . .
> Contre ces esprits insensez.
>
> (1.162)

(Use your friendliness less; you lose the title of just if you use too much pity. . . . I think that the sword's strokes are a salutary means. The honor of a just potentate is to ensure that in his state peace has firm roots: thereby must it be maintained . . . against these insane spirits.)

In the acceptance of this outlook through most of France in the later seventeenth century lies the end of the innovatory mood of the Reformation, an end aptly symbolized by the Revocation of the Edict of Nantes. Latent in the compensatory private satisfactions of libertines like St. Amant lay the seeds of Rousseau and Romanticism—but that is another phase of historical psychology.

﷯11﷯

Conclusion:
Literature and History

WHAT I HOPE TO HAVE SHOWN ARE THE NEGLECTED TRUTHS[1] THAT THE great literature of Renaissance France evolved under the pressures of intense adversary relations generated by religious controversy and that English literature profited from the exciting new distortions of behavior, ideas, values, and personality which resulted. Without the challenge of Anne Boleyn's alien personality, Thomas Wyatt would have lacked a catalyst of his art and self-awareness encouraging him to challenge archaic Petrarchan conventions. Without the self-assertion of Marot and Ronsard in the face of their opponents, Donne and Milton would have lacked precedents for their own self-development. If Henri de Navarre had not fought (and almost lost) the Battle of the Sexes mounted by Catherine de' Medici's *escadron volant*, Shakespeare would probably not have initiated that fascinating series of dynamic heroines which starts with the Princess and her ladies in *Love's Labour's Lost* and lends unexpected verisimilitude of detail to figures like Lady Macbeth and Cleopatra.

One of the most important results of the dislocation of French society by the Reformation was a shift in the roles of women, among the

1. See Richard J. Schoeck, "English Literature," in William M. Jones, ed., *The Present State of Scholarship in Sixteenth-Century Literature* (Columbia: University of Missouri Press, 1978), pp. 137–38.

372

upper classes and their artistic associates at least.[2] Much of this can be attributed to the personal impact of François I and his sister Marguerite. While society as a whole may have resisted change in sexual relationships, and while even Marguerite d'Angoulême, and Queen Elizabeth herself, may not have consciously emancipated themselves from many traditional female attitudes, nevertheless we can detect the unmistakable beginnings of a shift to our modern sense of the parity of the sexes in psychological and sociological interest, generated in the Valois courts at a time when social norms were no longer uniform. As a result, a representative figure like Brantôme is certainly a more comprehensive, sensitive, and sympathetic student of human sexuality and women's potentialities than Freud, or indeed than most modern psychiatrists; and Brantôme merely reflects in a meandering, gossipy way the raw material French society afforded for fresh literary endeavors plotting the new relationships of the sexes. If the increased status of women provoked John Knox to his diatribe, *The First Blast of the Trumpet against the Monstrous Regiment of Women*, and though such Calvinist hostility is also reflected in d'Aubigné's assaults on the Valois women, we must balance these repressive views against du Bartas' celebration of Marguerite de Navarre as Urania and Spenser's dynamic Britomart, who epitomizes in many ways the new self-assertiveness of sixteenth-century women. Far from being an evocation of the archaic pre-Roman matriarchies of ancient Britain, Britomart is based on current examples, afforded by many contemporary chronicles, including those of d'Aubigné himself, who celebrates, for example, madame de Saint-Balemon of Montauban: "Having trained a company of cavalry of sixty gentlemen, who followed her flag and that of love simultaneously (almost all burning with passion for her without any being able to boast of an unworthy caress), she made several forays against the king in lower Auvergne."[3] When besieged thereafter by an enemy force, she

2. While I acknowledge the anti-feminine attitudes documented by Natalie Davis' numerous studies of lower and middle class attitudes in provincial France, their display seems fruitless in comparison to recognizing the contrasting evolution of feminine roles at higher social levels, which led the way for modern views.

3. D'Aubigné, *Histoire Universelle*, vol. 4, pp. 346–47.

led her troop in a charge, herself galloping twenty yards ahead of the front ranks: she broke the enemy's nerve and killed their commander, Montal.

Comparably, the sister of Bussy d'Amboise, Renée, rivaled his flair and aggressiveness after his assassination, rallying her followers at the siege of Nevers in terms anticipating Shakespeare's Henry V: "Can you let yourselves be so overcome by foolish fears as to trust your hopes to a cruel enemy steeped in the blood of pillage, instead of in your courage and in these arms which we took up for the common good? Have you now anything more to fear from the enemy but the sound of his canons? The breach is so steep, so narrow, and so rough that their soldiers can never scale it. . . . Take heart then and have courage from the example of these brave French whom you see with arms in hand. You are safe among friends. . . . Follow me! Come fight with me on the breach. Come! We go on to victory!"[4] Failing in her defense of the city, Renée turned to her husband and said: "What is there left for you, Balagny, if you live after your sad misfortune, but to serve as laughter and spectacle for the world to point its finger at, falling from so great a glory, to which you have seen yourself raised, to a low fate, which I see prepared for you if you do not do as I? Learn then from me to die well and not submit to your misfortune and derision!"[5] It is reported that, whether by sword, poison, or self-starvation, "she died content, for she died a princess." Well might such a death be held "equal to the heroes of Plutarch," and perhaps it explains why the fate of Shakespeare's Cleopatra seems so authentic; for Shakespeare adds to his source in Plutarch the same fear of becoming a public spectacle displayed by Renée. Cleopatra fears to "be shown in Rome. . . . Mechanic slaves . . . shall / Uplift us to the view. . . . Scald rhymers / Ballad us out o' tune" (V.ii.209ff.). Similarly, among Othello's deepest fears is to become "a fixed figure for the time of scorn / To point his slow unmoving finger at!" (IV.ii.54–55).

Adversity is the touchstone of human mettle for such cases in Shake-

4. Claude Derblay, *Une Héroïne de Brantôme: Renée de Bussy d'Amboise* (Paris: Plon, 1935), pp. 218–19.

5. Derblay, pp. 225–28.

speare, as for many of his contemporaries. It is customary to see the Machiavellian "over-reacher" as the product of Renaissance interest in pagan models of heroism, but the more carefully we study the historical models for the Guise of Marlowe, the Berowne of Shakespeare, or the Bussy of Chapman, the more certain it becomes that these figures took root only after the religious schisms had cracked open society and allowed such exotic growths to flourish in the debris. They illustrate the curious fact that the Reformation was often a catalyst rather than a prime agent of psychological evolution. Neither Shakespeare's nor Chapman's version of Biron shows any more affinities with Reformation or Counter-Reformation values than does their historical original, yet it was this theological dichotomy which generated the "Bironic" spirit. Similarly Catherine de' Medici showed little consistent religious commitment, and her exploitative policies and those of her associates were usually expedient responses to the religious compulsions of others. Yet out of this skeptical perspective evolved not only the modern spirit of compromise of the Politique party, vindicated by the theories of Jean Bodin and the practice of Henri de Navarre as king of France, but also the sophisticated awareness of a Montaigne or a Théophile de Viau, which affected the outlook of a whole generation of Stuart intellectuals, from Bacon to Hobbes, not to discuss poets like Herrick, Carew, or Marvell.

Not least of the consequences of such disruptions of society and orthodoxy was the retreat of many of the subtlest spirits of the time into the haven of the private self. And it is significant that many of the minds now most valued from the era were those who could take at least periodic refuge in the supportive environment of some sympathetic provincial enclave with which their natures had intrinsic compatabilities, whether it was the Nérac that sheltered Marguerite d'Angoulême, Marot, du Bartas, d'Aubigné, and Henri de Navarre; or the Vendôme of Ronsard; or the Garonne of Théophile; or Montaigne's chateau. Similarly we find English intellectuals and artists more and more drawn, or forced, into seclusion: Herrick in Devon; Marvell and the Fairfaxes to Appleton House; Drayton, Cotton, and Walton to Derbyshire; Milton to Horton or suburban obscurity after the Restoration; and so on. The retreat of Petrarch from the corruption of Avignon to the peace of Vaucluse becomes a norm, anticipating the subjectivity of Rousseau and Wordsworth.[6]

The determining factors in the concerns and psychology of the art and literature of the sixteenth century are thus less the Renaissance manners imported from Italy to France than the practical consequences of the Reformation. Humanists have encouraged us to recognize the classical forms, rhetoric, and surface textures of Renaissance works, but they have relatively neglected the dynamics, themes, and attitudes that govern such works, which seem largely generated by the impact of the Reformation.[7] The *Heptameron* leads the way in seeking to review social relationships in this new context, and in this it lays the foundations for the ethical dilemmas in later writers such as Shakespeare. Without religious confrontations neither Ronsard nor Donne could have achieved their most memorable works, and without the religious precedents of du Bartas and d'Aubigné, driven into opposition to the secular state, the great iconoclastic enterprises of Milton would have lacked much of their basic assurance and definitiveness. Neglect of French history in the sixteenth century, that is essentially of the French Reformation which was its major concern, gives a false perspective of both the English Renaissance and its permanent contribution to human awareness in its art and literature, which truly mirrored the nature of contemporary society, as Shakespeare made Hamlet assert that they should, being "the abstract and brief chronicles of the time."

6. See my *Renaissance Landscapes* for detailed discussion of this progression.
7. See Richmond, *The Christian Revolutionary* for further illustration.

Bibliography

A SUMMARY ACCOUNT OF THE RANGE OF NATIONAL ARCHIVAL MATERIALS available for Europe in the Renaissance period is given by Charles Carter, *The Western European Powers, 1500–1700* (Ithaca: Cornell University Press, 1971). The best guide to surviving contemporary English data lies in the Public Records Office's numerous *Calendars of State Papers, Foreign and Domestic*, covering the reigns of the sixteenth century, though the foreign series lists relevant to France for the final years are not yet complete. A useful list of contemporary French journalistic material appears in Robert O. Lindsay and John Neu, *French Political Pamphlets, 1540–1648: a Catalogue of Major Collections in American Libraries* (Madison: University of Wisconsin, 1961). The most helpful sources of authentic French background materials are the numerous contemporary memoirs published in *Collection complète des mémoires relatifs à l'histoire de France depuis le règne de Philippe Auguste jusqu'à la paix de Paris*, ed. Claude B. Petitot et al. (Paris: Foucault, 1819–29) and *Nouvelle collection des mémoirs pour servir a l'histoire de France depuis le XIIIᵉ siècle jusqu'à la fin du XVIIIᵉ*, ed. Joseph F. Michaud and Jean J. F. Poujoulat (Paris: Firmin Didot, 1836–39). Helpful summary bibliographies of historical materials appear in J. D. Mackie, *The Earlier Tudors, 1485–1558* (Oxford: Clarendon Press, 1972) and J. B. Black, *The Reign of Elizabeth, 1558–1603* (Oxford: Clarendon Press, 1959). In terms of literary issues, Anne Lake Prescott's *French Poets and the English Renaissance: Studies in Fame and Transformation* (New Haven: Yale University Press, 1978) summarizes much of the recently published research, but it is not comprehensive and lacks an analytic bibliography.

Examination of the revised *Cambridge Bibliography of English Literature*, not to discuss the printed catalogues of the British Library, the Bibliothèque Nationale, and *The Short Title Catalogue of Printed Books*, will indicate the impossibility of exhausting specific references relevant to my topic here. What follows is a brief selection of those texts most used in my research which have provided rich and rewarding avenues of approach into Anglo-French literary relations in the sixteenth century. I have not attempted exhaustive documentation of the range of editions, but have indicated only the ones I have found most accessible or useful, among the innumerable choices available in many cases. The three sections cover: (1) Historical Background (Contemporary Sources, Modern Sources); (2) Literary Background; (3) Individual Literary and Political Figures (in chronological order). Some excessively long subtitles have been abbreviated.

Historical Background
Contemporary Sources: General

Bellay, Jean du. *Ambassades en Angleterre*. Edited by V. -L. Bourrilly and P. de Vaissière. Paris: Picard, 1905.

Bellot, Jacques. *The French Method*. Menston, Eng.: Scholar, 1970.

Bethune, Maximilien de, duc de Sully. *Memoirs*. Translated by Charlotte Lennox. London: Dodsley, 1763.

————. *Les Oeconomies royales*. Edited by David Buisseret and Bernard Barbiche. Paris: Klincksierck, 1970.

————. *Sages et royales economies d'estat*. Paris: Firmin Didot, 1837.

Brantôme, Pierre de Bourdeille, Seigneur de. *Oeuvres complètes*. Edited by Ludovic Lalanne. Paris: Renouard, 1873.

————. *Illustrious Dames of the Valois Kings*. Translated by Katherine P. Wormeley. New York: Lamb, 1912.

————. *Les Dames galantes*. Edited by Maurice Rat. Paris: Garnier, 1960.

————. *Memoires*. Leyden: Sambix, 1699.

————. *The Lives of Gallant Ladies*. Edited by Martin Turnell. Translated by Alec Brown. London: Elek, 1961.

Calvin, John. *Theological Treatises*. Edited and translated by J. K. S. Reid. London: Library of Christian Classics, 1954.

Colynet, Antony. *The True History of the Civill Warres of France*. London: Woodcock, 1591.

Coppie of the Anti-Spaniard, The. London: Wolfe, 1590.

Dallington, Robert. *The View of France*. London: Oxford University Press, 1936.

Davilla, H. C. *Historie of the Civill Warres of France*. London: Lee, 1647.

Discoverer of France to the Parisians and All the other French Nations, The. London: n.p., 1590.

Eliot, John. *Ortho-Epica Gallica*. London: Wolfe, 1592.

————. *Survey or Topographical Description of France*. London: Wolfe, 1592.

Erasmus and Luther, Martin. *Discourse on Free Will*. Translated by Ernst F. Winter. New York: Ungar, 1961.

Erondelle, Pierre. *The French Garden*. London: White, 1605.

Estienne, Henri. *A Meruaylous Discourse vpon the Lyfe of Katherine de Medicis, Queen Mother*. [London: Middleton], 1575.

Excellent Discourse upon the Now Present Estate of France. London: Wolfe, 1592.

Fenton, Sir Geoffrey. *A Discourse of the Civile Warres in France*. London: Bynneman, 1570.

Guistinian, Sebastian. *Fours years at the Court of Henry VIII*. London: Brown, 1854.

Henri III. *Lettres*. Edited by Michael François. Paris: Champion, 1959–72.

Herbert, Lord Edward, of Cherbury. *Autobiography*. Edited by Sidney Lee. London: Routledge, 1886.

Hurault, Michel. *An Excellent Discourse upon the now Present Estate of France*. London: Wolfe, 1592.

Lestoile, Pierre de. *Mémoires et Journal*. Edited by Champollion-Figéac. Paris: Firmin Didot, 1837.

Luther, Martin. *Selections from His Writings*. Edited by John Dillenberger. Chicago: Quadrangle, 1961.

Mark, Robert de la. *Mémoires*. Paris: Michaud, 1838.

Mezeray, François E. de. *Histoire de France*. Paris: Bureau Central, 1839.

Mornay, Philippe du. *Memoirs*. Translated by Lucy Crump. London: Routledge, n.d.

Olhagaray, Pierre. *Histoire de Foix, Béarne, et Navarre*. Paris: Douceur, 1609.

Perefixe, Hardouin. *Histoire du roy Henri le grand*. Amsterdam: Michiels, 1662.

Reaux, Tallement des. *Historiettes*. Paris: Pléiade, 1972.

Sanders, Nicolas. *De Origine ac Progressu Schismatis Anglicani*. Ingolstadt: Ederus, 1588.

Tour d'Auvergne, Henri de la. *Mémoires*. Paris: Guignard, 1666.

Williams, Roger. *A Briefe Discourse of Warre*. London: Orwin, 1590.

Wilson, Thomas. *The Arte of Rhetorique*. Oxford: Clarendon Press, 1909.

Modern Sources

Aguerre, L. *Histoire de l'établisement du Protestantisme en France*. Paris: Fischbacher, 1882–86.

Armstrong, Edward. *The French Wars of Religion: Their Political Aspect*. London: Percival, 1892.

Biographie Universelle. Paris: Desplaces, 1843.

Black, John B. *The Reign of Elizabeth, 1558–1603*. Oxford: Clarendon Press, 1959.

Braudel, Fernand, *The Mediterranean and the Mediterranean World in the Age of Philip II*. New York: Harper, 1972.

Caillou, George. *Nérac*. Nérac: Berceron, 1977.

Champion, Pierre. *Paganism et réforme: fin du règne de François 1er*. Paris: Calmann-Lévy, 1936.

Chapman, Hester W. *The Last Tudor King: A Study of Edward VI*. London: Cape, 1961.

Charlanne, Louis. *L'Influence française en Angleterre au XVIIe siècle*. Paris: Société Francaise, 1906.

Charlotte, Catherine (Lady Jackson). *The Last of the Valois and the Accession of Henry of Navarre*. London: Bentley, 1888.

Clavière, R. de Maulde la. *Les Femmes de la Renaissance*. Paris: Perrin, 1904.

Decrue de Stoutz, Francis. *Le Parti des politiques*. Paris: Plon, 1892.

———. *La Cour de France et la société au XVIe siècle*. Paris: Firmin Didot, 1888.

Delumeau, Jean. *Naissance et affirmation de la Réforme.* Paris: Presses Universitaires, 1965.

Derblay, Claude. *Une Héroine de Brantôme: Renée de Bussy d'Amboise.* Paris: Plon, 1935.

Dickens, Arthur G. *The English Reformation.* London: Batsford, 1964.

————. *Reformation and Society.* New York: Harcourt Brace, 1966.

————. "The Elizabethans and St. Bartholomew." In *International Archives of the History of Ideas.* Hague: Nighoff, 1975.

Dunn, Richard S. *The Age of Religious Wars, 1559–1689.* New York: Norton, 1970.

Elton, G., ed. *New Cambridge Modern History.* Vol. 2, *The Reformation.* Cambridge: Cambridge University Press, 1958.

Erlanger, Philippe. *Henri III.* Paris: Gallimard, 1935.

Green, V. H. H. *Luther and the Reformation.* London: Methuen, 1969.

Hoeffer, ed. *Nouvelle Biographie Générale.* Paris: Didot, 1858–78.

Jacobsen, Brigitte: *Florent Chrestien.* Munich: Fink, 1972.

Kinsman, Robert, ed. *The Darker Vision of the Renaissance.* Berkeley and Los Angeles: University of California Press, 1974.

Leibrecht, Walter, ed. *Religion and Culture: Essays in Honor of Paul Tillich.* New York: Harper, 1959.

Lloyd, Howell A. *The Rouen Campaign, 1590–1592.* Oxford: Clarendon, 1973.

Parker, T. H. L. *John Calvin.* London: Dent, 1975.

Plumb, J. M. *The Renaissance.* Harmondsworth: Penguin, 1964.

Prévost, M., ed. *Dictionnaire Biographie Française.* Paris: Letouzey, 1954.

Romier, Lucien. *Catholiques et Huguenots à la cour de Charles IX.* Paris: Perrin, 1924.

————. *Le Royaume de Catherine de Medicis.* Paris: Perrin, 1922.

————. *Origines politiques des guerres de religion.* Paris: Perrin, 1913.

Rose, Hugh J., ed. *New General Biographical Dictionary.* London: Fellowes, 1847.

Saint-Amand, Imbert de. *Women of the Valois Court.* New York: Scribners, 1895.

381

Salmon, John H. M. *The French Religious Wars in English Political Thought*. Oxford: Clarendon Press, 1959.

Schleiner, Winfried. "Divina Virago: Queen Elizabeth as an Amazon." *Studies in Philology* 75 (1978): 163–80.

Shaaber, Matthais. *Some Forerunners of the Newspaper in England, 1476–1622*. Philadelphia: University of Pennsylvania Press, 1929.

Sichel, Edith. *Women and Men of the French Renaissance*. Port Washington: Kennicat Press, 1970.

Stephen, Leslie, ed. *Dictionary of National Biography*. London: Macmillan, 1908–9.

Thompson, James W. *The Wars of Religion in France, 1559–76*. Chicago: University of Chicago Press, 1915.

Watson, Forster. *Notes and Materials on Religious Refugees in Their Relation to Education in England Before . . . 1685*. London: Huguenot Society, 1911.

Wernham, Richard B. *Before the Armada: The Growth of English Foreign Policy, 1485–1588*. London: Cape, 1966.

Literary Background

Bairciez, Edouard E. J. *Les Moeurs polies et la littérature de cour sous Henri II*. Paris: Hachette, 1886.

Bastide, Charles. *The Anglo-French Entente in the Seventeenth Century*. London: Lane, 1914.

Berdan, John M. *Early Tudor Poetry*. New York: Macmillan, 1920.

Bever, Adolphe van. *Les Poètes du terroir du xve siècle au xxe siècle*. Paris: Delagrave, 1909–14.

Bevington, David. *Tudor Drama and Politics*. Cambridge: Harvard University Press, 1968.

Charbonnier, abbé F. *La Poèsie française et les guerres de religion (1560–1574)*. Paris: Revue des Oeuvres Nouvelles, 1919.

Colie, Rosalie. *The Resources of Kind*. Berkeley and Los Angeles: University of California Press, 1973.

Eliot, T. S. *Selected Essays*. New York: Harcourt Brace, 1950.

Ellrodt, Robert. *L'Inspiration personelle et l'esprit du temps chez les poètes métaphysiques anglais*. Paris: Corti, 1960.

Highet, Gilbert. *The Migration of Ideas*. New York: Oxford University Press, 1954.

Jones, William M., ed. *The Present State of Sixteenth Century Scholarship*. Columbia: University of Missouri Press, 1978.

Kastner, L. E. "The Elizabethan Sonneteers and the French Poets." *Modern Language Review* 3 (1907–8): 268–77.

Lambley, Kathleen. *The Teaching and Cultivation of the French Language in England During Tudor and Stuart Times*. Manchester: Longmans, 1920.

Lee, Sidney. *The French Renaissance in England*. New York: Octagon, 1968.

Magnus, Laurie. *English Literature in its Foreign Relations, 1300–1800*. New York: Dutton, 1927.

Mason, Harold A. *Humanism and Poetry in the Early Tudor Period*. London: Routledge, 1959.

McClung, William. *The Country House in English Renaissance Poetry*. Berkeley and Los Angeles: University of California Press, 1977.

McFarlane, Ian D. *A Literary History of France: Renaissance France, 1470–1589*. London: Benn, 1974.

Praz, Mario. *Chronache letterarie anglosassoni*. Roma: Storia e letteratura, 1950–51.

———. *Marinismo e seicentismo in Inghilterra*. Firenze: La Voce, 1925.

Prescott, Anne Lake. *French Poets and the English Renaissance: Studies in Fame and Transformation*. New Haven: Yale University Press, 1978.

———. "The Reception of du Bartas in England." *Studies in the Renaissance* 15 (1968): 144–73.

Richmond, Hugh M. *Renaissance Landscapes: English Lyrics in a European Tradition*. Hague: Mouton, 1973.

———. "Personal Identity and Literary Personae: A Study in Historical Psychology." *PMLA* 90 (1975): 209–21.

———. "The Intangible Mistress." *Modern Philology* 56 (1959): 217–23.

———. *The School of Love: The Evolution of the Stuart Love Lyric*. Princeton: Princeton University Press, 1964.

Saintsbury, George. *A Short History of French Literature*. Oxford: Clarendon Press, 1901.

Sattersthwaite, A. W. *Spenser, Ronsard, and du Bellay*. Princeton: Princeton University Press, 1960.

Schelling, Felix. *Elizabethan Drama, 1558–1642*. New York: Houghton Mifflin, 1908.

Schmidt, Albert-Marie, ed. *Poètes du XVIe siècle*. Paris: Gallimard, 1969.

Scott, Janet G. *Les Sonnets elizabéthains, les sources et l'apport personel*. Paris: Champion, 1929.

Stevens, John E. *Music and Poetry in the Early Tudor Court*. London: Methuen, 1961.

"The Pléiade and the Elizabethans." *Edinburgh Review* 205 (1907): 336.

Thompson, John. *The Founding of English Metre*. New York: Columbia University Press, 1961.

Upham, Alfred H. *The French Influence on English Literature from the Accession of Elizabeth to the Restoration*. New York: Octagon, 1965.

White, Harry O. *Plagiarism and Imitation During the Renaissance*. Cambridge: Harvard University Press, 1935.

Yates, Frances. *The French Academies of the Sixteenth Century*. London: Warburg, 1947.

Individual Bibliographies in Chronological Order

Marguerite d'Angoulême and the Court of François I

Ambrière, Francis. *Le Favori de François Ier: Gouffier de Bonnivet, amiral de France*. Paris: Hachette, 1936.

Blind, Henri A. *Marguerite de Navarre dans ses rapports avec la Réforme*. Strasbourg: Heitz, 1868.

Bordeaux, Paul H. *Louise de Savoie*. Paris: Plon, 1954.

Capafigue, Jean B. H. R. *François Ier et la Renaissance, 1515–1547*. Paris: Amyot, 1845.

Durand, Victor. *Marguerite de Valois à la cour de Francois 1ᵉʳ*. Paris: Imprimeurs Unis, 1849.

Febvre, Lucien. *Amour sacré, amour profane, autour de l'Heptameron*. Paris: Gallimard, 1944.

Freer, Martha W. *Life of Marguerite de Navarre*. London: Hunt and Blackett, 1856.

Jourda, Pierre. *Marguerite d'Angoulême, reine de Navarre (1492–1549)*. Paris: Champion, 1930.

Marguerite [d'Angoulême, reine] de Navarre. *L'Heptameron*. Edited by Michel François. Paris: Garnier, 1967.

————. *Les Marguerites de la Marguerite des Princesses*. Edited by Félix Franc. Geneva: Slatkine, 1970.

————. *Lettres*. Edited by F. Génin. Paris: Renouard, 1841.

————. *Tales*. London: Oxenbridge, 1597.

————. *The Mirror of the Sinful Soul*. Translated by [Princess] Elizabeth [Tudor], later Queen. Edited by Percy W. Ames. London: Asher, 1847.

Mirepoix, duc de Levis, *François 1ᵉʳ*. Paris: Éditions de France, 1931.

Painter, William. *The Palace of Pleasure*. Edited by Joseph Jacobs. New York: Dover, 1966.

Peyre, Roger. *Une Princesse de la Renaissance: Marguerite de France*. Paris: Émile-Paul, 1902.

Robinson, A. Mary F. *Margaret of Angoulême, Queen of Navarre*. London: Allen, 1886.

Savoie, Louise de. *Journal*. Edited by Joseph F. Michaud and Jean J. F. Poujoulat. Paris: Féchoz et Letouzey, 1881.

Seward, Desmond. *Prince of the Renaissance: The Life of François I*. London: Cardinal, 1974.

Telle, Émile V. *L'Oeuvre de Marguerite d'Angoulême, reine de Navarre, et la querelle des femmes*. Toulouse: Lion, 1937.

Tetel, Marcel. *Marguerite de Navarre's "Heptameron": Themes, Language, and Structure*. Durham: Duke University Press, 1973.

Clément Marot

Bentley-Cranch, Dana. "La Réputation de Clément Marot en Angleterre." *Studi Francesi* 17 (1973): 201–21.

Borland, Lois. "The Influence of Marot on English Poetry." M.A. Thesis: University of Chicago, 1913.

Douen, Emmanuel O. *Clément Marot et le psautier huguenot*. Paris: Imprimerie Nationale, 1878.

Griffin, Robert. *Clément Marot and the Inflections of Poetic Voice*. Berkeley and Los Angeles: University of California Press, 1974.

Guy, Henry. *Clément Marot et son école*. Paris: Champion, 1926.

Jourda, Pierre. *Marot*. Paris: Hatier, 1956.

Leblanc, P. *La Poésie religieuse de Clément Marot*. Paris: Nizet, 1955.

Marot, Clément. *Les Épigrammes*. Edited by C. A. Mayer. London: Athlone, 1970.

———. *Les Épîtres*. Edited by C. A. Mayer. London: Athlone, 1958.

———. *Oeuvres diverses*. Edited by C. A. Mayer. London: Athlone, 1966.

———. *Oeuvres lyriques*. Edited by C. A. Mayer. London: Athlone, 1964.

———. *Oeuvres satiriques*. Edited by C. A. Mayer. London: Athlone, 1962.

Mayer, C. A. *Clément Marot*. Paris: Seghers, 1964.

———. *La Religion de Marot*. Geneva: Droz, 1960.

Plattard, Jean. *Marot, sa carrière politique et son oeuvre*. Paris: B.R.C.G., 1938.

Smith, Pauline M. *Clément Marot, Poet of the French Renaissance*. London: Athlone, 1970.

Villey, Pierre. *Marot et Rabelais*. Paris: Champion, 1923.

Wyatt, Anne Boleyn, and Henry VIII

Baldi, Sergio. *La Poesia di Sir Thomas Wyatt*. Florence: Le Monnier, 1953.

Berdan, John M. "Wyatt and the French Sonneteers." *Modern Language Review* 4 (1908–9): 240–49.

Bruce, Mary L. *Anne Boleyn*. New York: Warner, 1973.

Cavendish, George. *The Life and Death of Cardinal Wolsey*. New Haven: Yale University Press, 1962.

Foxwell, A. K. *A Study of Sir Thomas Wyatt's Poems*. London: London University Press, 1911.

Friedman, Donald M. "The Mind in the Poem: Wyatt's 'They Fle From Me.'" *Studies in English Literature* 7 (1967): 1–13.

————. "Wyatt's *Amoris Personae*." *Modern Language Quarterly* 27 (1966): 136–46.

Gairdner, James. "Mary and Anne Boleyn." *English Historical Review* 8 (1893): 53–60.

Harrier, Richard C. "Notes on Wyatt and Anne Boleyn." *Journal of English and Germanic Philology* 53 (1954): 581–84.

————. *The Canon of Sir Thomas Wyatt's Poetry*. Cambridge: Harvard University Press, 1975.

Herbert, Lord Edward, of Cherbury. *The Life and Raigne of King Henry VIII*. London: Whitaker, 1649.

Jacqueton, Gilbert. *La Politique exterieure de Louise de Savoie*. Paris: Bouillon, 1892.

Kamholtz, Jonathan Z. "Thomas Wyatt's Poetry: The Politics of Love." *Criticism* 20 (1978): 349–65.

Mason, H. A. *Humanism and Poetry in the Early Tudor Period*. London: Routledge and Kegan Paul, 1954.

McCanles, Michael. "Love and Power in the Poetry of Sir Thomas Wyatt." *Modern Language Quarterly* 29 (1968): 145–60.

McConica, J. K. *English Humanists and Reformation Politics under Henry VIII and Edward VI*. Oxford: Clarendon Press, 1965.

Muir, Kenneth. *Life and Letters of Sir Thomas Wyatt*. Liverpool: Liverpool University Press, 1963.

Round, J. H. *The Early Life of Anne Boleyn*. London: Stock, 1886.

Savage, Henry, ed. *The Love Letters of Henry VIII*. London: Wingate, 1949.

Scarisbrick, J. J. *Henry VIII*. Berkeley and Los Angeles: University of California Press, 1968.

Sergeant, Philip W. *Anne Boleyn: A Study*. London: Hutchinson, 1934.

Southall, Raymond. *The Courtly Maker: An Essay on the Poetry of Wyatt and His Contemporaries*. Oxford: Blackwell, 1964.

Thomson, Patricia. *Sir Thomas Wyatt and His Background*. Stanford: Stanford University Press, 1964.

Tjernagel, Neelaks. *Henry VIII and the Lutherans*. St. Louis: Corcordia, 1965.

Wiatt, William H. "Sir Thomas Wyatt and Anne Boleyn." *English Language Notes* 6 (1968): 94–102.

Wyatt, George. *The Papers*. Edited by D. M. Loader. London: Royal Historical Society, 1968.

Wyatt, Sir Thomas. *Collected Poems*. Edited by Joost Daalder. London: Oxford, 1975.

————. *Collected Poems*. Edited by Kenneth Muir and Patricia Thomson. Liverpool: Liverpool University Press, 1969. (See also his earlier edition, in the Muses Library, Cambridge: Harvard University Press, 1949.)

————. *The Complete Poems*. Edited by Ronald A. Rebholz. Harmondsworth: Penguin, 1978.

Ronsard and the Court of Catherine de' Medici

Armstrong, Elizabeth. *Ronsard and the Age of Gold*. Cambridge: Cambridge University Press, 1968.

Castelnau, Jacques. *Catherine de Médicis*. Paris: Hachette, 1954.

Castor, G. "The Theme of Illusion in Ronsard's *Sonnets pour Hélène*." *Forum for Modern Language Studies* (1971): 361–73.

Catherine de' Medici. *Lettres*. Edited by Baguenault de Puchesse, etc. Paris: Imprimerie Nationale, 1880–1943.

Cave, Terence, ed. *Ronsard the Poet*. London: Methuen, 1973.

Charbonnier, abbé F. *Pamphlets protestants contre Ronsard (1560–1577)*. Paris: Champion, 1923.

Dassonville, Michel. *Ronsard: Étude historique et littéraire*. Geneva: Droz, 1968–.

Denonay, Fernand. *Ronsard, poète de l'amour*. Brussels: ARLLRB, 1952–59.

Dyke, Paul van. *Catherine de Médicis*. New York: Scribners, 1922.

Franchet, Henri. *Le Poète et son oeuvre d'après Ronsard*. Paris: Champion, 1923.

Gendre, André. *Ronsard, poète de la conquête amoureuse*. Neuchatel: Baconniere, 1970.

Heritier, Jean. *Catherine de Médicis*. Paris: Fayard, 1959.

Mahoney, Irene. *Madame Catherine*. New York: Coward, 1975.

Mariéjol, Jean H. *A Daughter of the Medicis*. New York: Harper, 1930.

Neale, J. E. *The Age of Catherine de' Medici*. London: Cape, 1943.

Nolhac, Pierre de. *Ronsard et l'humanisme*. Paris: Champion, 1921.

Perdrizet, Pierre. *Ronsard et la reforme*. Paris: Feschbacher, 1902.

Pineaux, Jacques, ed. *La Polémique protestant contre Ronsard*. Paris: Didier, 1973.

Puchasse, G. Baguenault de. "Catherine de Médicis et les négotiations de Nérac, 1578-79." *Revue des Questions Historiques* 61 (1897).

Richmond, Hugh M. "Ronsard and the English Renaissance." *Comparative Literature Studies* 7 (1970): 141-60.

Roeder, Ralph. *Catherine de' Medici and the Lost Revolution*. London: Harrap, 1937.

Ronsard, Pierre de. *Oeuvres complètes*. Edited by Gustave Cohen. Paris: Gallimard, Pléiade, 1950.

————. *Oeuvres complètes*. Edited by Paul Laumonier. Paris: Didier, 1914-70.

————. *Oeuvres complètes*. Edited by Hugues Vaganay. Paris: Garnier, 1924.

Sichel, Edith. *Catherine de' Medici and the French Reformation*. London: Constable, 1905.

Silver, Isidore. *The Intellectual Evolution of Ronsard*. St. Louis: Washington University Press, 1969-.

Smith, M. C. "Ronsard and Elizabeth." *Bibliothèque d'humanisme et renaissance* (1967): 93-119.

Stevens, Irma N. R. "Ronsard and Stuart Lyric Poetry." Dissertation: Florida State University, 1973.

Stone, Donald. *Ronsard's Sonnet Cycles*. New Haven: Yale University Press, 1966.

Williamson, Hugh R., *Catherine de' Medici*. London: Joseph, 1973.

Henri IV, Marguerite de Navarre, and Their Courts

Andrieux, Maurice. *Henri IV dans ses années pacifiques*. Paris: n.p., 1954.

Antoine, A. *La Jeunesse de Henri IV*. Paris: Blanchard, 1824.

L'Atheisme de Henri de Valoys. Paris: Hayes, 1589.

Batz-Trenquelléon, Charles de. *Henri IV en Gascogne*. Paris: Oudin, 1885.

Biron, Roger de Gontaut. *Armand de Gontaut, premier maréchal de Biron*. Paris: Plon, 1950.

Black, John B. *Elizabeth and Henry IV*. Oxford: Blackwell's, 1914.

Blair, Edward T. *Henri of Navarre and the Religious Wars*. Philadelphia: Lippincott, 1895.

Chamberlain, E. R. *Marguerite of Navarre*. New York: Dial, 1974.

Droz, Eugénie. *La Reine Marguerite de Navarre et la vie littéraire à la cour de Nérac (1579-1582)*. Bordeaux: Taffard, 1964.

Dumaître, Paul. *La Jeunesse d'Henri IV*. Paris: Nathan, 1968.

Erlanger, Philippe. *La Reine Margot*. Paris: Perrin, 1972.

————. *La Vie quotidienne sous Henri IV*. Paris: Hachette, 1958.

Gerard, Jo. *Henri IV: Le plus vert des galants*. Paris: Dargaut, 1967.

Gontaut, Armand de, [duc de] Biron. *Letters and Documents*. Edited by James W. Thompson. Berkeley and Los Angeles: University of California Press, 1936.

H., Alice. *Les Amours de Catherine de Bourbon*. Paris: Hurtsel, 1879.

Henri IV. *Lettres d'amour*. Paris: Madeleine, 1932.

————. *Lettres d'amour et de guèrre*. Edited by André Lamandé. Paris: Jonquieres, 1928.

————. *Receuil de lettres missives*. Edited by Berger de Xivrey. Paris: Imprimerie Royale, 1843-76.

Lagrèze, G. B. de. *Henri IV*. Paris: Fermin Didot, 1885.

Lauzun, Philippe. *Itinéraire raisonné de Marguerite de Valois en Gascogne*. Paris: Picard, 1902.

Lévis-Mirepoix, duc de. *Henri IV, roi de France et de Navarre*. Paris: Perrin, 1971.

Marguerite de Valois [reine de Navarre]. *Mémoires et lettres*. Edited by M. F. Guissard. Paris: Renouard, 1842.

————. *Memoirs*. Translated by Violet Fane. London: Nimmo, 1892.

Mariéjol, Jean H. *La Vie de Marguerite de Valois*. Paris: Hachette, 1928.

————. *A Daughter of the Medicis*. London: Harper, 1930.

Montigny, Charles de. *Le Maréchal de Biron, sa vie, son procés, sa mort, 1562-1602*. Paris: Hachette, 1861.

Nabonne, Bernard. *Jeanne d'Albret, reine des Huguenots*. Paris: Hachette, 1945.

Poirson, M. A. *Histoire du règne de Henri IV*. Paris: Colas, 1862.

Ritter, Raymond. *Henri IV lui-même, l'homme*. Paris: Michel, 1944.

Russell, Lord, of Liverpool. *Henry of Navarre*. New York: Praeger, 1970.

Savine, Albert. *La Vraie reine Margot*. Paris: Michaud, 1922.

Stuck, Johan W. *Carolus Magnus Redivivus, Hoc est Caroli Magni ... cum Henrico M. Gallorum et Navarorum ... Comparatio*. Tigurino: Wolphium, 1592.

True and Perfect Discourse of the Practises and Treasons of Marshall Biron, A. London: P.S., 1602.

Willert, Paul F. *Henry of Navarre and the Huguenots*. New York: Putnam, 1893.

Shakespeare and France

Allen, Percy. *The Plays of Shakespeare and Chapman in Relation to French History*. London: Archer, 1933.

Bastide, Charles. *La France et les français dans le théâtre de Shakespeare. EDDA* 3 (1916): 112–123.

Bullough, Geoffrey, ed. *Narrative and Dramatic Sources of Shakespeare*. London: Routledge and Kegan Paul, 1968–75.

Chambers, E. K. *William Shakespeare*. Oxford: Clarendon Press, 1930.

Chambrun, Clara Longworth de. *Essential Documents Never Yet Presented in the Shakespeare Case*. Bordeaux: Delmas, 1934.

————. "Influences françaises dans la *Tempête* de Shakespeare." *Revue de la Littérature Comparée* 5 (1929).

————. *Shakespeare, Actor-Poet*. New York: Appleton, 1927.

————. "Shakespeare et Florio: étude de vieux documents." *La Revue* (1 May 1916).

Cooper, Duff. *Sergeant Shakespeare*. New York: Viking, 1950.

Harman, Alice. "How Great was Shakespeare's Debt to Montaigne?" *PMLA* 57 (1942): 988–1008.

Jusserand, J. J. *Shakespeare in France Under the Ancien Régime*. London: Unwin, 1899.

Lefranc, Abel. *A la Découverte de Shakespeare*. Paris: Michel, 1950.

————. "Les Élements Français de *Peines d'Amour Perdues*." *Revue Historique* (1936).

Leishman, J. B. *Themes and Variations in Shakespeare's Sonnets*. New York: Harper and Row, 1966.

Richmond, Hugh M. "Much Ado About Notables." *Shakespeare Studies* 12 (1979), pp. 49–63.

———. "Shakespeare's Navarre." *Huntington Library Quarterly* 42 (1979): 193–216.

———. " 'To be or not to be' and the *Hymne de la Mort*." *Shakespeare Quarterly* 13 (1962): 317–20.

Schoenbaum, Samuel. *Shakespeare's Lives*. Oxford: Clarendon Press, 1970.

———. *William Shakespeare: a Documentary Life*. Oxford: Clarendon Press, 1975.

Shakespeare, William. *Complete Works*. Edited by Alfred Harbage. Baltimore: Penguin, 1969.

———. *Love's Labour's Lost*. Edited by Richard David. London: Methuen, 1968.

———. *Love's Labour's Lost*. Edited by John Dover Wilson. Cambridge: Cambridge University Press, 1962.

Yates, Frances. *A Study of "Love's Labour's Lost."* Cambridge: Cambridge University Press, 1936.

Donne, Milton, Marvell, etc.

Carew, Thomas. *The Poems*. Edited by Rhodes Dunlap. Oxford: Clarendon Press, 1957.

Chapman, George. *The Plays and Poems*. Edited by Thomas M. Parrott. London: Routledge, 1910–14.

Colie, Rosalie. *My Echoing Song: Andrew Marvell's Poetry of Criticism*. Princeton: Princeton University Press, 1970.

Donne, John. *The Elegies and the Songs and Sonnets*. Edited by Helen Gardner. Oxford: Clarendon Press, 1965.

———. *The Divine Poems*. Edited by Helen Gardner. Oxford: Clarendon Press, 1959.

———. *The Satires, Epigrams and Verse Letters*. Edited by W. Milgate. Oxford: Clarendon Press, 1967.

Guss, Donald L. *John Donne, Petrarchist: Italianate Conceits and Love*

Theory in the "Songs and Sonets." Detroit: Wayne State University Press, 1966.

Herbert, George. *The Works.* Edited by F. E. Hutchinson. Oxford: Clarendon Press, 1964.

Jonson, Ben. [*The Works.*] Edited by C. H. Herford and Percy Simpson. Oxford: Clarendon Press, 1925–52.

Legouis, Pierre. *Andrew Marvell, Poet, Puritan, Patriot.* Oxford: Clarendon Press, 1965.

Lein, Clayton D. "Donne and Ronsard." *Notes and Queries* 21 (1974): 90–92.

Marvell, Andrew. *Poems and Letters.* Edited by H. M. Margoliouth. Oxford: Clarendon Press, 1971.

Milton, John. *Complete Poems and Major Prose.* Edited by Merrit Y. Hughes. New York: Odyssey, 1957.

Richmond, Hugh M. "Donne and Ronsard." *Notes and Queries* n.s. 5 (1958): 534–36.

Taylor, George C. *Milton's Use of du Bartas.* Cambridge: Harvard University Press, 1934.

Wallace, John M. *Destiny His Choice: The Loyalism of Andrew Marvell.* London: Cambridge University Press, 1968.

Waller, Edmund. *The Poems.* Edited by G. Thorn Drury. London: Routledge, 1895.

Wolledge, G. "St. Amant, Fairfax, and Marvell." *Modern Language Review* 25 (1930): 481–83.

D'Aubigné, Théophile de Viau, etc.

Adam, Antoine. *Les Libertins au XVIIe siècle.* Paris: Buchet-Chastel, 1964.

——. *Théophile de Viau et la libre pensée française en 1620.* Geneva: Slatkine, 1965.

Aubigné, Agrippa d'. *Histoire Universelle.* Edited by Alphonse d'Aubigné. Paris: Renouard, 1891.

——. *Oeuvres.* Edited by Henri Weber. Paris: Gallimard, Pléiade, 1969.

Durand-Lapie, Paul. *Un Académicien du XVIIe siècle: Saint-Amant.* Paris: Delagrave, 1898.

Garnier, Armand. *Agrippa d'Aubigné et le parti protestant.* Paris: Fischbacher, 1928.

Lachèvre, Frederic. *Le Prince des libertins du XVIIe siècle: Jacques Vallée des Barreaux.* Paris: Leclerc, 1907.

Montaigne, Michel de. *Essays.* Translated by John Florio. London: Dent, 1942.

Scève, Maurice. *The "Délie."* Edited by Ian D. McFarlane. Cambridge: Cambridge University Press, 1966.

Stone, Donald. "Théophile's *La Solitude*: An Appreciation of Poem and Poet." *French Review* 60 (1966): 321–28.

Viau, Théophile de. *Oeuvres poétiques.* Edited by Jeanne Streicher. Geneva: Droz, 1951.

Index

Shakespeare, William, 5, 8, 27, 30, 32, 33, 39, 46, 47, 48, 53, 56, 93, 94, 107, 110, 112, 148, 173–74, 184–95, 224, 297–339, 376; *All's Well*, 91, 126, 298, 299; *Antony and Cleopatra*, 118, 325, 340, 372, 374; *As You Like It*, 91–93, 107, 298; *Comedy of Errors*, 52; *Hamlet*, 134–35, 313, 376; *Henry IV, Part I*, 43, 133, 188–90, 192, 208, 275, 300, 337–38; *Henry V*, 94, 189, 192, 233, 274, 298–99, 321–22, 337–38, 347–48; *Henry VIII*, 14, 157; *Love's Labour's Lost*, 9, 13, 14, 48, 71, 74–75, 77–80, 82, 91, 94, 118, 131–32, 154, 297–337, 340, 372; *Macbeth*, 343, 346–67, 372; *Measure for Measure*, 51, 64–73, 99–100, 116, 126, 137; *Merchant of Venice*, 85, 137–38; *Midsummer Night's Dream*, 50, 126–31; *Much Ado*, 12, 34–36, 48, 51, 83, 84, 131–32, 339; *Othello*, 83–91, 118, 132, 135, 137, 185, 374; *Richard III*, 134, 345; *Romeo and Juliet*, 50, 86; *Sonnets*, 9, 48, 57–64, 111, 116, 118, 122, 124, 125, 152, 162, 338; *Troilus and Cressida*, 193–95
Shirley, James, 12
Sichel, Edith, 9, 324
Sidney, Sir Philip, 110, 118
Silver, Isidore, 2
Skinner, Cyriac, 262
Sorbonne, 27, 29, 75, 93, 144
Southampton, earl of, 297
Spenser, Edmund, 4, 13, 50, 74, 95, 97, 115, 117, 141, 225, 251, 342, 373
Spooner, F. C., 29, 139
Stafford, Sir Edward, 316, 317
Stanley, Thomas, 253, 369
Sterling-Maxwell, William, 118
Stoutz, Francis D. de, 31
Streicher, J., 2, 359
Stuck, Johan, 302
Suckling, Sir John, 253, 360, 370

Suffolk, duke of, 157–58
Surgères, Hélène de, 218–19
Surrey, Henry Howard, earl of, 95, 117, 149, 159

Tasso, 4, 223–24
Telle, Emile V., 30, 41
Terence, 160
Tetel, Marcel, 29, 38, 39, 45–49, 51
Theocritus, 106
Thompson, James W., 312
Thomson, Patricia, 159
Tignonvile, mlle. de, 328
Tottel, Richard, 173
Touard, Claude, 64–65
Tournon, Hélène de, 125
Turenne, Henri de la Tour d'Auvergne, vicomte de, 31, 302, 310, 316, 327, 329

Upham, Alfred H., 6, 7
Ussac, baron d', 309, 316

Vanini, Lucilio, 355
Vautrollier, Jacqueline, 298
Vergil, Polydore, 23
Viau, Théophile de, 2, 8, 79, 101, 259, 352–71, Plate 14
Vigne, André de la, 128, 130
Villey, Pierre, 96, 98
Villon, François, 110
Virgil, 106, 148
Vorstius, 354

Waller, Edmund, 146, 369
Walsingham, Sir Francis, 303, 316, 317
Ward, A. W., 306
Wernham, Richard B., 321
Whetstone, George, 11, 65
Wiatt, William H., 158
Williams, Roger, 313, 321
Williamson, George, 223

Designer: Wolfgang Lederer
Compositor: Heritage Printers, Inc.
Printer: Heritage Printers, Inc.
Binder: The Delmar Companies
Text: Linotype Granjon
Display: Monotype Bembo